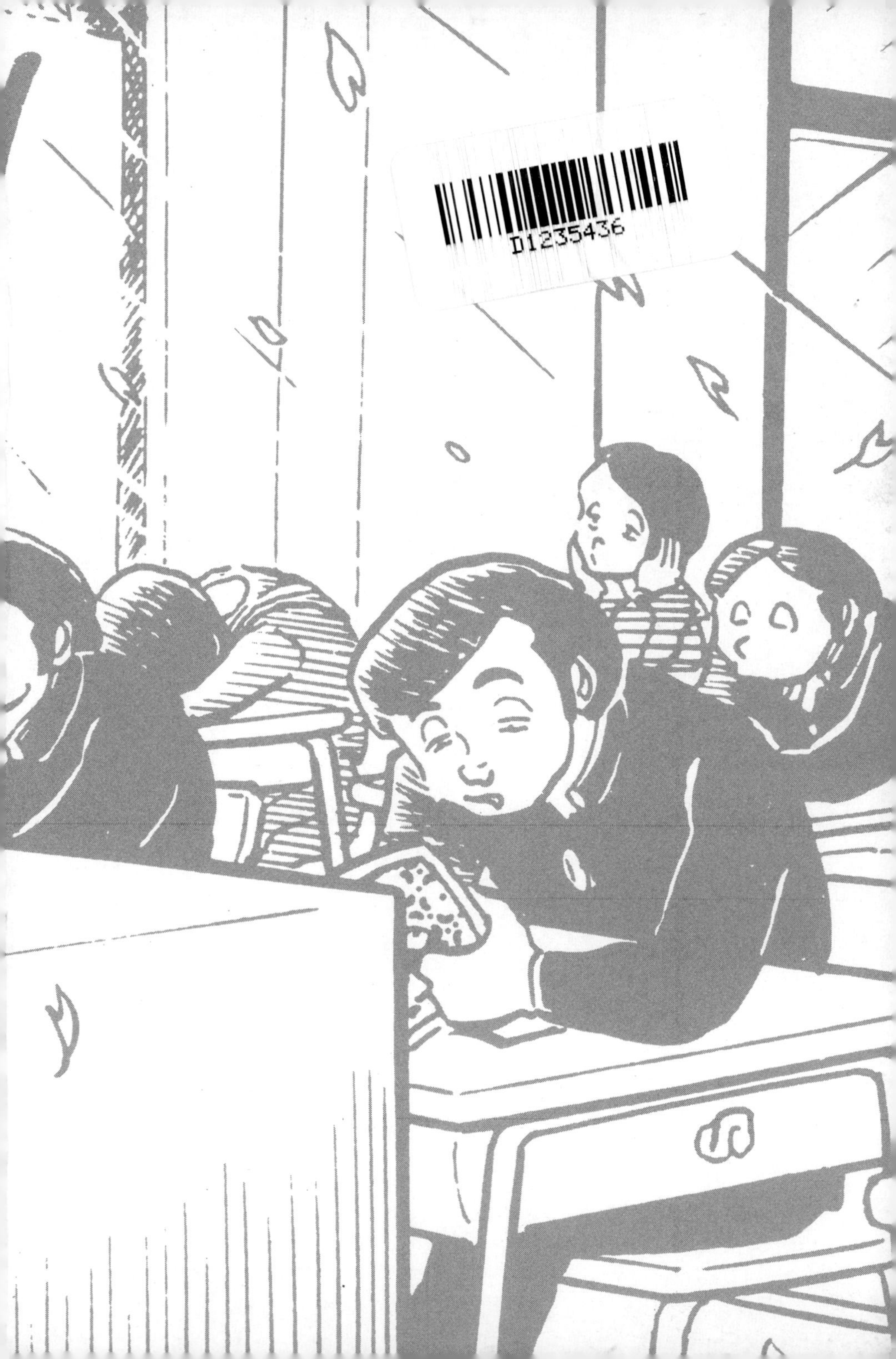

VIZ GRAPHIC NOVEL

THE RETURN OF LUM™

STORY & ART BY
RUMIKO TAKAHASHI

CONTENTS

PART ONE	Trouble Drops In	5
PART TWO	Zodiac-Go-Round	25
PART THREE	Spring Fever	45
PART FOUR	On the Horns of Passion	61
PART FIVE	Even Though I Wait for You...	77
PART SIX	Diary of Tears	93
PART SEVEN	What Child Is This?	109
PART EIGHT	A-Mazed!	125
PART NINE	Waking to a Nightmare	141
PART TEN	Shooting the Fourth Dimension	157
PART ELEVEN	A Flying Start	173
PART TWELVE	Since You Went Away	193

This volume contains all the LUM * URUSEI YATSURA installments from ANIMERICA, Anime & Manga Monthly Vol. 1, No. 10 through Vol. 2, No. 11 in their entirety.

STORY & ART BY RUMIKO TAKAHASHI

English Adaptation/Gerard Jones
Touch-up Art and Lettering/Wayne Truman
Cover Design/Viz Graphics
Editors/Trish Ledoux & Annette Roman
Assistant Editor/Toshifumi Yoshida
Managing Editor/Satoru Fujii
Executive Editor/Seiji Horibuchi
Publisher/Keizo Inoue

First Published by Shogakukan, Inc. in Japan
Executive Editor/Katsuya Shirai

Published by Viz Communications, Inc.
P.O. Box 77010, San Francisco, CA 94107

Part 1
Trouble Drops In

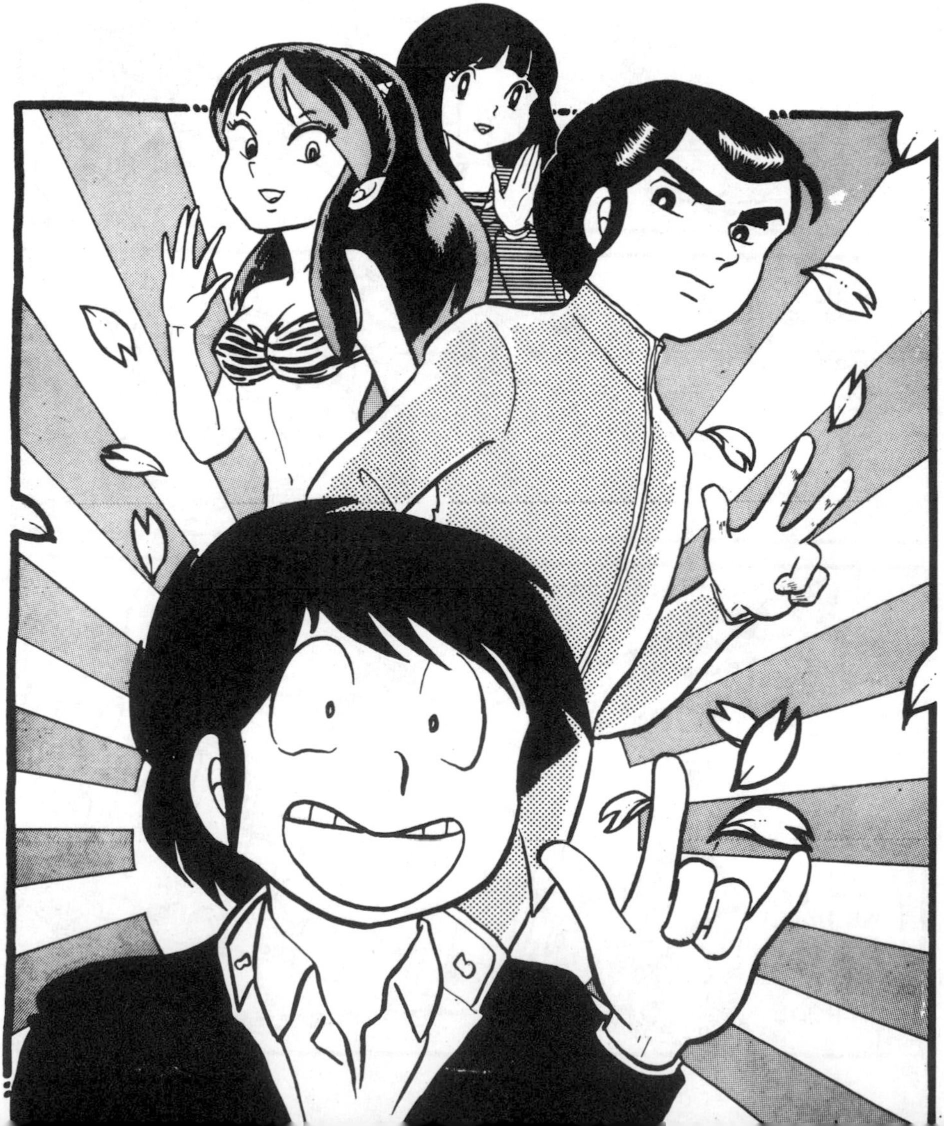

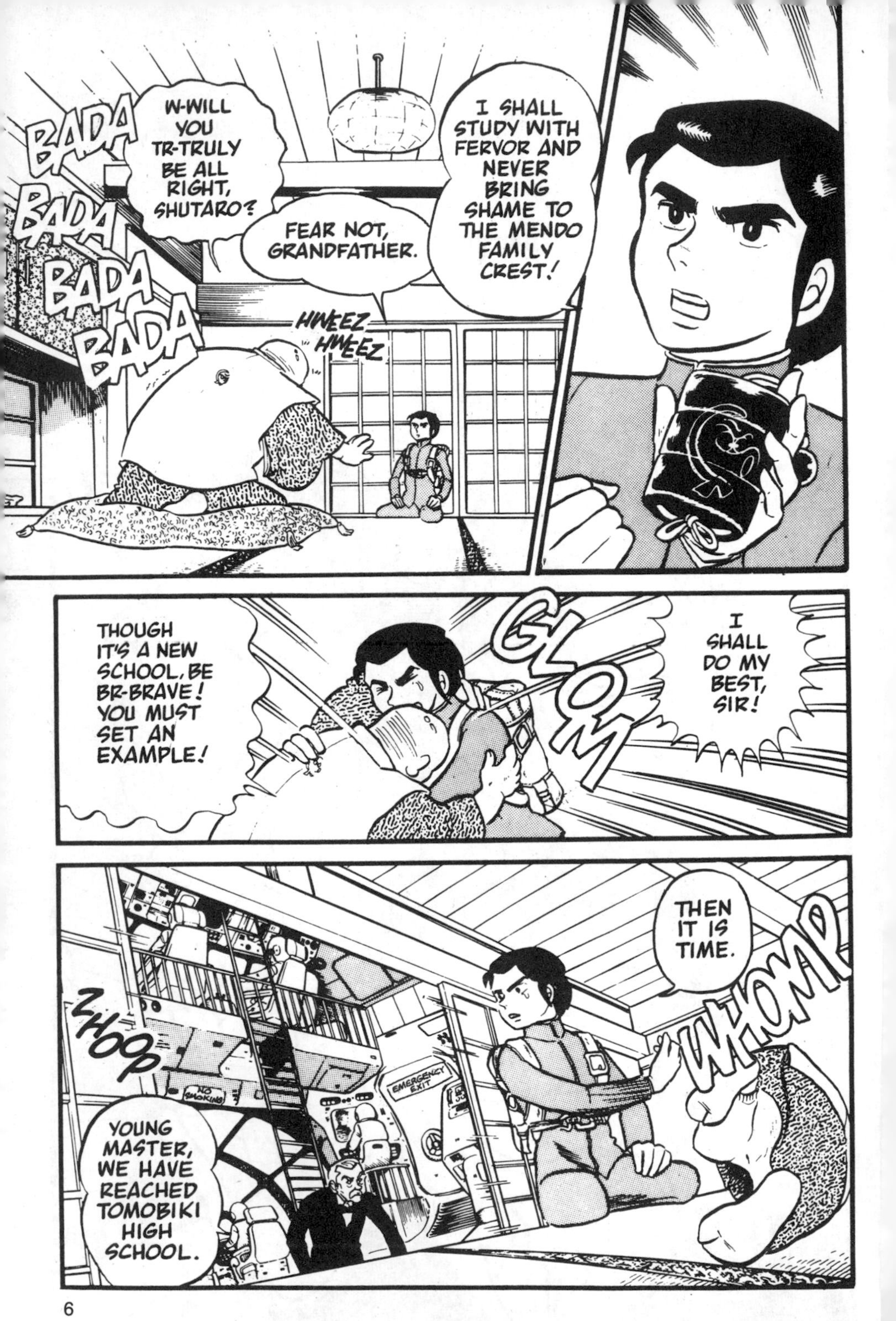
BADA BADA BADA BADA
W-WILL YOU TR-TRULY BE ALL RIGHT, SHUTARO?
FEAR NOT, GRANDFATHER.
I SHALL STUDY WITH FERVOR AND NEVER BRING SHAME TO THE MENDO FAMILY CREST!
HWEEZ HWEEZ
THOUGH IT'S A NEW SCHOOL, BE BR-BRAVE! YOU MUST SET AN EXAMPLE!
GLOM
I SHALL DO MY BEST, SIR!
ZHOOP
NO SMOKING
EMERGENCY EXIT
YOUNG MASTER, WE HAVE REACHED TOMOBIKI HIGH SCHOOL.
THEN IT IS TIME.
WHOMP

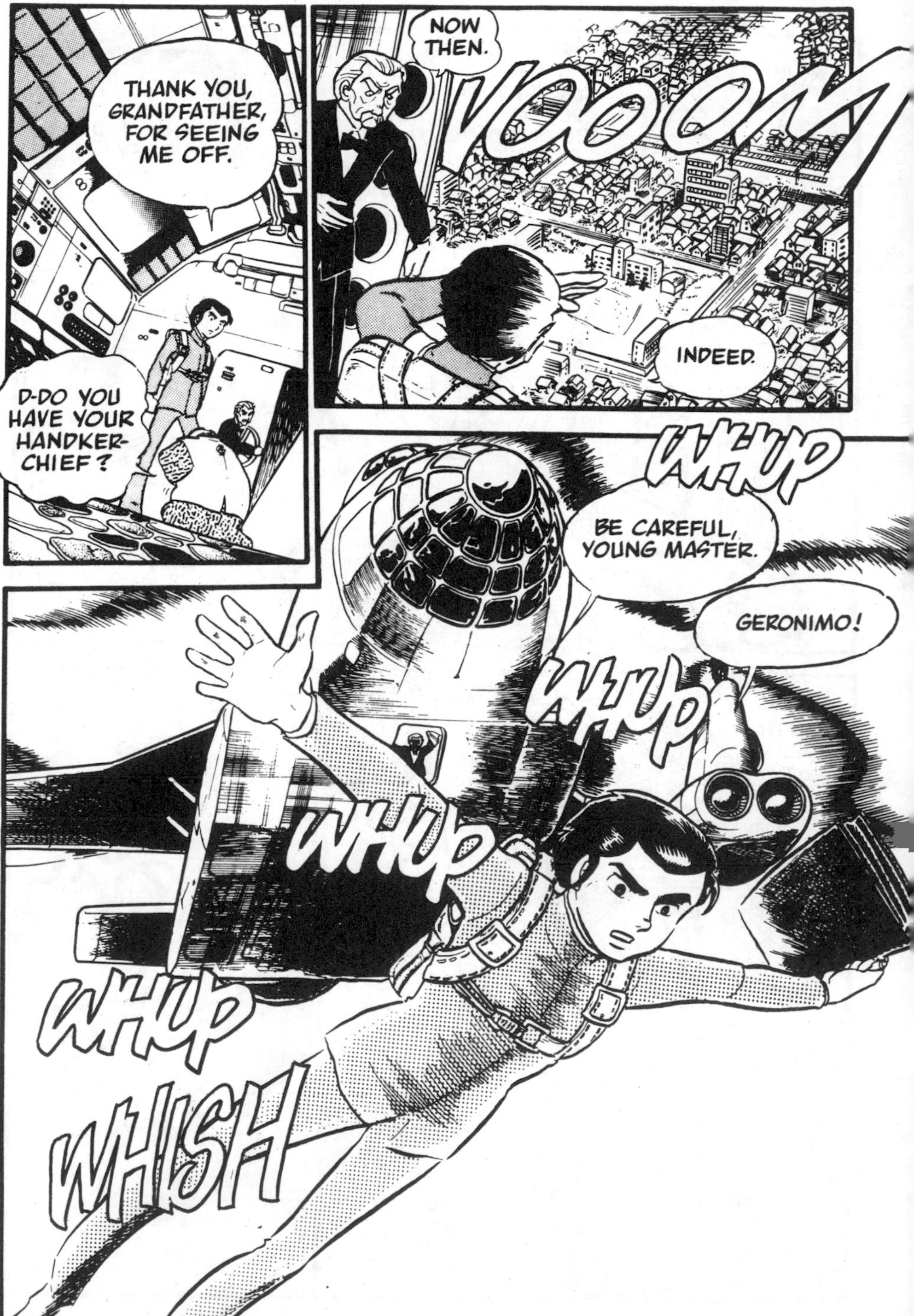
THANK YOU, GRANDFATHER, FOR SEEING ME OFF.
D-DO YOU HAVE YOUR HANDKER-CHIEF?
NOW THEN.
VOOOM
INDEED.
WHUP
BE CAREFUL, YOUNG MASTER.
GERONIMO!
WHUP
WHUP
WHUP
WHISH

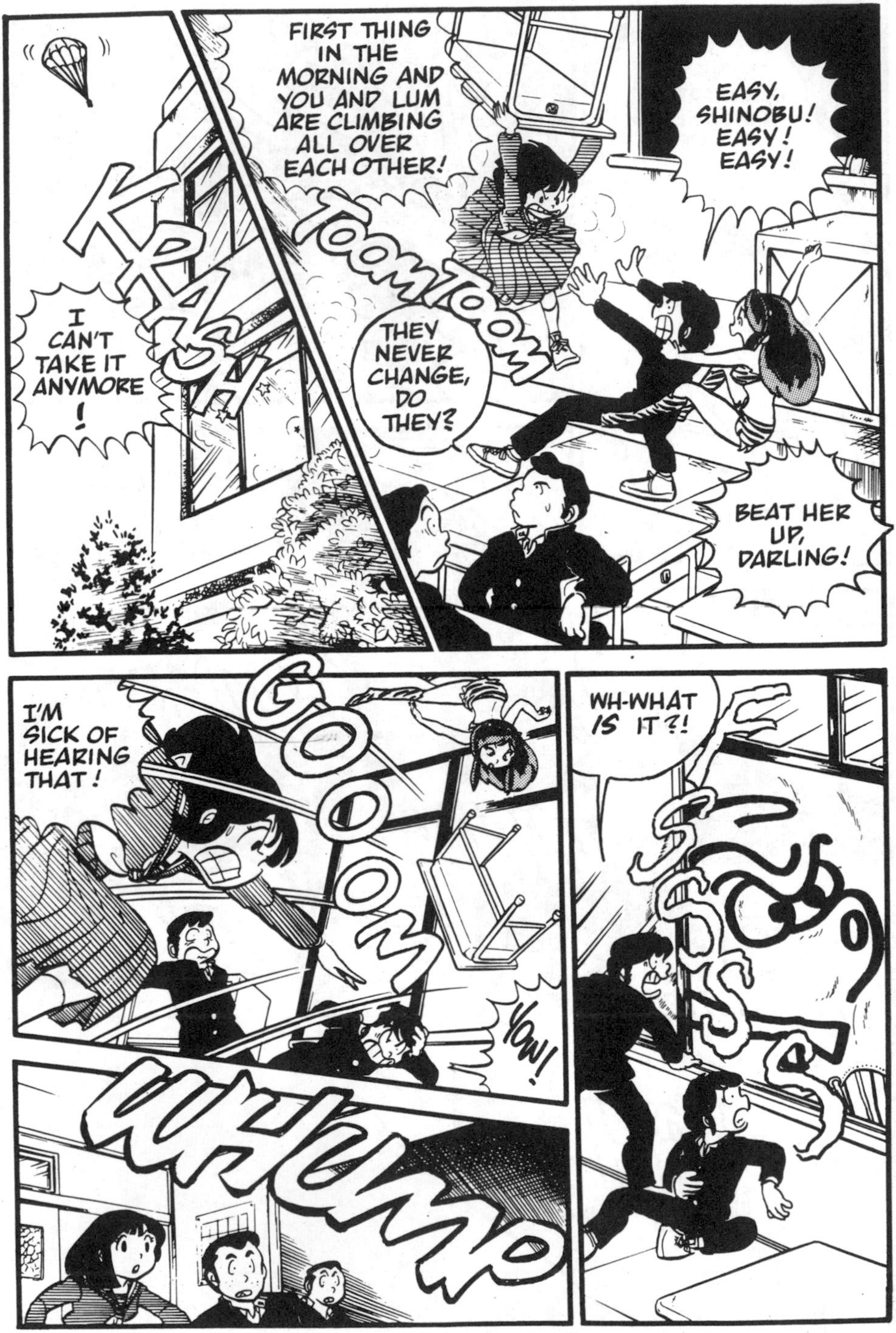

KRASH
I CAN'T TAKE IT ANYMORE!
FIRST THING IN THE MORNING AND YOU AND LUM ARE CLIMBING ALL OVER EACH OTHER!
TOOMTOOM
THEY NEVER CHANGE, DO THEY?
EASY, SHINOBU! EASY! EASY!
BEAT HER UP, DARLING!
I'M SICK OF HEARING THAT!
GOOOOM
YOW!
WH-WHAT IS IT?!
SSSS
WHUMP

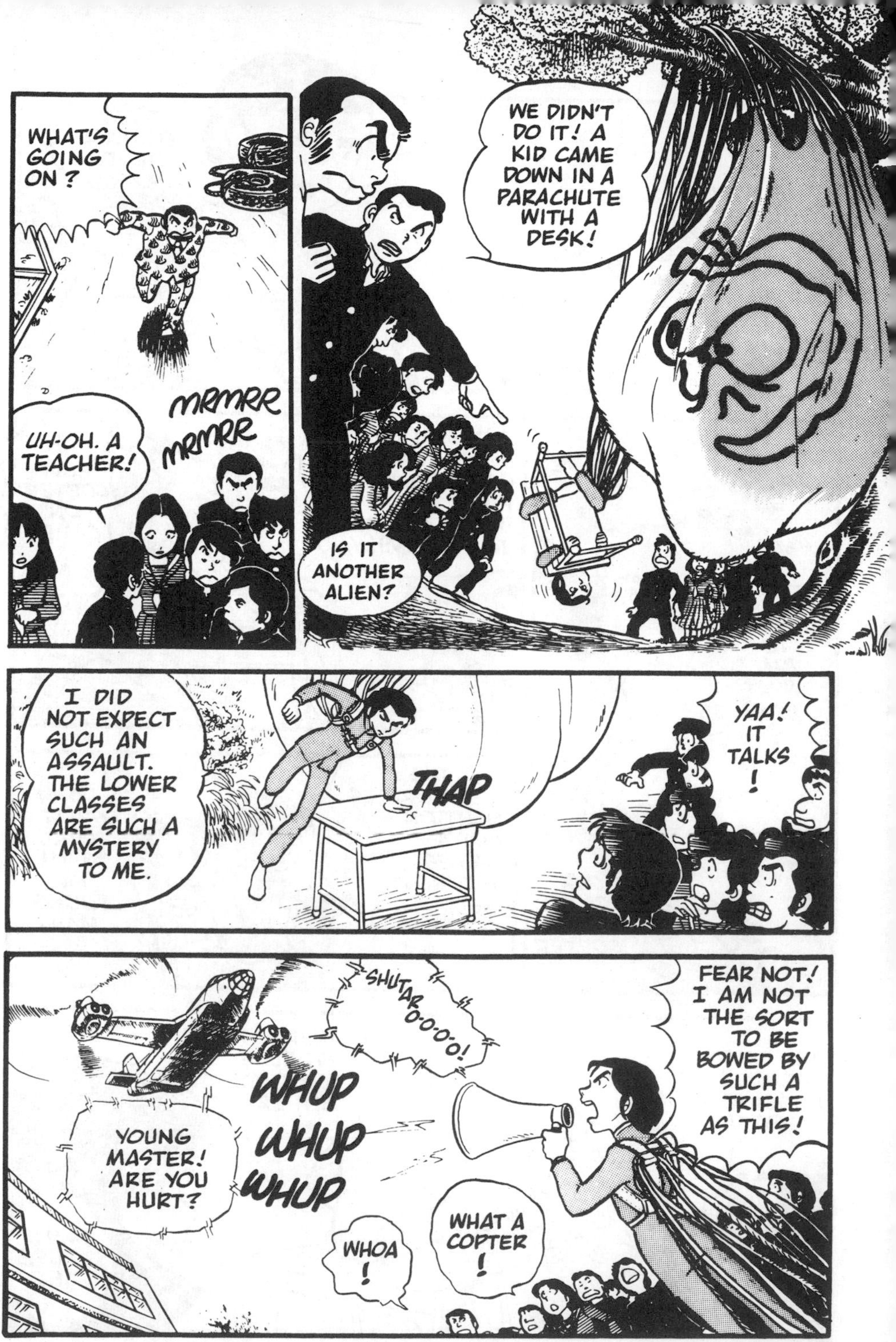
WHAT'S GOING ON?
UH-OH. A TEACHER!
MRMRR MRMRR
WE DIDN'T DO IT! A KID CAME DOWN IN A PARACHUTE WITH A DESK!
IS IT ANOTHER ALIEN?
I DID NOT EXPECT SUCH AN ASSAULT. THE LOWER CLASSES ARE SUCH A MYSTERY TO ME.
THAP
YAA! IT TALKS!
SHUTARO-O-O-O!
YOUNG MASTER! ARE YOU HURT?
WHUP WHUP WHUP
FEAR NOT! I AM NOT THE SORT TO BE BOWED BY SUCH A TRIFLE AS THIS!
WHOA!
WHAT A COPTER!

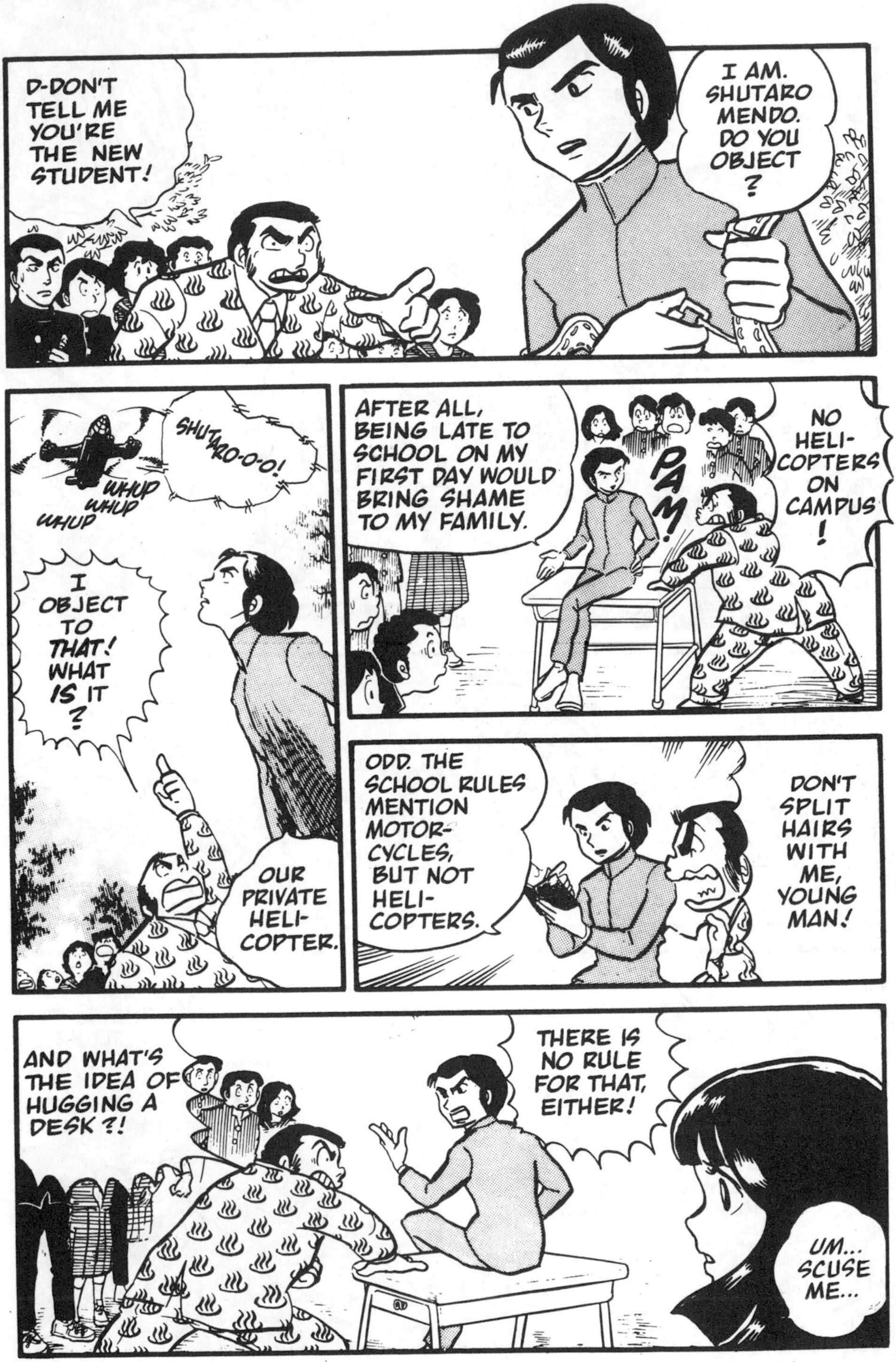
D-DON'T TELL ME YOU'RE THE NEW STUDENT!
I AM. SHUTARO MENDO. DO YOU OBJECT?
SHUTARO-O-O!
WHUP WHUP WHUP
I OBJECT TO THAT! WHAT IS IT?
OUR PRIVATE HELI-COPTER.
AFTER ALL, BEING LATE TO SCHOOL ON MY FIRST DAY WOULD BRING SHAME TO MY FAMILY.
PAM!
NO HELI-COPTERS ON CAMPUS!
ODD. THE SCHOOL RULES MENTION MOTOR-CYCLES, BUT NOT HELI-COPTERS.
DON'T SPLIT HAIRS WITH ME, YOUNG MAN!
AND WHAT'S THE IDEA OF HUGGING A DESK?!
THERE IS NO RULE FOR THAT, EITHER!
UM... SCUSE ME...

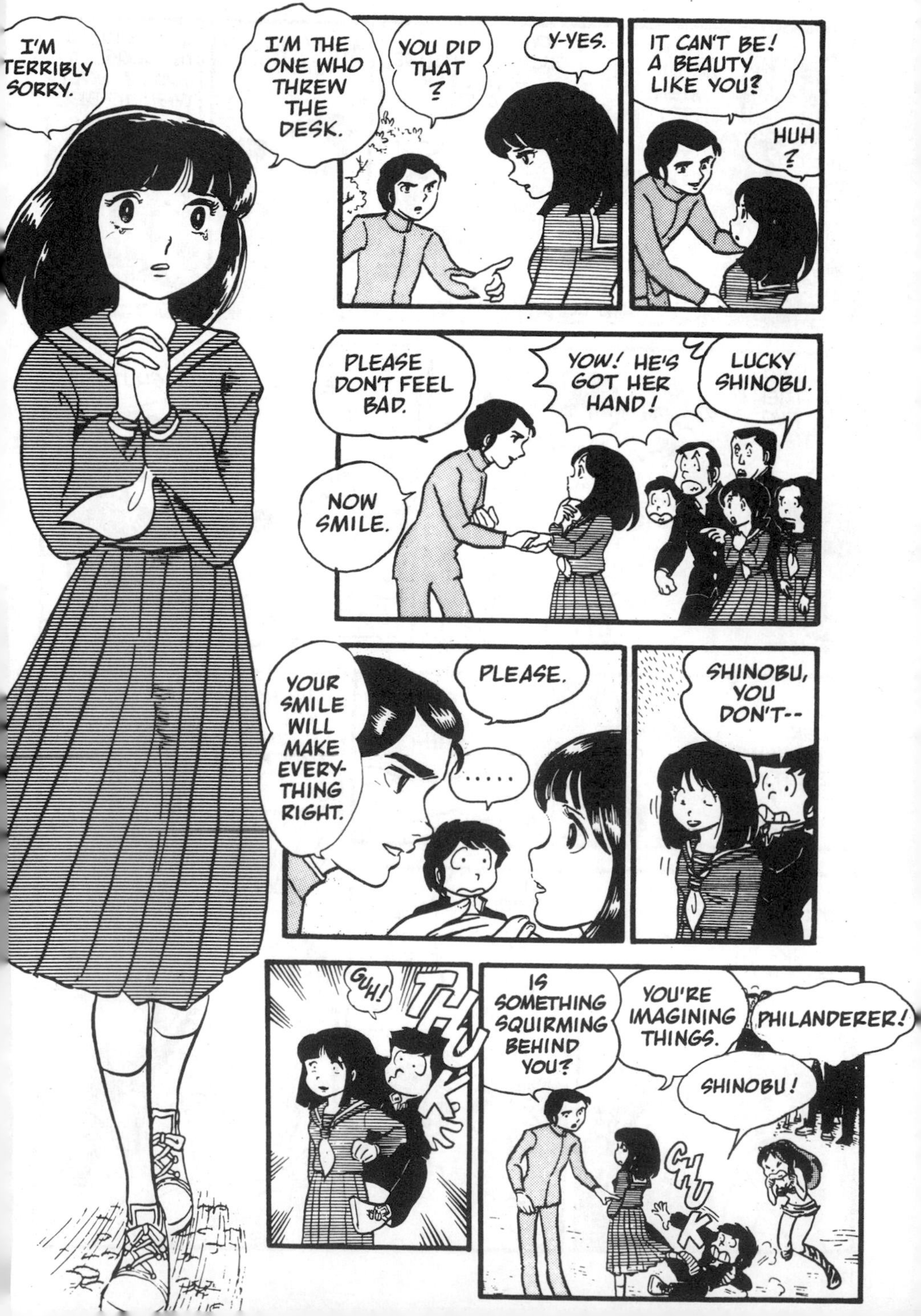
I'M TERRIBLY SORRY.
I'M THE ONE WHO THREW THE DESK.
YOU DID THAT?
Y-YES.
IT CAN'T BE! A BEAUTY LIKE YOU?
HUH?
PLEASE DON'T FEEL BAD.
YOW! HE'S GOT HER HAND!
LUCKY SHINOBU.
NOW SMILE.
YOUR SMILE WILL MAKE EVERY-THING RIGHT.
PLEASE.
......
SHINOBU, YOU DON'T--
GUH!
THUK
IS SOMETHING SQUIRMING BEHIND YOU?
YOU'RE IMAGINING THINGS.
PHILANDERER!
SHINOBU!
CHUK

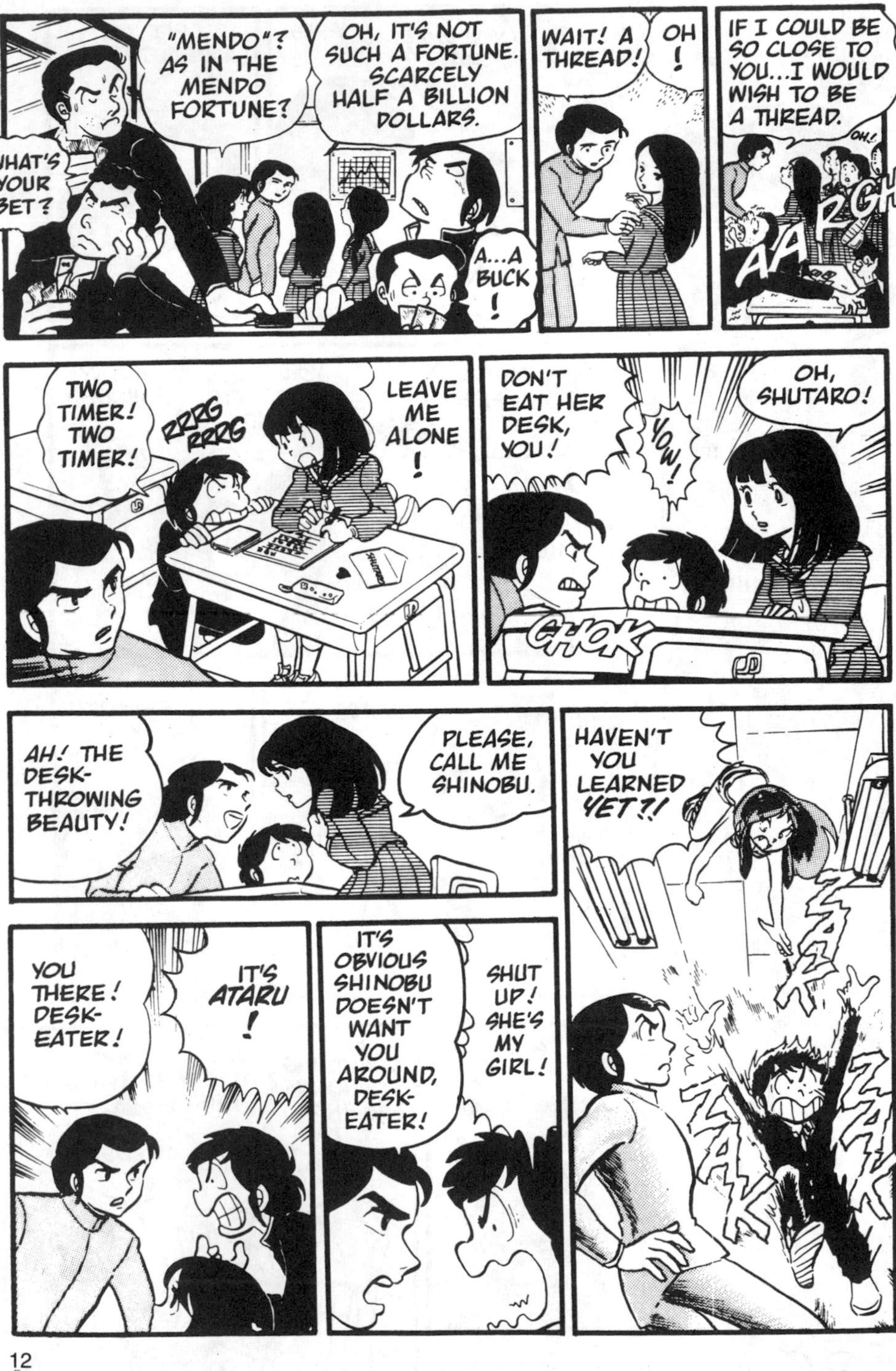
"MENDO"? AS IN THE MENDO FORTUNE?
OH, IT'S NOT SUCH A FORTUNE. SCARCELY HALF A BILLION DOLLARS.
WHAT'S YOUR BET?
A...A BUCK!
WAIT! A THREAD!
OH!
IF I COULD BE SO CLOSE TO YOU...I WOULD WISH TO BE A THREAD.
OH!
AARGH
TWO TIMER! TWO TIMER!
RRRG RRRG
LEAVE ME ALONE!
DON'T EAT HER DESK, YOU!
YOW!
OH, SHUTARO!
CHOK
AH! THE DESK-THROWING BEAUTY!
PLEASE, CALL ME SHINOBU.
YOU THERE! DESK-EATER!
IT'S ATARU!
IT'S OBVIOUS SHINOBU DOESN'T WANT YOU AROUND, DESK-EATER!
SHUT UP! SHE'S MY GIRL!
HAVEN'T YOU LEARNED YET?!

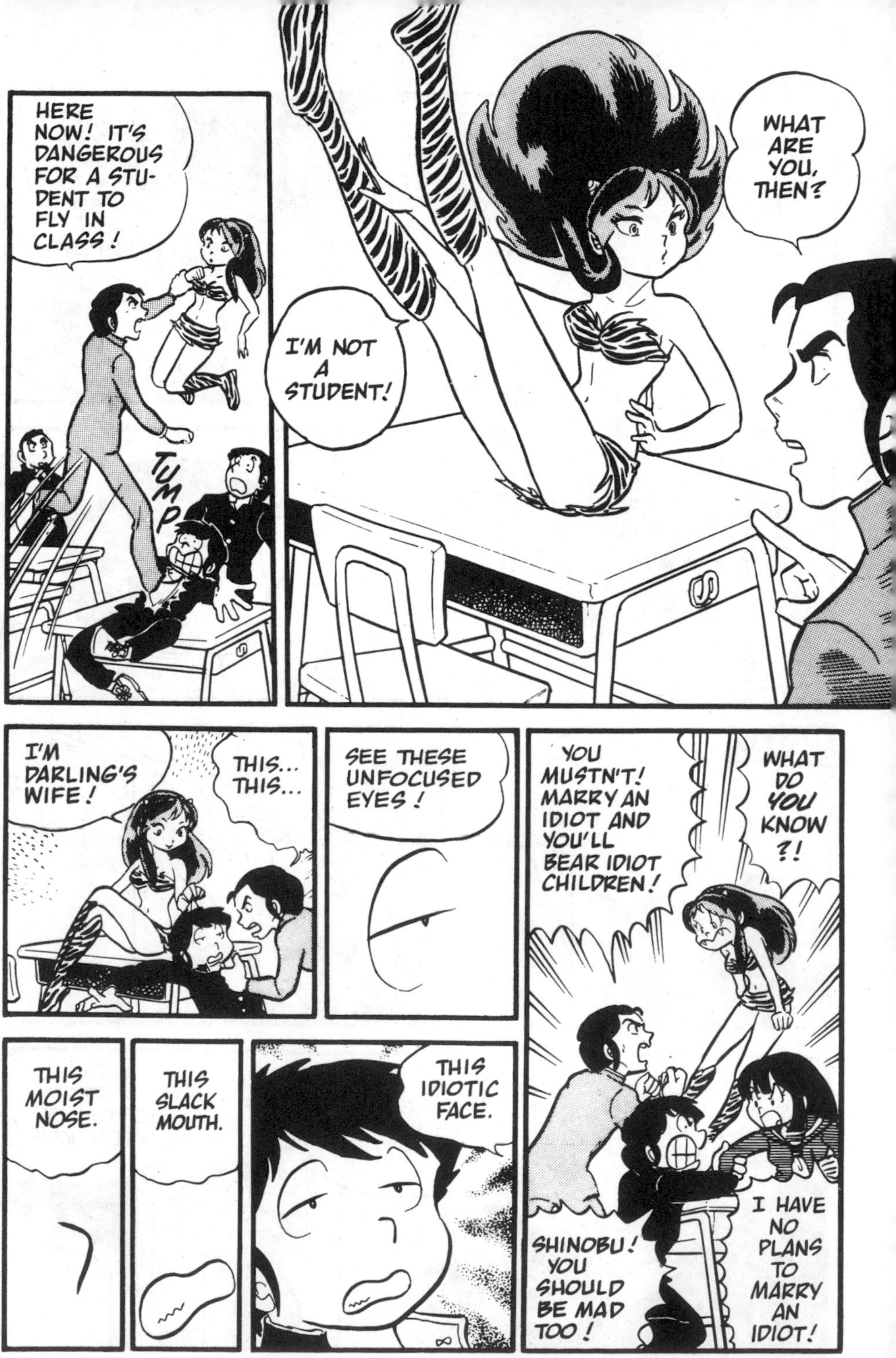
HERE NOW! IT'S DANGEROUS FOR A STUDENT TO FLY IN CLASS!
TUMP
I'M NOT A STUDENT!
WHAT ARE YOU, THEN?
I'M DARLING'S WIFE!
THIS... THIS...
SEE THESE UNFOCUSED EYES!
YOU MUSTN'T! MARRY AN IDIOT AND YOU'LL BEAR IDIOT CHILDREN!
WHAT DO YOU KNOW?!
THIS MOIST NOSE.
THIS SLACK MOUTH.
THIS IDIOTIC FACE.
SHINOBU! YOU SHOULD BE MAD TOO!
I HAVE NO PLANS TO MARRY AN IDIOT!

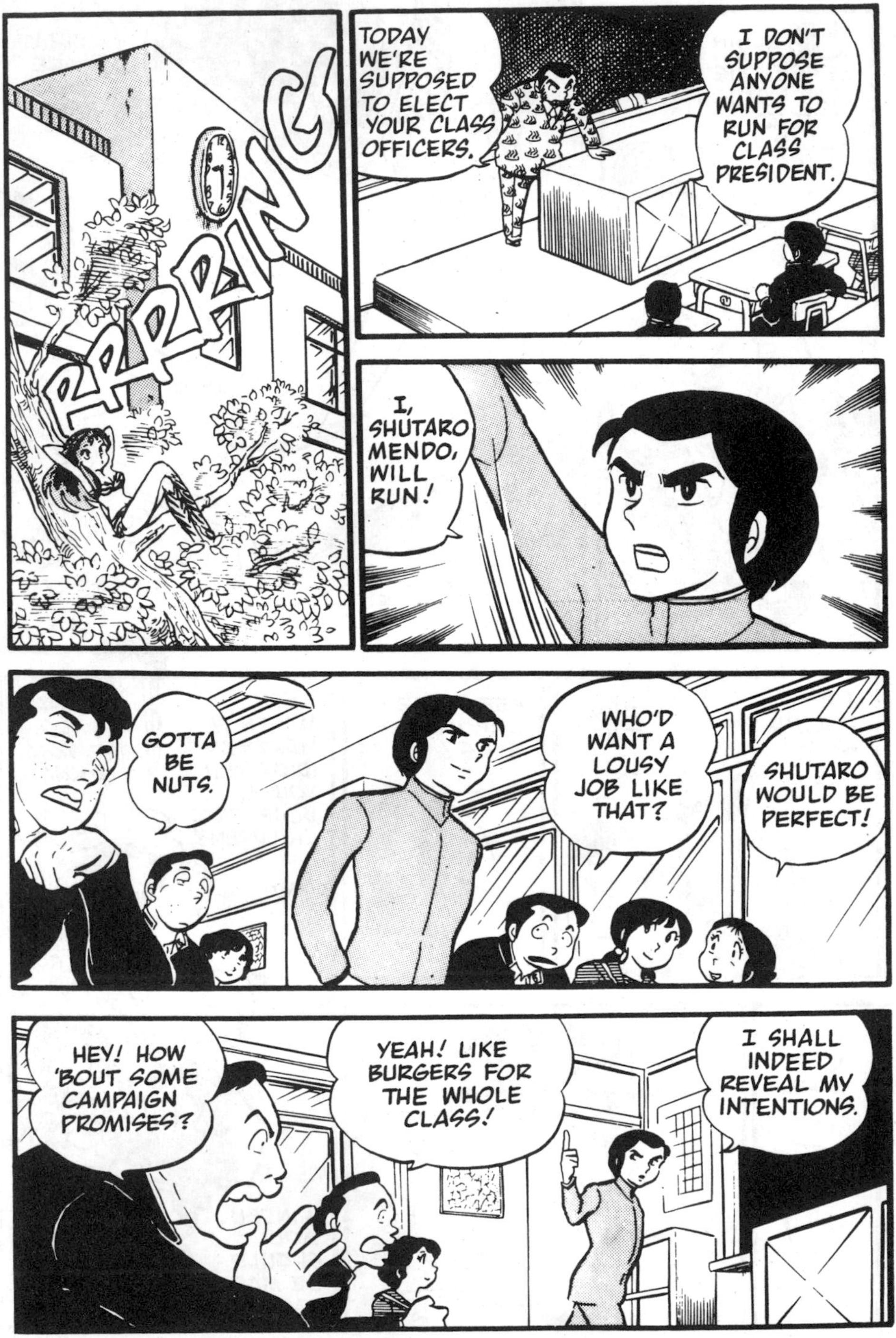
RRRRING
TODAY WE'RE SUPPOSED TO ELECT YOUR CLASS OFFICERS.
I DON'T SUPPOSE ANYONE WANTS TO RUN FOR CLASS PRESIDENT.
I, SHUTARO MENDO, WILL RUN!
GOTTA BE NUTS.
WHO'D WANT A LOUSY JOB LIKE THAT?
SHUTARO WOULD BE PERFECT!
HEY! HOW 'BOUT SOME CAMPAIGN PROMISES?
YEAH! LIKE BURGERS FOR THE WHOLE CLASS!
I SHALL INDEED REVEAL MY INTENTIONS.

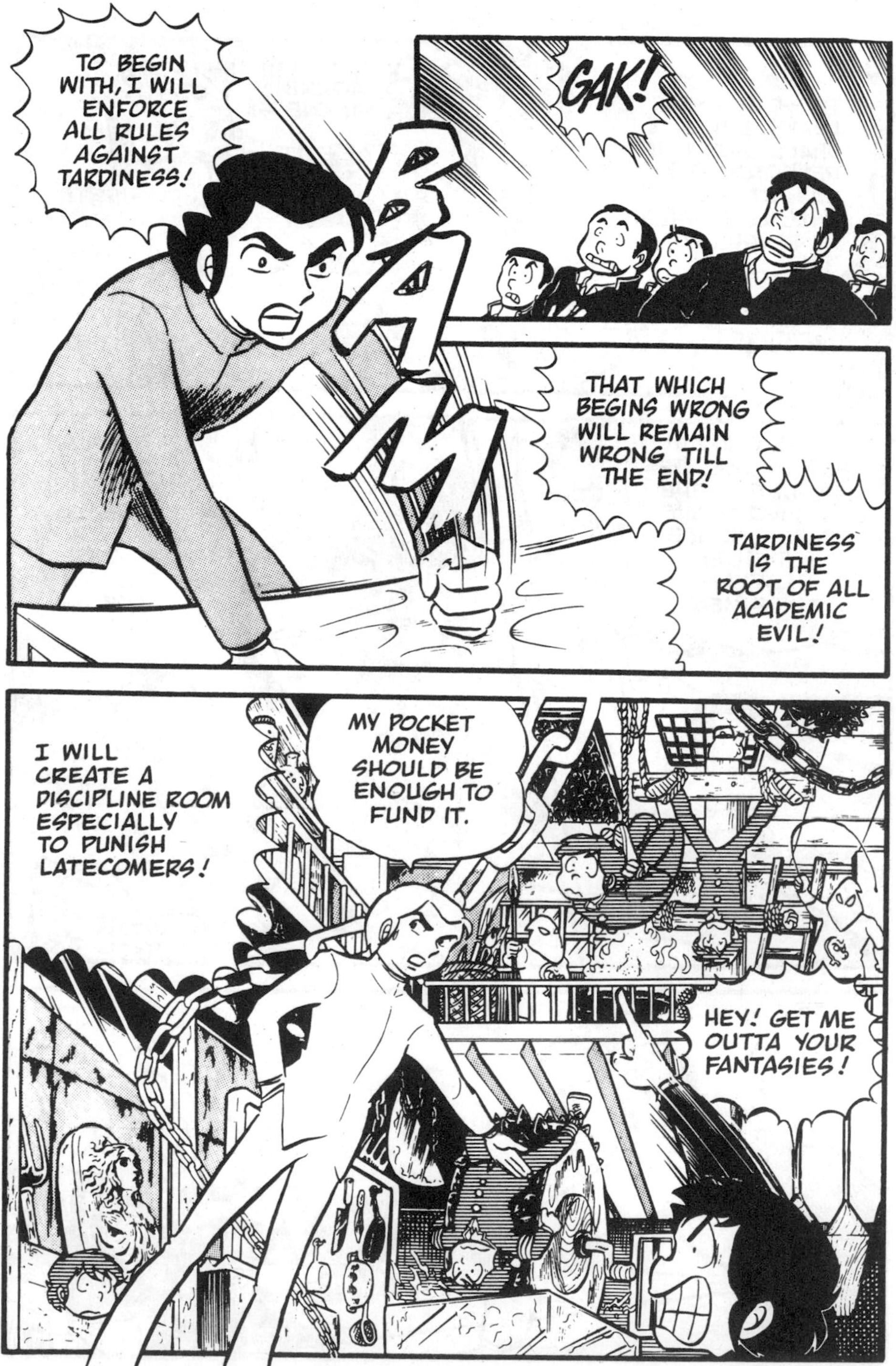
TO BEGIN WITH, I WILL ENFORCE ALL RULES AGAINST TARDINESS!
BAM
GAK!
THAT WHICH BEGINS WRONG WILL REMAIN WRONG TILL THE END!
TARDINESS IS THE ROOT OF ALL ACADEMIC EVIL!
I WILL CREATE A DISCIPLINE ROOM ESPECIALLY TO PUNISH LATECOMERS!
MY POCKET MONEY SHOULD BE ENOUGH TO FUND IT.
HEY! GET ME OUTTA YOUR FANTASIES!

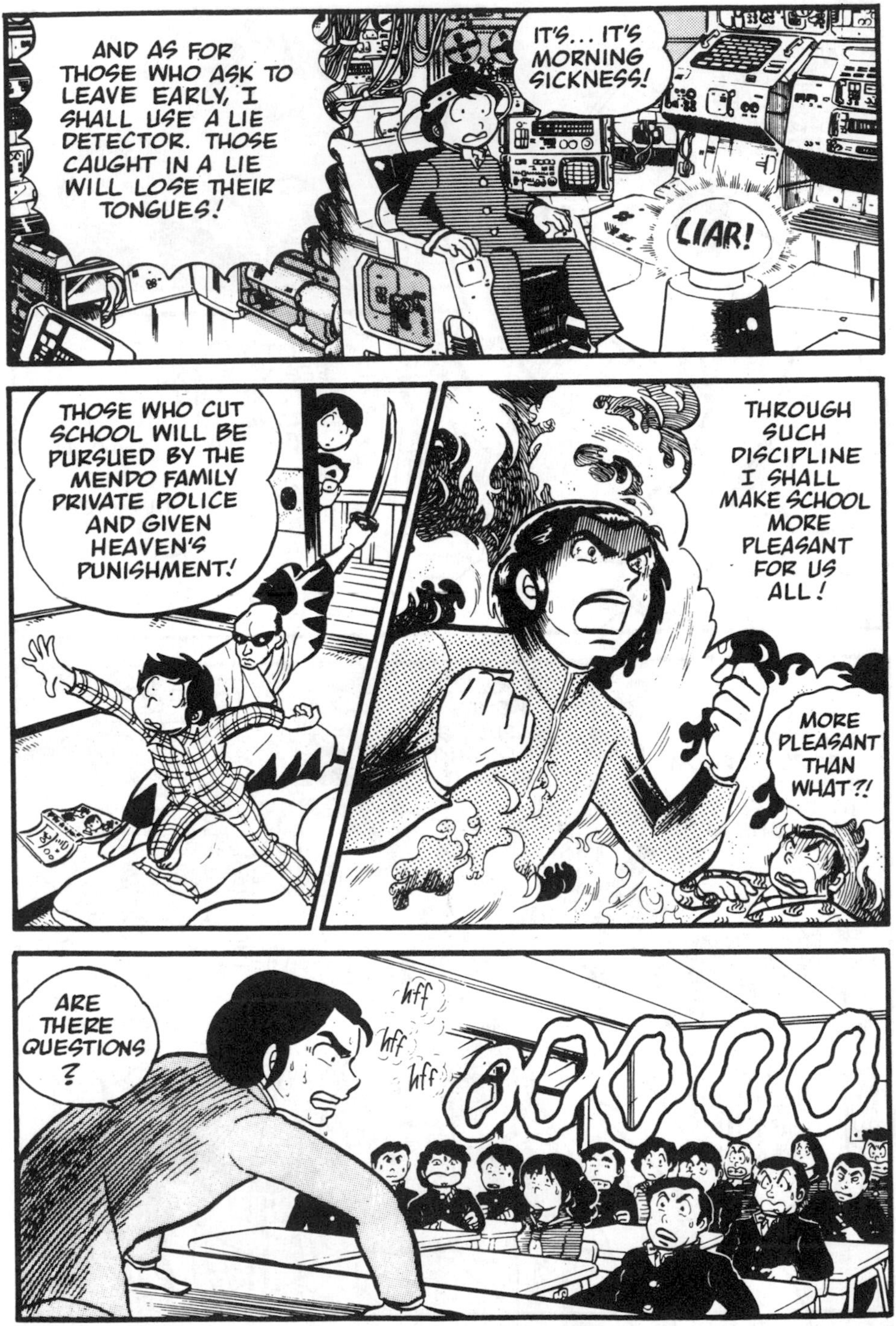
AND AS FOR THOSE WHO ASK TO LEAVE EARLY, I SHALL USE A LIE DETECTOR. THOSE CAUGHT IN A LIE WILL LOSE THEIR TONGUES!
IT'S... IT'S MORNING SICKNESS!
LIAR!
THOSE WHO CUT SCHOOL WILL BE PURSUED BY THE MENDO FAMILY PRIVATE POLICE AND GIVEN HEAVEN'S PUNISHMENT!
THROUGH SUCH DISCIPLINE I SHALL MAKE SCHOOL MORE PLEASANT FOR US ALL!
MORE PLEASANT THAN WHAT?!
ARE THERE QUESTIONS ?
hff
hff
hff

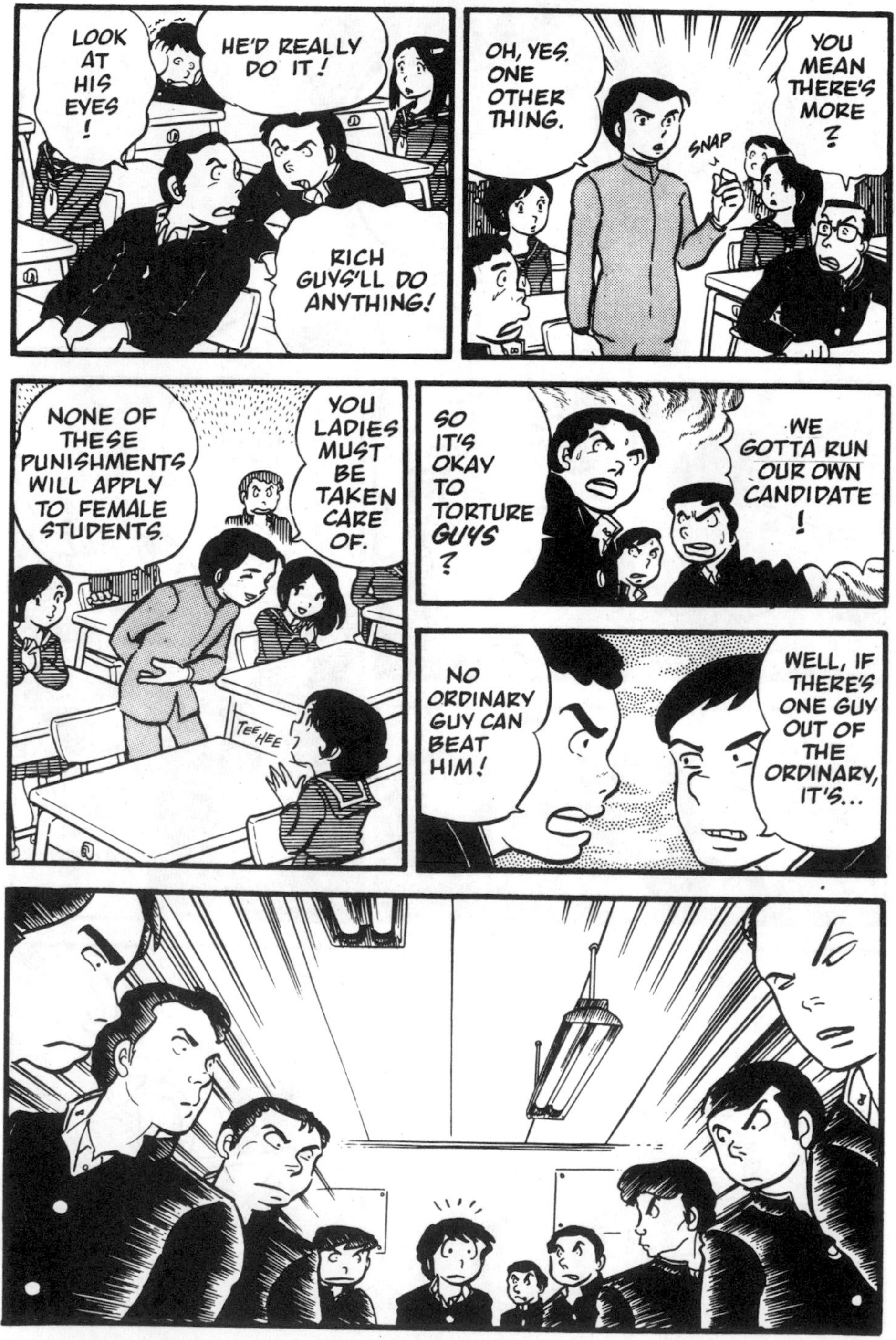
LOOK AT HIS EYES!
HE'D REALLY DO IT!
RICH GUYS'LL DO ANYTHING!
OH, YES. ONE OTHER THING.
SNAP
YOU MEAN THERE'S MORE?
NONE OF THESE PUNISHMENTS WILL APPLY TO FEMALE STUDENTS.
YOU LADIES MUST BE TAKEN CARE OF.
TEE HEE
SO IT'S OKAY TO TORTURE GUYS?
WE GOTTA RUN OUR OWN CANDIDATE!
NO ORDINARY GUY CAN BEAT HIM!
WELL, IF THERE'S ONE GUY OUT OF THE ORDINARY, IT'S...

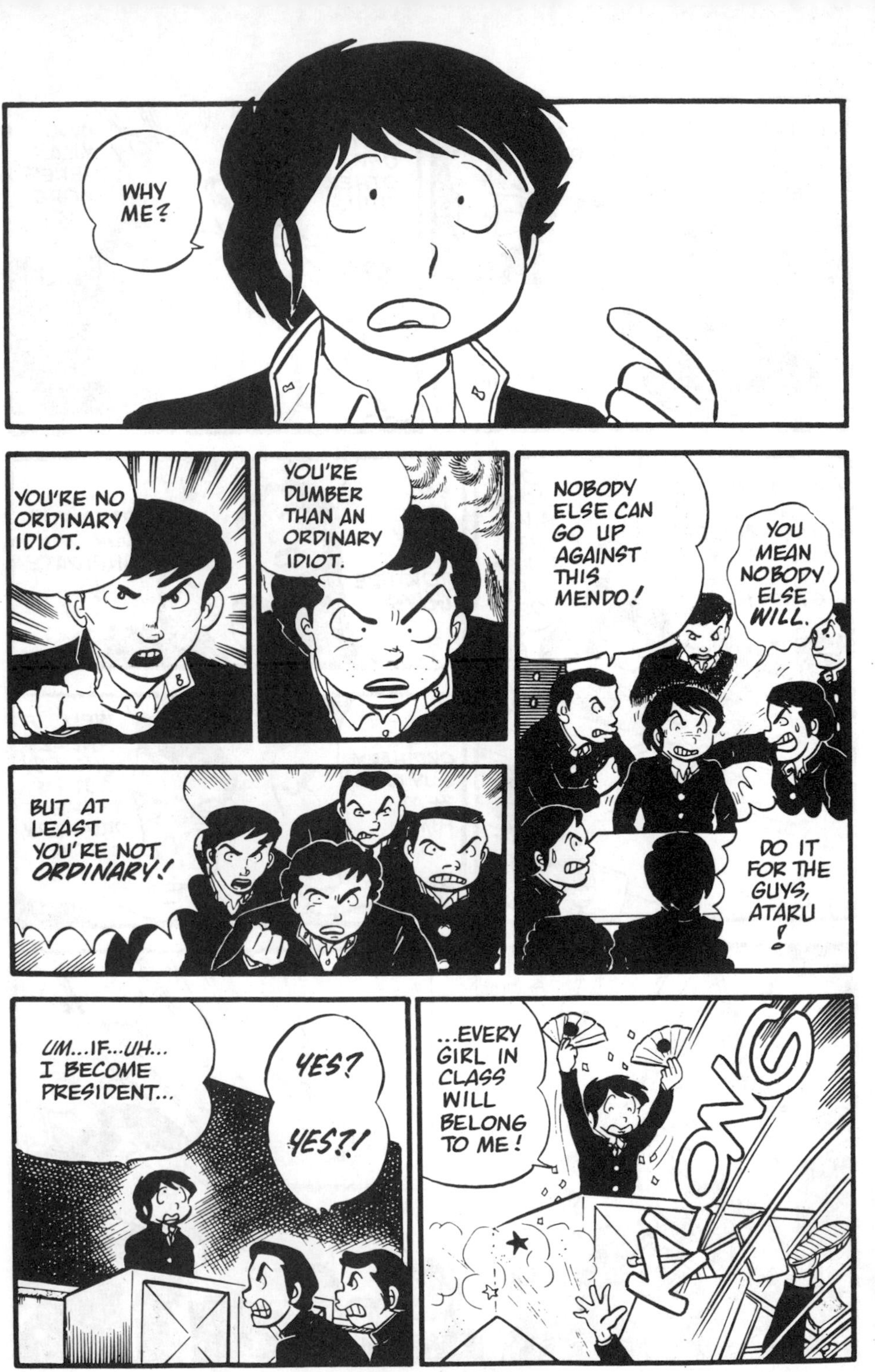
WHY ME?
YOU'RE NO ORDINARY IDIOT.
YOU'RE DUMBER THAN AN ORDINARY IDIOT.
NOBODY ELSE CAN GO UP AGAINST THIS MENDO!
YOU MEAN NOBODY ELSE WILL.
BUT AT LEAST YOU'RE NOT ORDINARY!
DO IT FOR THE GUYS, ATARU!
UM...IF...UH... I BECOME PRESIDENT...
YES?
YES?!
...EVERY GIRL IN CLASS WILL BELONG TO ME!
KLONG

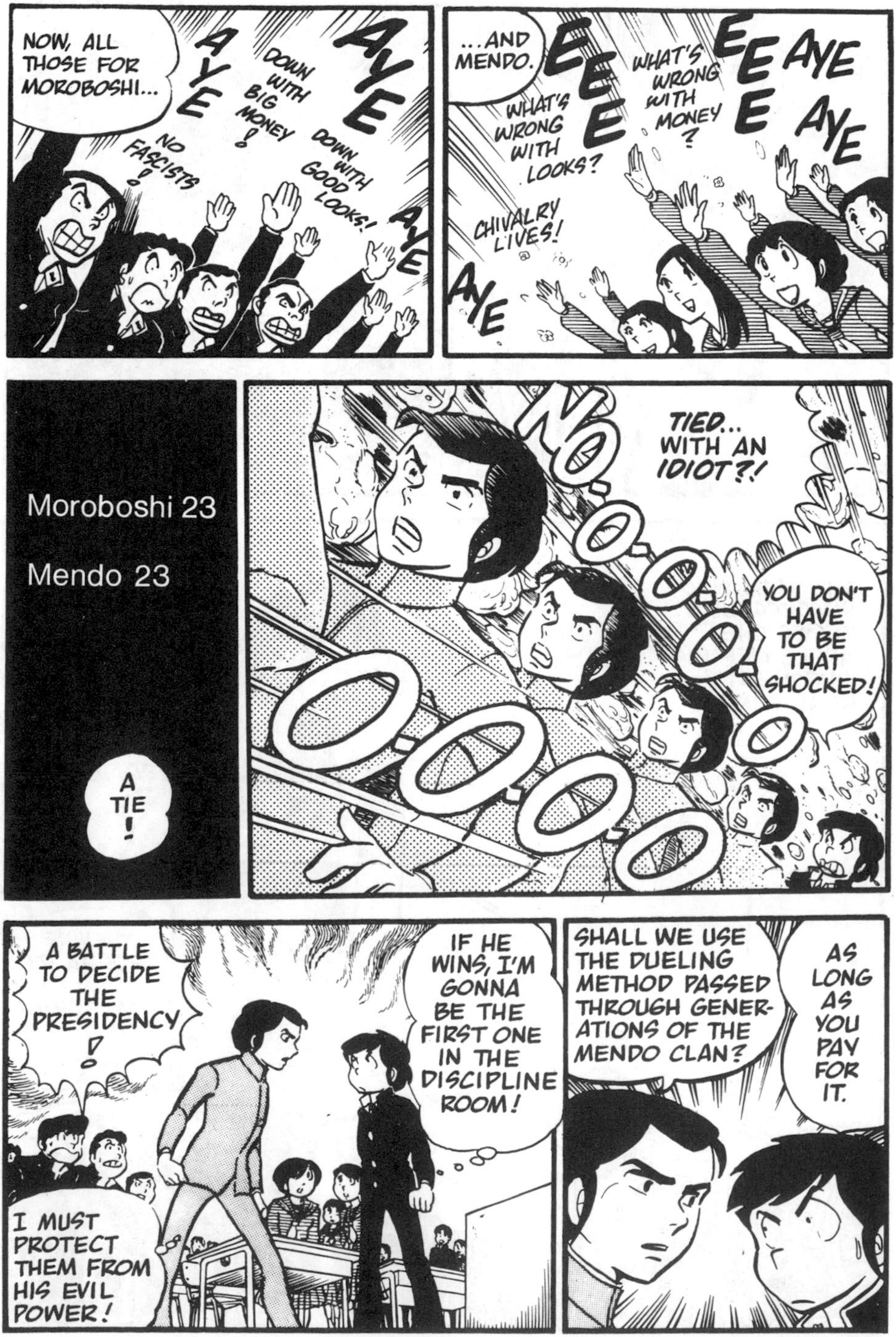

NOW, ALL THOSE FOR MOROBOSHI...
AYE
AYE
DOWN WITH BIG MONEY!
NO FASCISTS!
DOWN WITH GOOD LOOKS!
AYE
...AND MENDO.
EEE
WHAT'S WRONG WITH LOOKS?
WHAT'S WRONG WITH MONEY?
EEE
AYE
AYE
CHIVALRY LIVES!
AYE
Moroboshi 23
Mendo 23
A TIE!
NO...O...O...O...O...O...O...O...O...O
TIED... WITH AN IDIOT?!
YOU DON'T HAVE TO BE THAT SHOCKED!
A BATTLE TO DECIDE THE PRESIDENCY!
I MUST PROTECT THEM FROM HIS EVIL POWER!
IF HE WINS, I'M GONNA BE THE FIRST ONE IN THE DISCIPLINE ROOM!
SHALL WE USE THE DUELING METHOD PASSED THROUGH GENERATIONS OF THE MENDO CLAN?
AS LONG AS YOU PAY FOR IT.

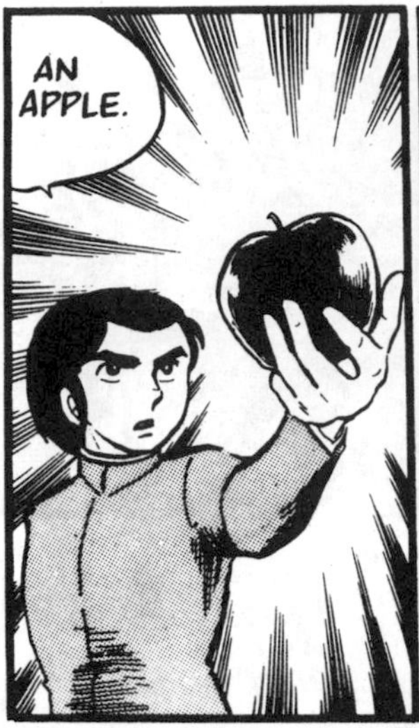
AN APPLE.

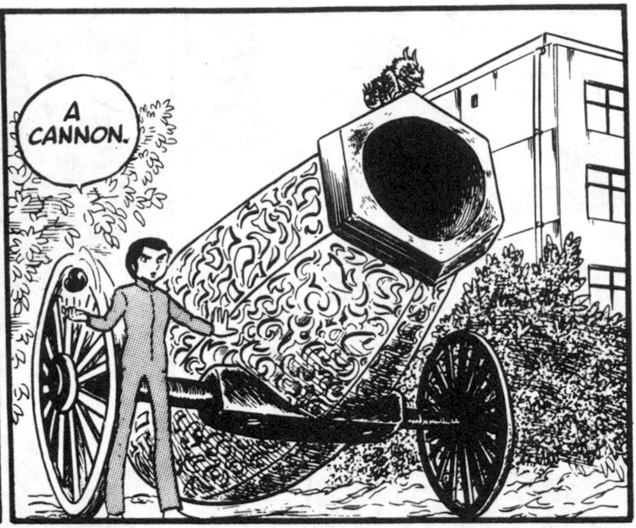
A CANNON.

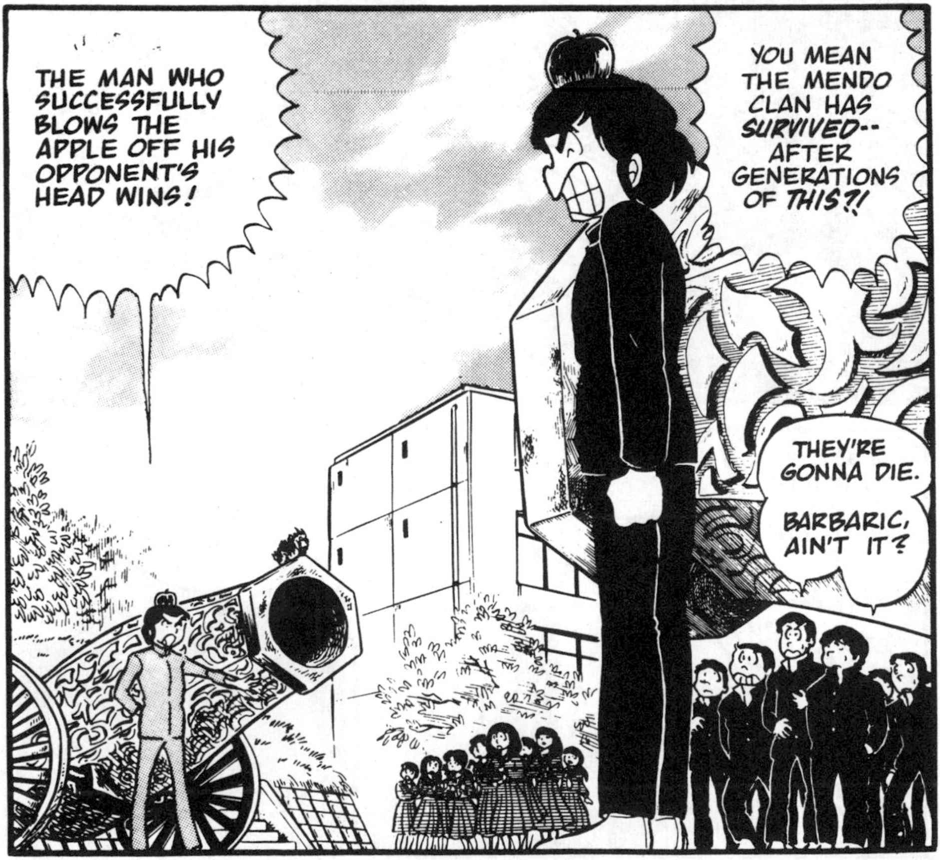
THE MAN WHO SUCCESSFULLY BLOWS THE APPLE OFF HIS OPPONENT'S HEAD WINS!
YOU MEAN THE MENDO CLAN HAS SURVIVED-- AFTER GENERATIONS OF THIS?!
THEY'RE GONNA DIE.
BARBARIC, AIN'T IT?

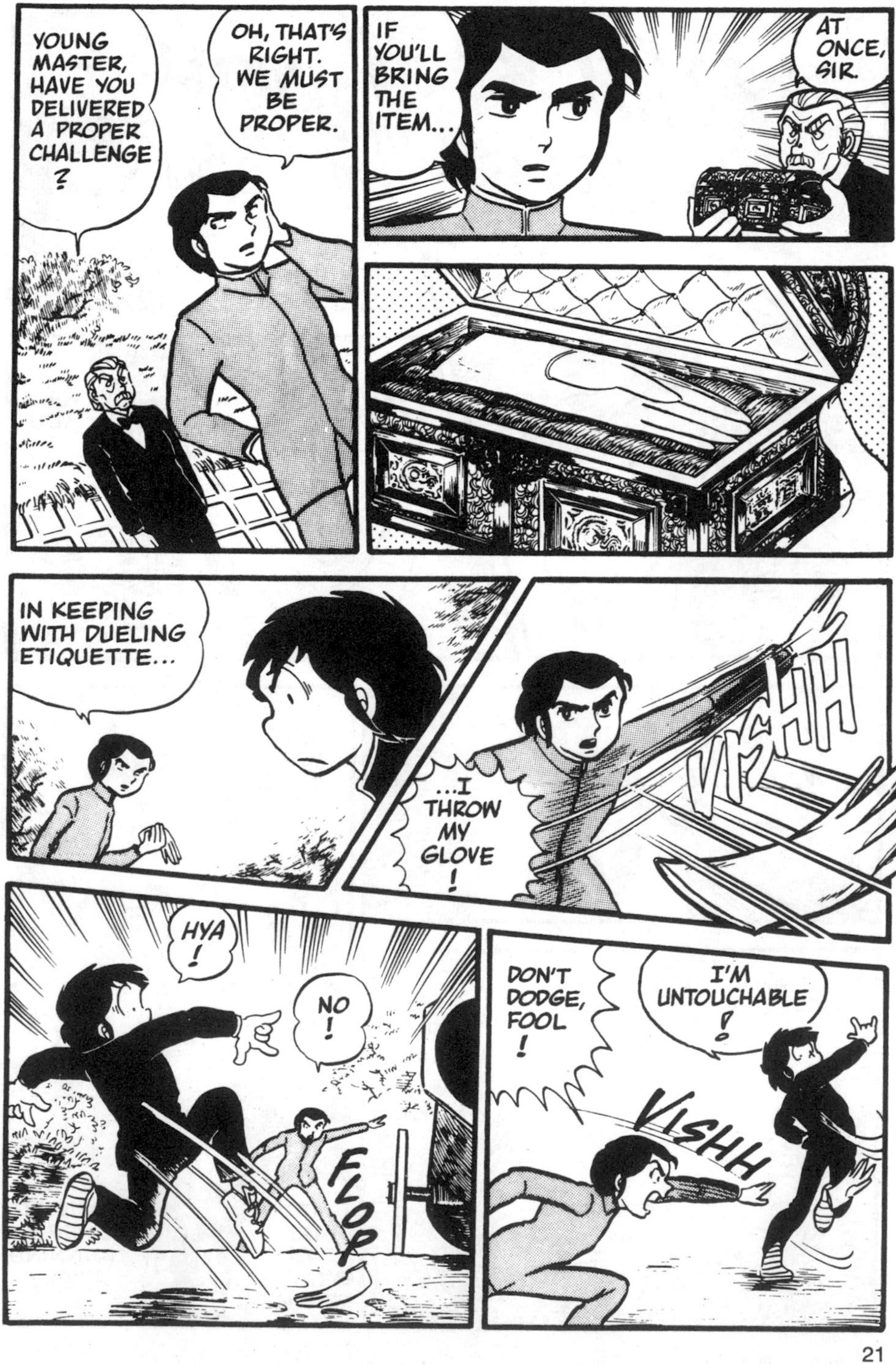
YOUNG MASTER, HAVE YOU DELIVERED A PROPER CHALLENGE?
OH, THAT'S RIGHT. WE MUST BE PROPER.
IF YOU'LL BRING THE ITEM...
AT ONCE, SIR.
IN KEEPING WITH DUELING ETIQUETTE...
...I THROW MY GLOVE!
VISHH
HYA!
NO!
FLOP
DON'T DODGE, FOOL!
I'M UNTOUCHABLE!
VISHH

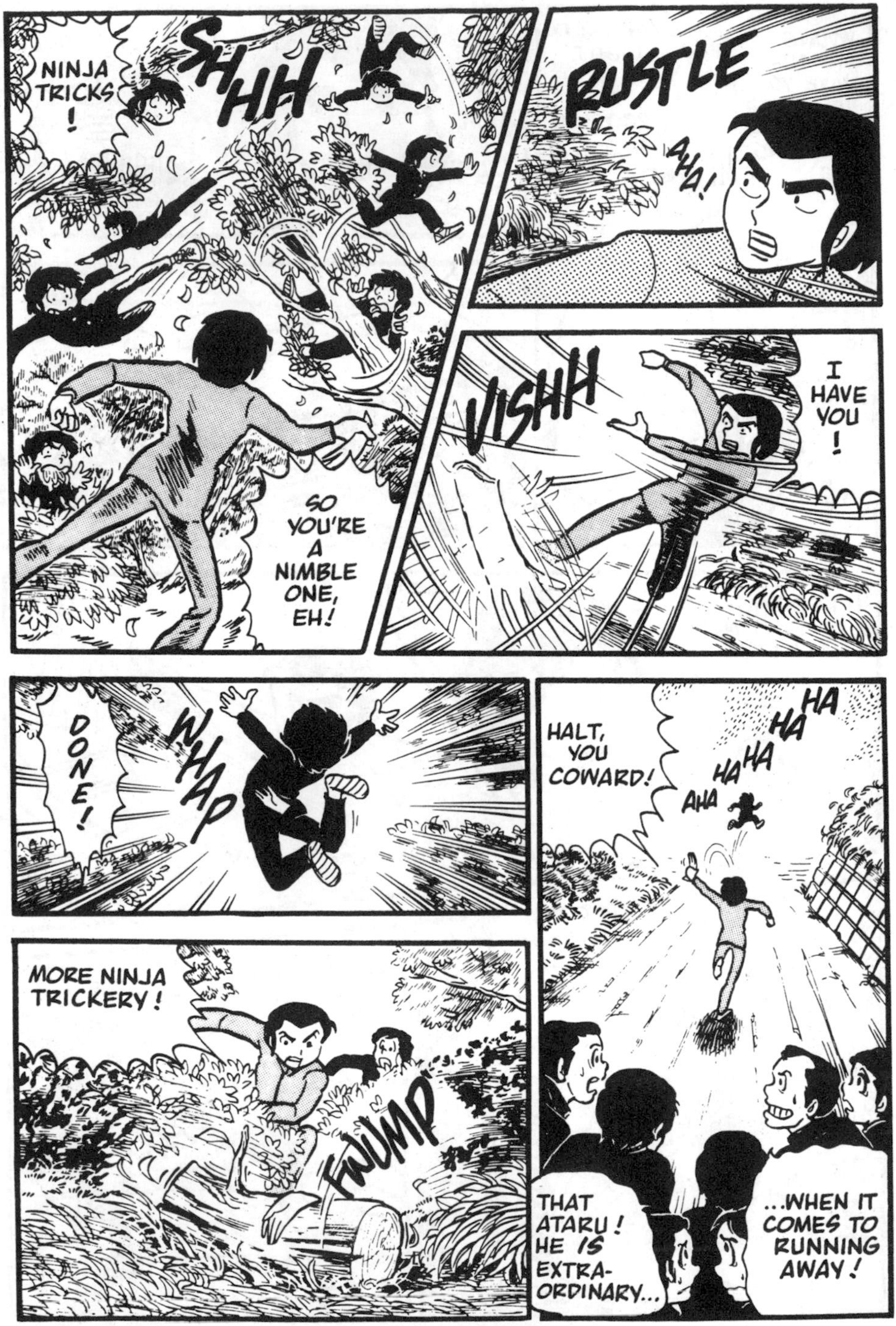
NINJA TRICKS!
SHHH
SO YOU'RE A NIMBLE ONE, EH!
RUSTLE
AHA!
VISHH
I HAVE YOU!
DONE!
WHAP
MORE NINJA TRICKERY!
FWUMP
HALT, YOU COWARD!
AHA HA HA HA HA
THAT ATARU! HE IS EXTRA-ORDINARY...
...WHEN IT COMES TO RUNNING AWAY!

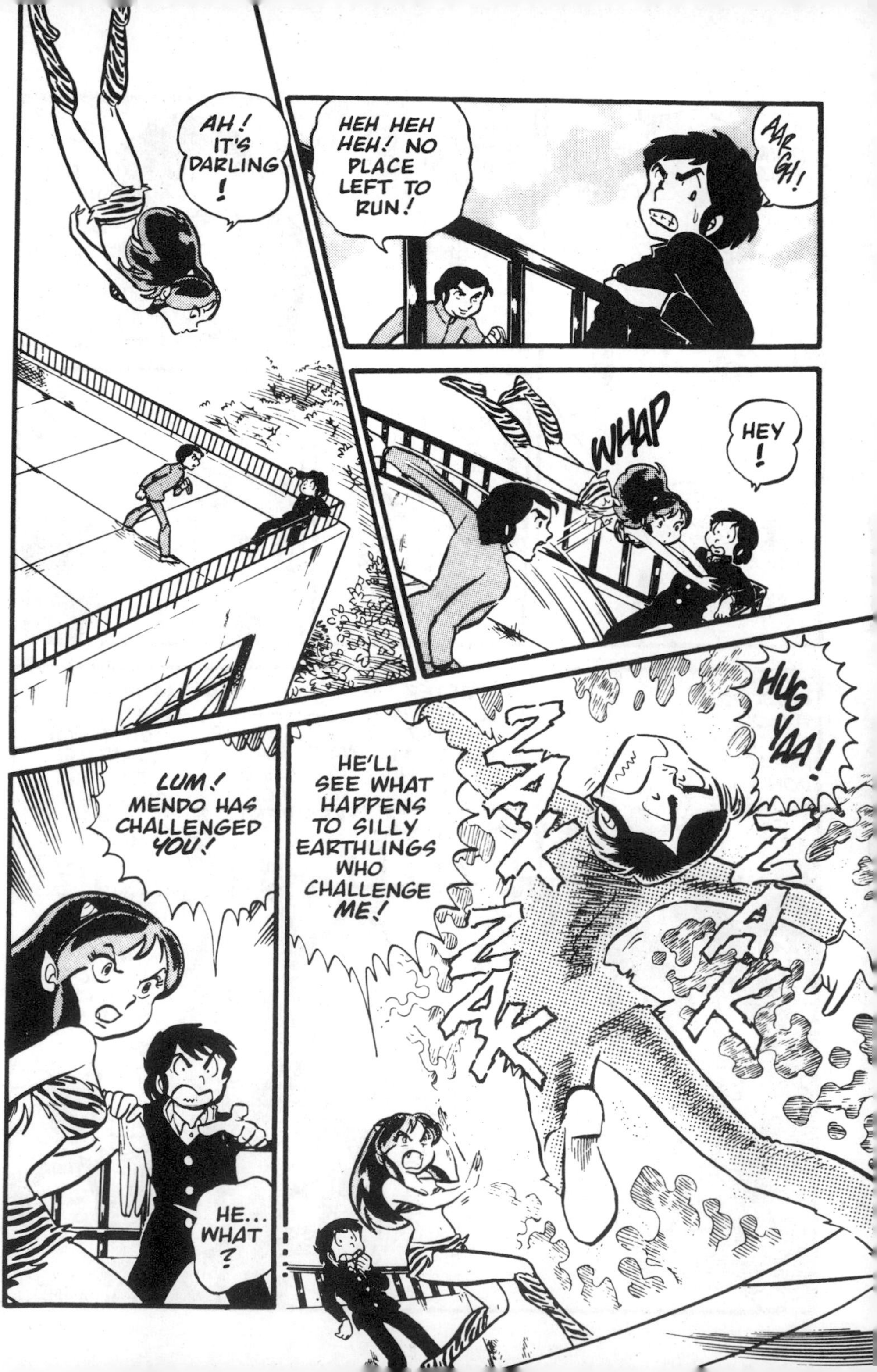
AH! IT'S DARLING!
HEH HEH HEH! NO PLACE LEFT TO RUN!
AARGH!
WHAP
HEY!
LUM! MENDO HAS CHALLENGED YOU!
HE... WHAT?
HE'LL SEE WHAT HAPPENS TO SILLY EARTHLINGS WHO CHALLENGE ME!
HUG YAA!
ZAK ZAK
ZAK ZAK

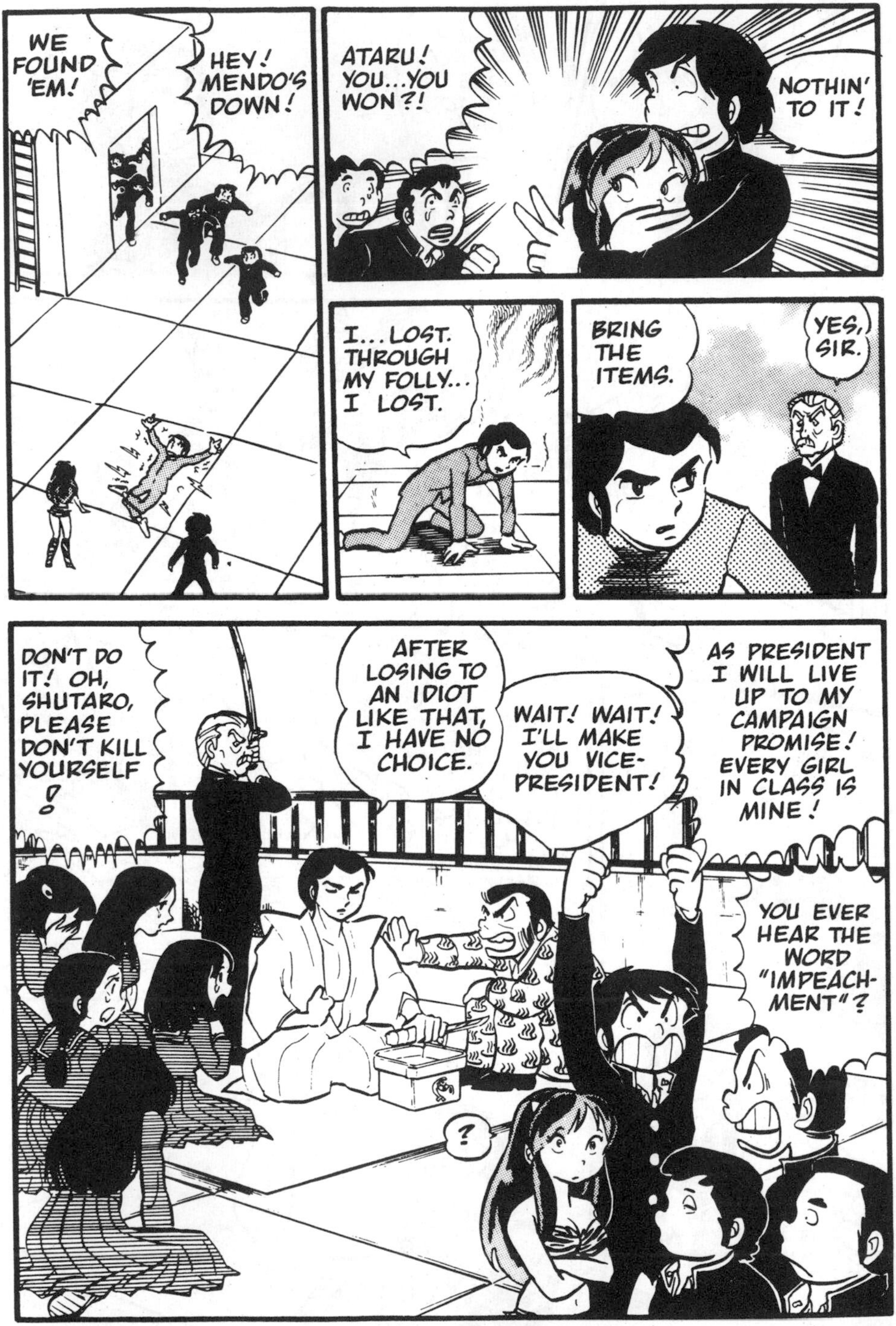
WE FOUND 'EM!
HEY! MENDO'S DOWN!
ATARU! YOU...YOU WON?!
NOTHIN' TO IT!
I...LOST. THROUGH MY FOLLY... I LOST.
BRING THE ITEMS.
YES, SIR.
DON'T DO IT! OH, SHUTARO, PLEASE DON'T KILL YOURSELF!
AFTER LOSING TO AN IDIOT LIKE THAT, I HAVE NO CHOICE.
WAIT! WAIT! I'LL MAKE YOU VICE-PRESIDENT!
AS PRESIDENT I WILL LIVE UP TO MY CAMPAIGN PROMISE! EVERY GIRL IN CLASS IS MINE!
YOU EVER HEAR THE WORD "IMPEACHMENT"?
?

Part 2
Zodiac-Go-Round

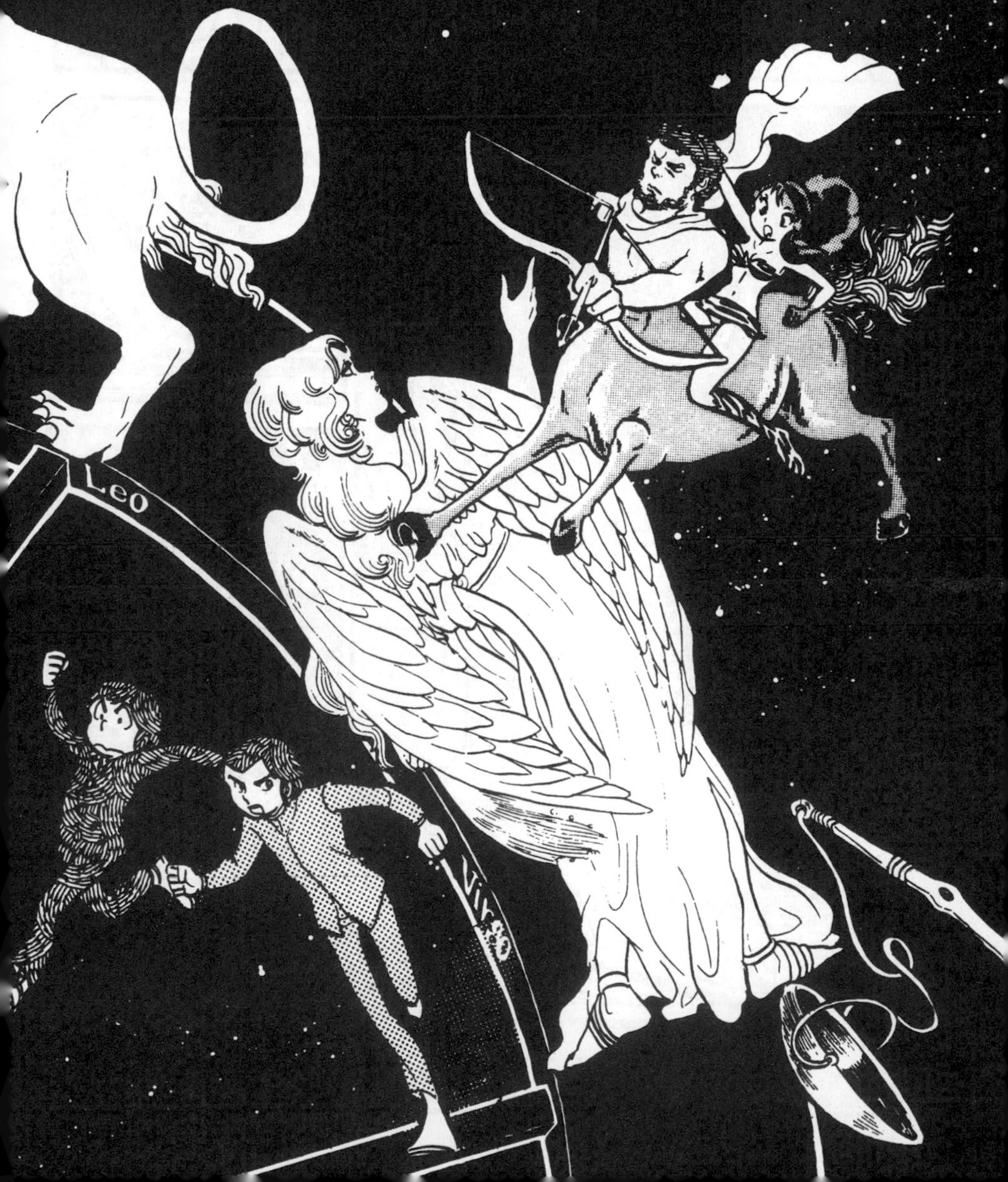
Leo

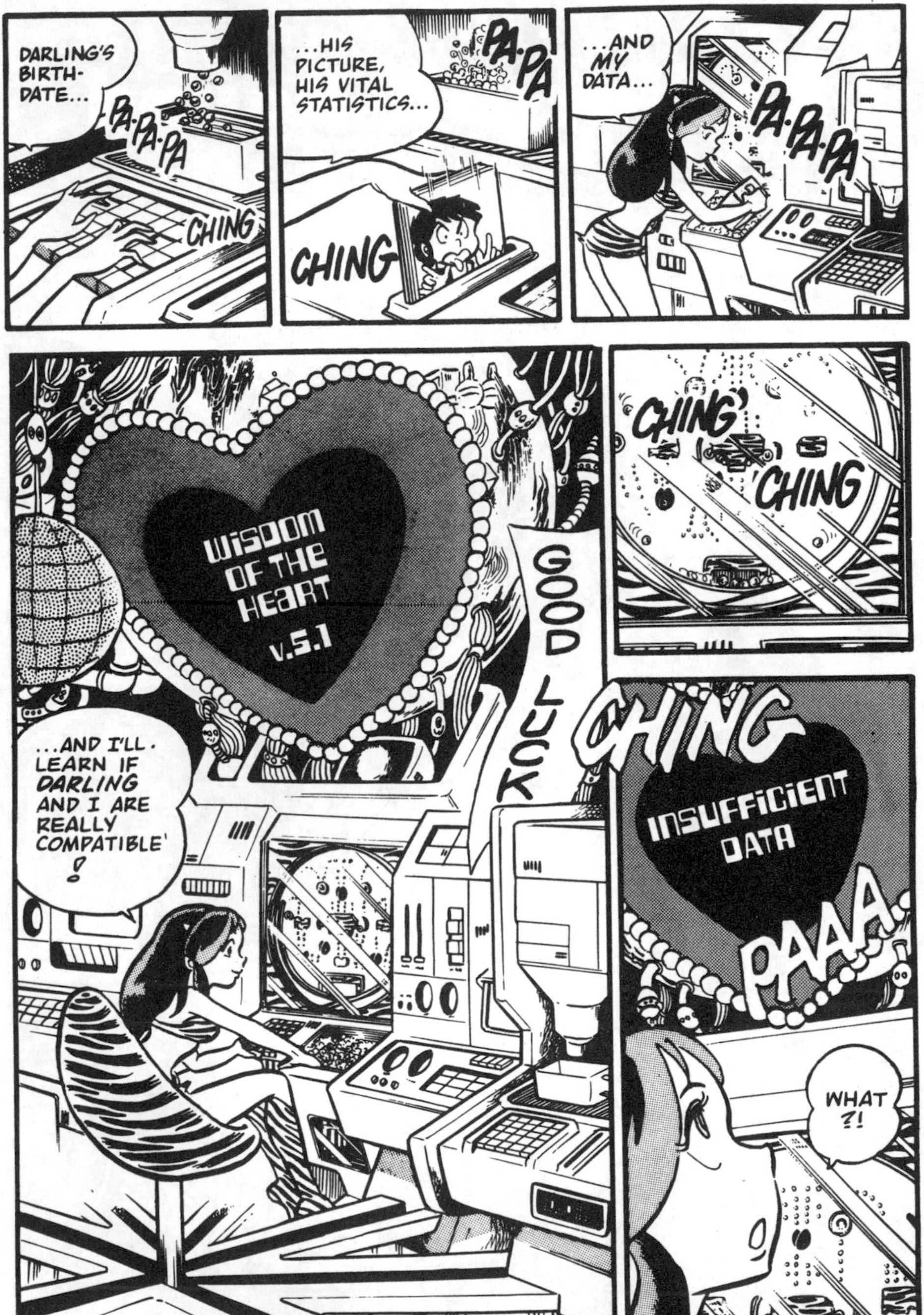

DARLING'S BIRTH-DATE...
PA-PA-PA
CHING
...HIS PICTURE, HIS VITAL STATISTICS...
PA-PA
CHING
...AND MY DATA...
PA-PA-PA-PA
WISDOM OF THE HEART v.5.1
GOOD LUCK
...AND I'LL LEARN IF DARLING AND I ARE REALLY COMPATIBLE!
CHING
CHING
CHING
INSUFFICIENT DATA
PAAA
WHAT ?!

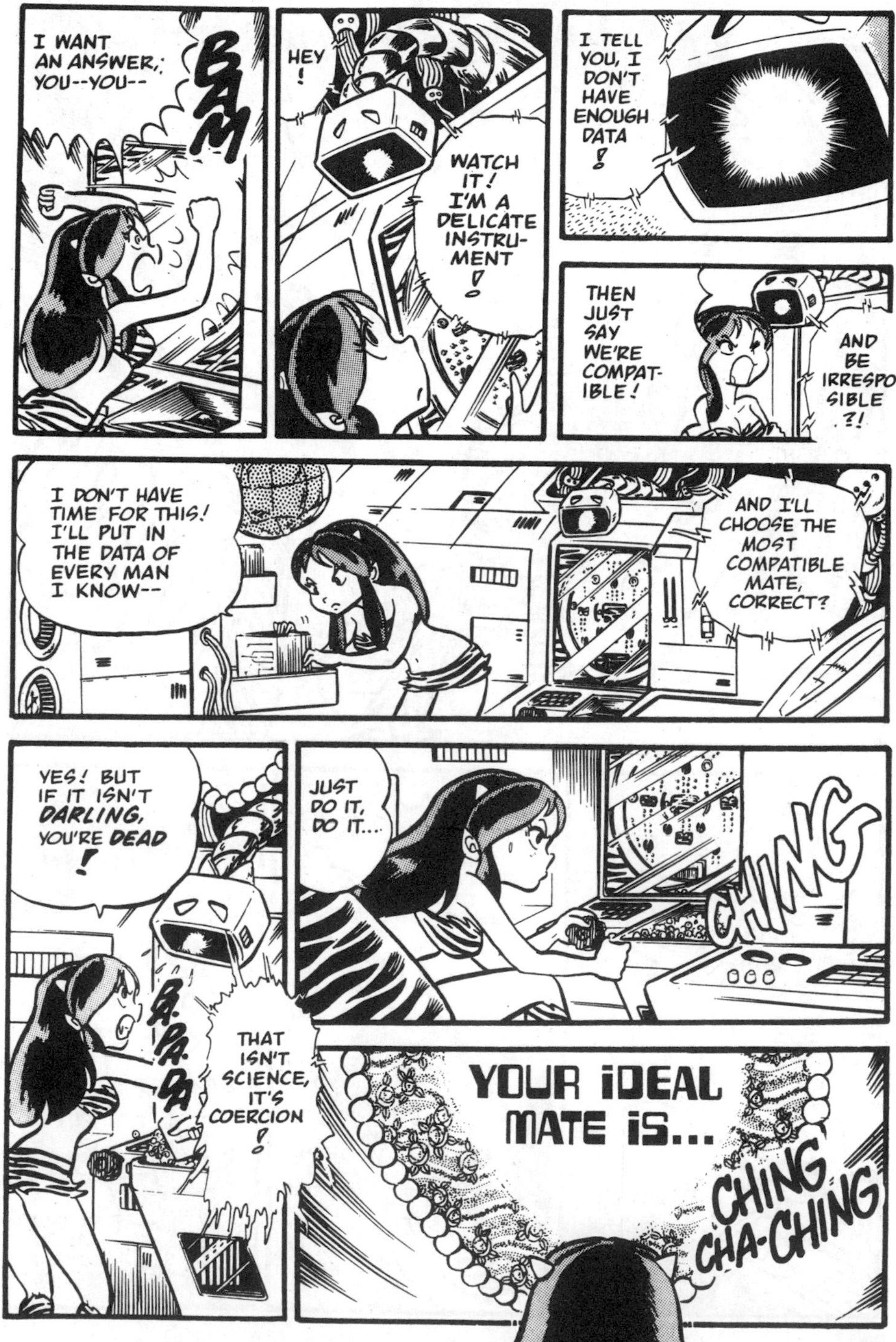
I WANT AN ANSWER, YOU--YOU--
BAM
HEY!
WATCH IT! I'M A DELICATE INSTRUMENT!
I TELL YOU, I DON'T HAVE ENOUGH DATA!
THEN JUST SAY WE'RE COMPATIBLE!
AND BE IRRESPONSIBLE?!
I DON'T HAVE TIME FOR THIS! I'LL PUT IN THE DATA OF EVERY MAN I KNOW--
AND I'LL CHOOSE THE MOST COMPATIBLE MATE, CORRECT?
YES! BUT IF IT ISN'T DARLING, YOU'RE DEAD!
BA-PA-DA
THAT ISN'T SCIENCE, IT'S COERCION!
JUST DO IT, DO IT...
CHING
YOUR iDEAL MATE iS...
CHING CHA-CHING

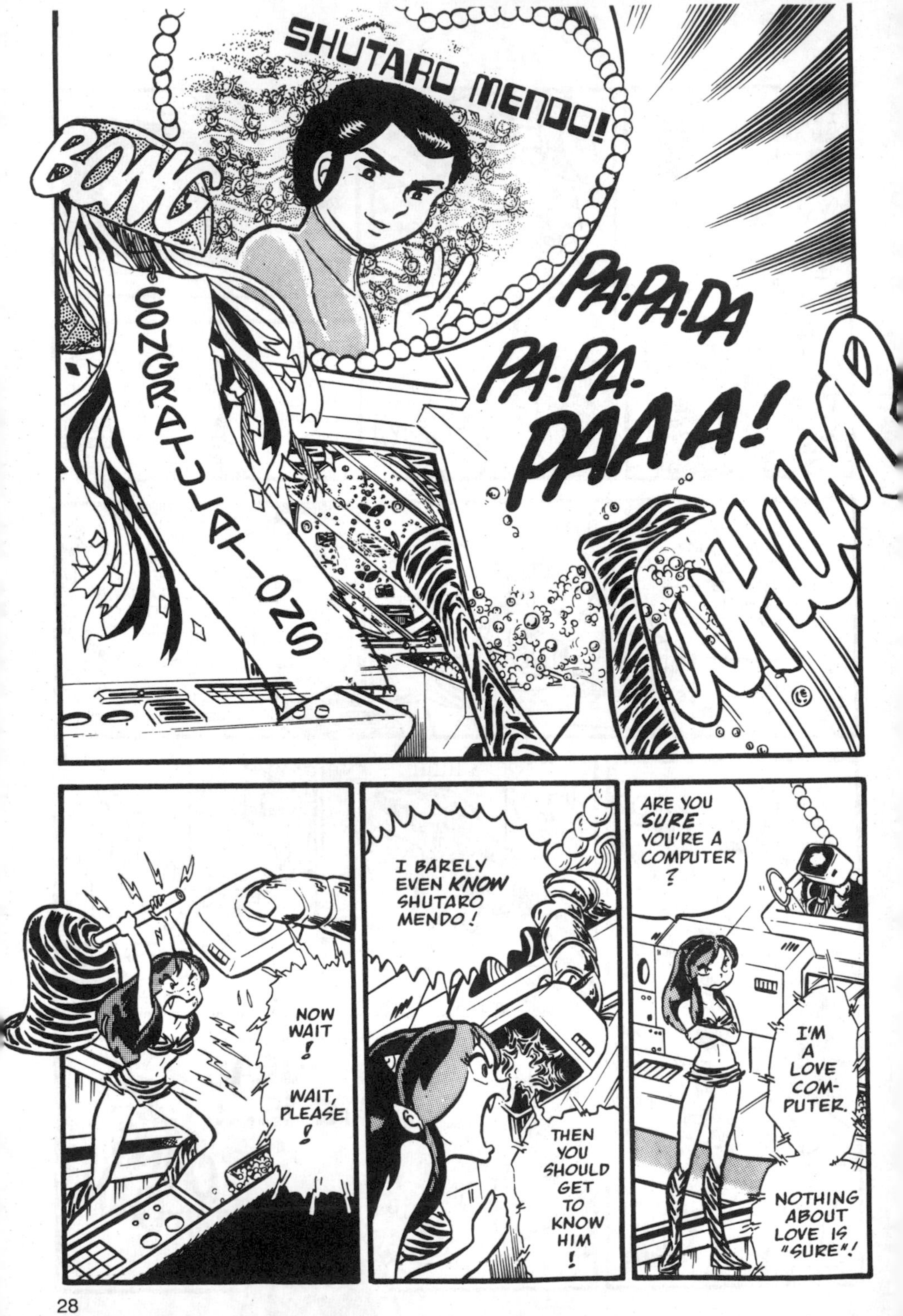
SHUTARO MENDO!
BONG
CONGRATULATIONS
PA-PA-DA
PA-PA-
PAAA A!
CHUMP
NOW WAIT!
WAIT, PLEASE!
I BARELY EVEN KNOW SHUTARO MENDO!
THEN YOU SHOULD GET TO KNOW HIM!
ARE YOU SURE YOU'RE A COMPUTER?
I'M A LOVE COM-PUTER.
NOTHING ABOUT LOVE IS "SURE"!

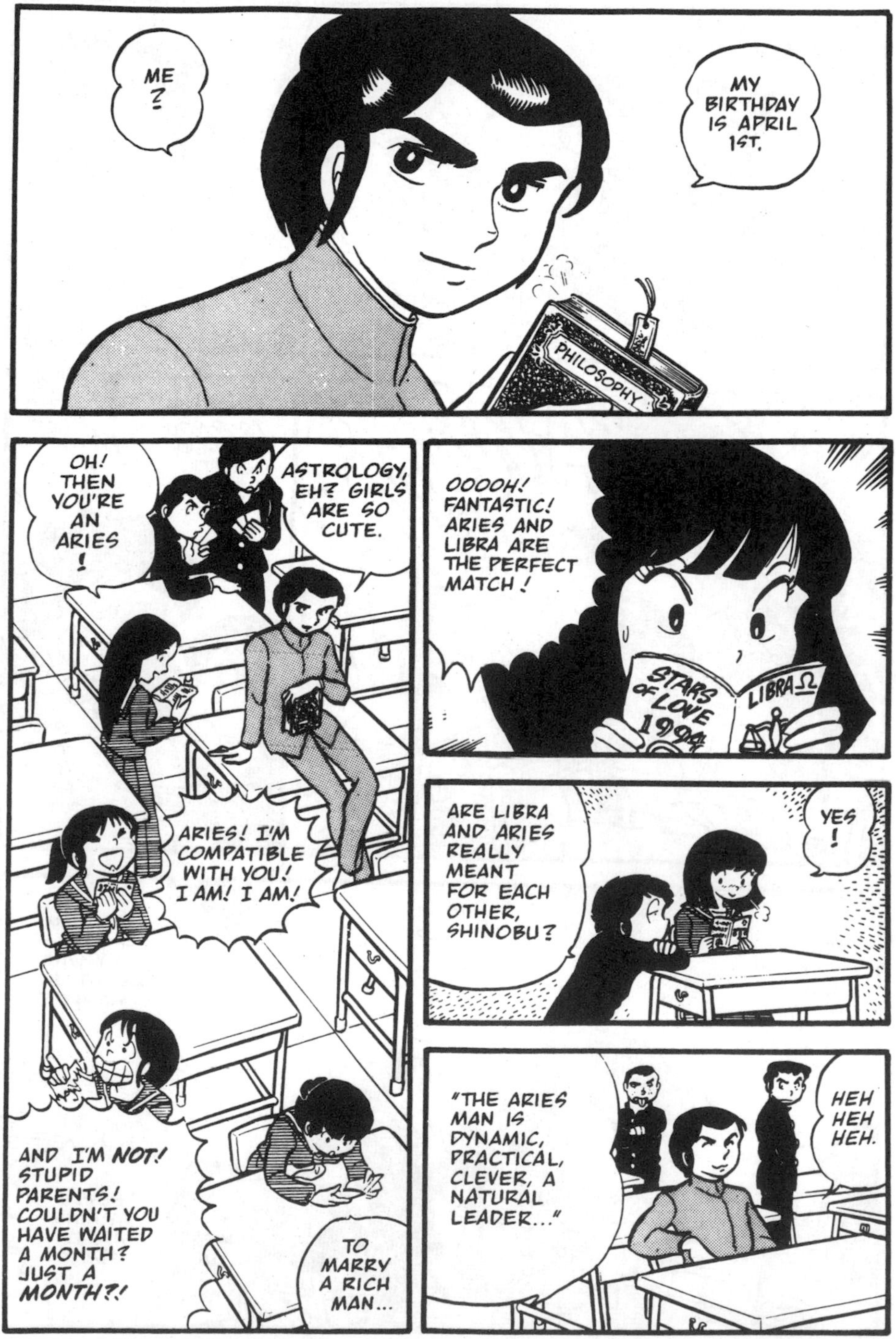
ME?
MY BIRTHDAY IS APRIL 1ST.
PHILOSOPHY
OH! THEN YOU'RE AN ARIES!
ASTROLOGY, EH? GIRLS ARE SO CUTE.
ARIES! I'M COMPATIBLE WITH YOU! I AM! I AM!
AND I'M *NOT*! STUPID PARENTS! COULDN'T YOU HAVE WAITED A MONTH? JUST A *MONTH*?!
TO MARRY A RICH MAN...
OOOOH! FANTASTIC! ARIES AND LIBRA ARE THE PERFECT MATCH!
STARS OF LOVE 1994
LIBRA Ω
ARE LIBRA AND ARIES REALLY MEANT FOR EACH OTHER, SHINOBU?
YES!
"THE ARIES MAN IS DYNAMIC, PRACTICAL, CLEVER, A NATURAL LEADER..."
HEH HEH HEH.

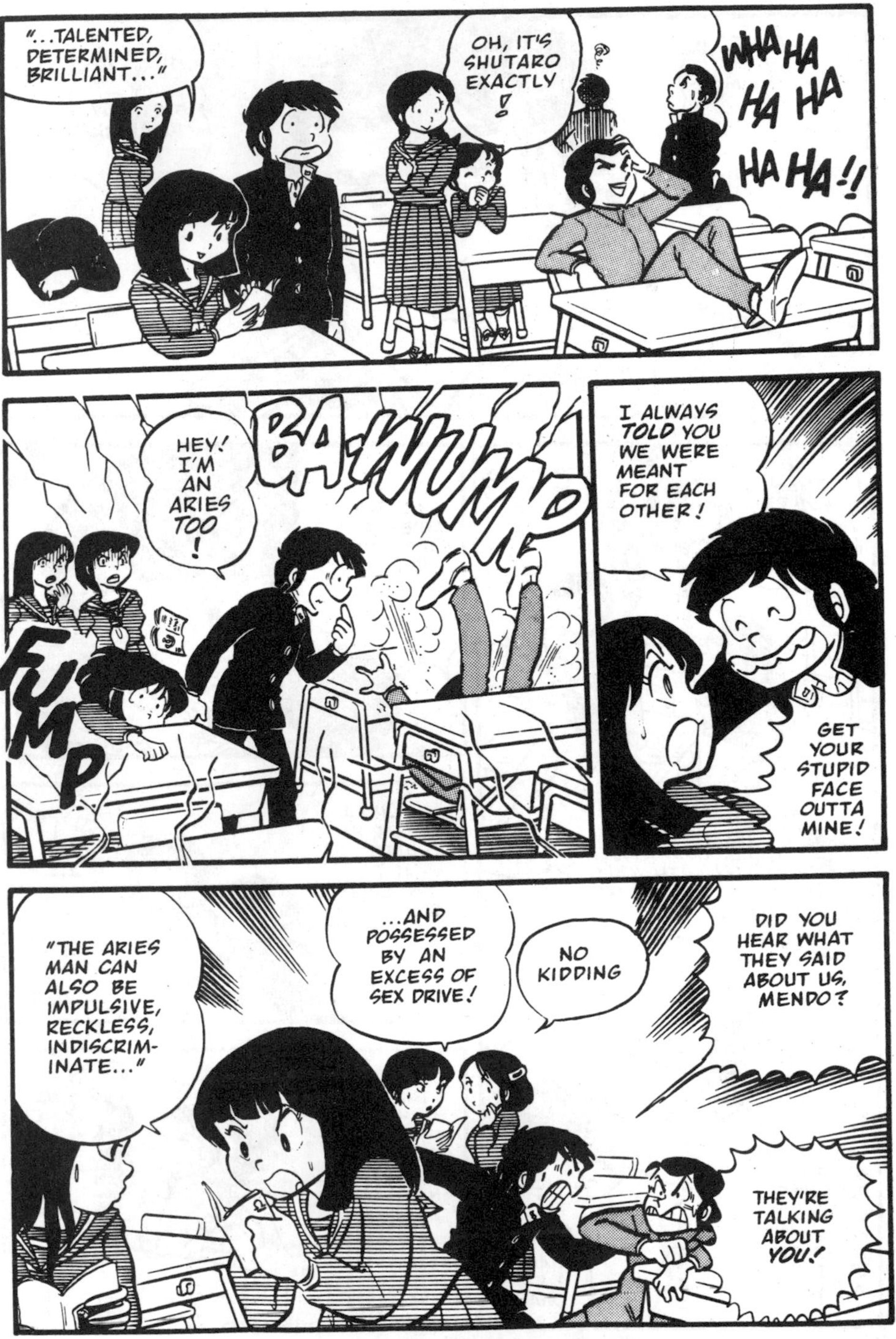
"...TALENTED, DETERMINED, BRILLIANT..."
OH, IT'S SHUTARO EXACTLY!
WHA HA HA HA HA HA HA HA!!
HEY! I'M AN ARIES TOO!
BA-WUMP
FUMP
I ALWAYS TOLD YOU WE WERE MEANT FOR EACH OTHER!
GET YOUR STUPID FACE OUTTA MINE!
"THE ARIES MAN CAN ALSO BE IMPULSIVE, RECKLESS, INDISCRIMINATE..."
...AND POSSESSED BY AN EXCESS OF SEX DRIVE!
NO KIDDING
DID YOU HEAR WHAT THEY SAID ABOUT US, MENDO?
THEY'RE TALKING ABOUT YOU!

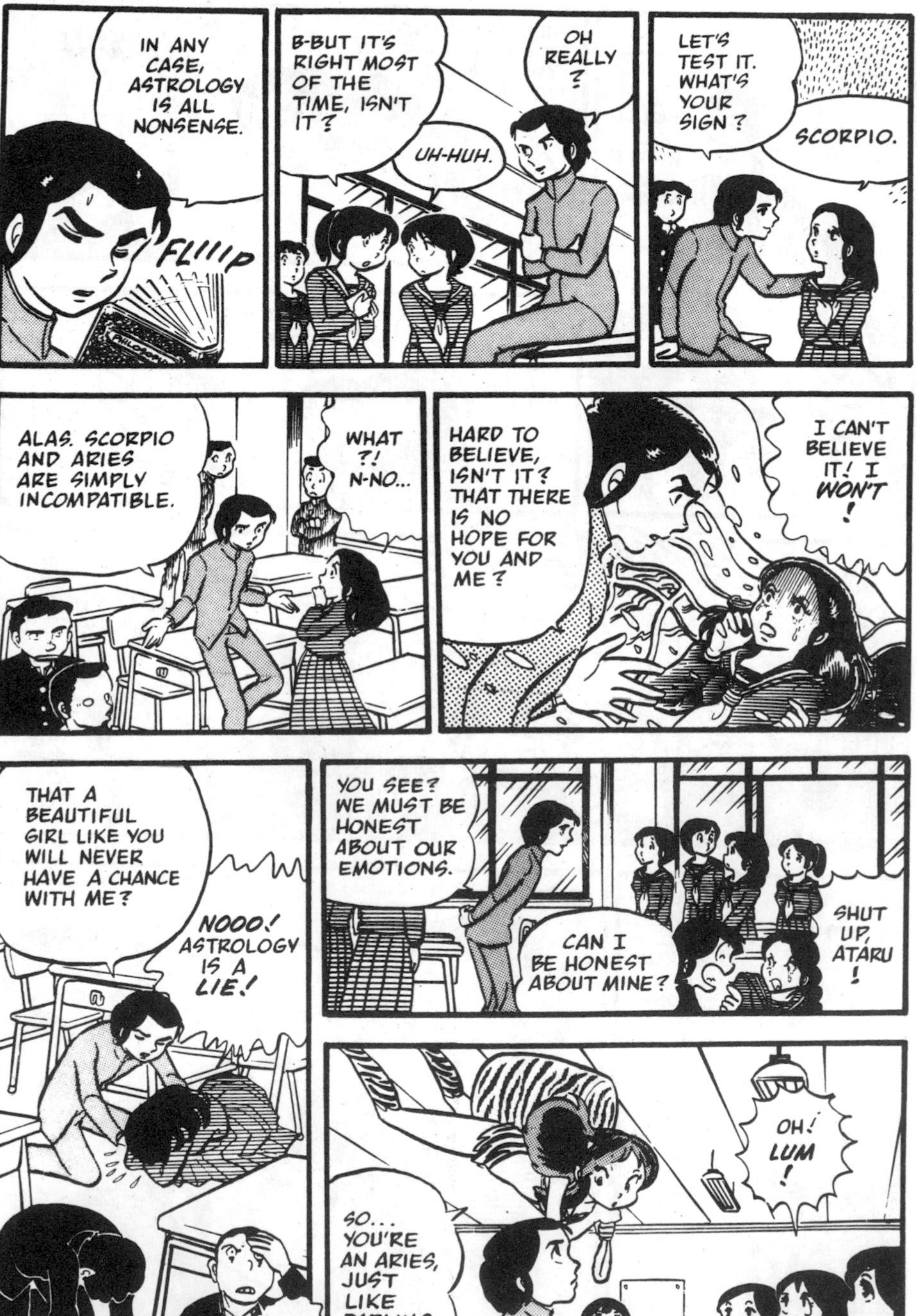
IN ANY CASE, ASTROLOGY IS ALL NONSENSE.
FLIIIP
B-BUT IT'S RIGHT MOST OF THE TIME, ISN'T IT?
UH-HUH.
OH REALLY?
LET'S TEST IT. WHAT'S YOUR SIGN?
SCORPIO.
ALAS. SCORPIO AND ARIES ARE SIMPLY INCOMPATIBLE.
WHAT?! N-NO...
HARD TO BELIEVE, ISN'T IT? THAT THERE IS NO HOPE FOR YOU AND ME?
I CAN'T BELIEVE IT! I WON'T!
THAT A BEAUTIFUL GIRL LIKE YOU WILL NEVER HAVE A CHANCE WITH ME?
NOOO! ASTROLOGY IS A LIE!
I FEEL ILL...
YOU SEE? WE MUST BE HONEST ABOUT OUR EMOTIONS.
CAN I BE HONEST ABOUT MINE?
SHUT UP, ATARU!
OH! LUM!
SO... YOU'RE AN ARIES, JUST LIKE DARLING, HM?

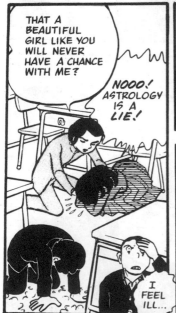

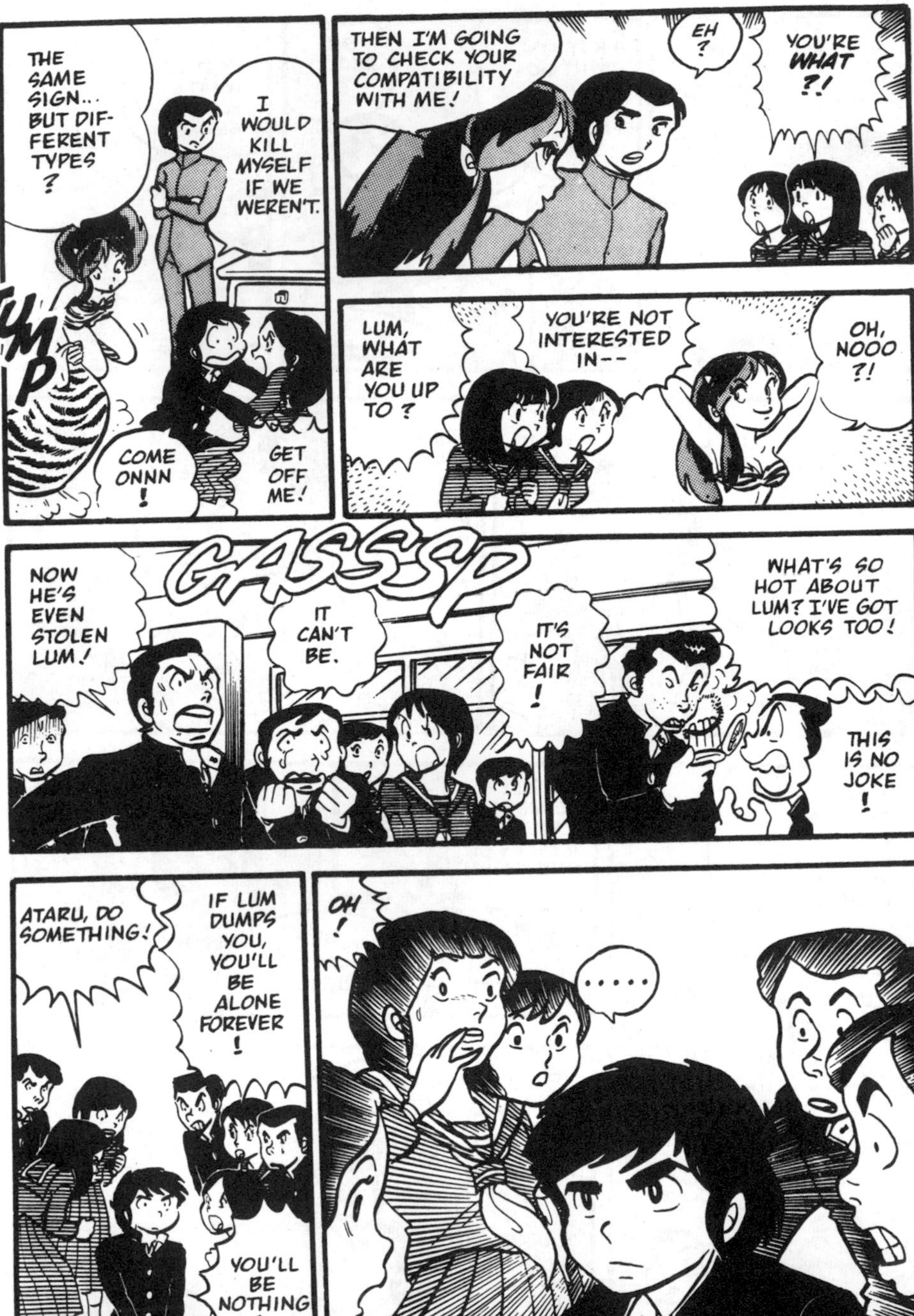
THE SAME SIGN... BUT DIFFERENT TYPES?
I WOULD KILL MYSELF IF WE WEREN'T.
TUMP
COME ONNN!
GET OFF ME!
THEN I'M GOING TO CHECK YOUR COMPATIBILITY WITH ME!
EH?
YOU'RE WHAT?!
LUM, WHAT ARE YOU UP TO?
YOU'RE NOT INTERESTED IN--
OH, NOOO?!
GASSSP
NOW HE'S EVEN STOLEN LUM!
IT CAN'T BE.
IT'S NOT FAIR!
WHAT'S SO HOT ABOUT LUM? I'VE GOT LOOKS TOO!
THIS IS NO JOKE!
ATARU, DO SOMETHING!
IF LUM DUMPS YOU, YOU'LL BE ALONE FOREVER!
YOU'LL BE NOTHING!
OH!
.....

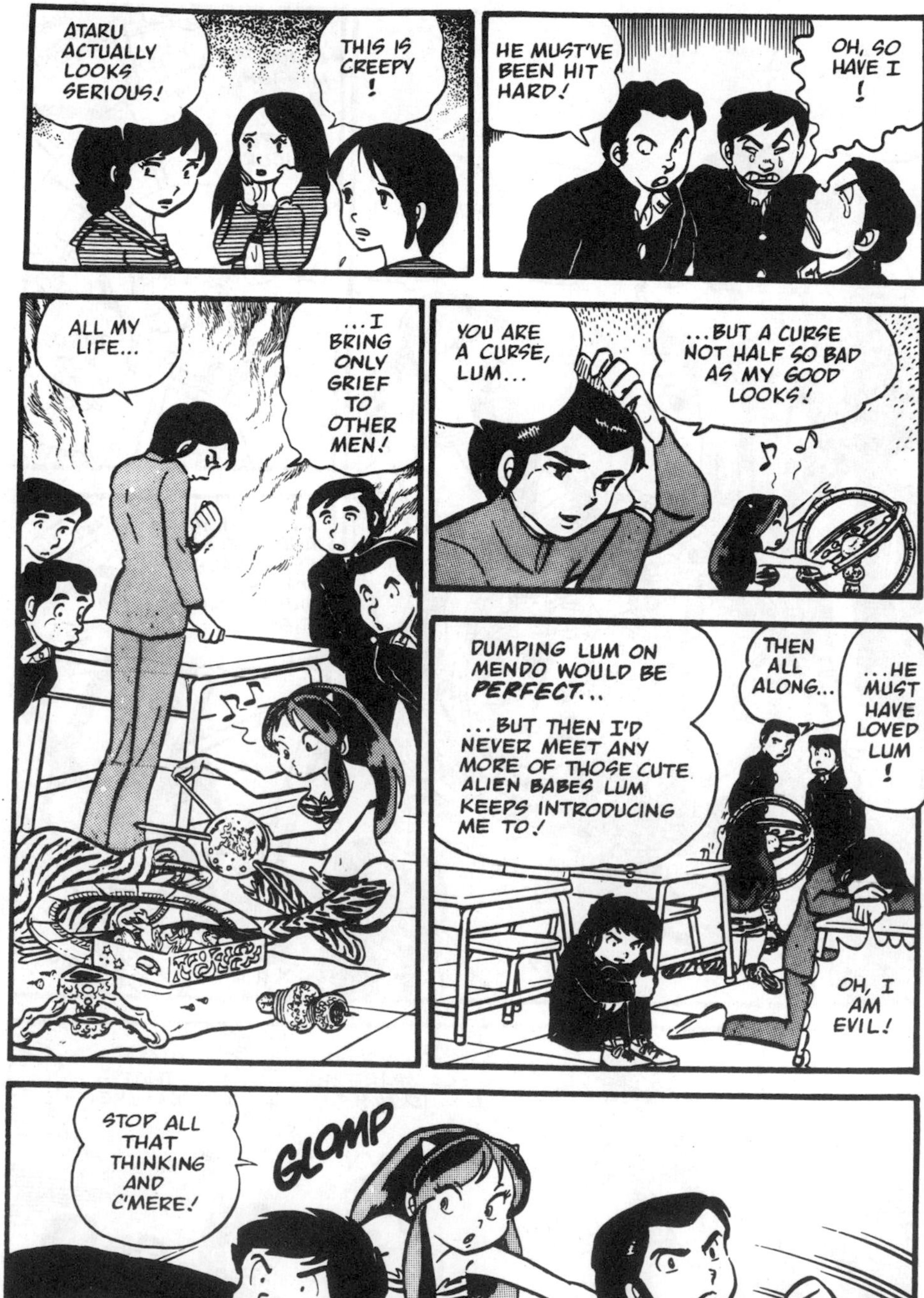
ATARU ACTUALLY LOOKS SERIOUS!
THIS IS CREEPY!
HE MUST'VE BEEN HIT HARD!
OH, SO HAVE I!
ALL MY LIFE...
...I BRING ONLY GRIEF TO OTHER MEN!
YOU ARE A CURSE, LUM...
...BUT A CURSE NOT HALF SO BAD AS MY GOOD LOOKS!
DUMPING LUM ON MENDO WOULD BE PERFECT...
...BUT THEN I'D NEVER MEET ANY MORE OF THOSE CUTE ALIEN BABES LUM KEEPS INTRODUCING ME TO!
THEN ALL ALONG...
...HE MUST HAVE LOVED LUM!
OH, I AM EVIL!
STOP ALL THAT THINKING AND C'MERE!
GLOMP

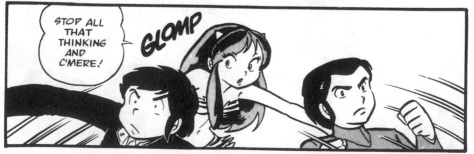

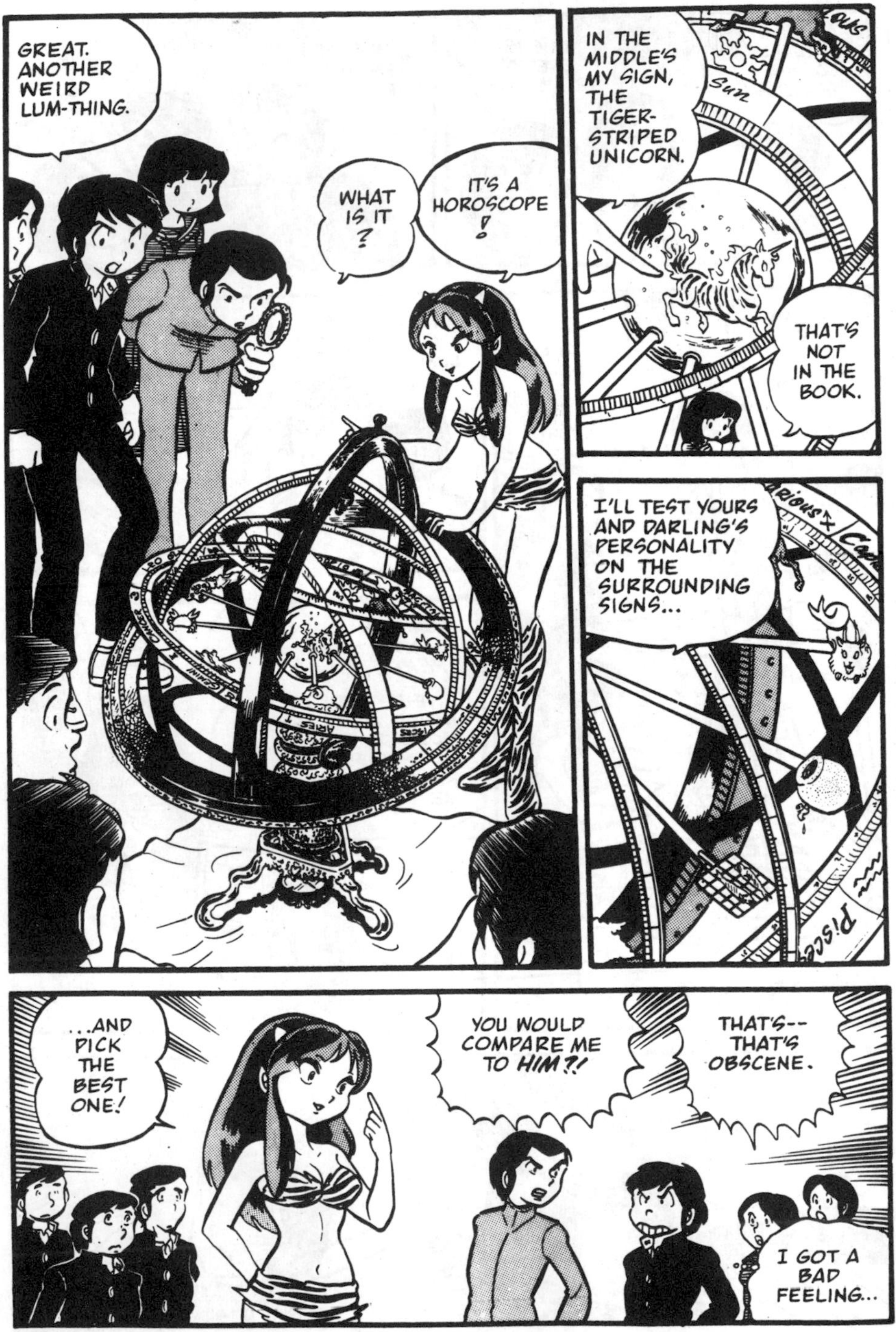
GREAT. ANOTHER WEIRD LUM-THING.
WHAT IS IT?
IT'S A HOROSCOPE!
IN THE MIDDLE'S MY SIGN, THE TIGER-STRIPED UNICORN.
Sun
THAT'S NOT IN THE BOOK.
I'LL TEST YOURS AND DARLING'S PERSONALITY ON THE SURROUNDING SIGNS...
...AND PICK THE BEST ONE!
YOU WOULD COMPARE ME TO HIM?!
THAT'S-- THAT'S OBSCENE.
I GOT A BAD FEELING...

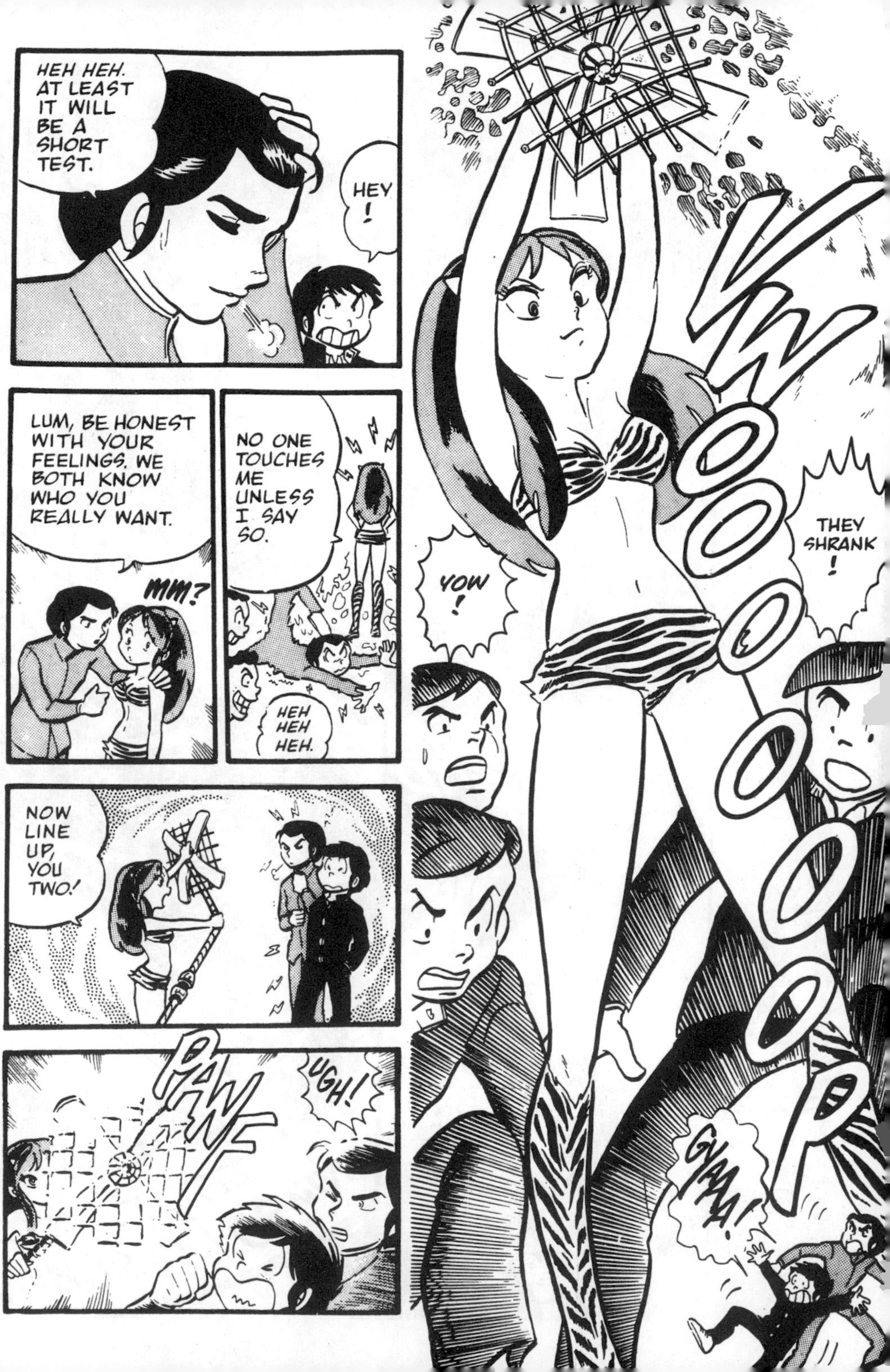
HEH HEH. AT LEAST IT WILL BE A SHORT TEST.
HEY!
LUM, BE HONEST WITH YOUR FEELINGS. WE BOTH KNOW WHO YOU REALLY WANT.
MM?
NO ONE TOUCHES ME UNLESS I SAY SO.
HEH HEH HEH.
NOW LINE UP, YOU TWO!
PAWF
UGH!
VWOOOOOOOOP
YOW!
THEY SHRANK!
GYAAA!

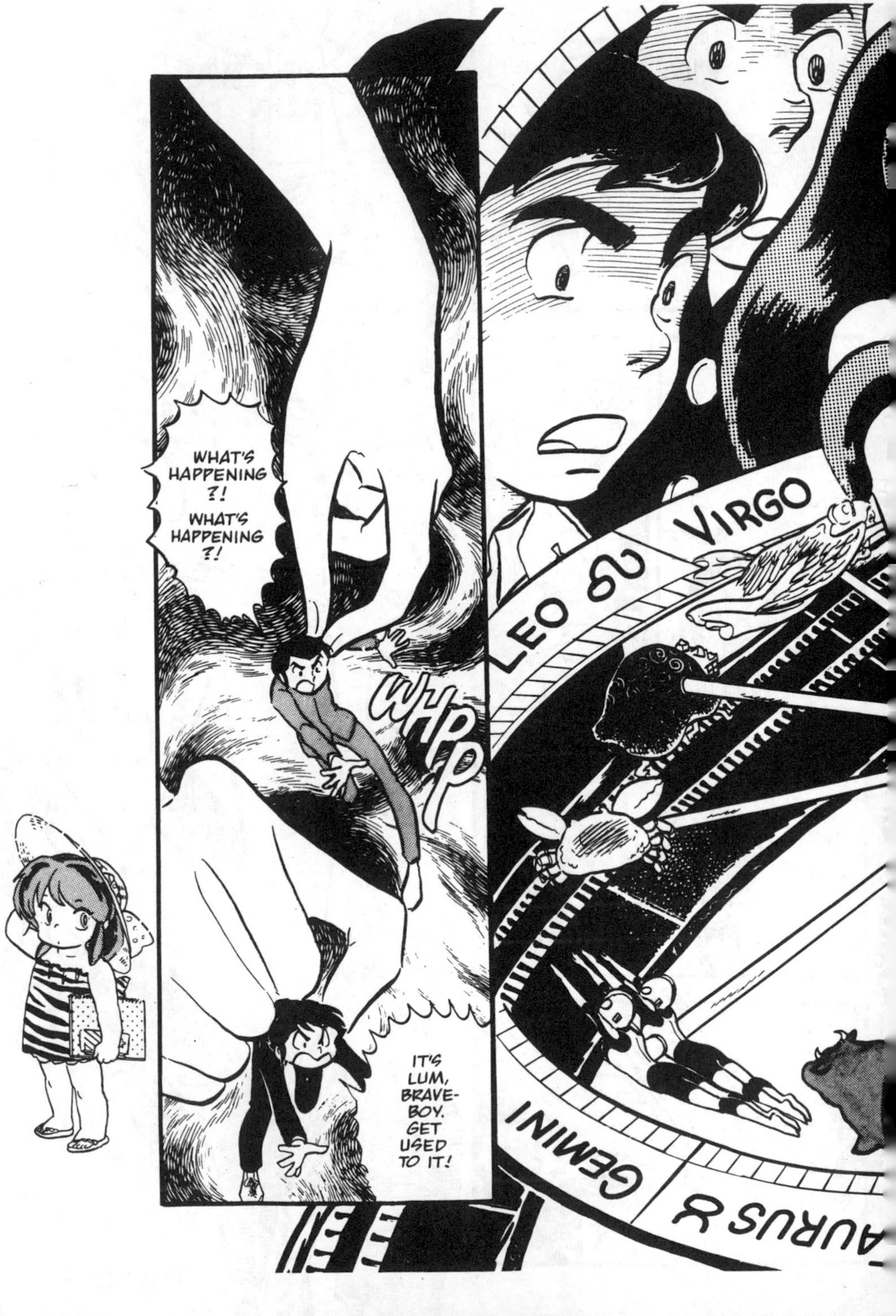
WHAT'S HAPPENING ?! WHAT'S HAPPENING ?!
WHPP
IT'S LUM, BRAVE-BOY. GET USED TO IT!
LEO
VIRGO
GEMINI
AURUS

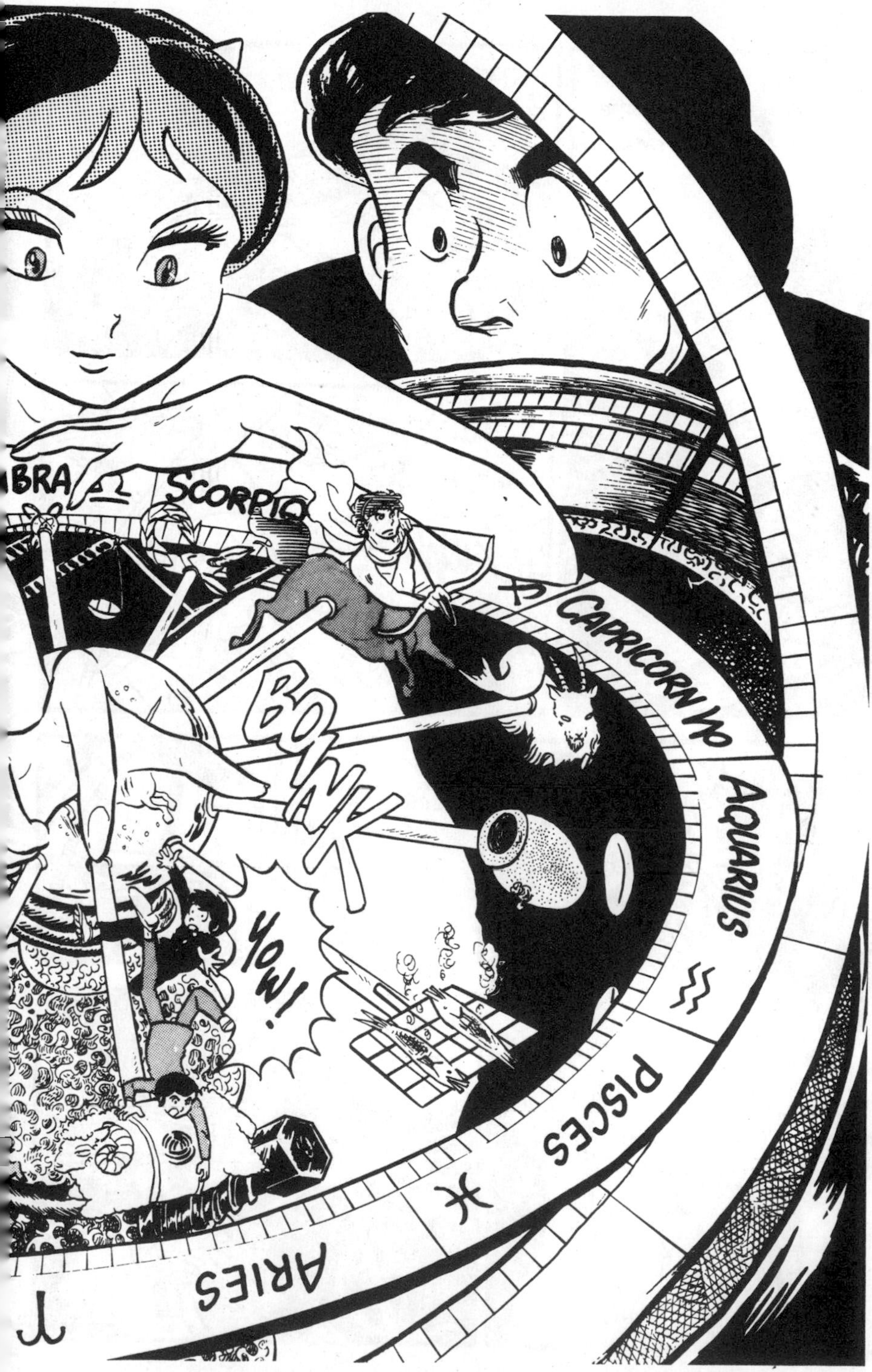

LIBRA ♎
SCORPIO
CAPRICORN ♑
AQUARIUS
♒
PISCES
♓
ARIES
♈
BONK
YOW!

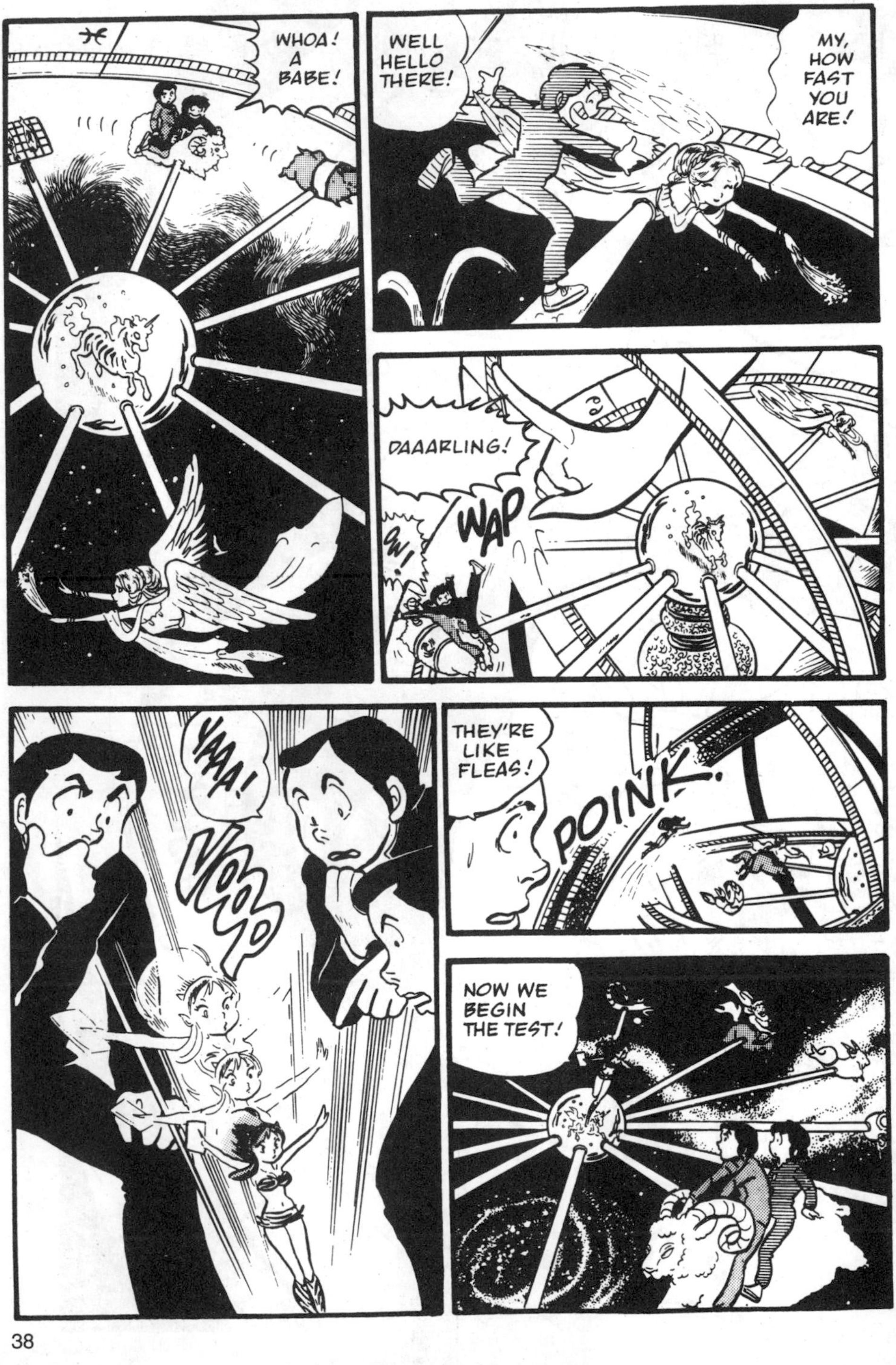

WHOA! A BABE!
WELL HELLO THERE!
MY, HOW FAST YOU ARE!
DAAARLING!
WAP
OW!
YAAAA!
VOOOOP
THEY'RE LIKE FLEAS!
POINK
NOW WE BEGIN THE TEST!

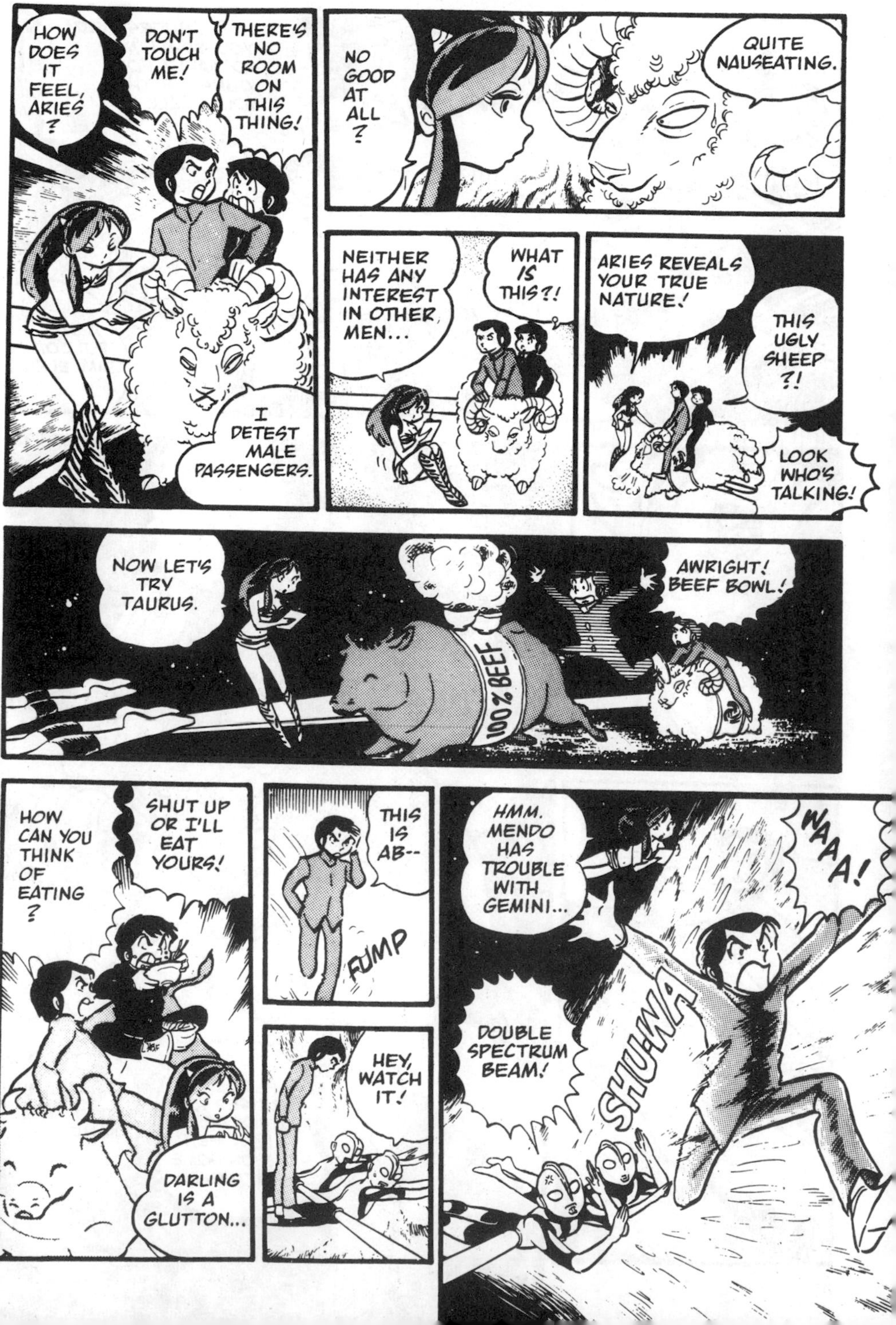
HOW DOES IT FEEL, ARIES?
DON'T TOUCH ME!
THERE'S NO ROOM ON THIS THING!
I DETEST MALE PASSENGERS.
NO GOOD AT ALL?
QUITE NAUSEATING.
NEITHER HAS ANY INTEREST IN OTHER MEN...
WHAT IS THIS?!
ARIES REVEALS YOUR TRUE NATURE!
THIS UGLY SHEEP?!
LOOK WHO'S TALKING!
NOW LET'S TRY TAURUS.
100% BEEF
AWRIGHT! BEEF BOWL!
HOW CAN YOU THINK OF EATING?
SHUT UP OR I'LL EAT YOURS!
DARLING IS A GLUTTON...
THIS IS AB--
FUMP
HEY, WATCH IT!
HMM. MENDO HAS TROUBLE WITH GEMINI...
WAAAA!
DOUBLE SPECTRUM BEAM!
SHUWA

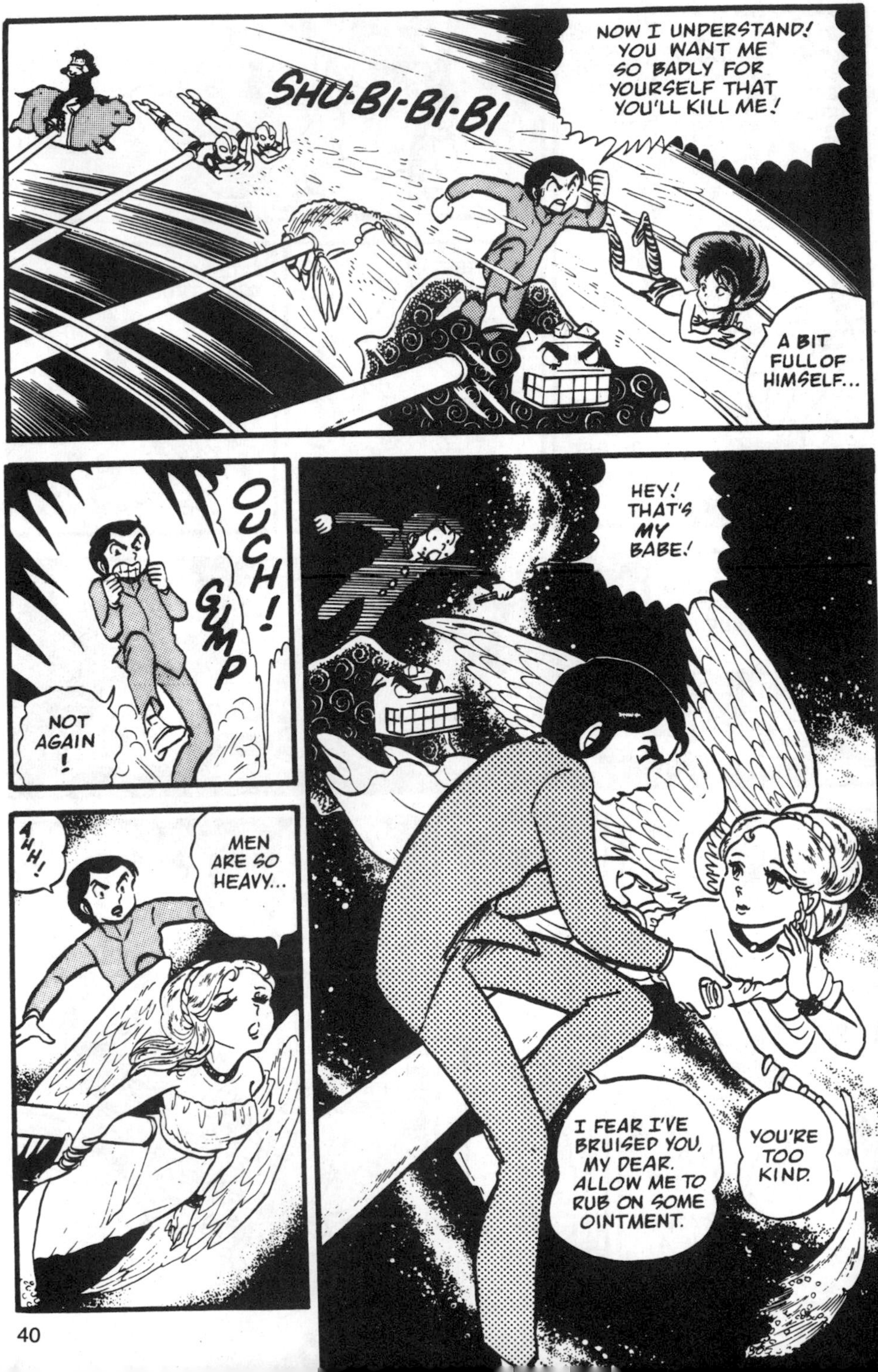
SHU-BI-BI-BI
NOW I UNDERSTAND! YOU WANT ME SO BADLY FOR YOURSELF THAT YOU'LL KILL ME!
A BIT FULL OF HIMSELF...
OUCH!
GUMP
NOT AGAIN!
AHH!
MEN ARE SO HEAVY...
HEY! THAT'S MY BABE!
I FEAR I'VE BRUISED YOU, MY DEAR. ALLOW ME TO RUB ON SOME OINTMENT.
YOU'RE TOO KIND.

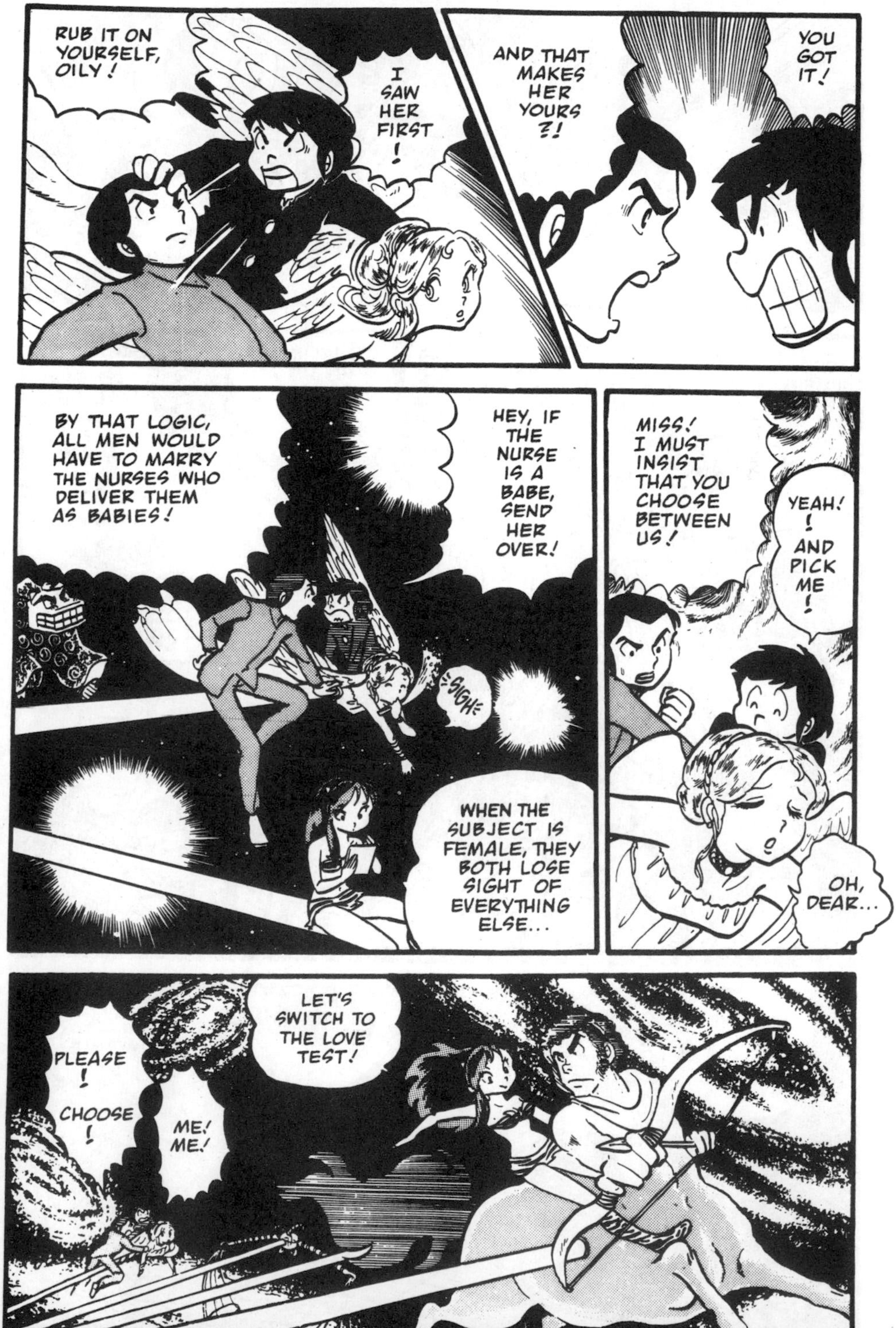
RUB IT ON YOURSELF, OILY!
I SAW HER FIRST!
AND THAT MAKES HER YOURS?!
YOU GOT IT!
BY THAT LOGIC, ALL MEN WOULD HAVE TO MARRY THE NURSES WHO DELIVER THEM AS BABIES!
HEY, IF THE NURSE IS A BABE, SEND HER OVER!
SIGH
WHEN THE SUBJECT IS FEMALE, THEY BOTH LOSE SIGHT OF EVERYTHING ELSE...
MISS! I MUST INSIST THAT YOU CHOOSE BETWEEN US!
YEAH!! AND PICK ME!
OH, DEAR...
PLEASE! CHOOSE!
LET'S SWITCH TO THE LOVE TEST!
ME! ME!

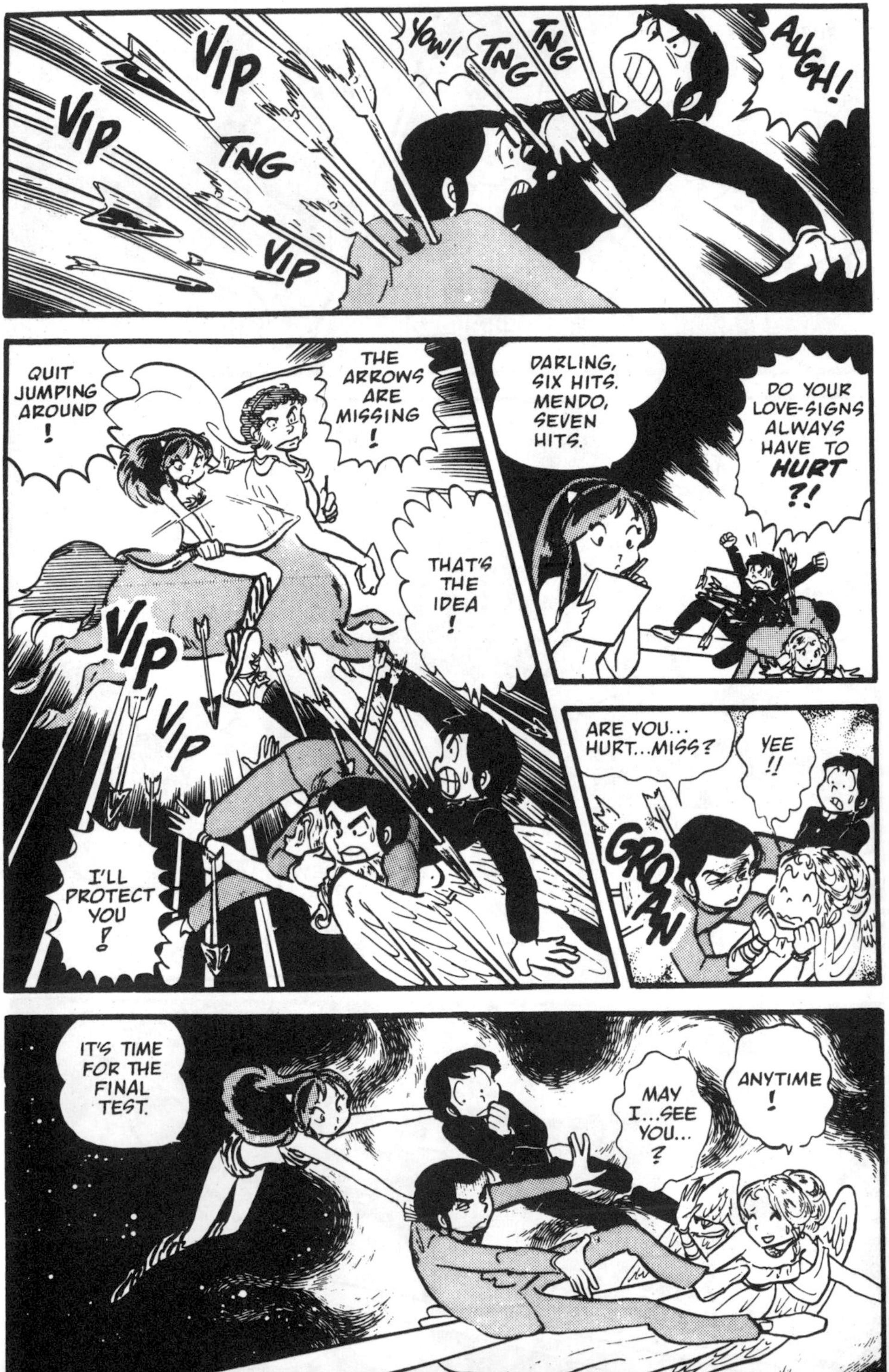
VIP
VIP
TNG
VIP
YOW!
TNG
TNG
AUGH!
QUIT JUMPING AROUND!
THE ARROWS ARE MISSING!
THAT'S THE IDEA!
VIP
VIP
I'LL PROTECT YOU!
DARLING, SIX HITS. MENDO, SEVEN HITS.
DO YOUR LOVE-SIGNS ALWAYS HAVE TO HURT?!
ARE YOU... HURT...MISS?
YEE!!
GROAN
IT'S TIME FOR THE FINAL TEST.
MAY I...SEE YOU...?
ANYTIME!

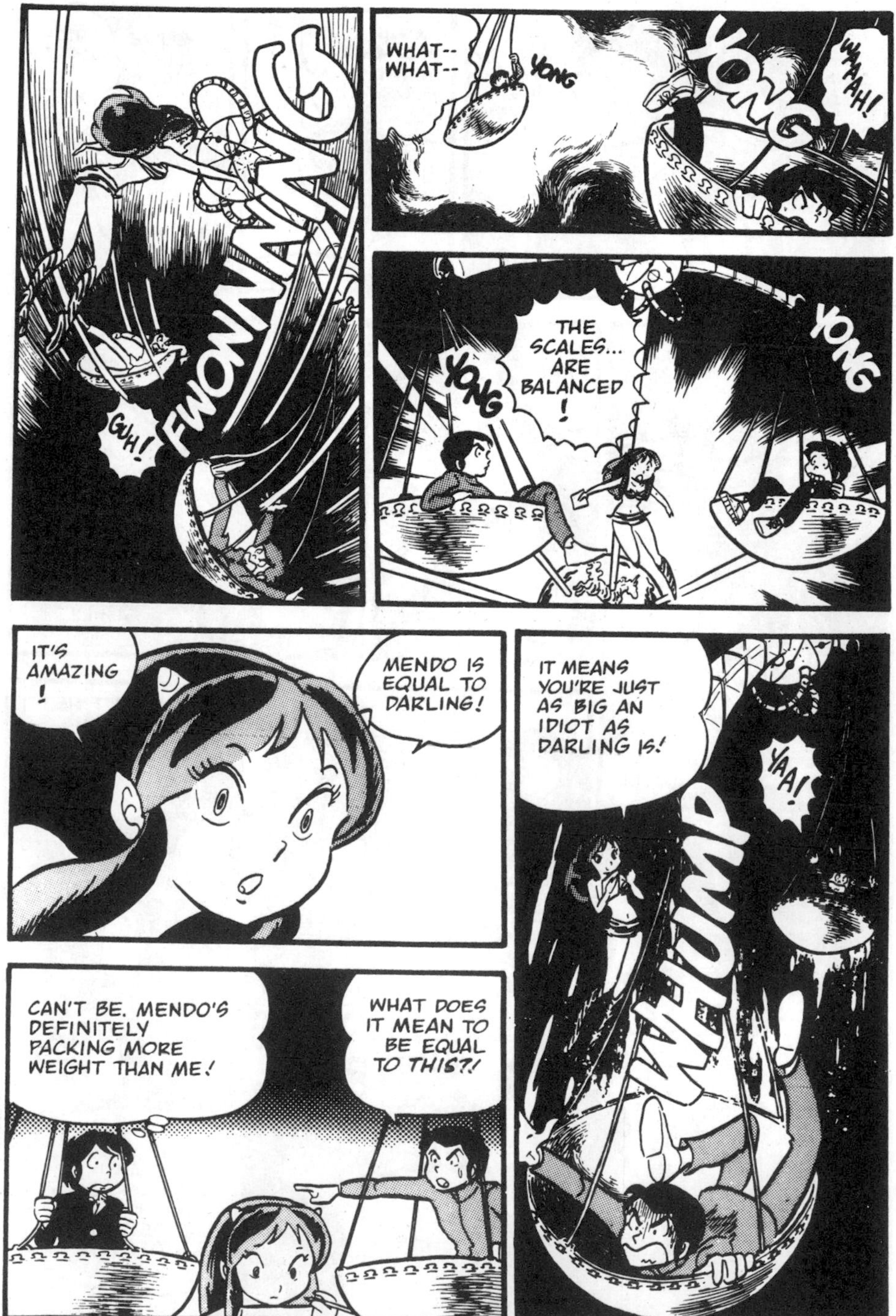
FWONNNG
GUH!
WHAT--
WHAT--
YONG
YONG
WAAAAH!
THE SCALES... ARE BALANCED!
YONG
YONG
IT'S AMAZING!
MENDO IS EQUAL TO DARLING!
CAN'T BE. MENDO'S DEFINITELY PACKING MORE WEIGHT THAN ME!
WHAT DOES IT MEAN TO BE EQUAL TO *THIS?!*
IT MEANS YOU'RE JUST AS BIG AN IDIOT AS DARLING IS!
YAAA!
WHUMP

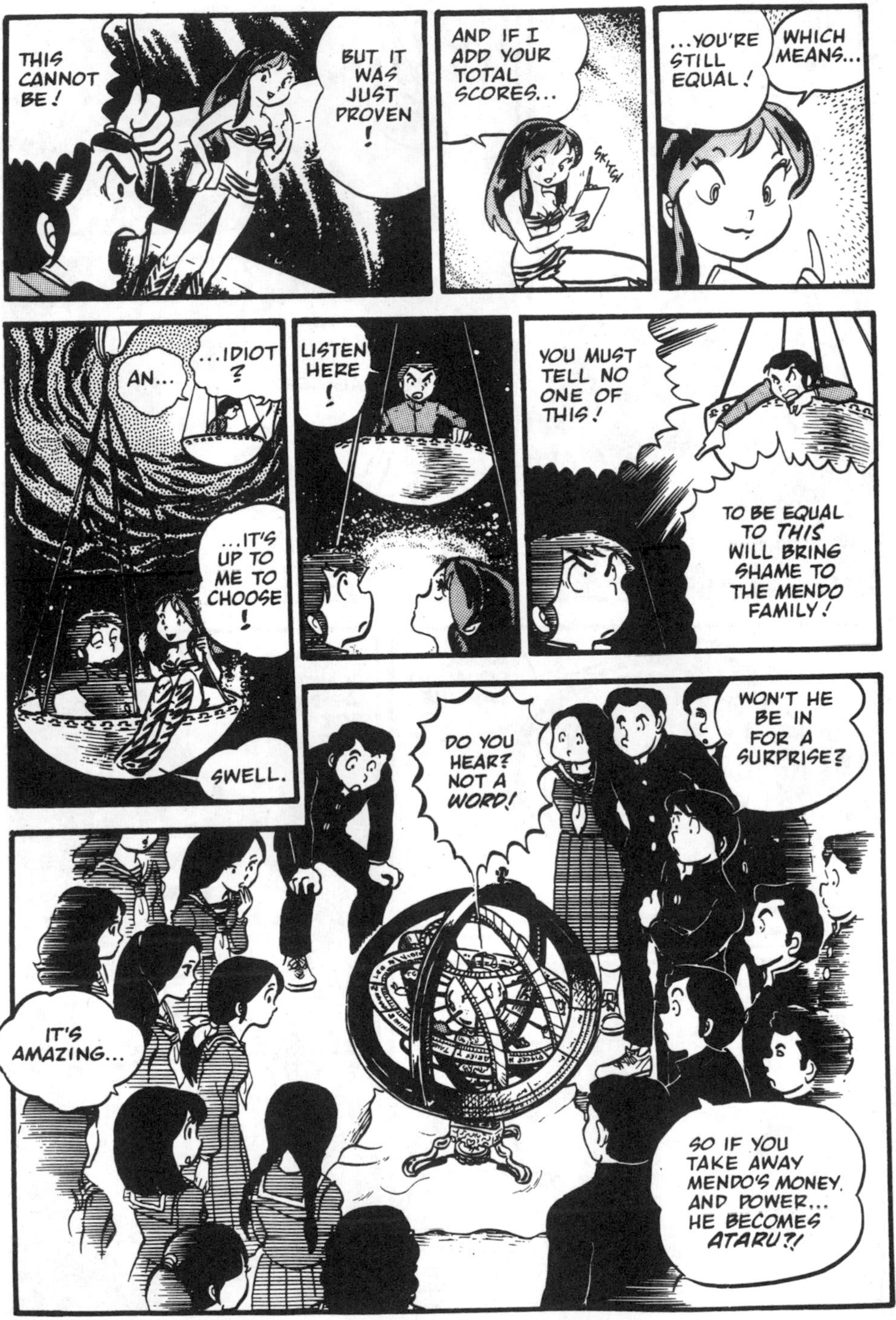
THIS CANNOT BE!
BUT IT WAS JUST PROVEN!
AND IF I ADD YOUR TOTAL SCORES...
...YOU'RE STILL EQUAL!
WHICH MEANS...
AN...
...IDIOT?
...IT'S UP TO ME TO CHOOSE!
SWELL.
LISTEN HERE!
YOU MUST TELL NO ONE OF THIS!
TO BE EQUAL TO *THIS* WILL BRING SHAME TO THE MENDO FAMILY!
DO YOU HEAR? NOT A *WORD!*
WON'T HE BE IN FOR A SURPRISE?
IT'S AMAZING...
SO IF YOU TAKE AWAY MENDO'S MONEY AND POWER... HE BECOMES *ATARU?!*

Part 3
Spring Fever

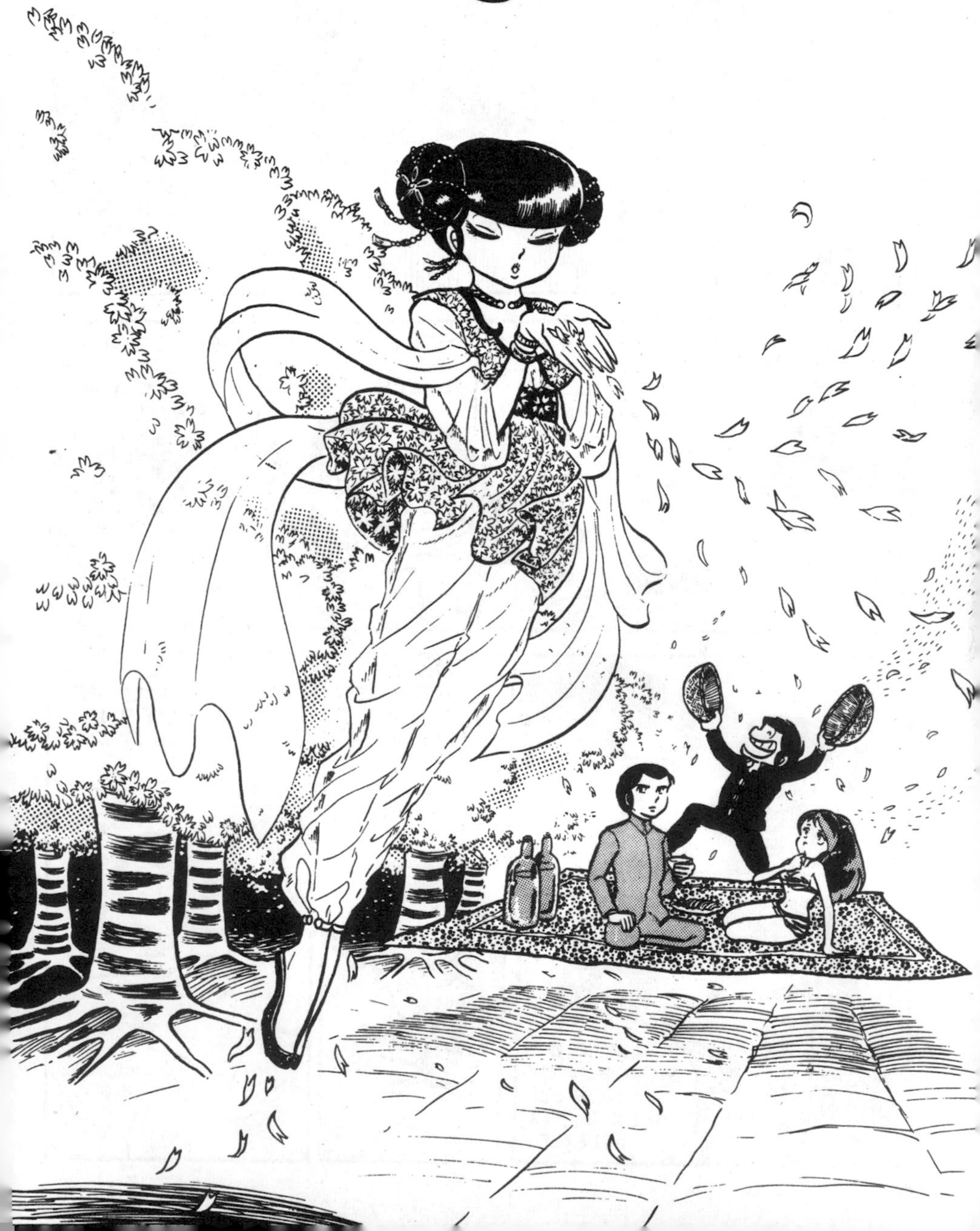

AND... SO THE... UHHHHH... SO THE PRONOUN IS...

SIGH

SIGH SIGH

HEY. LET'S (YAWN) LET'S WAKE UP OUT THERE.

IT MAY BE SPRING, BUT IT'S STILL SCHOOL.

SO... SO SLEEPY...

MUSTN'T...GIVE IN.

I'M A STRAIGHT A STU...

RUB RUB

GASP!

LOOK AT MOROBOSHI! HE'S SO ALERT! SO INTENT!

NOW MY PRIDE IS ON THE LINE! I MUST HAVE CAFFEINE! I WILL NOT SLEEP!

PLOK

I WON'T BE OUTDONE BY THAT BUFFOON!

SHLRP SHLRP

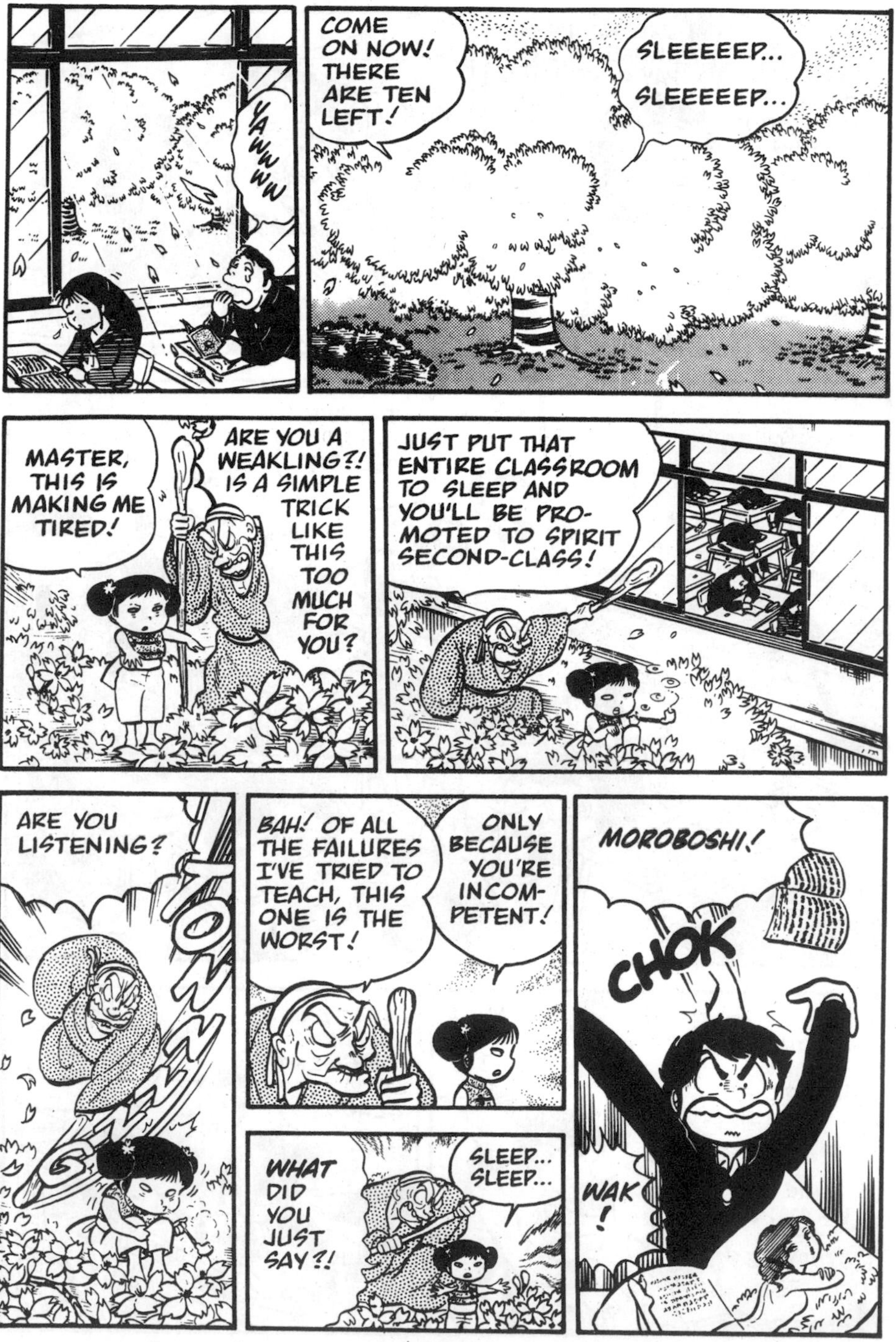
YAWWWW
COME ON NOW! THERE ARE TEN LEFT!
SLEEEEEP... SLEEEEEP...
MASTER, THIS IS MAKING ME TIRED!
ARE YOU A WEAKLING?! IS A SIMPLE TRICK LIKE THIS TOO MUCH FOR YOU?
JUST PUT THAT ENTIRE CLASSROOM TO SLEEP AND YOU'LL BE PRO-MOTED TO SPIRIT SECOND-CLASS!
ARE YOU LISTENING?
YOWWWNNN
BAH! OF ALL THE FAILURES I'VE TRIED TO TEACH, THIS ONE IS THE WORST!
ONLY BECAUSE YOU'RE INCOM-PETENT!
WHAT DID YOU JUST SAY?!
SLEEP... SLEEP...
MOROBOSHI!
CHOK
WAK!

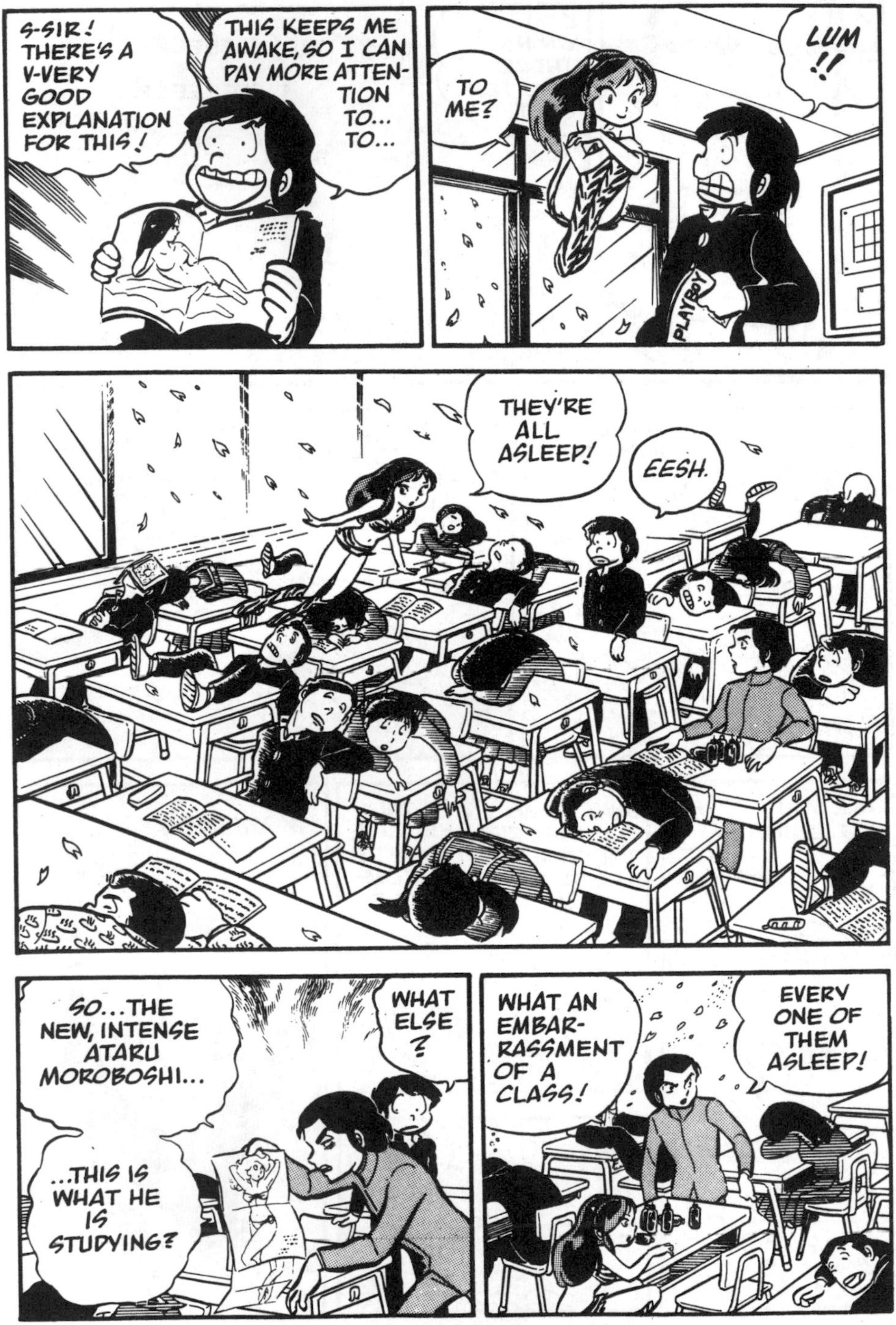
S-SIR! THERE'S A V-VERY GOOD EXPLANATION FOR THIS!
THIS KEEPS ME AWAKE, SO I CAN PAY MORE ATTENTION TO... TO...
TO ME?
LUM!!
PLAYBOY
THEY'RE ALL ASLEEP!
EESH.
SO...THE NEW, INTENSE ATARU MOROBOSHI...
...THIS IS WHAT HE IS STUDYING?
WHAT ELSE?
WHAT AN EMBARRASSMENT OF A CLASS!
EVERY ONE OF THEM ASLEEP!

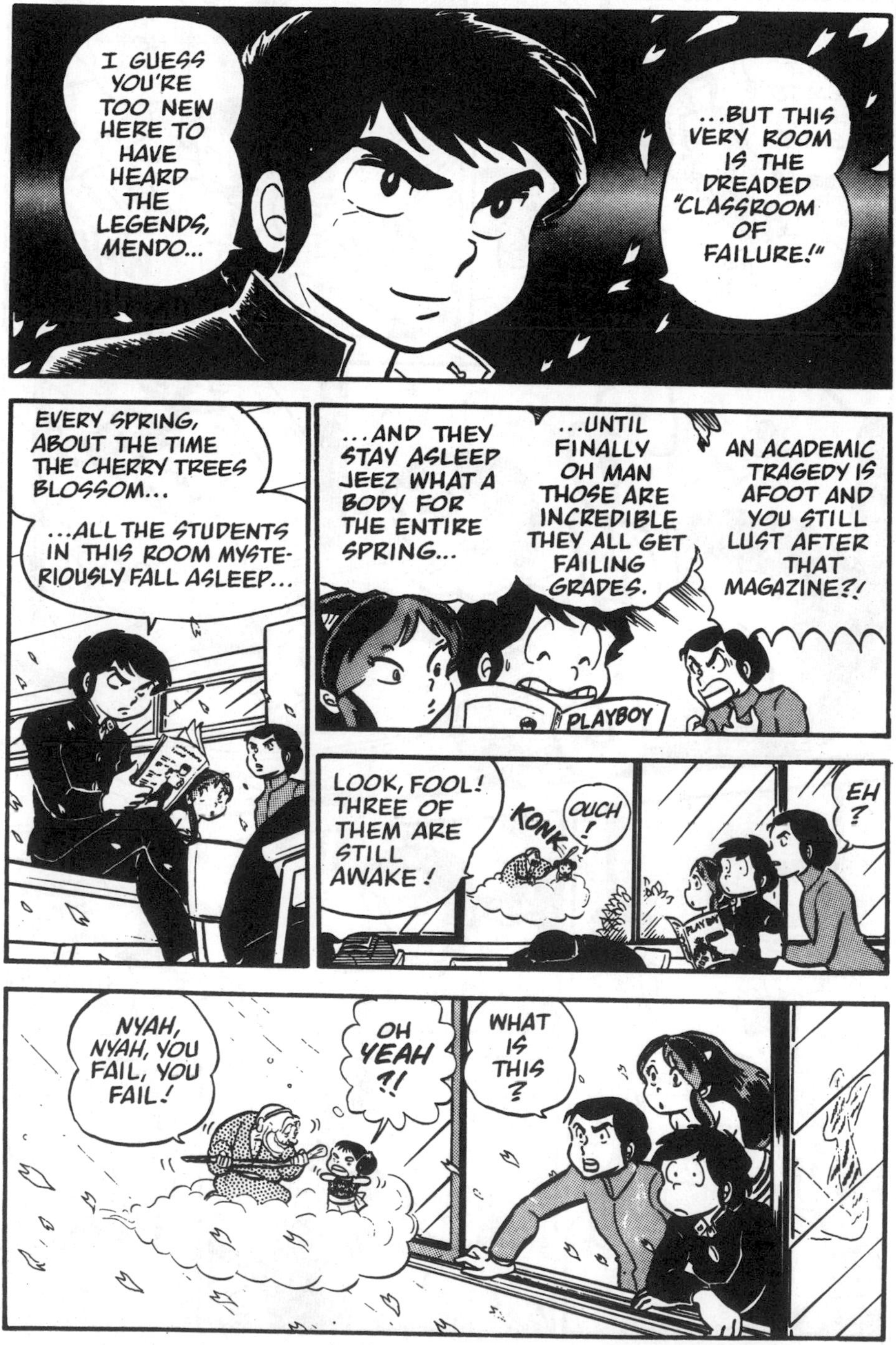
I GUESS YOU'RE TOO NEW HERE TO HAVE HEARD THE LEGENDS, MENDO...
...BUT THIS VERY ROOM IS THE DREADED "CLASSROOM OF FAILURE!"
EVERY SPRING, ABOUT THE TIME THE CHERRY TREES BLOSSOM...
...ALL THE STUDENTS IN THIS ROOM MYSTERIOUSLY FALL ASLEEP...
...AND THEY STAY ASLEEP JEEZ WHAT A BODY FOR THE ENTIRE SPRING...
...UNTIL FINALLY OH MAN THOSE ARE INCREDIBLE THEY ALL GET FAILING GRADES.
AN ACADEMIC TRAGEDY IS AFOOT AND YOU STILL LUST AFTER THAT MAGAZINE?!
PLAYBOY
LOOK, FOOL! THREE OF THEM ARE STILL AWAKE!
KONK
OUCH!
EH?
NYAH, NYAH, YOU FAIL, YOU FAIL!
OH YEAH ?!
WHAT IS THIS ?

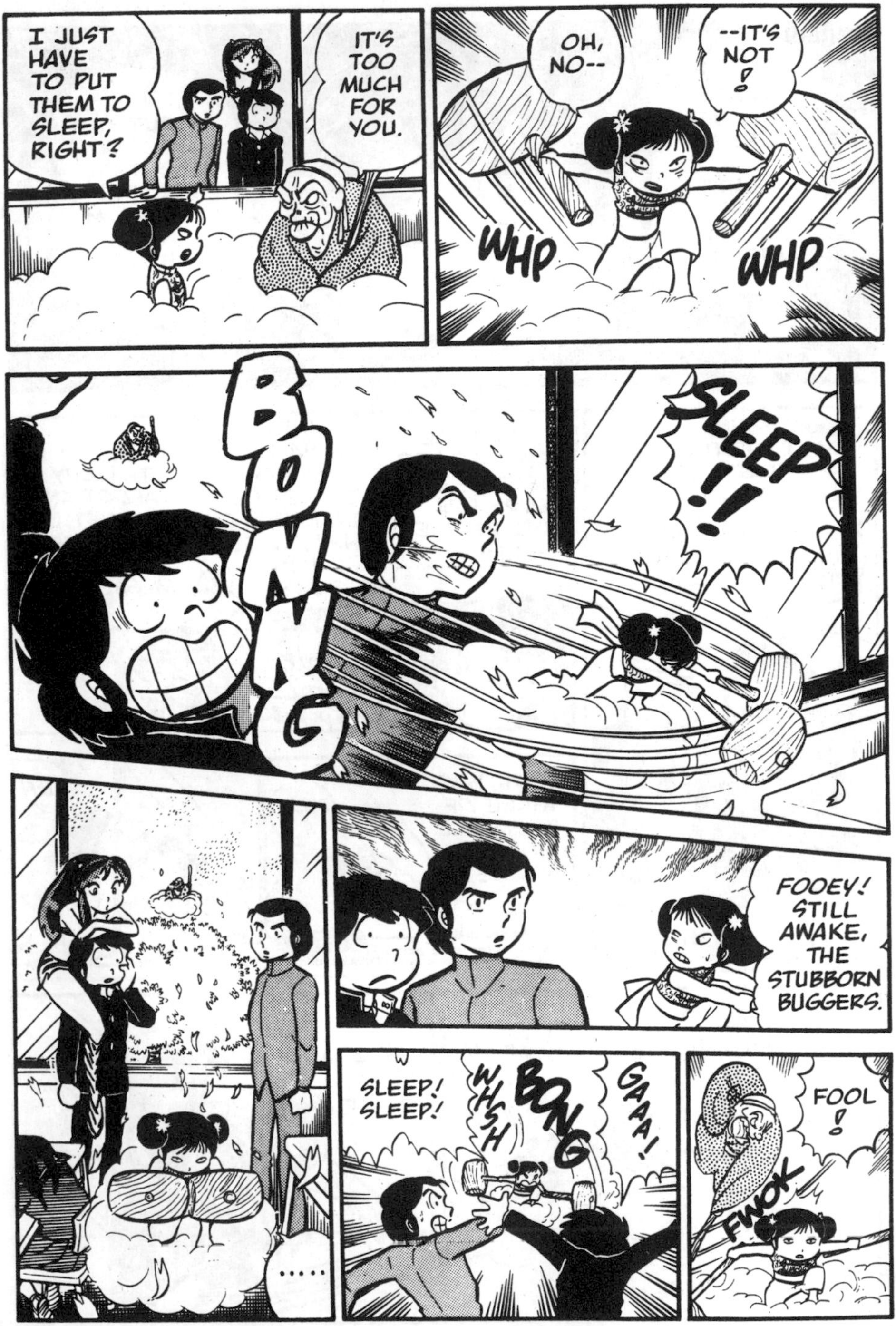
I JUST HAVE TO PUT THEM TO SLEEP, RIGHT?
IT'S TOO MUCH FOR YOU.
OH, NO--
--IT'S NOT!
WHP
WHP
BONNNG
SLEEP!!!
.....
FOOEY! STILL AWAKE, THE STUBBORN BUGGERS.
SLEEP! SLEEP!
WHSH
BONG
GAAA!
FOOL!
FWOK

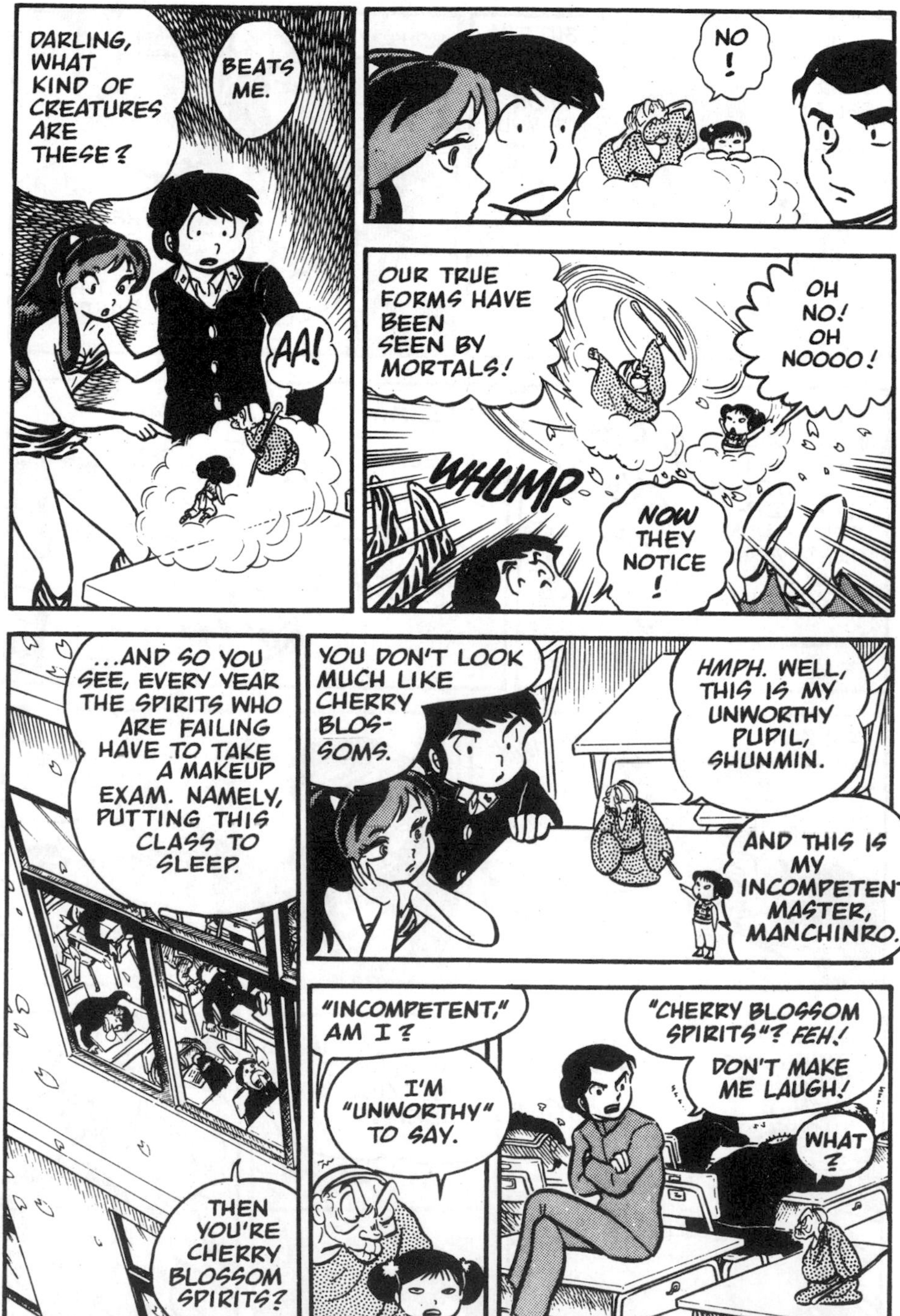
DARLING, WHAT KIND OF CREATURES ARE THESE?
BEATS ME.
AA!
NO!
OUR TRUE FORMS HAVE BEEN SEEN BY MORTALS!
OH NO! OH NOOOO!
WHUMP
NOW THEY NOTICE!
...AND SO YOU SEE, EVERY YEAR THE SPIRITS WHO ARE FAILING HAVE TO TAKE A MAKEUP EXAM. NAMELY, PUTTING THIS CLASS TO SLEEP.
THEN YOU'RE CHERRY BLOSSOM SPIRITS?
YOU DON'T LOOK MUCH LIKE CHERRY BLOS-SOMS.
HMPH. WELL, THIS IS MY UNWORTHY PUPIL, SHUNMIN.
AND THIS IS MY INCOMPETENT MASTER, MANCHINRO.
"INCOMPETENT," AM I?
I'M "UNWORTHY" TO SAY.
"CHERRY BLOSSOM SPIRITS"? FEH!
DON'T MAKE ME LAUGH!
WHAT?

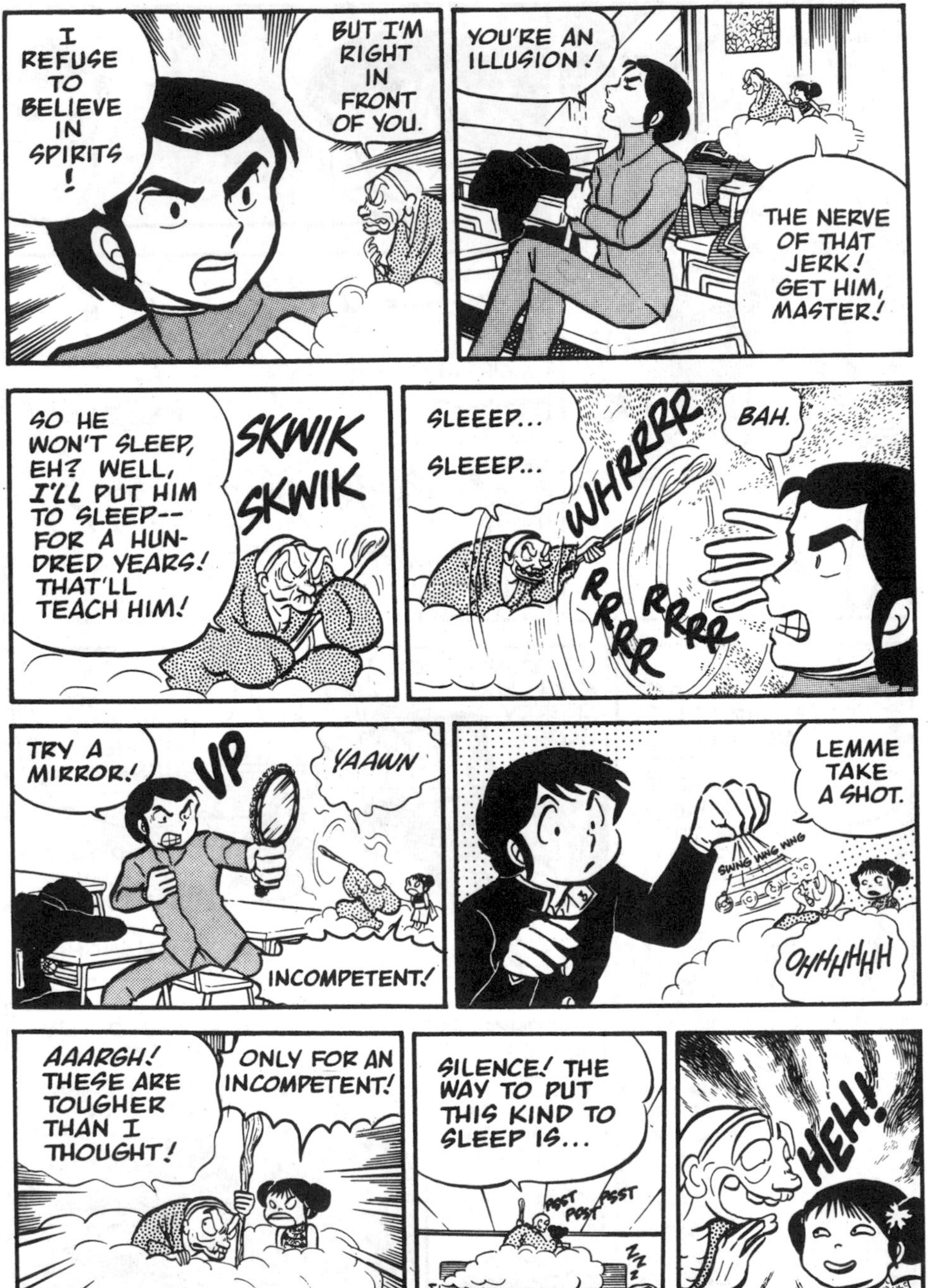
I REFUSE TO BELIEVE IN SPIRITS!
BUT I'M RIGHT IN FRONT OF YOU.
YOU'RE AN ILLUSION!
THE NERVE OF THAT JERK! GET HIM, MASTER!
SO HE WON'T SLEEP, EH? WELL, I'LL PUT HIM TO SLEEP-- FOR A HUN-DRED YEARS! THAT'LL TEACH HIM!
SKWIK SKWIK
SLEEEP... SLEEEP...
WHRRRR
BAH.
TRY A MIRROR!
VP
YAAWN
INCOMPETENT!
LEMME TAKE A SHOT.
SWING WING WING
OHHHHHH
AAARGH! THESE ARE TOUGHER THAN I THOUGHT!
ONLY FOR AN INCOMPETENT!
SILENCE! THE WAY TO PUT THIS KIND TO SLEEP IS...
PSST PSST PSST
HEH!

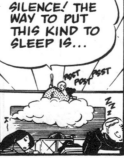

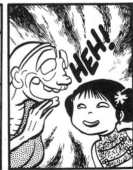

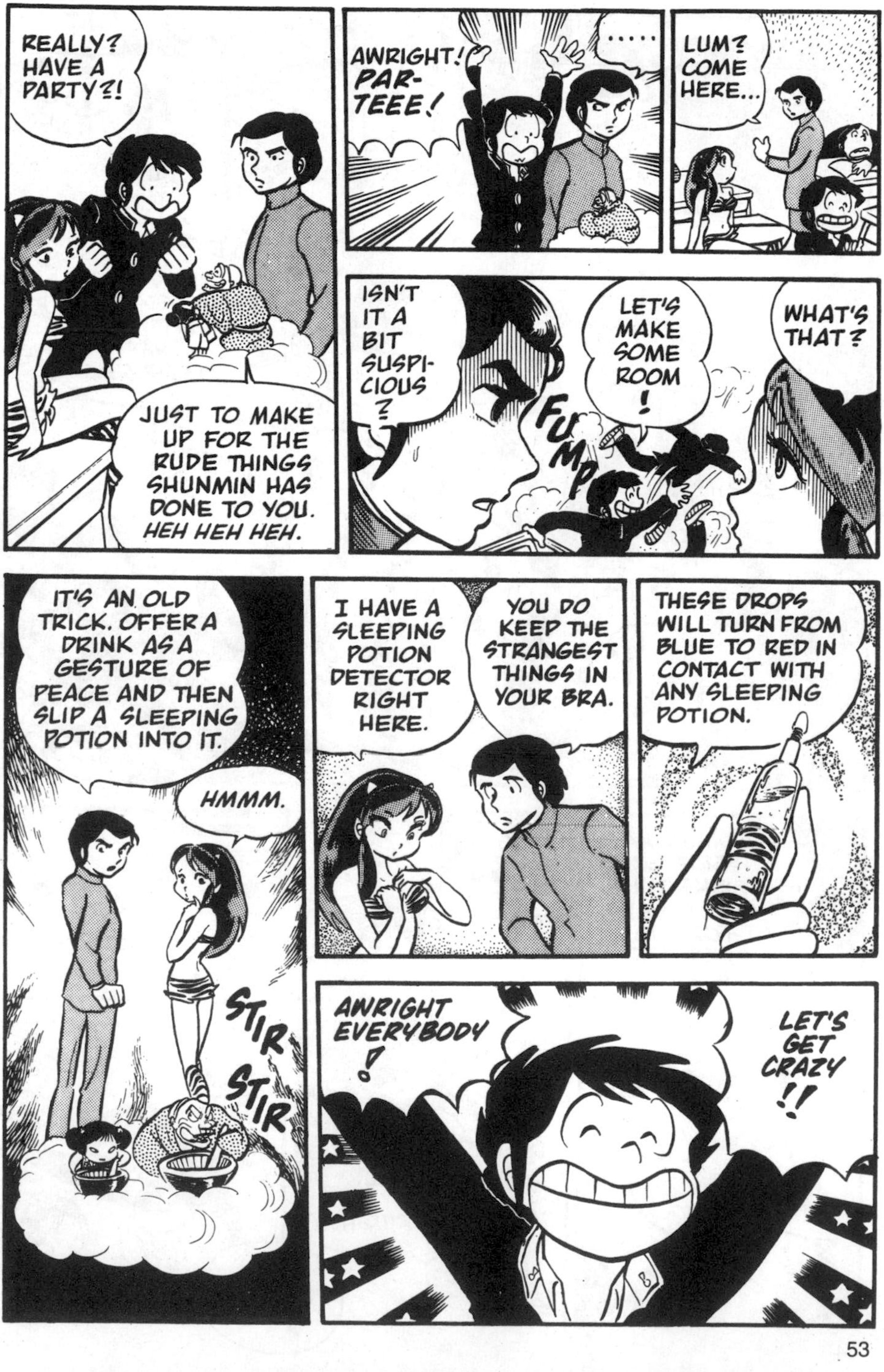

REALLY? HAVE A PARTY?!
JUST TO MAKE UP FOR THE RUDE THINGS SHUNMIN HAS DONE TO YOU. HEH HEH HEH.
AWRIGHT! PAR-TEEE!
.....
LUM? COME HERE...
ISN'T IT A BIT SUSPICIOUS?
LET'S MAKE SOME ROOM!
FUMP
WHAT'S THAT?
IT'S AN OLD TRICK. OFFER A DRINK AS A GESTURE OF PEACE AND THEN SLIP A SLEEPING POTION INTO IT.
HMMM.
STIR STIR
I HAVE A SLEEPING POTION DETECTOR RIGHT HERE.
YOU DO KEEP THE STRANGEST THINGS IN YOUR BRA.
THESE DROPS WILL TURN FROM BLUE TO RED IN CONTACT WITH ANY SLEEPING POTION.
AWRIGHT EVERYBODY!
LET'S GET CRAZY!!

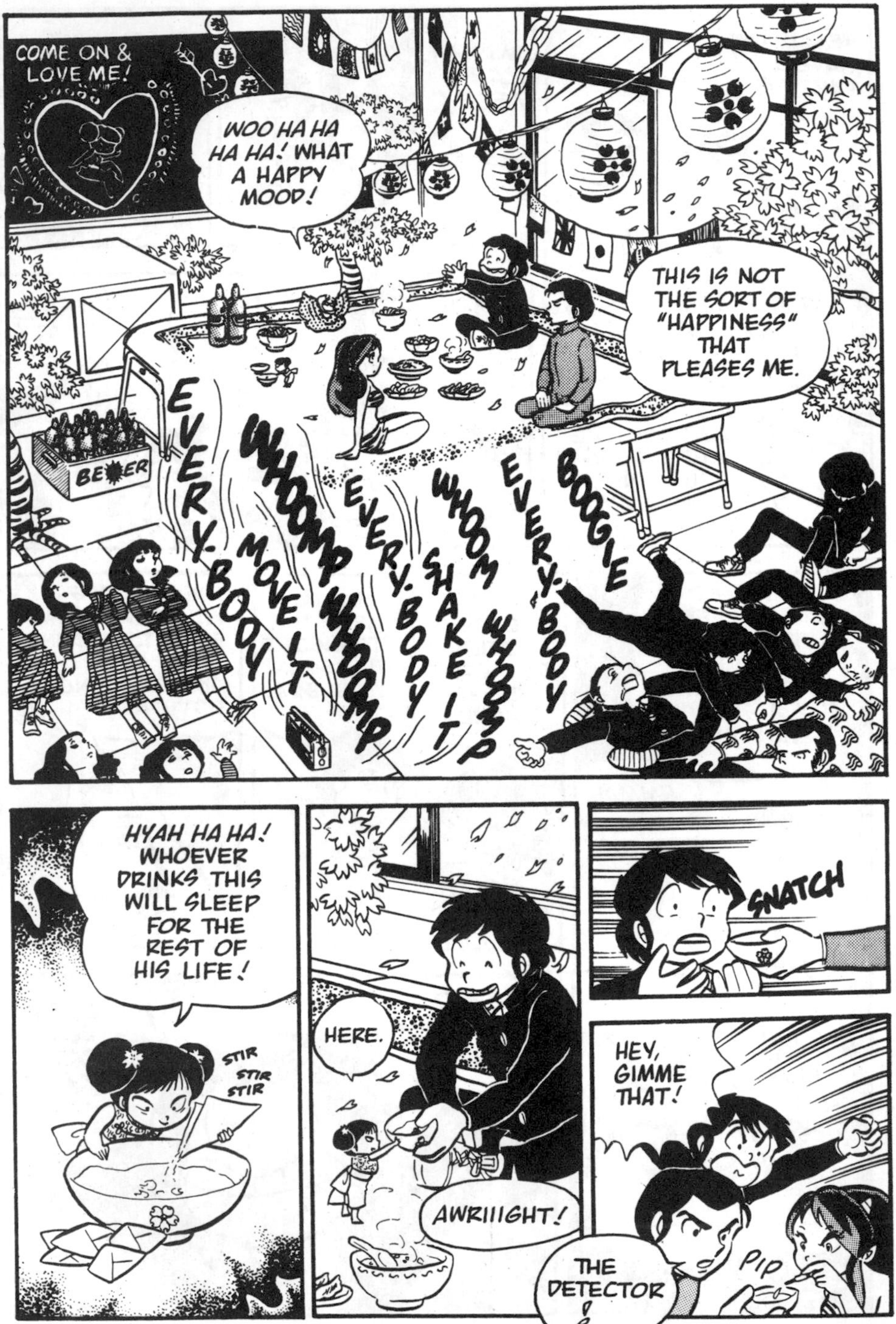
COME ON & LOVE ME!
WOO HA HA HA HA! WHAT A HAPPY MOOD!
THIS IS NOT THE SORT OF "HAPPINESS" THAT PLEASES ME.
EVERY-BODY
MOVE IT
WHOOMP WHOOMP WHOOMP
EVERY-BODY
SHAKE IT
WHOOM WHOOMP
EVERY-BODY
BOOGIE
HYAH HA HA! WHOEVER DRINKS THIS WILL SLEEP FOR THE REST OF HIS LIFE!
STIR STIR STIR
HERE.
AWRIIIGHT!
SNATCH
HEY, GIMME THAT!
THE DETECTOR!
PIP

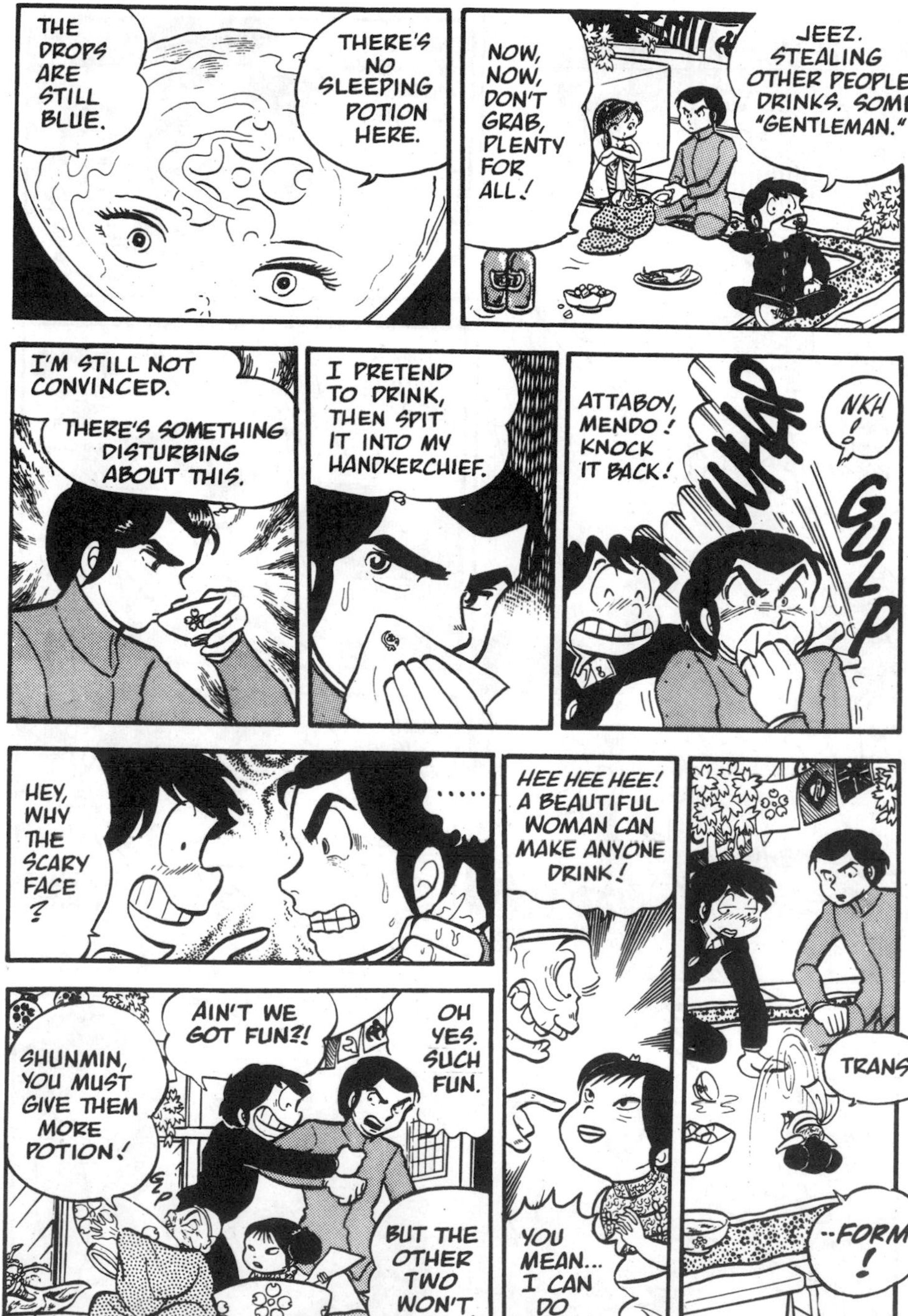
THE DROPS ARE STILL BLUE.
THERE'S NO SLEEPING POTION HERE.
NOW, NOW, DON'T GRAB, PLENTY FOR ALL!
JEEZ. STEALING OTHER PEOPLE'S DRINKS. SOME "GENTLEMAN."
I'M STILL NOT CONVINCED.
THERE'S SOMETHING DISTURBING ABOUT THIS.
I PRETEND TO DRINK, THEN SPIT IT INTO MY HANDKERCHIEF.
ATTABOY, MENDO! KNOCK IT BACK!
WHAP
NKH!
GULP
HEY, WHY THE SCARY FACE?
.....
AIN'T WE GOT FUN?!
OH YES. SUCH FUN.
SHUNMIN, YOU MUST GIVE THEM MORE POTION!
BUT THE OTHER TWO WON'T DRINK!
HEE HEE HEE! A BEAUTIFUL WOMAN CAN MAKE ANYONE DRINK!
YOU MEAN... I CAN DO THAT?!
TRANS-
--FORM!

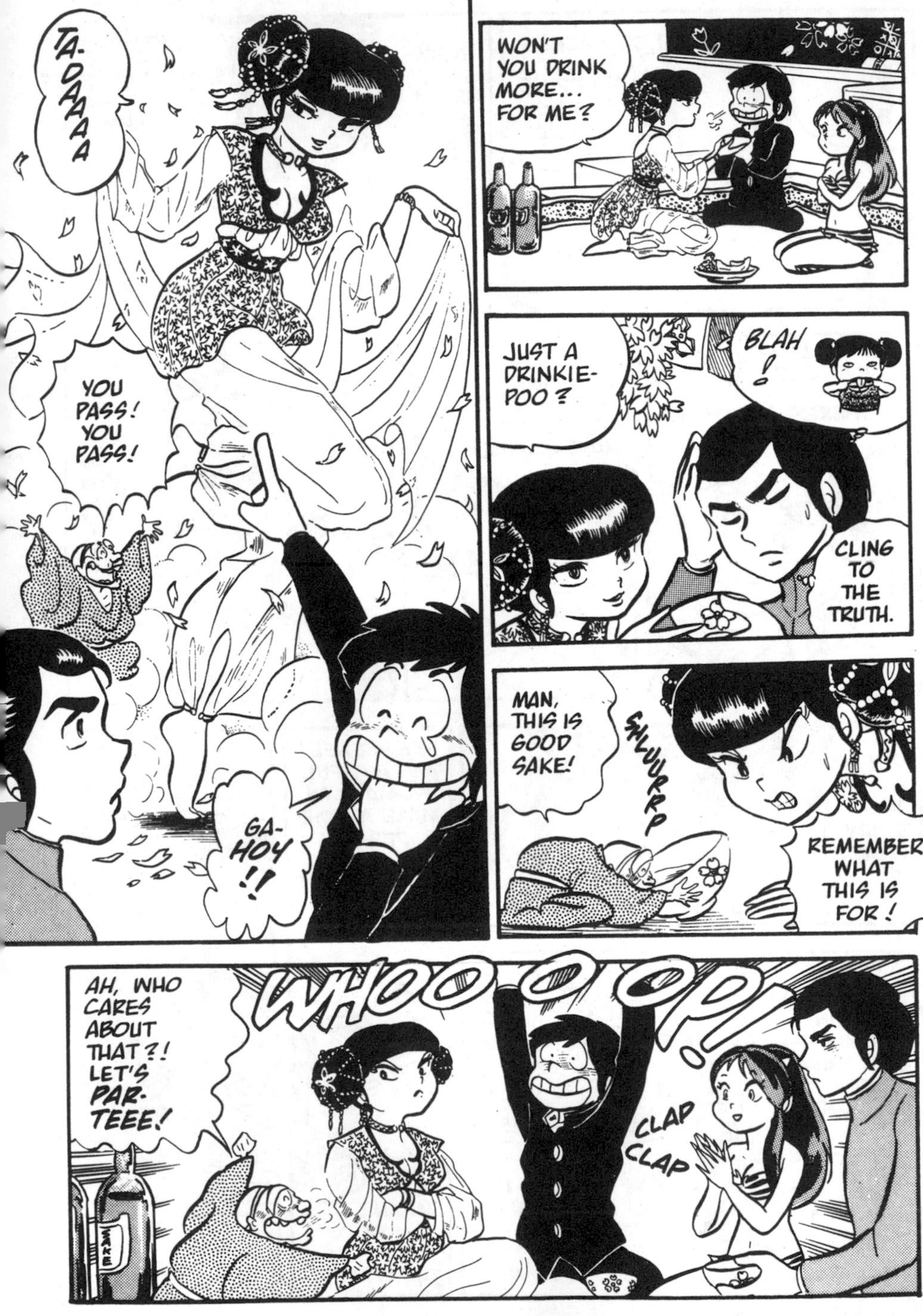
TA-DAAAAA
YOU PASS! YOU PASS!
GA-HOY!!
WON'T YOU DRINK MORE... FOR ME?
JUST A DRINKIE-POO?
BLAH!
CLING TO THE TRUTH.
MAN, THIS IS GOOD SAKE!
SHLUURRP
REMEMBER WHAT THIS IS FOR!
AH, WHO CARES ABOUT THAT?! LET'S PAR-TEEE!
WHOOOOP!
CLAP CLAP
SAKE

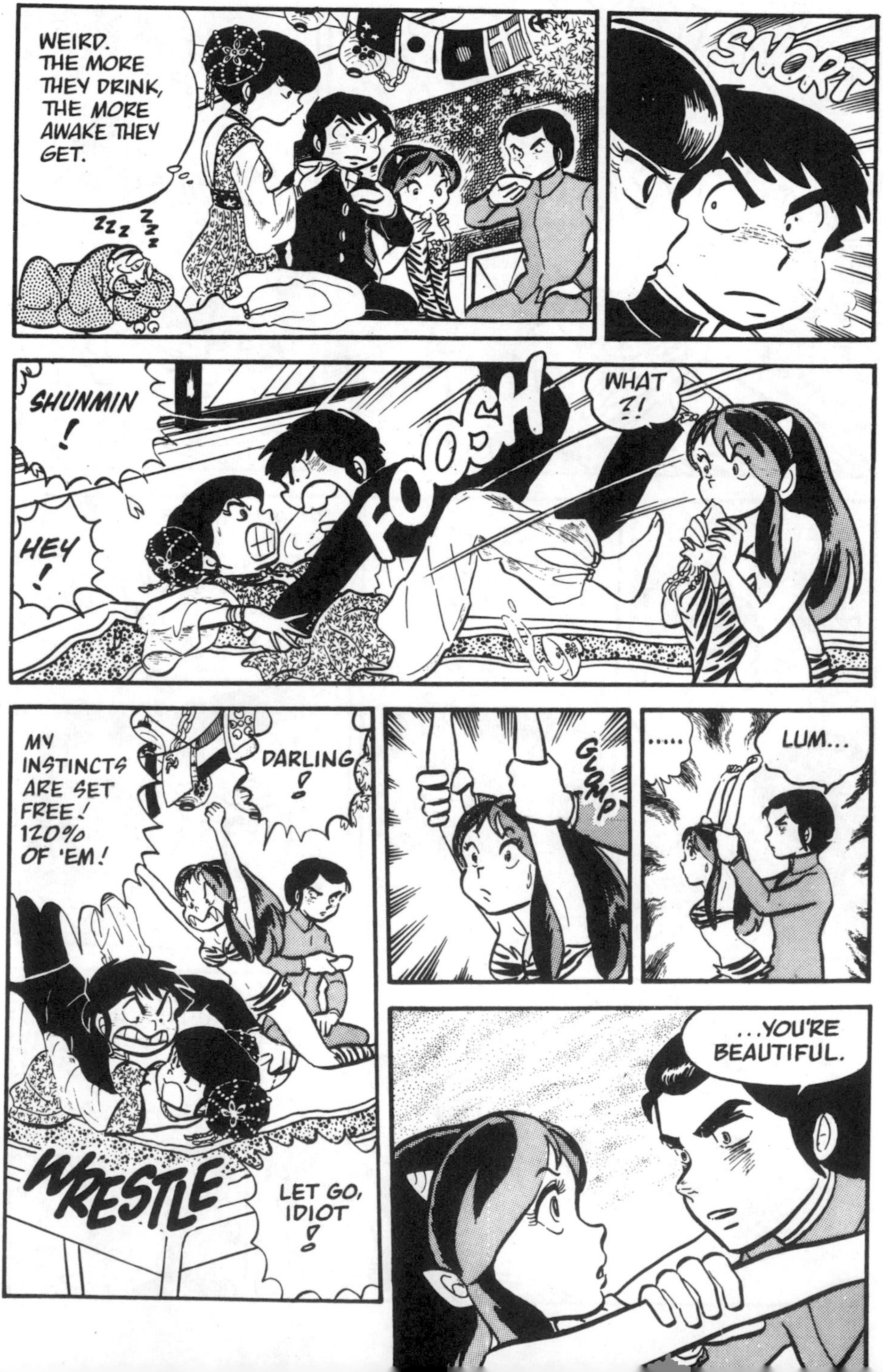
WEIRD. THE MORE THEY DRINK, THE MORE AWAKE THEY GET.
ZZZ ZZZ
SNORT
SHUNMIN !
HEY !
FOOSH
WHAT ?!
MY INSTINCTS ARE SET FREE! 120% OF 'EM!
DARLING !
WRESTLE
LET GO, IDIOT !
GLOMP
.....
LUM...
...YOU'RE BEAUTIFUL.

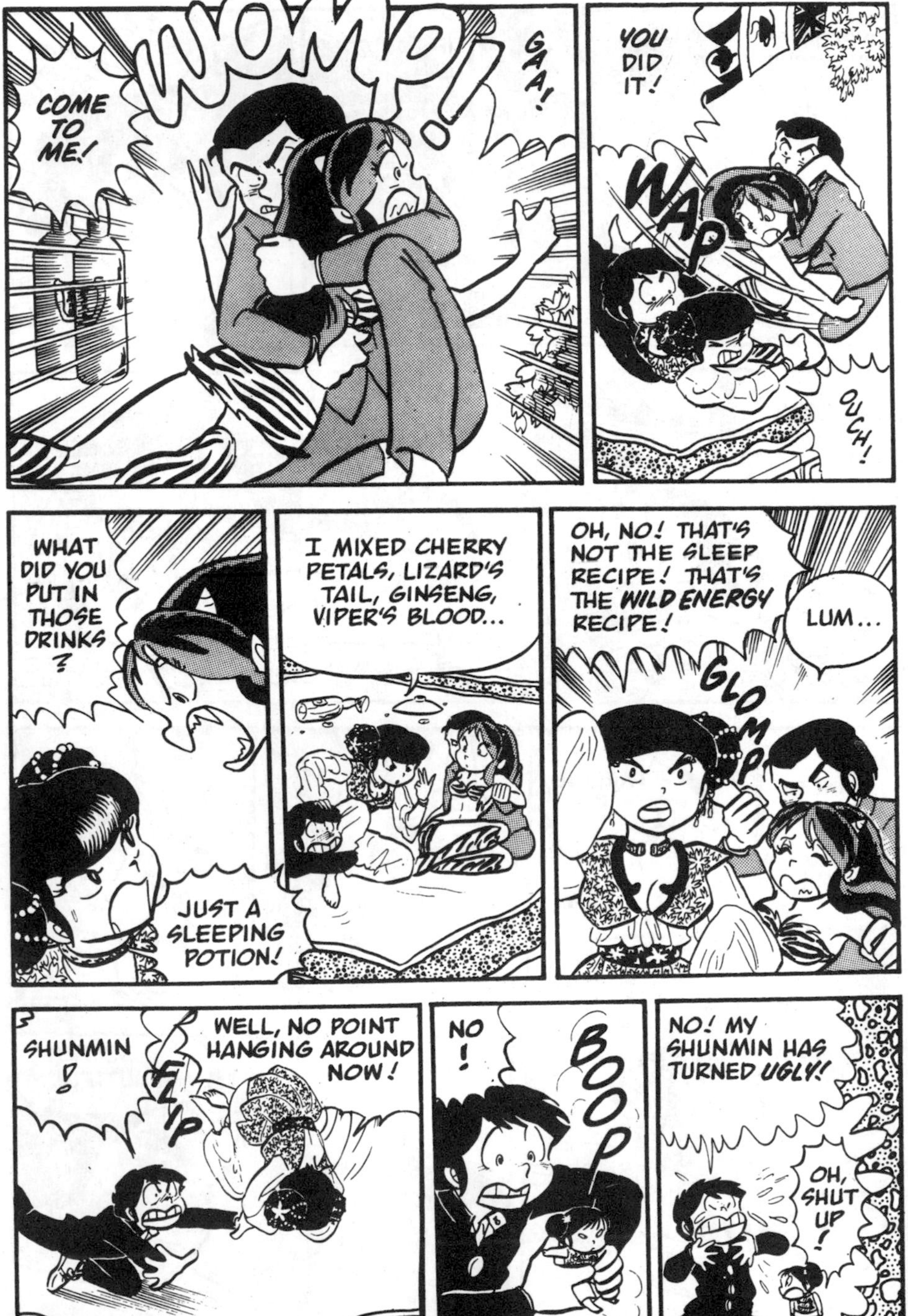
WOMP!
COME TO ME!
GAAA!
YOU DID IT!
WAP
OUCH!
WHAT DID YOU PUT IN THOSE DRINKS?
JUST A SLEEPING POTION!
I MIXED CHERRY PETALS, LIZARD'S TAIL, GINSENG, VIPER'S BLOOD...
OH, NO! THAT'S NOT THE SLEEP RECIPE! THAT'S THE WILD ENERGY RECIPE!
LUM...
GLOMP
SHUNMIN!
WELL, NO POINT HANGING AROUND NOW!
FLIP
NO!
BOOP
NO! MY SHUNMIN HAS TURNED UGLY!
OH, SHUT UP!

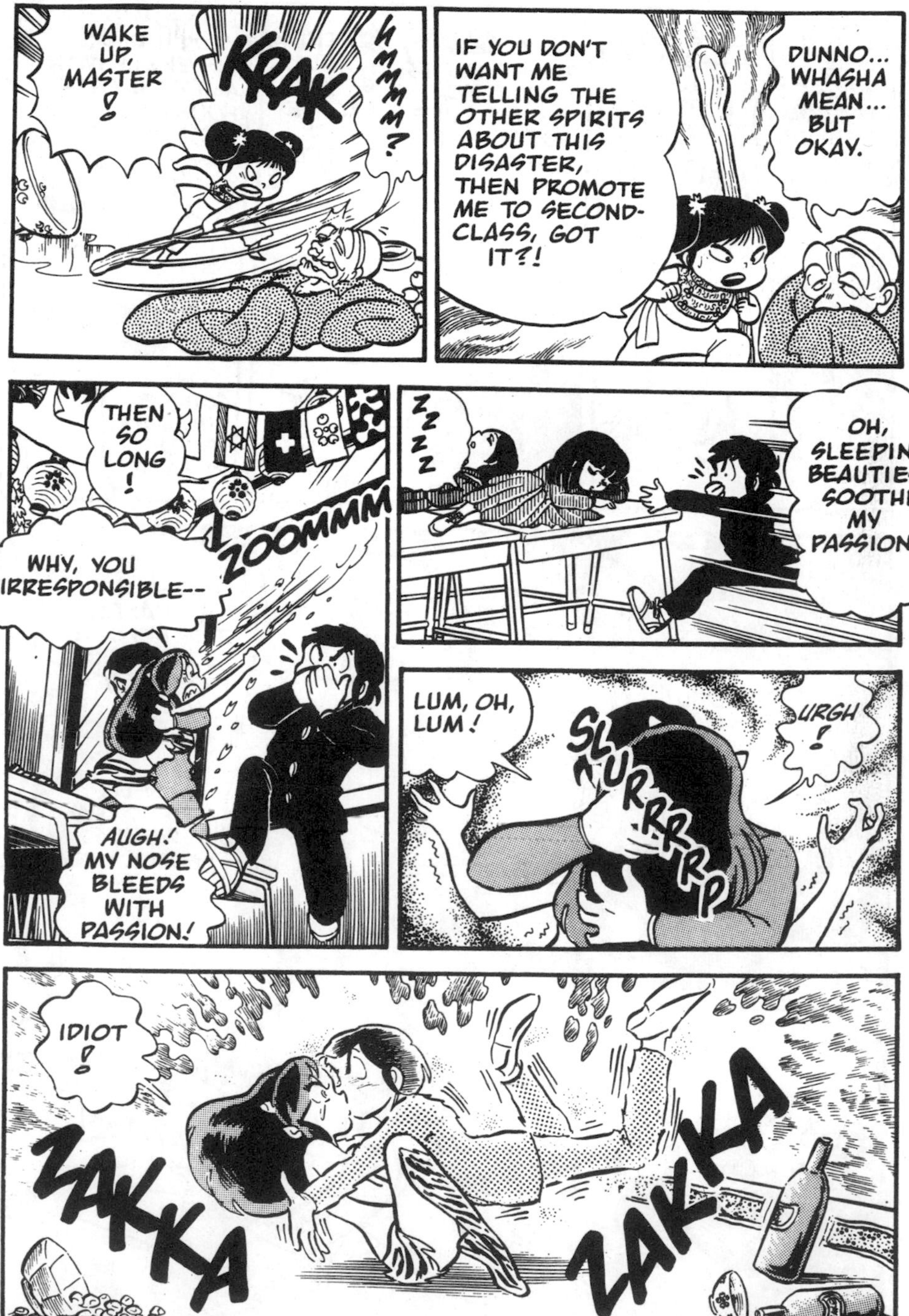
WAKE UP, MASTER!
KRAK
HMMMM?
IF YOU DON'T WANT ME TELLING THE OTHER SPIRITS ABOUT THIS DISASTER, THEN PROMOTE ME TO SECOND-CLASS, GOT IT?!
DUNNO... WHASHA MEAN... BUT OKAY.
THEN SO LONG!
ZOOMMM
WHY, YOU IRRESPONSIBLE--
AUGH! MY NOSE BLEEDS WITH PASSION!
ZZZZ
OH, SLEEPING BEAUTIES! SOOTHE MY PASSION!
LUM, OH, LUM!
SLURRRRP
URGH!
IDIOT!
ZAKKA
ZAKKA

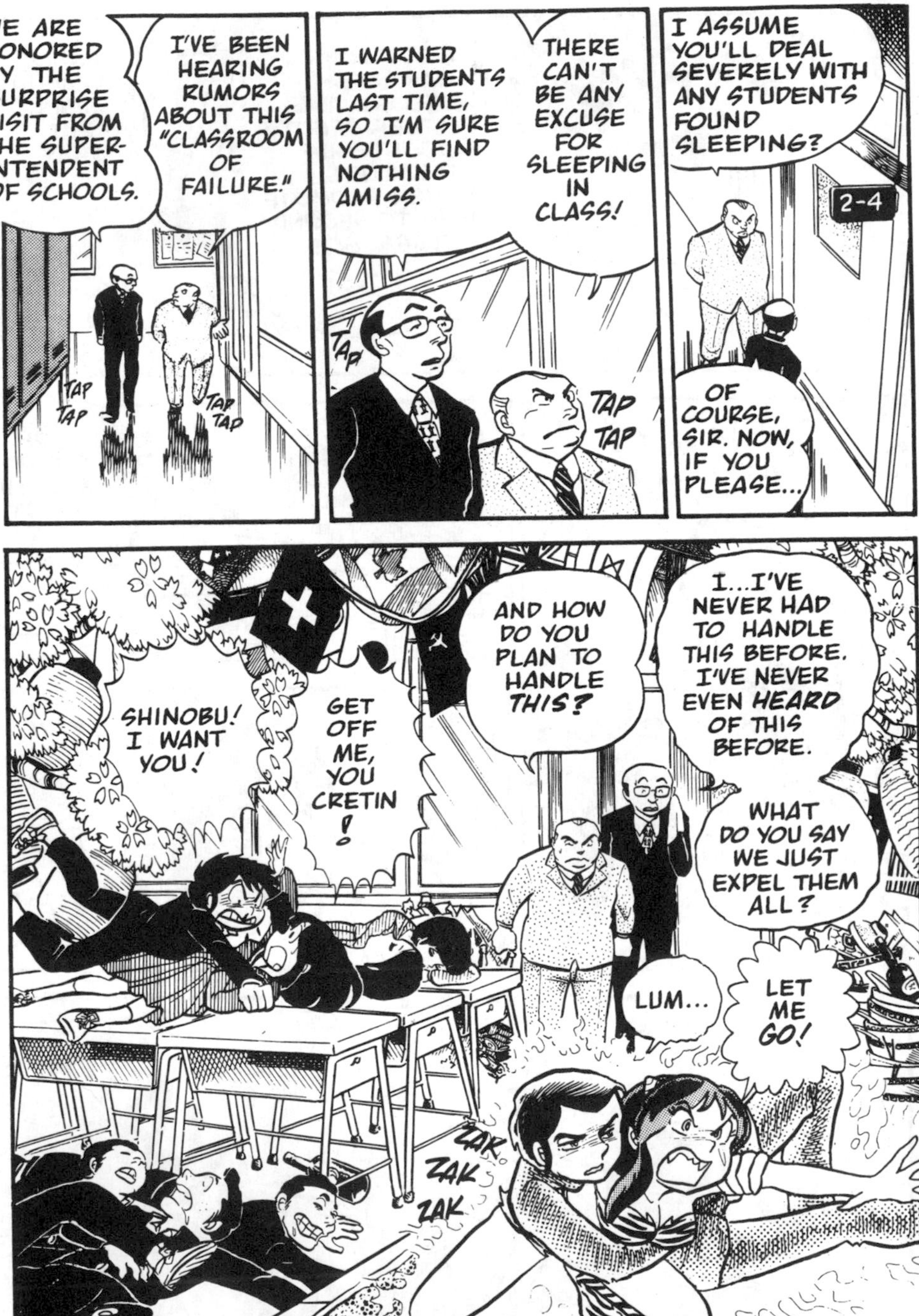

WE ARE HONORED BY THE SURPRISE VISIT FROM THE SUPER-INTENDENT OF SCHOOLS.
I'VE BEEN HEARING RUMORS ABOUT THIS "CLASSROOM OF FAILURE."
TAP TAP
TAP TAP
I WARNED THE STUDENTS LAST TIME, SO I'M SURE YOU'LL FIND NOTHING AMISS.
THERE CAN'T BE ANY EXCUSE FOR SLEEPING IN CLASS!
TAP
TAP TAP
I ASSUME YOU'LL DEAL SEVERELY WITH ANY STUDENTS FOUND SLEEPING?
2-4
OF COURSE, SIR. NOW, IF YOU PLEASE...
SHINOBU! I WANT YOU!
GET OFF ME, YOU CRETIN!
AND HOW DO YOU PLAN TO HANDLE THIS?
I...I'VE NEVER HAD TO HANDLE THIS BEFORE. I'VE NEVER EVEN HEARD OF THIS BEFORE.
WHAT DO YOU SAY WE JUST EXPEL THEM ALL?
LUM...
LET ME GO!
ZAK ZAK ZAK

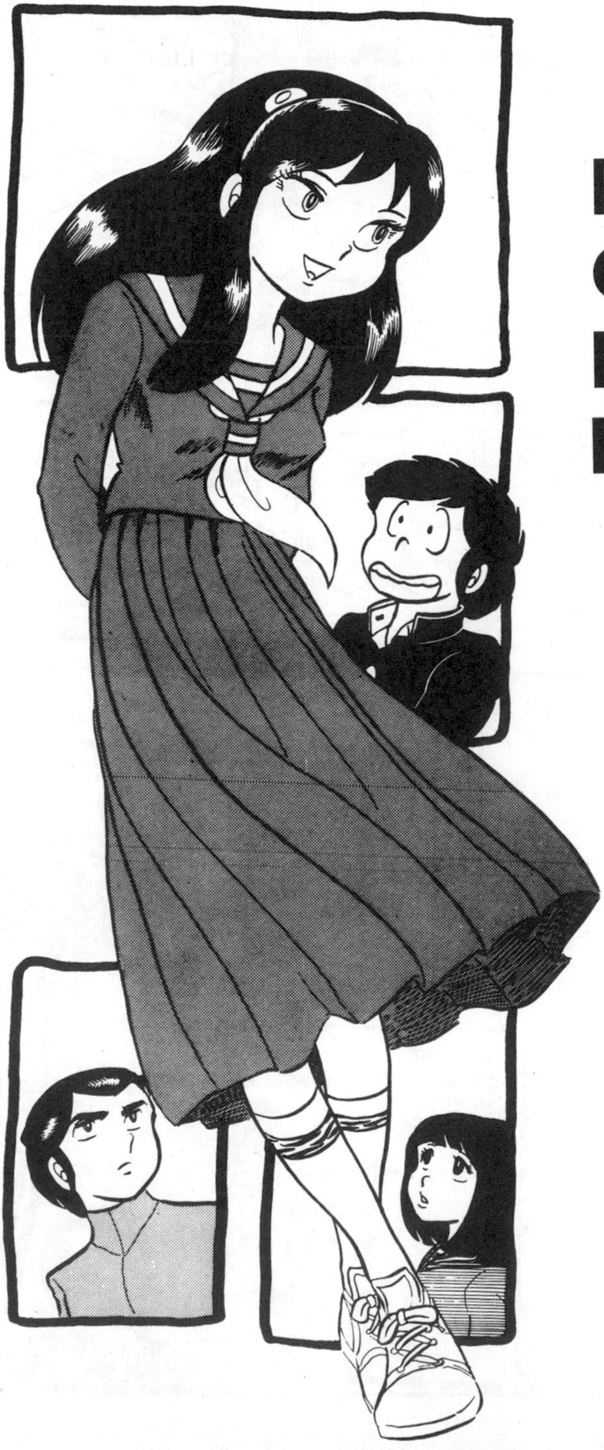

Part 4
On the Horns of Passion

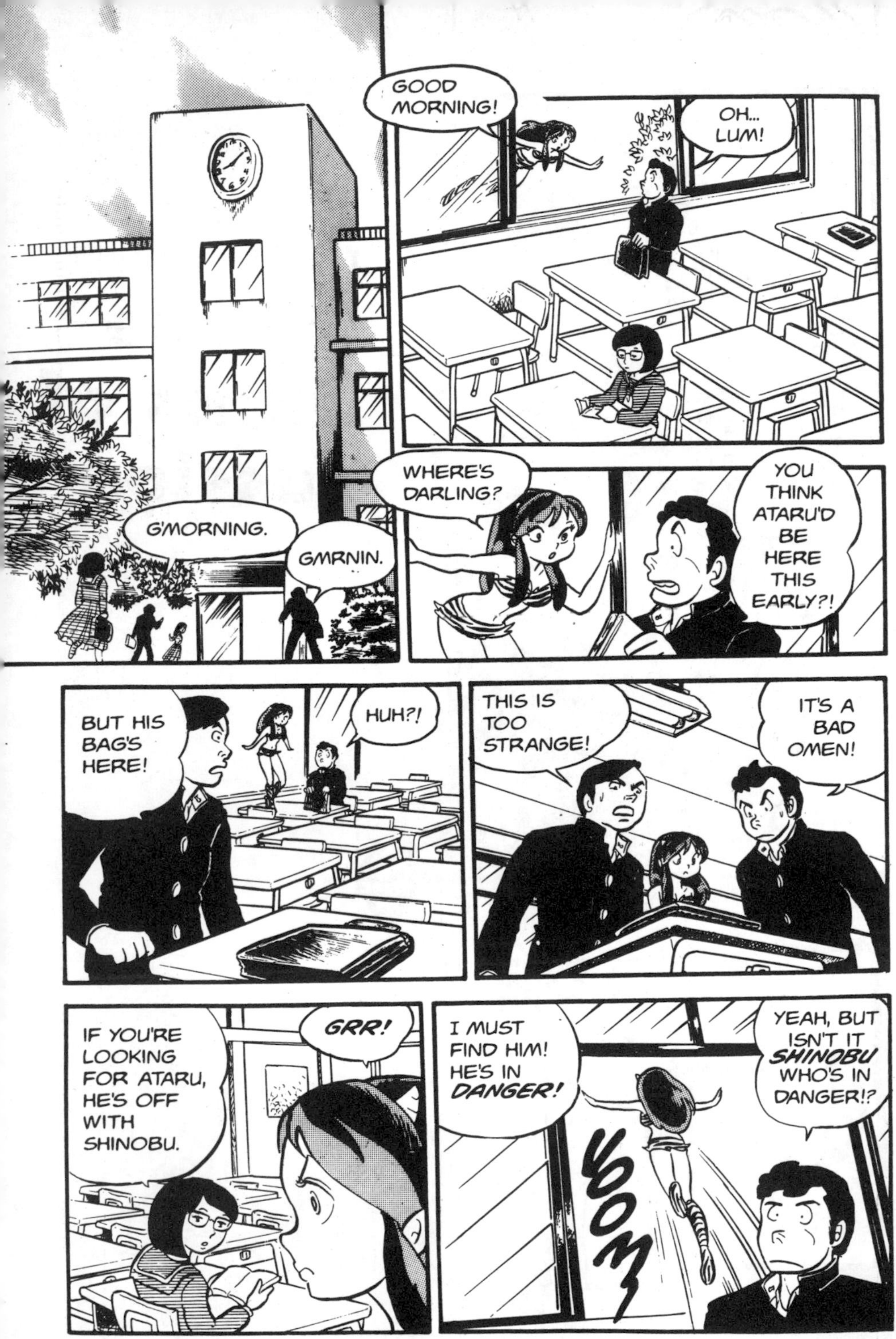
G'MORNING.
GMRNIN.
GOOD MORNING!
OH... LUM!
WHERE'S DARLING?
YOU THINK ATARU'D BE HERE THIS EARLY?!
BUT HIS BAG'S HERE!
HUH?!
THIS IS TOO STRANGE!
IT'S A BAD OMEN!
IF YOU'RE LOOKING FOR ATARU, HE'S OFF WITH SHINOBU.
GRR!
I MUST FIND HIM! HE'S IN DANGER!
VOOM
YEAH, BUT ISN'T IT SHINOBU WHO'S IN DANGER!?

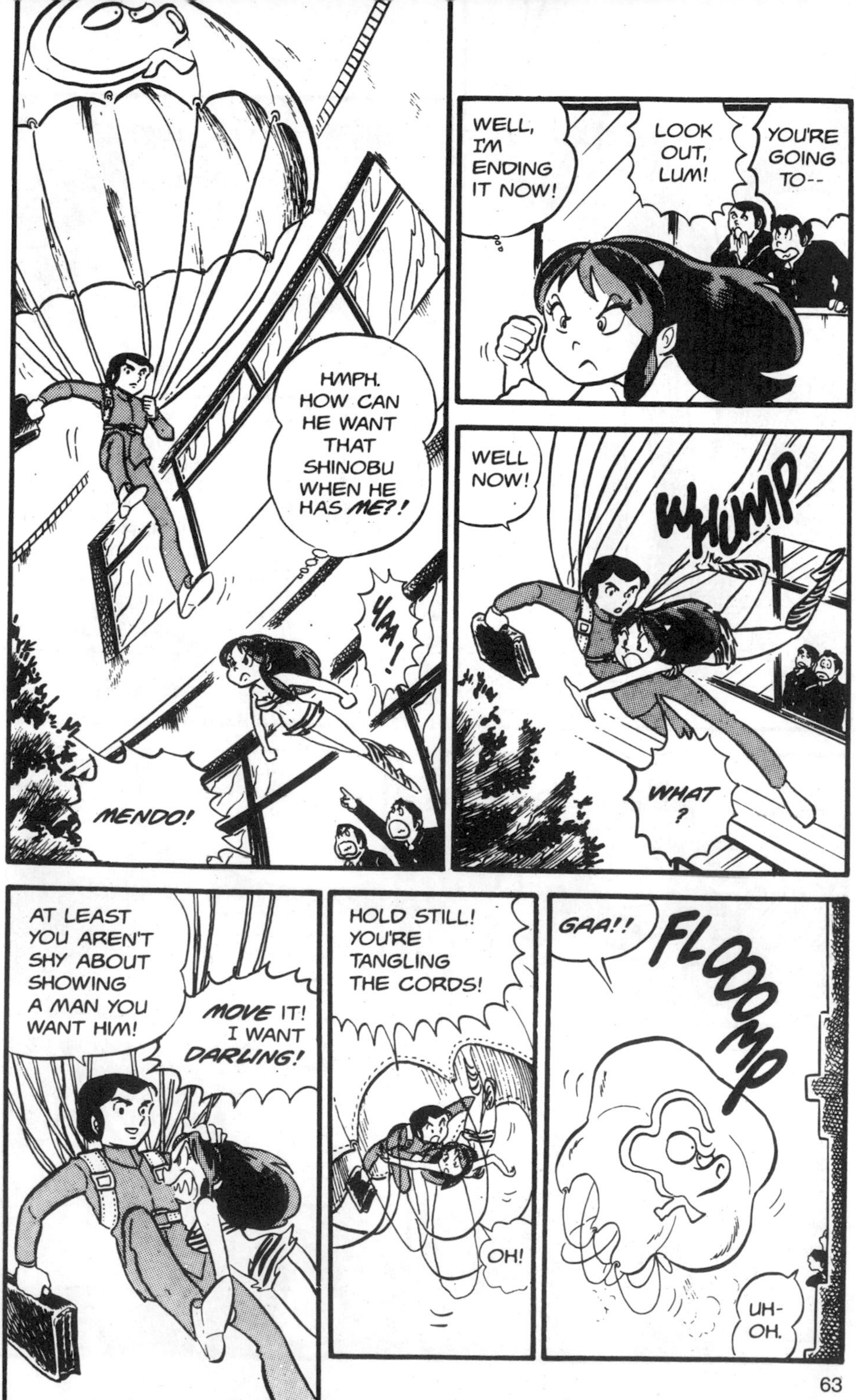
HMPH. HOW CAN HE WANT THAT SHINOBU WHEN HE HAS ME?!
YAA!
MENDO!
WELL, I'M ENDING IT NOW!
LOOK OUT, LUM!
YOU'RE GOING TO--
WELL NOW!
WHUMP
WHAT?
AT LEAST YOU AREN'T SHY ABOUT SHOWING A MAN YOU WANT HIM!
MOVE IT! I WANT DARLING!
HOLD STILL! YOU'RE TANGLING THE CORDS!
OH!
GAA!!
FLOOOMP
UH-OH.

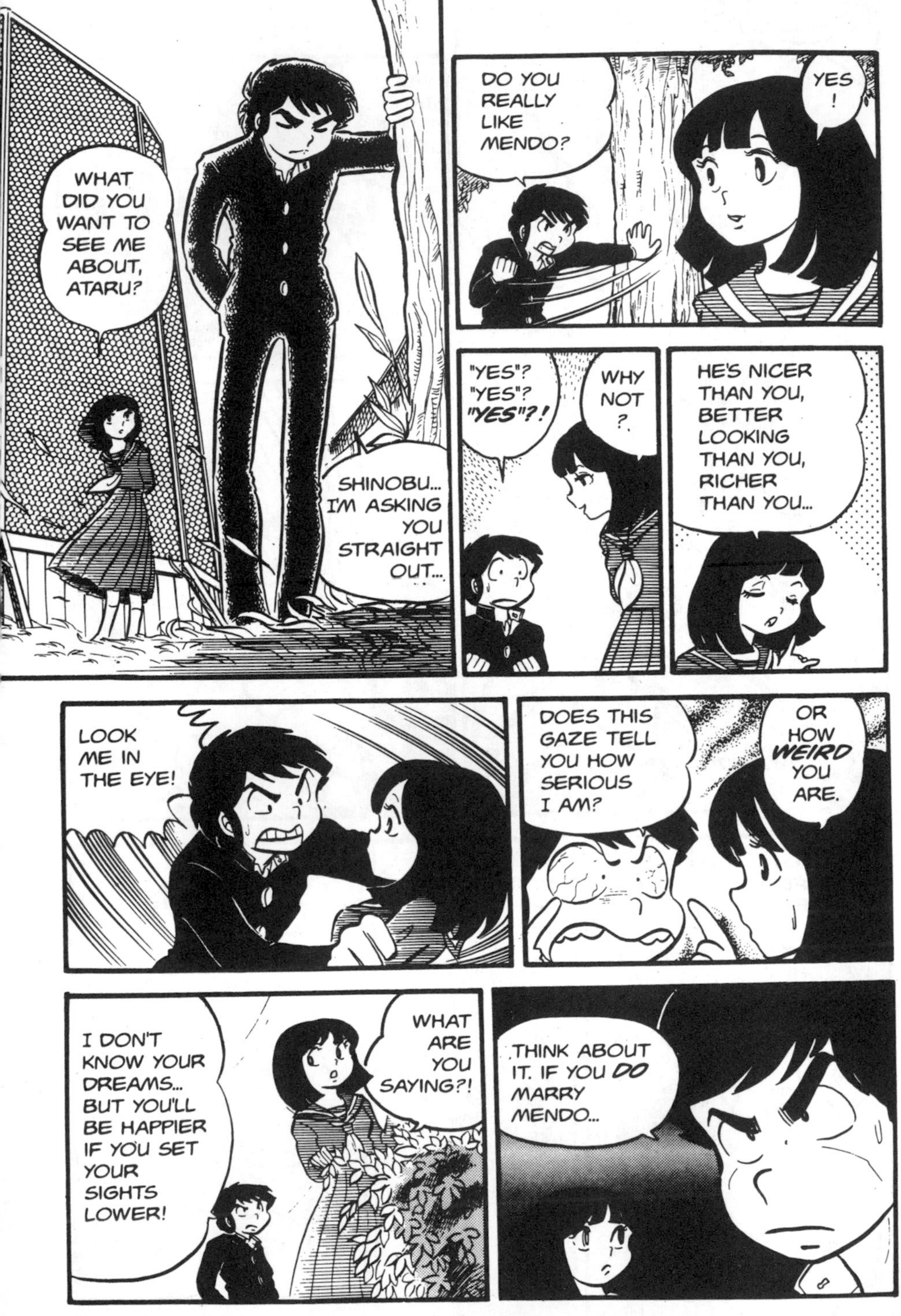

WHAT DID YOU WANT TO SEE ME ABOUT, ATARU?
SHINOBU... I'M ASKING YOU STRAIGHT OUT...
DO YOU REALLY LIKE MENDO?
YES!
"YES"? "YES"? **"YES"?!**
WHY NOT?
HE'S NICER THAN YOU, BETTER LOOKING THAN YOU, RICHER THAN YOU...
LOOK ME IN THE EYE!
DOES THIS GAZE TELL YOU HOW SERIOUS I AM?
OR HOW ***WEIRD*** YOU ARE.
I DON'T KNOW YOUR DREAMS... BUT YOU'LL BE HAPPIER IF YOU SET YOUR SIGHTS LOWER!
WHAT ARE YOU SAYING?!
THINK ABOUT IT. IF YOU ***DO*** MARRY MENDO...

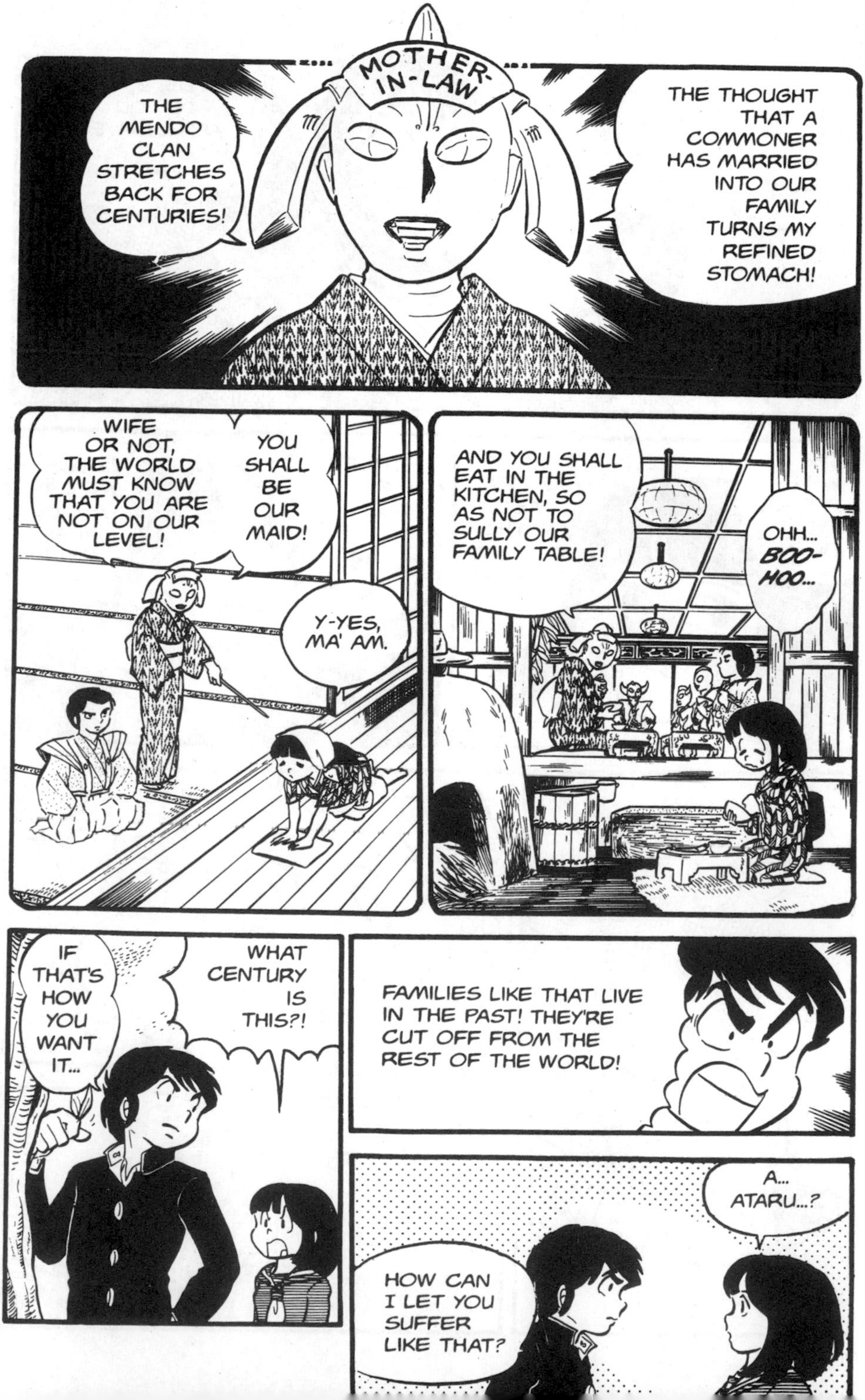
MOTHER-IN-LAW
THE MENDO CLAN STRETCHES BACK FOR CENTURIES!
THE THOUGHT THAT A COMMONER HAS MARRIED INTO OUR FAMILY TURNS MY REFINED STOMACH!
WIFE OR NOT, THE WORLD MUST KNOW THAT YOU ARE NOT ON OUR LEVEL!
YOU SHALL BE OUR MAID!
Y-YES, MA' AM.
AND YOU SHALL EAT IN THE KITCHEN, SO AS NOT TO SULLY OUR FAMILY TABLE!
OHH... BOO-HOO...
IF THAT'S HOW YOU WANT IT...
WHAT CENTURY IS THIS?!
FAMILIES LIKE THAT LIVE IN THE PAST! THEY'RE CUT OFF FROM THE REST OF THE WORLD!
A... ATARU...?
HOW CAN I LET YOU SUFFER LIKE THAT?

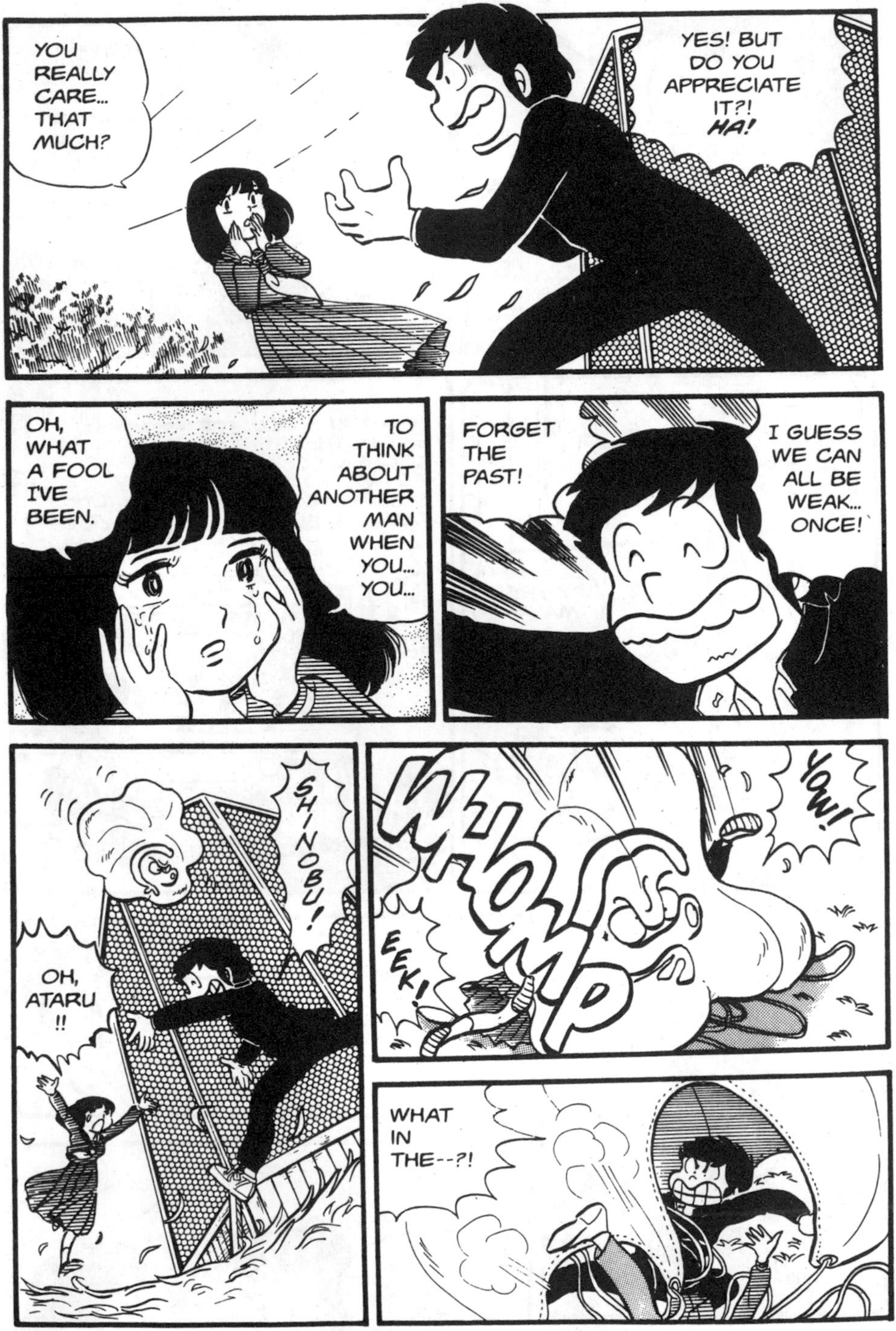
YOU REALLY CARE... THAT MUCH?
YES! BUT DO YOU APPRECIATE IT?! HA!
OH, WHAT A FOOL I'VE BEEN.
TO THINK ABOUT ANOTHER MAN WHEN YOU... YOU...
FORGET THE PAST!
I GUESS WE CAN ALL BE WEAK... ONCE!
SHINOBU!
OH, ATARU !!
WHOMP
YOW!
EEK!
WHAT IN THE--?!

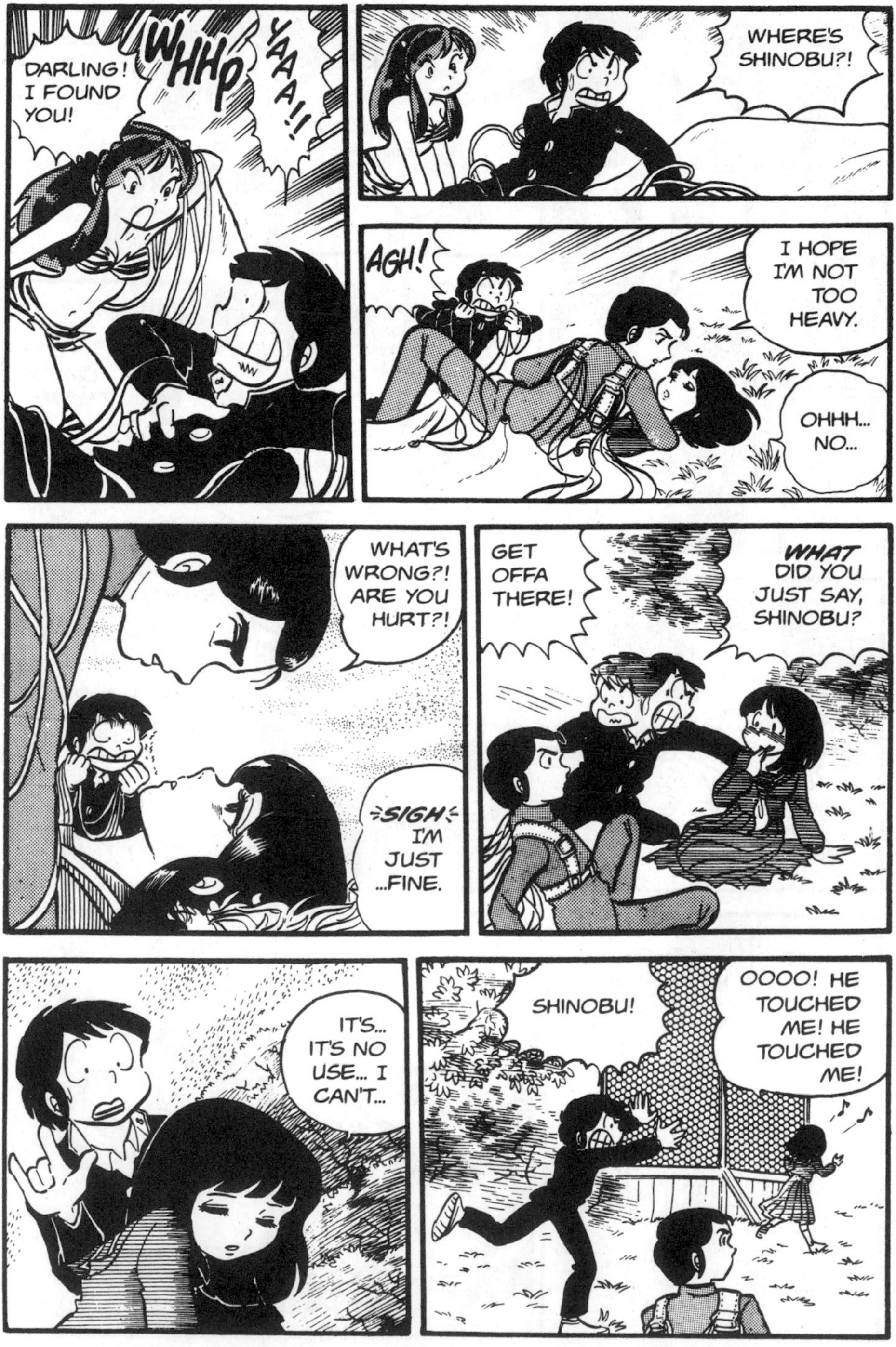
WHHP
YAAAA!!
DARLING! I FOUND YOU!
WHERE'S SHINOBU?!
AGH!
I HOPE I'M NOT TOO HEAVY.
OHHH... NO...
WHAT'S WRONG?! ARE YOU HURT?!
SIGH I'M JUST ...FINE.
GET OFFA THERE!
WHAT DID YOU JUST SAY, SHINOBU?
IT'S... IT'S NO USE... I CAN'T...
SHINOBU!
OOOO! HE TOUCHED ME! HE TOUCHED ME!

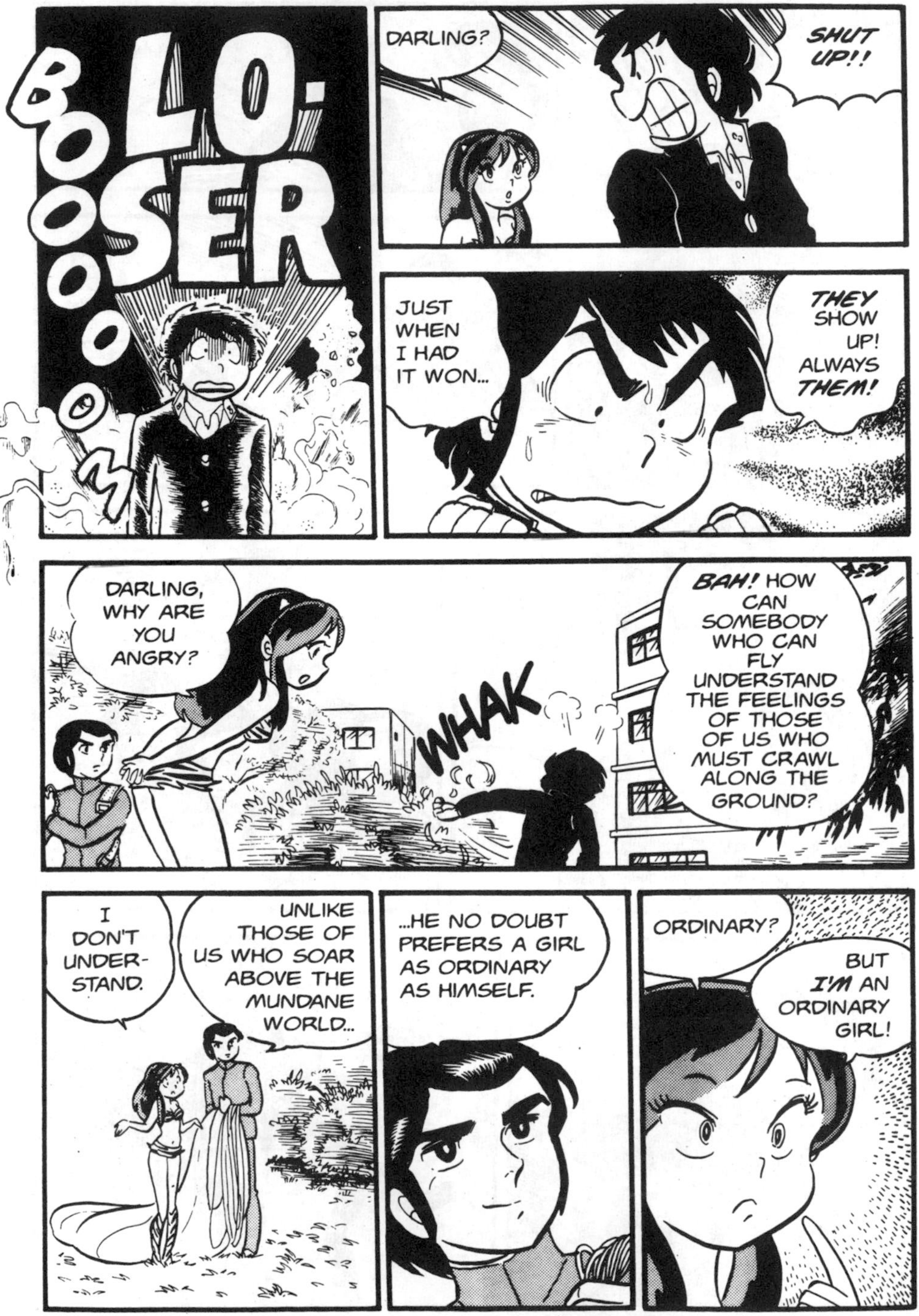
BOOOOOM
LO-SER
DARLING?
SHUT UP!!
JUST WHEN I HAD IT WON...
THEY SHOW UP! ALWAYS THEM!
DARLING, WHY ARE YOU ANGRY?
WHAK
BAH! HOW CAN SOMEBODY WHO CAN FLY UNDERSTAND THE FEELINGS OF THOSE OF US WHO MUST CRAWL ALONG THE GROUND?
I DON'T UNDER-STAND.
UNLIKE THOSE OF US WHO SOAR ABOVE THE MUNDANE WORLD...
...HE NO DOUBT PREFERS A GIRL AS ORDINARY AS HIMSELF.
ORDINARY?
BUT I'M AN ORDINARY GIRL!

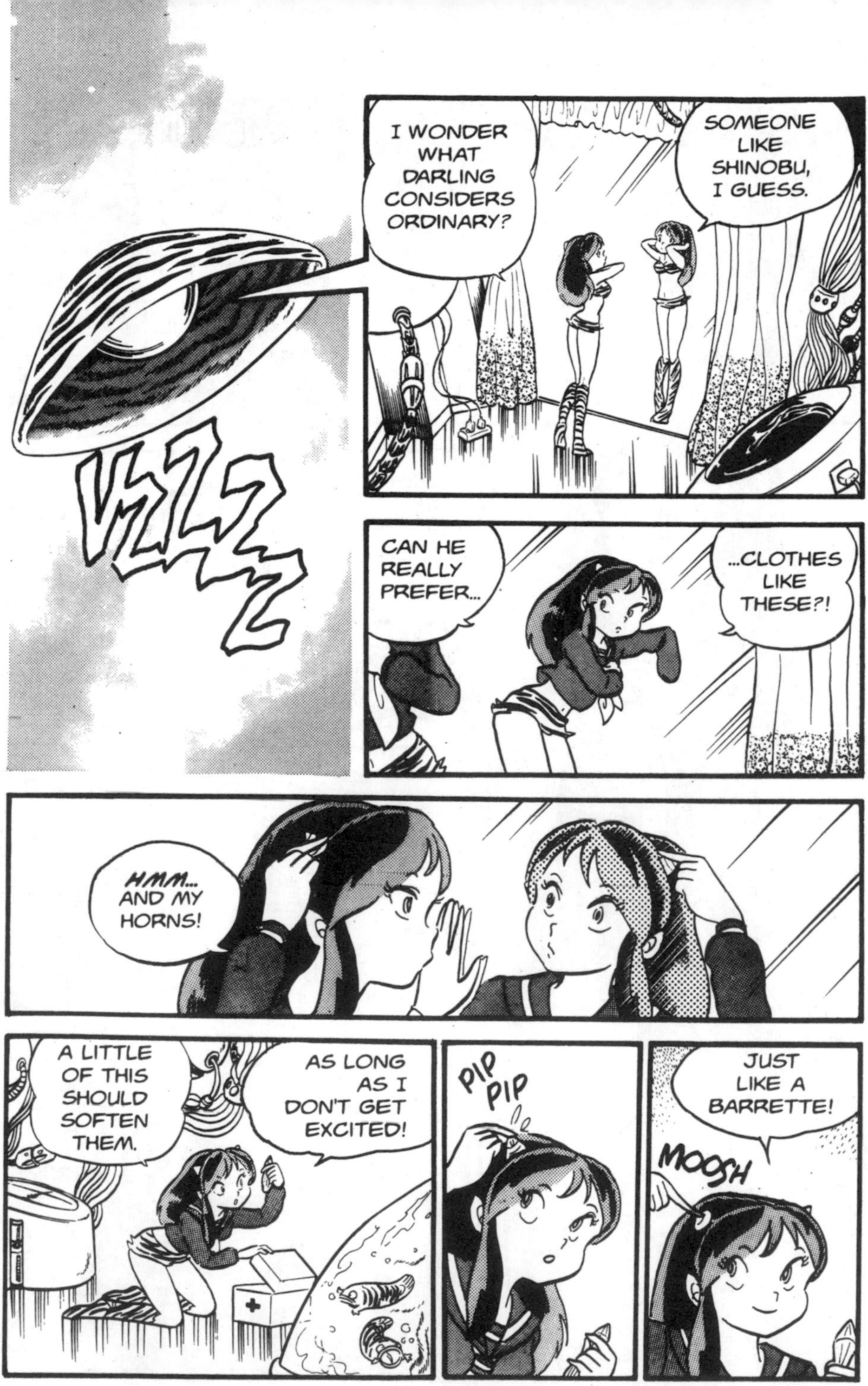
VZZZ
I WONDER WHAT DARLING CONSIDERS ORDINARY?
SOMEONE LIKE SHINOBU, I GUESS.
CAN HE REALLY PREFER...
...CLOTHES LIKE THESE?!
HMM... AND MY HORNS!
A LITTLE OF THIS SHOULD SOFTEN THEM.
AS LONG AS I DON'T GET EXCITED!
PIP PIP
JUST LIKE A BARRETTE!
MOOSH

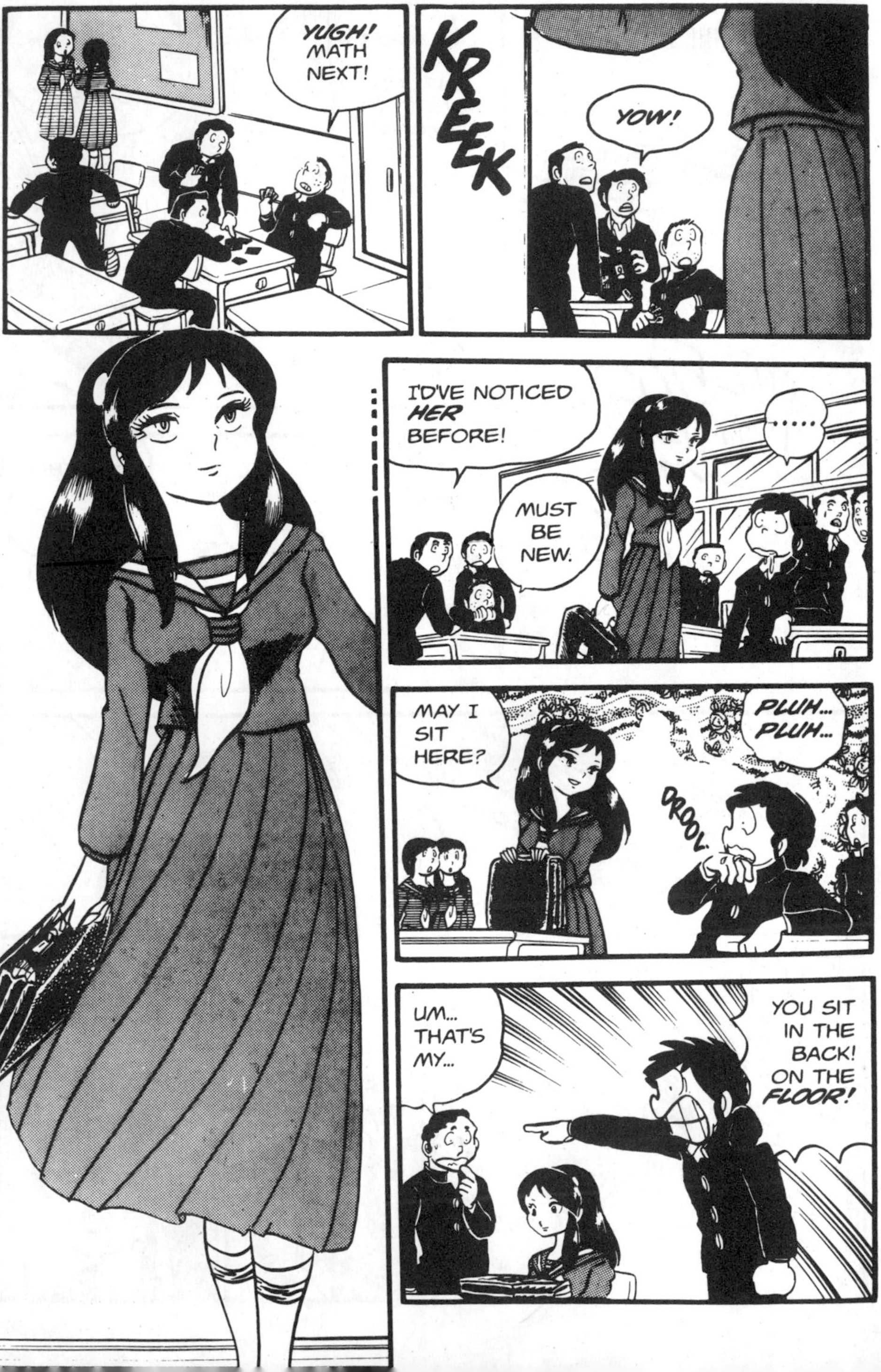
YUGH! MATH NEXT!
KREEEK
YOW!
I'D'VE NOTICED HER BEFORE!
MUST BE NEW.
......
MAY I SIT HERE?
PLUH... PLUH...
DROOL
UM... THAT'S MY...
YOU SIT IN THE BACK! ON THE FLOOR!

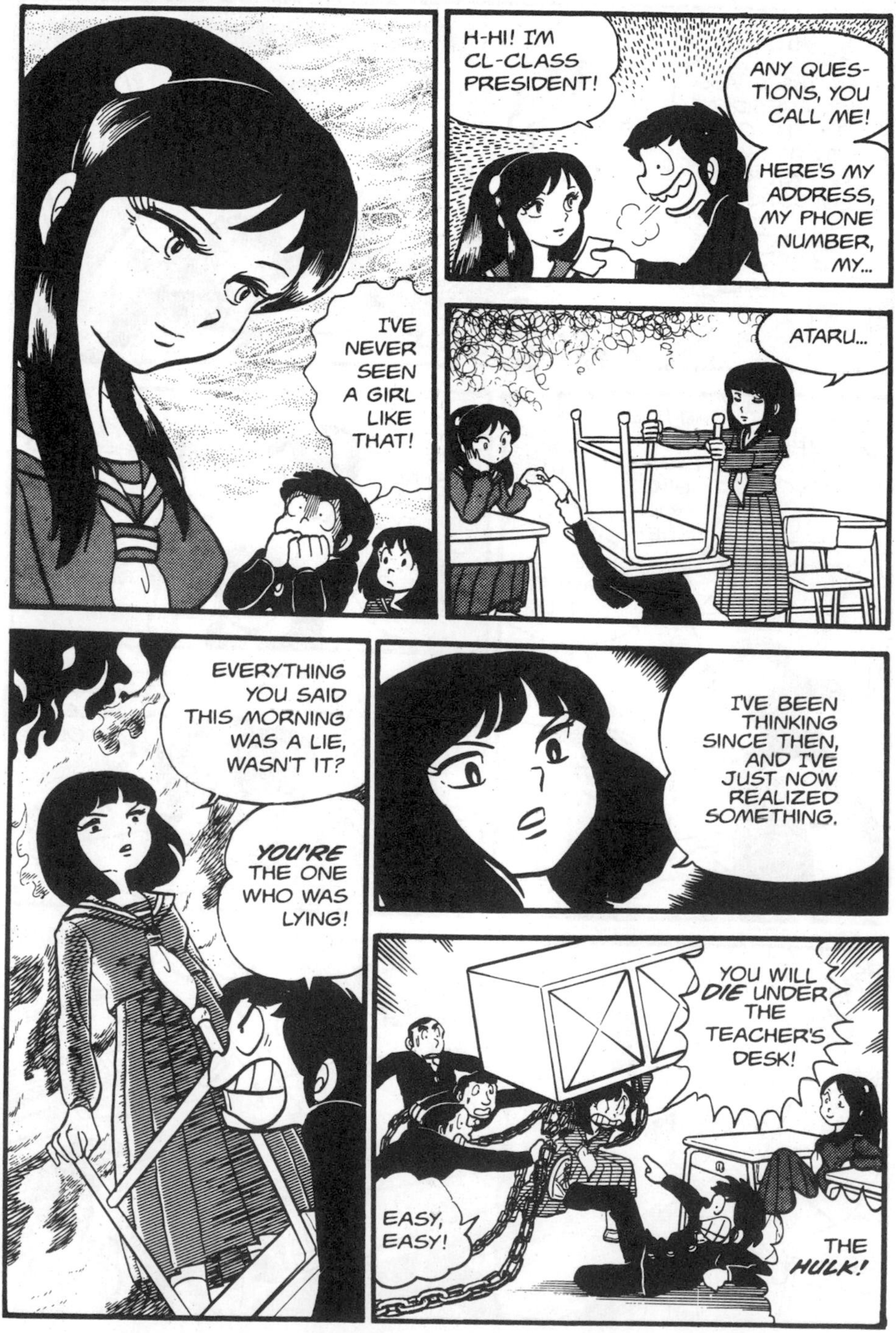
I'VE NEVER SEEN A GIRL LIKE THAT!
H-HI! I'M CL-CLASS PRESIDENT!
ANY QUESTIONS, YOU CALL ME!
HERE'S MY ADDRESS, MY PHONE NUMBER, MY...
ATARU...
EVERYTHING YOU SAID THIS MORNING WAS A LIE, WASN'T IT?
YOU'RE THE ONE WHO WAS LYING!
I'VE BEEN THINKING SINCE THEN, AND I'VE JUST NOW REALIZED SOMETHING.
YOU WILL DIE UNDER THE TEACHER'S DESK!
EASY, EASY!
THE HULK!

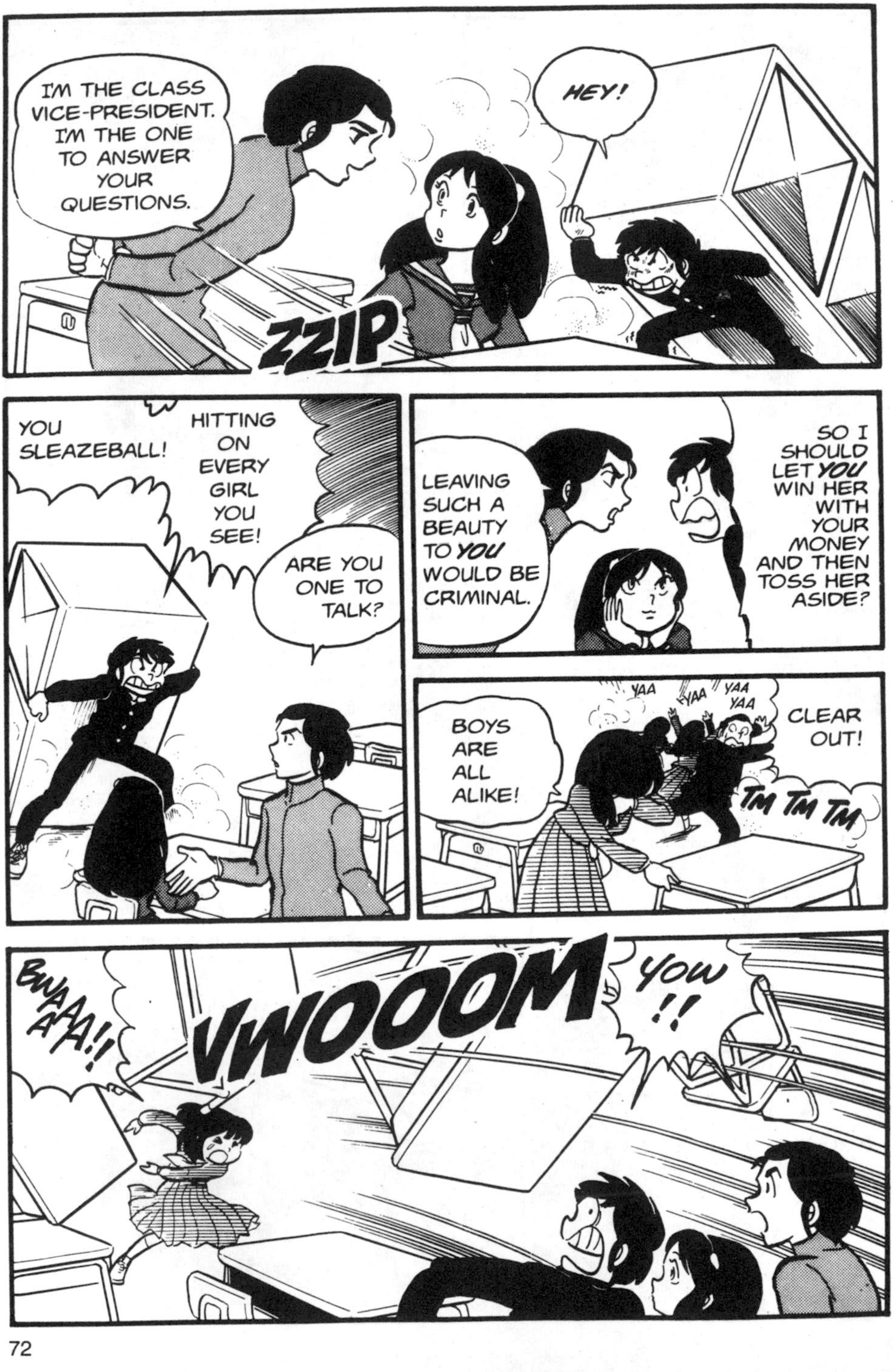

I'M THE CLASS VICE-PRESIDENT. I'M THE ONE TO ANSWER YOUR QUESTIONS.
HEY!
ZZIP
YOU SLEAZEBALL!
HITTING ON EVERY GIRL YOU SEE!
ARE YOU ONE TO TALK?
LEAVING SUCH A BEAUTY TO YOU WOULD BE CRIMINAL.
SO I SHOULD LET YOU WIN HER WITH YOUR MONEY AND THEN TOSS HER ASIDE?
BOYS ARE ALL ALIKE!
YAA YAA YAA YAA
CLEAR OUT!
TM TM TM
BWAAAAA!!
VWOOOM
YOW!!

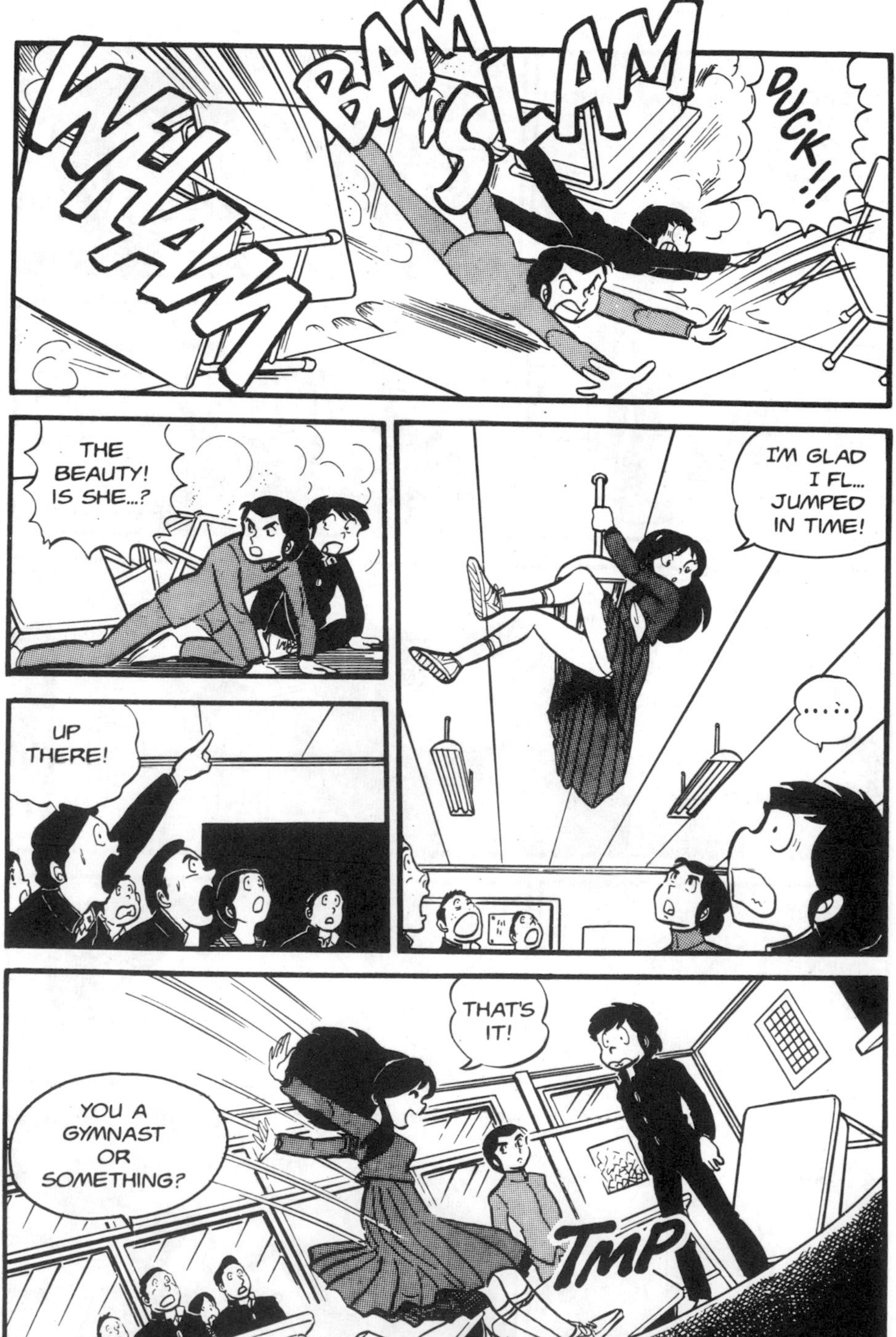
WHAM
BAM
SLAM
DUCK!!!
THE BEAUTY! IS SHE...?
UP THERE!
I'M GLAD I FL... JUMPED IN TIME!
....?
THAT'S IT!
YOU A GYMNAST OR SOMETHING?
TMP

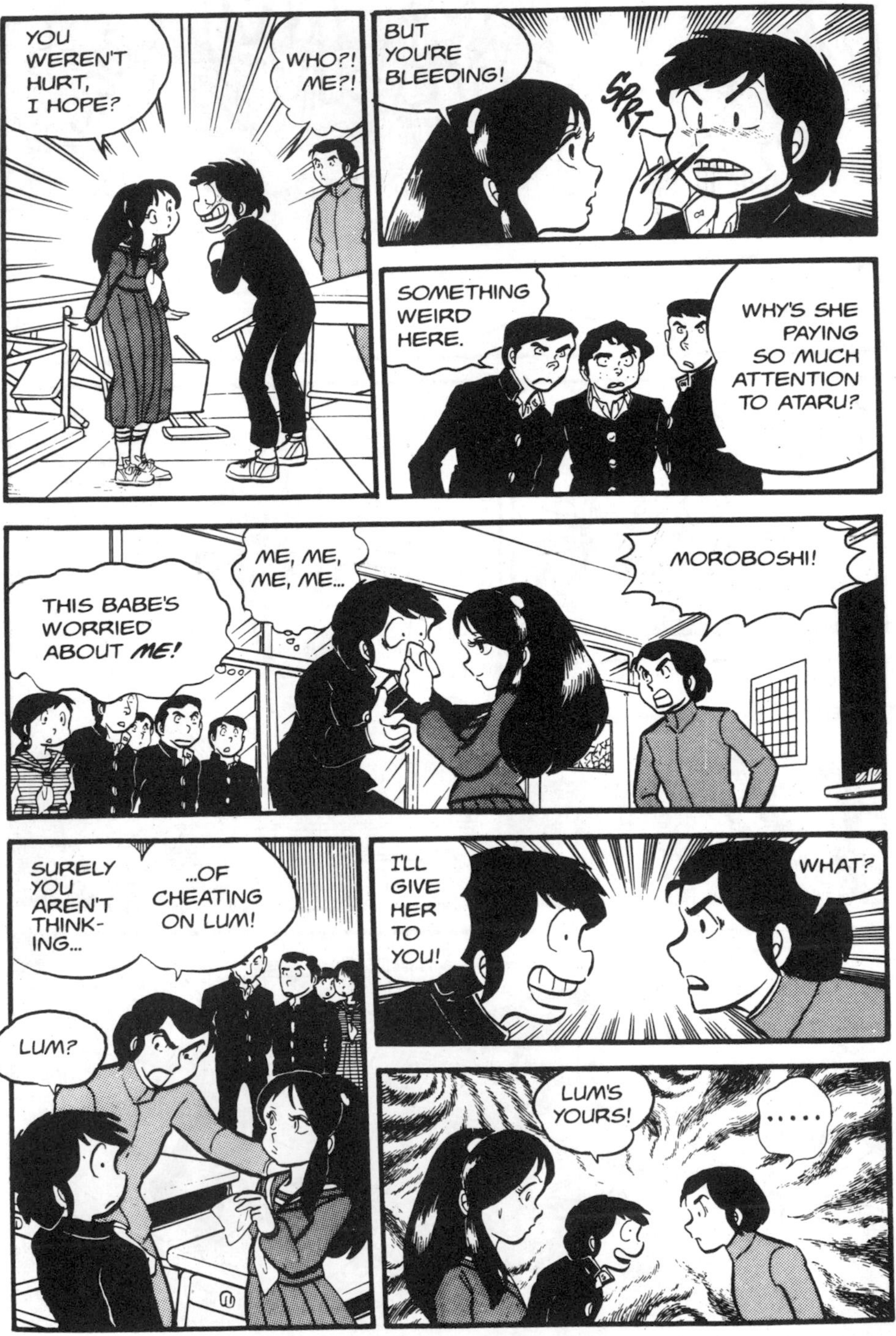
YOU WEREN'T HURT, I HOPE?
WHO?! ME?!
BUT YOU'RE BLEEDING!
SPRY
SOMETHING WEIRD HERE.
WHY'S SHE PAYING SO MUCH ATTENTION TO ATARU?
THIS BABE'S WORRIED ABOUT *ME!*
ME, ME, ME, ME...
MOROBOSHI!
SURELY YOU AREN'T THINK-ING...
...OF CHEATING ON LUM!
LUM?
I'LL GIVE HER TO YOU!
WHAT?
LUM'S YOURS!
.....

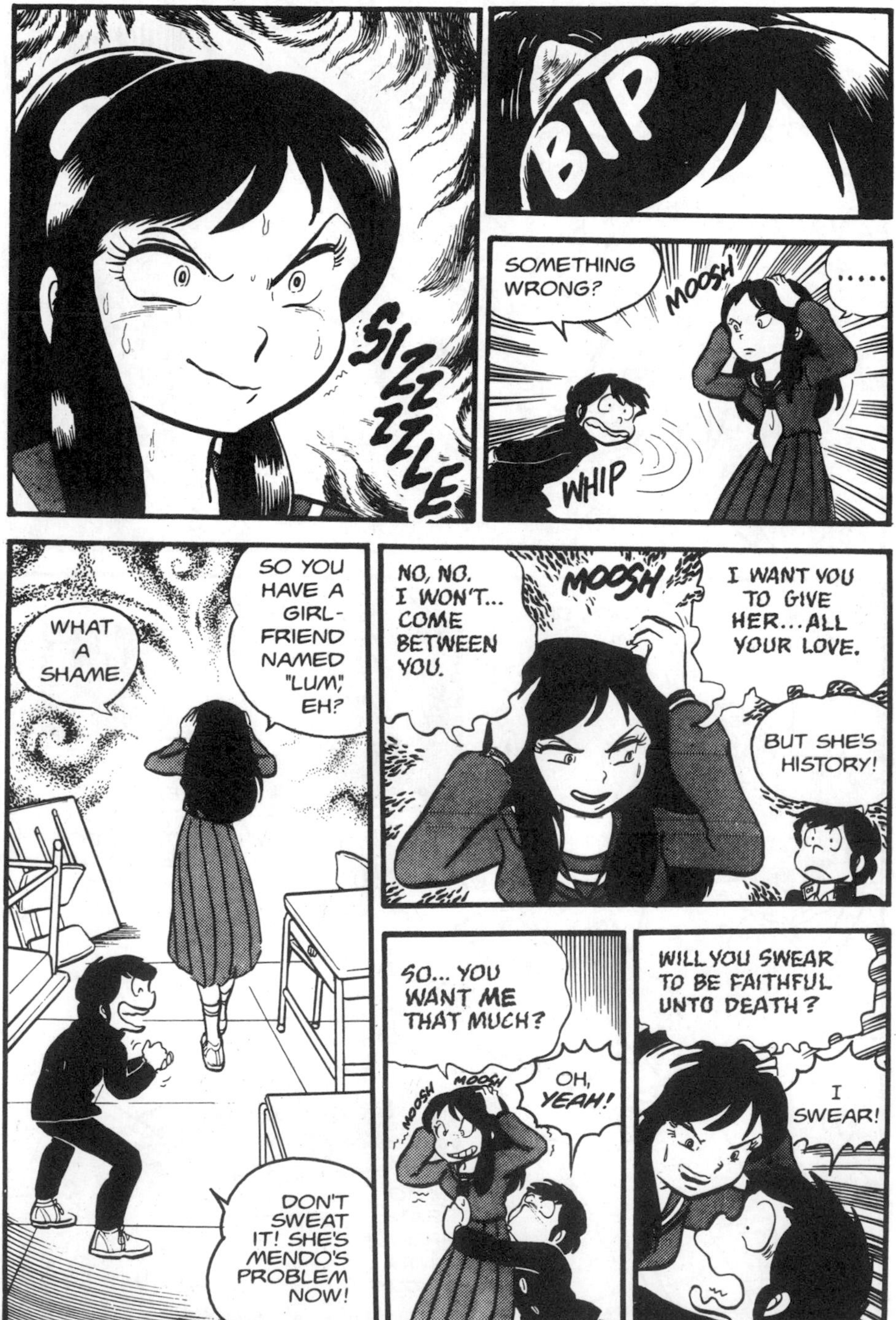
SIZZZZLE
BIP
SOMETHING WRONG?
MOOSH
.....
WHIP
WHAT A SHAME.
SO YOU HAVE A GIRL-FRIEND NAMED "LUM," EH?
DON'T SWEAT IT! SHE'S MENDO'S PROBLEM NOW!
NO, NO. I WON'T... COME BETWEEN YOU.
MOOSH
I WANT YOU TO GIVE HER... ALL YOUR LOVE.
BUT SHE'S HISTORY!
SO... YOU WANT ME THAT MUCH?
MOOSH
MOOSH
OH, YEAH!
WILL YOU SWEAR TO BE FAITHFUL UNTO DEATH?
I SWEAR!

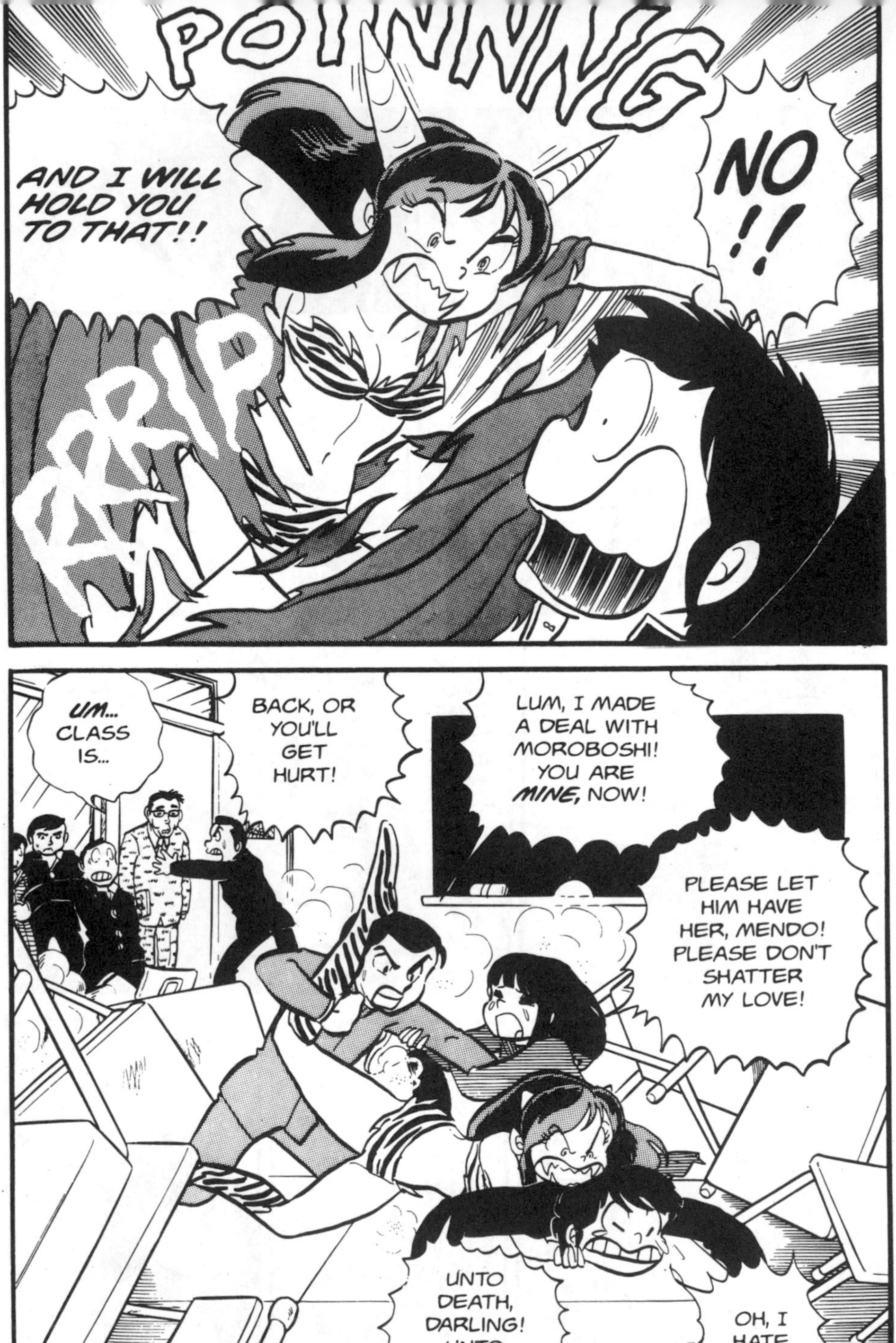
POINNNG
AND I WILL HOLD YOU TO THAT!!
NO!!
RRIP
UM... CLASS IS...
BACK, OR YOU'LL GET HURT!
LUM, I MADE A DEAL WITH MOROBOSHI! YOU ARE MINE, NOW!
PLEASE LET HIM HAVE HER, MENDO! PLEASE DON'T SHATTER MY LOVE!
UNTO DEATH, DARLING! UNTO DEATH!
OH, I HATE THIS!

Part 5
Even Though I Wait for You...

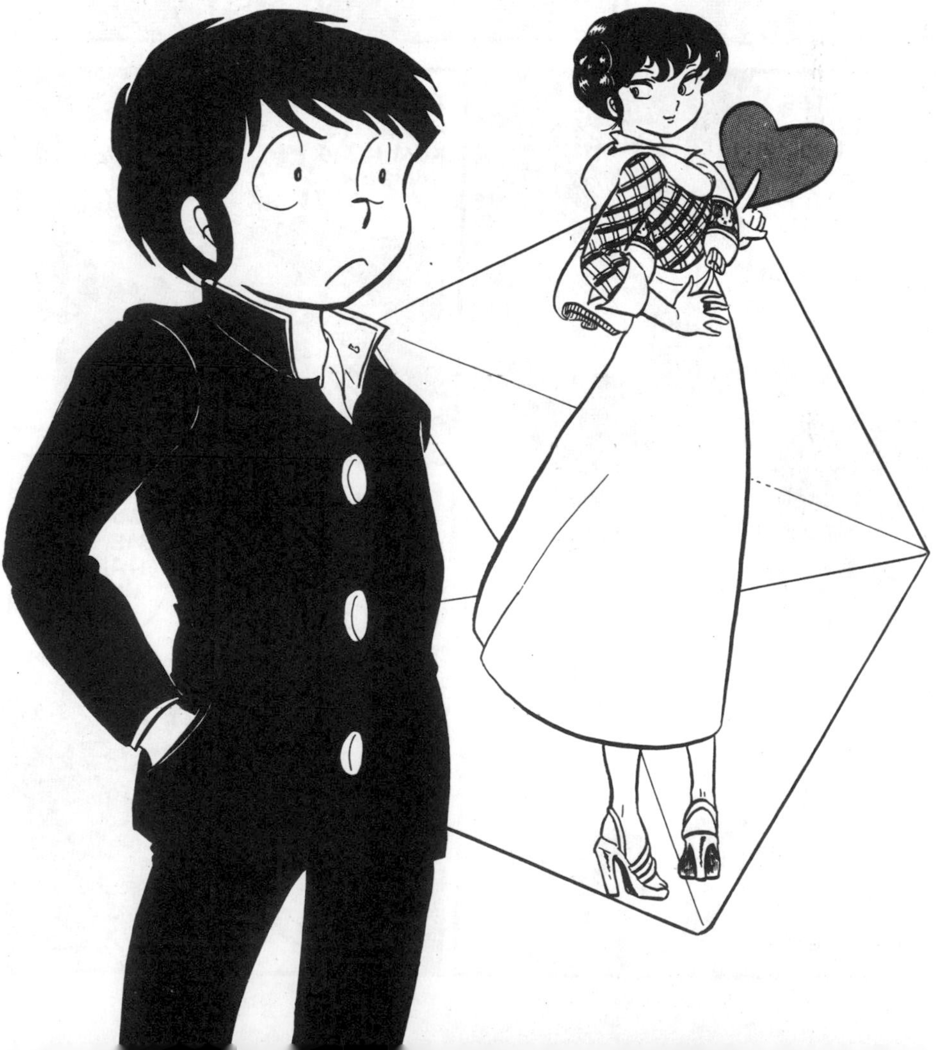

FIRST PLACE... KUMIKO!

SECOND PLACE... MOMOE!

THIRD PLACE... SHINOBU!

THE VOTES ARE IN! THE ROOM 4 BABE-DEBATE IS SETTLED!

MASAKO ||||
HIROMI ||||| |
SHINOBU ||||| |||
MOMOE ||||| ||||| |
KUMIKO ||||| ||||| ||||

DISGUSTING.

THERE'S MORE TO A WOMAN THAN LOOKS!

I ALWAYS KNEW IT! KUMIKO IS NUMBER 1!

NO *WAY* MOMOE IS NUMBER 2!

KUMIKO... THIS LETTER...

YOU'VE MADE ME SO HAPPY, MENDO!

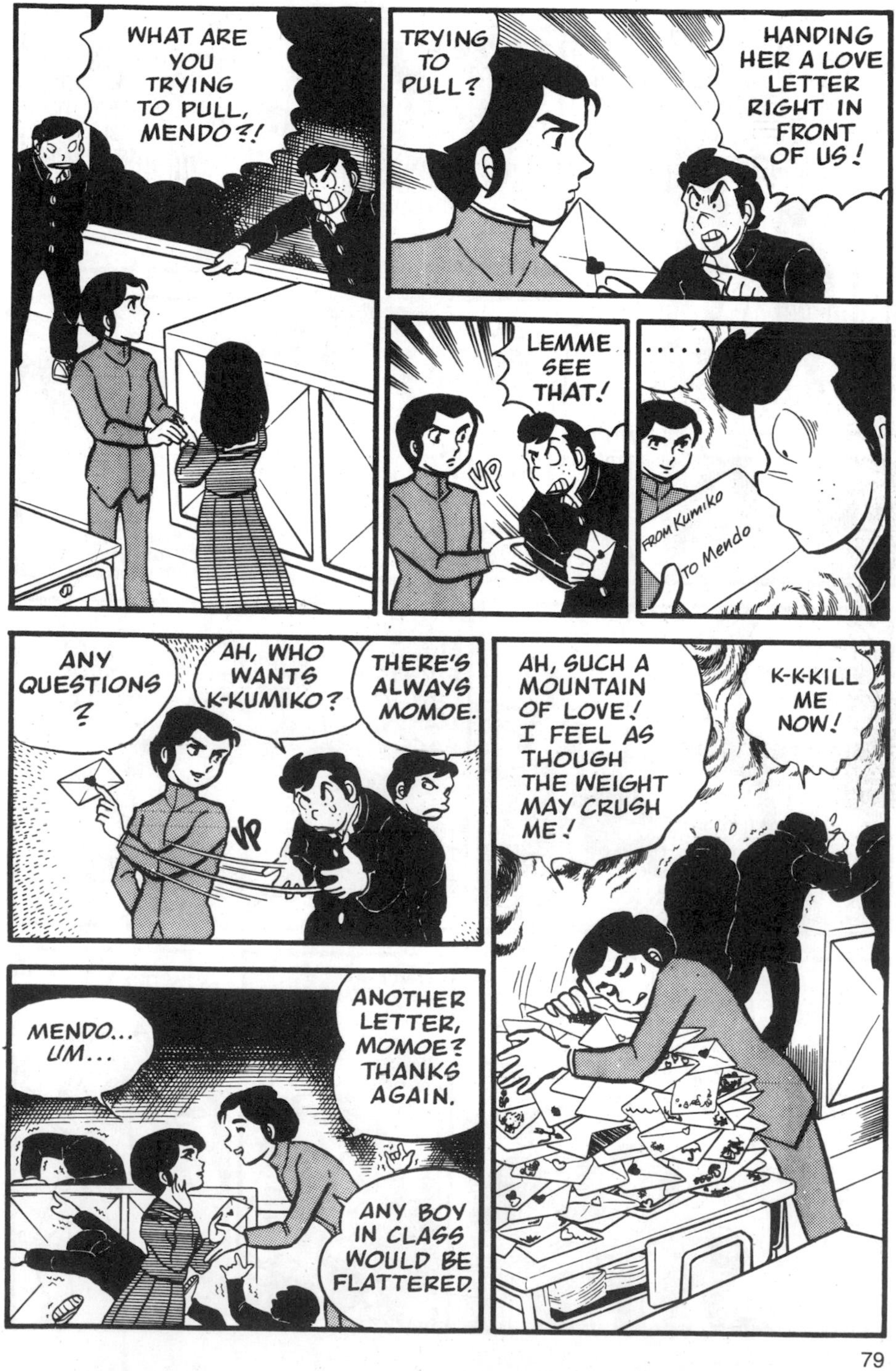
WHAT ARE YOU TRYING TO PULL, MENDO?!
TRYING TO PULL?
HANDING HER A LOVE LETTER RIGHT IN FRONT OF US!
LEMME SEE THAT!
VP
.....
FROM Kumiko
TO Mendo
ANY QUESTIONS?
VP
AH, WHO WANTS K-KUMIKO?
THERE'S ALWAYS MOMOE.
AH, SUCH A MOUNTAIN OF LOVE! I FEEL AS THOUGH THE WEIGHT MAY CRUSH ME!
K-K-KILL ME NOW!
MENDO... UM...
ANOTHER LETTER, MOMOE? THANKS AGAIN.
ANY BOY IN CLASS WOULD BE FLATTERED.

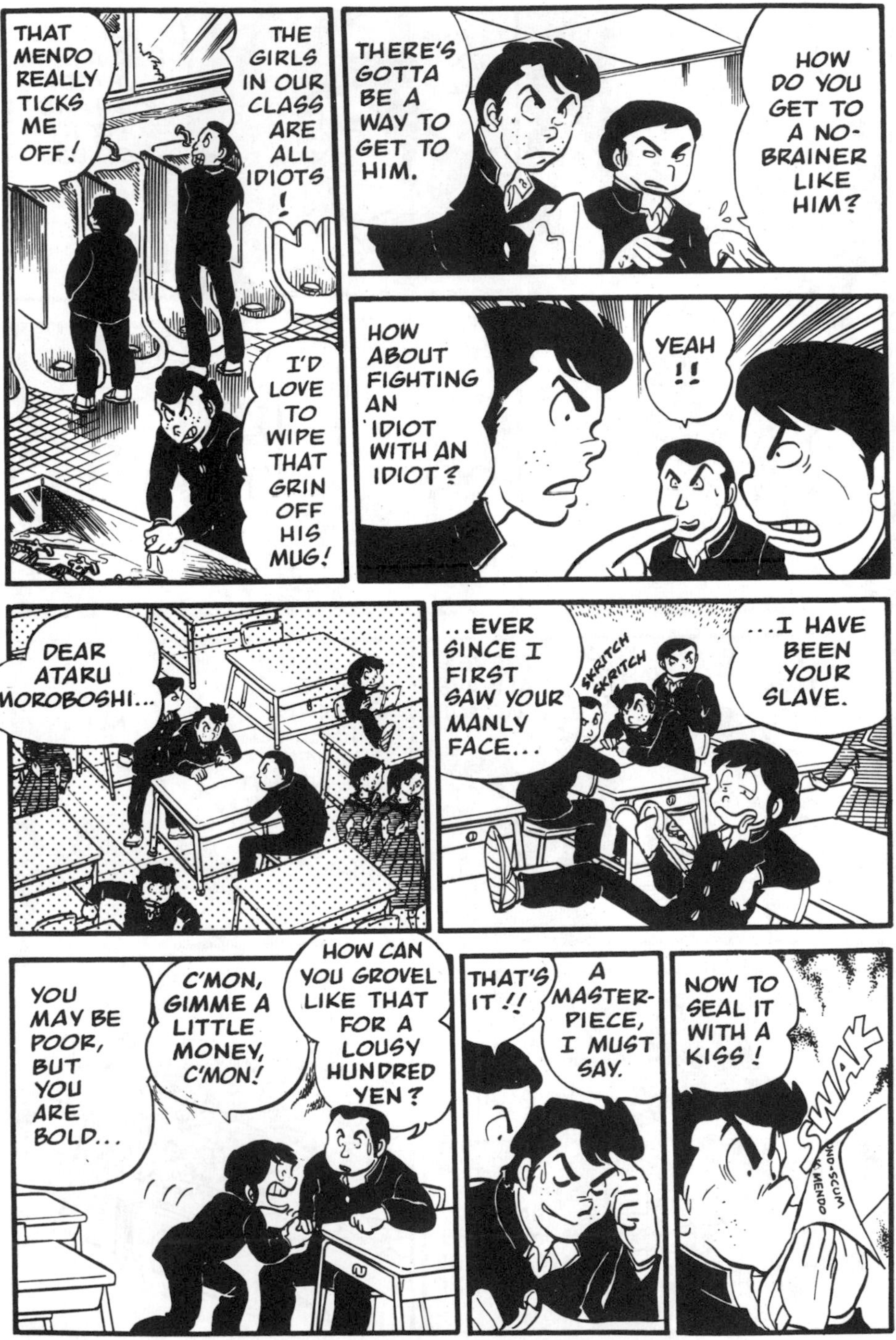
THAT MENDO REALLY TICKS ME OFF!
THE GIRLS IN OUR CLASS ARE ALL IDIOTS!
I'D LOVE TO WIPE THAT GRIN OFF HIS MUG!
THERE'S GOTTA BE A WAY TO GET TO HIM.
HOW DO YOU GET TO A NO-BRAINER LIKE HIM?
HOW ABOUT FIGHTING AN IDIOT WITH AN IDIOT?
YEAH!!
DEAR ATARU MOROBOSHI...
...EVER SINCE I FIRST SAW YOUR MANLY FACE...
SKRITCH SKRITCH
...I HAVE BEEN YOUR SLAVE.
YOU MAY BE POOR, BUT YOU ARE BOLD...
C'MON, GIMME A LITTLE MONEY, C'MON!
HOW CAN YOU GROVEL LIKE THAT FOR A LOUSY HUNDRED YEN?
THAT'S IT!!
A MASTER-PIECE, I MUST SAY.
NOW TO SEAL IT WITH A KISS!
SWAK
MENDO

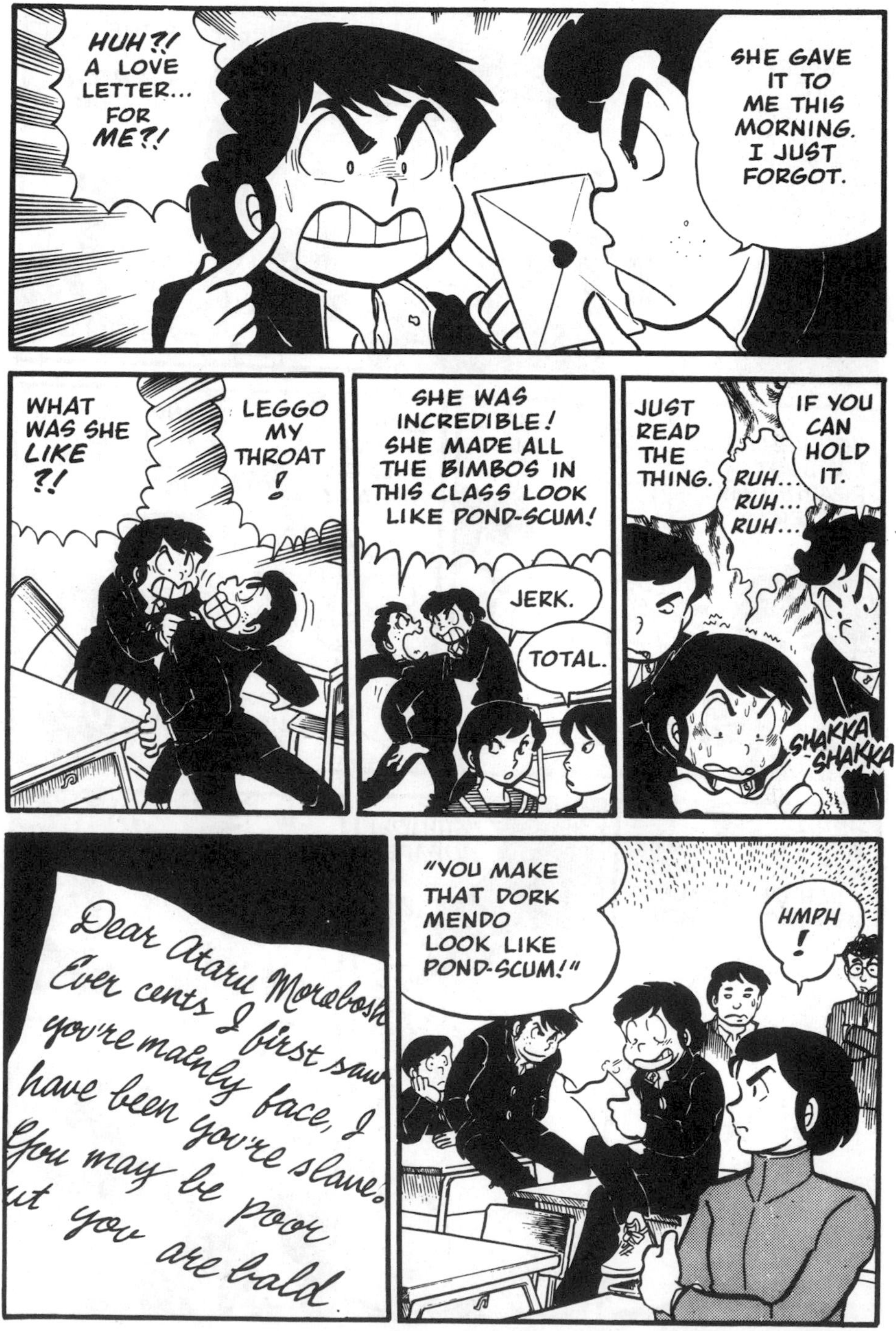
HUH?! A LOVE LETTER... FOR ME?!
SHE GAVE IT TO ME THIS MORNING. I JUST FORGOT.
WHAT WAS SHE LIKE?!
LEGGO MY THROAT!
SHE WAS INCREDIBLE! SHE MADE ALL THE BIMBOS IN THIS CLASS LOOK LIKE POND-SCUM!
JERK.
TOTAL.
JUST READ THE THING.
IF YOU CAN HOLD IT.
RUH... RUH... RUH...
SHAKKA SHAKKA
Dear Ataru Morobosh
Ever cents I first saw
you're mainly face, I
have been you're slave.
You may be poor
ut you are bald
"YOU MAKE THAT DORK MENDO LOOK LIKE POND-SCUM!"
HMPH!

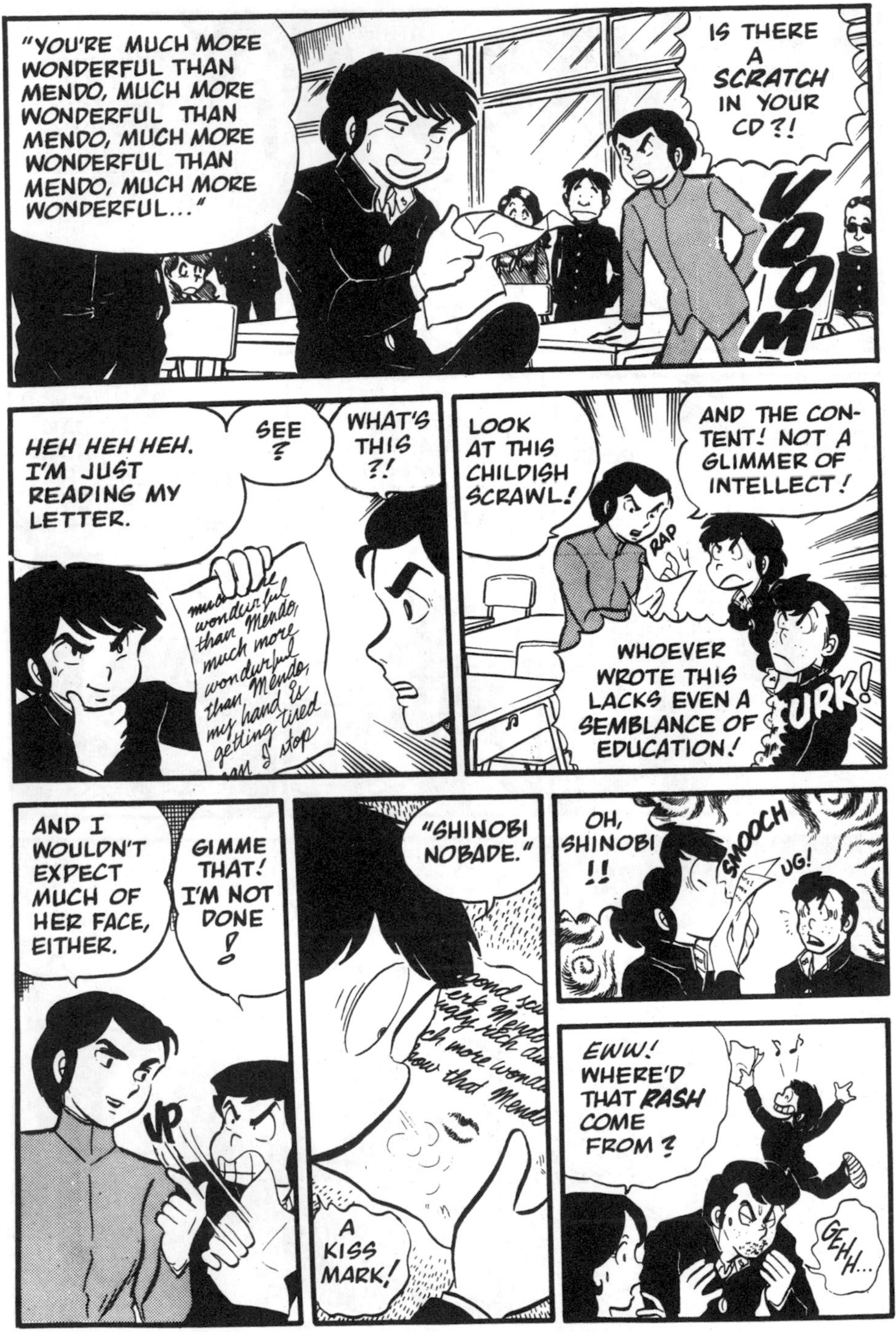
"YOU'RE MUCH MORE WONDERFUL THAN MENDO, MUCH MORE WONDERFUL THAN MENDO, MUCH MORE WONDERFUL THAN MENDO, MUCH MORE WONDERFUL..."
IS THERE A SCRATCH IN YOUR CD?!
VOOM
HEH HEH HEH. I'M JUST READING MY LETTER.
SEE?
WHAT'S THIS?!
wonderful than Mendo, much more wonderful than Mendo, my hand is getting tired
LOOK AT THIS CHILDISH SCRAWL!
AND THE CONTENT! NOT A GLIMMER OF INTELLECT!
RAP
WHOEVER WROTE THIS LACKS EVEN A SEMBLANCE OF EDUCATION!
URK!
AND I WOULDN'T EXPECT MUCH OF HER FACE, EITHER.
GIMME THAT! I'M NOT DONE!
YP
"SHINOBI NOBADE."
A KISS MARK!
OH, SHINOBI!!
SMOOCH
UG!
EWW! WHERE'D THAT RASH COME FROM?
GEHH...

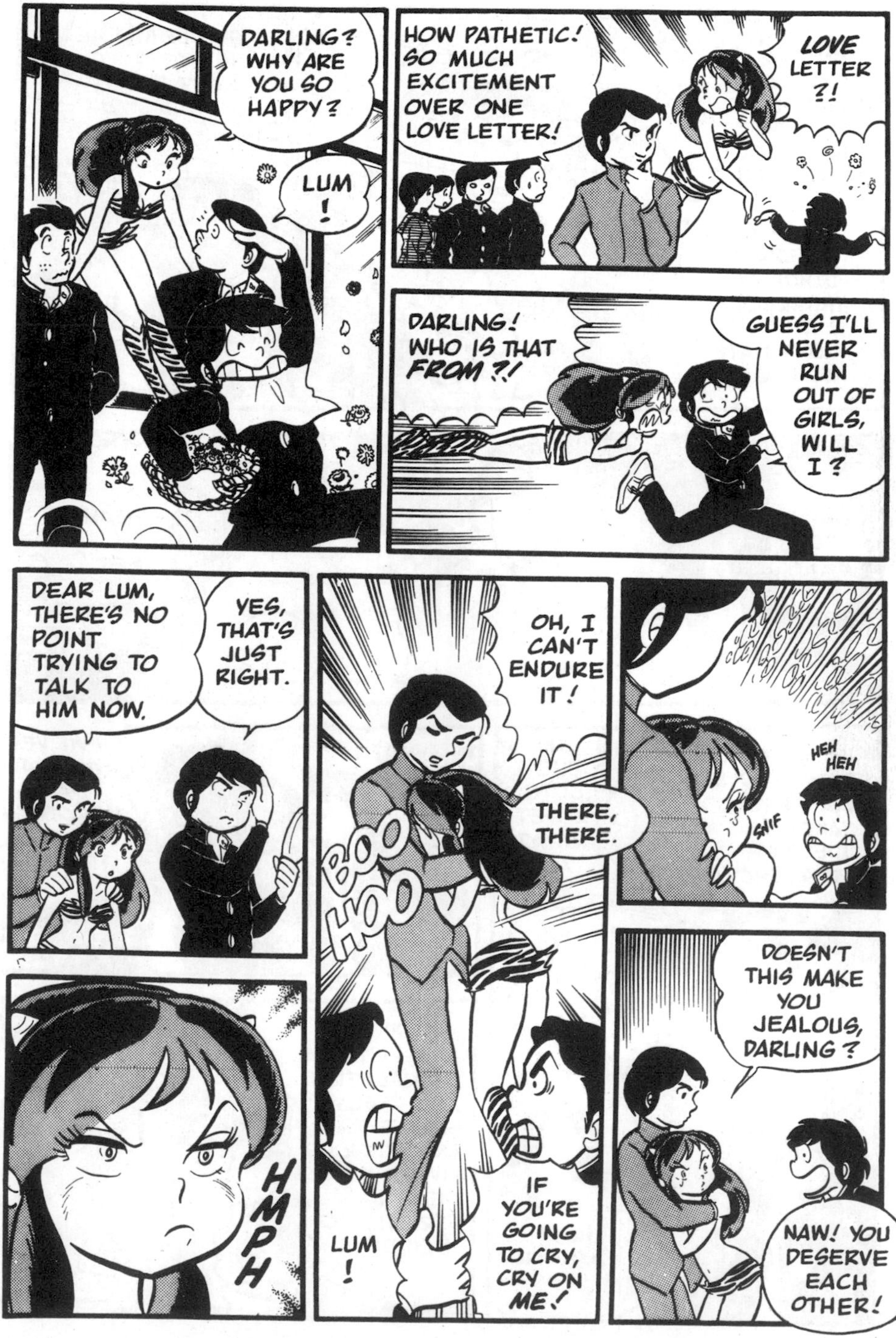
DARLING? WHY ARE YOU SO HAPPY?
LUM!
HOW PATHETIC! SO MUCH EXCITEMENT OVER ONE LOVE LETTER!
LOVE LETTER?!
DARLING! WHO IS THAT FROM?!
GUESS I'LL NEVER RUN OUT OF GIRLS, WILL I?
DEAR LUM, THERE'S NO POINT TRYING TO TALK TO HIM NOW.
YES, THAT'S JUST RIGHT.
HMPH
OH, I CAN'T ENDURE IT!
THERE, THERE.
BOO HOO
LUM!
IF YOU'RE GOING TO CRY, CRY ON ME!
HEH HEH
SNIF
DOESN'T THIS MAKE YOU JEALOUS, DARLING?
NAW! YOU DESERVE EACH OTHER!

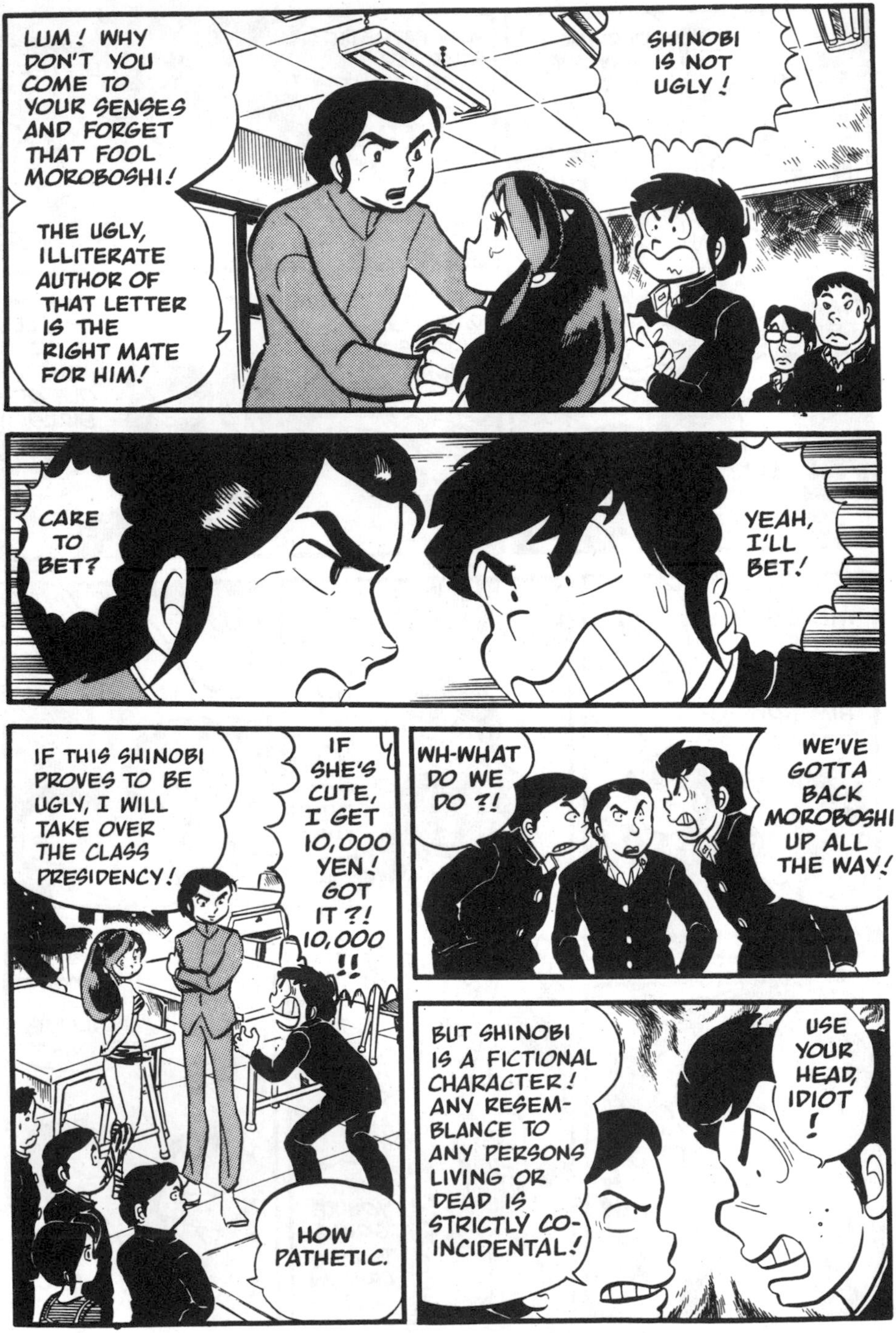
LUM! WHY DON'T YOU COME TO YOUR SENSES AND FORGET THAT FOOL MOROBOSHI!
THE UGLY, ILLITERATE AUTHOR OF THAT LETTER IS THE RIGHT MATE FOR HIM!
SHINOBI IS NOT UGLY!
CARE TO BET?
YEAH, I'LL BET!
IF THIS SHINOBI PROVES TO BE UGLY, I WILL TAKE OVER THE CLASS PRESIDENCY!
IF SHE'S CUTE, I GET 10,000 YEN! GOT IT?! 10,000!!
HOW PATHETIC.
WH-WHAT DO WE DO?!
WE'VE GOTTA BACK MOROBOSHI UP ALL THE WAY!
BUT SHINOBI IS A FICTIONAL CHARACTER! ANY RESEMBLANCE TO ANY PERSONS LIVING OR DEAD IS STRICTLY COINCIDENTAL!
USE YOUR HEAD, IDIOT!

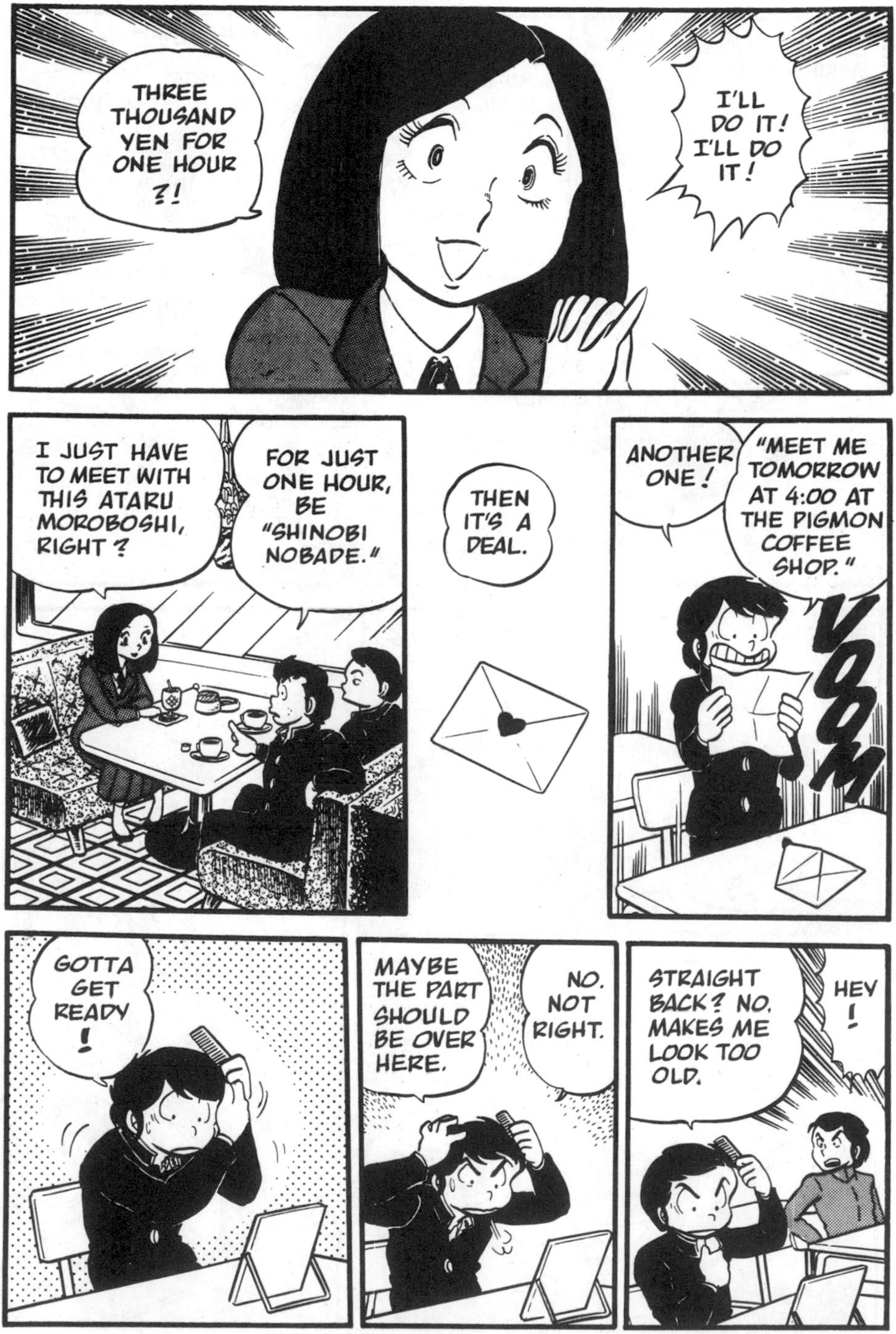

THREE THOUSAND YEN FOR ONE HOUR ?!
I'LL DO IT! I'LL DO IT!
I JUST HAVE TO MEET WITH THIS ATARU MOROBOSHI, RIGHT?
FOR JUST ONE HOUR, BE "SHINOBI NOBADE."
THEN IT'S A DEAL.
ANOTHER ONE!
"MEET ME TOMORROW AT 4:00 AT THE PIGMON COFFEE SHOP."
VOOM
GOTTA GET READY!
MAYBE THE PART SHOULD BE OVER HERE.
NO. NOT RIGHT.
STRAIGHT BACK? NO. MAKES ME LOOK TOO OLD.
HEY!

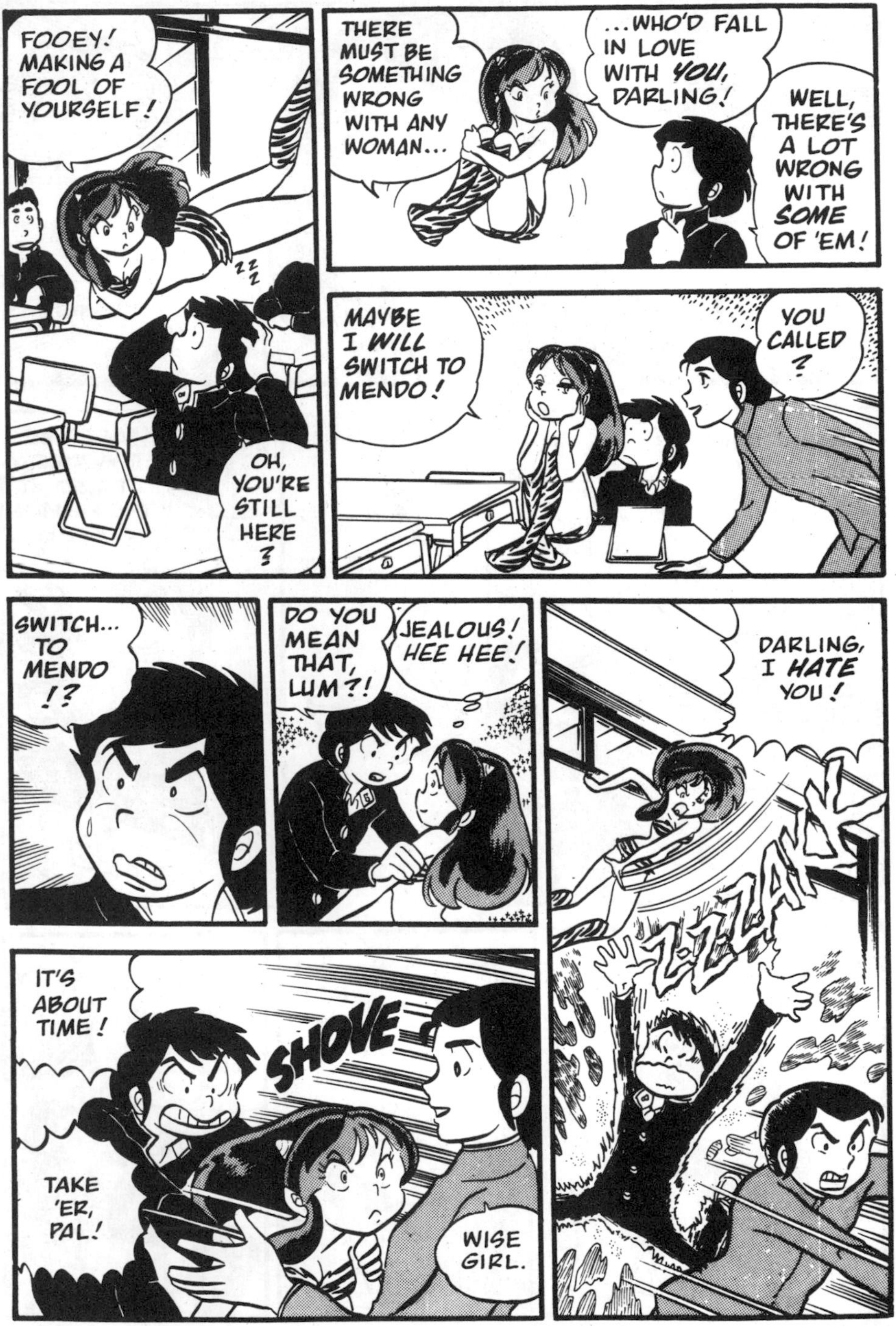
FOOEY! MAKING A FOOL OF YOURSELF!
Z Z Z
OH, YOU'RE STILL HERE?
THERE MUST BE SOMETHING WRONG WITH ANY WOMAN...
...WHO'D FALL IN LOVE WITH YOU, DARLING!
WELL, THERE'S A LOT WRONG WITH SOME OF 'EM!
MAYBE I WILL SWITCH TO MENDO!
YOU CALLED?
SWITCH... TO MENDO!?
DO YOU MEAN THAT, LUM?!
JEALOUS! HEE HEE!
IT'S ABOUT TIME!
SHOVE
TAKE 'ER, PAL!
WISE GIRL.
DARLING, I HATE YOU!
Z-ZZZAAK

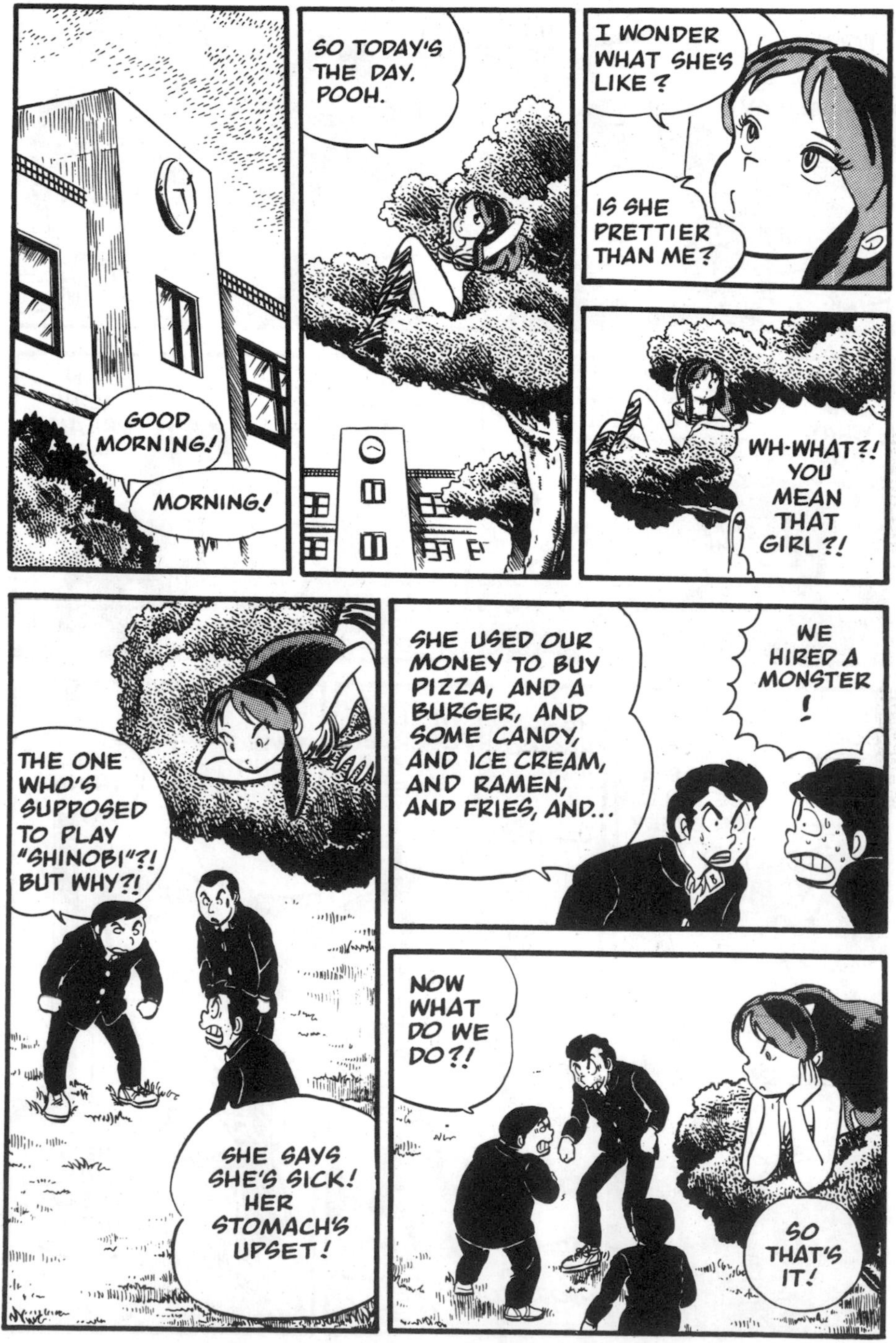

GOOD MORNING!
MORNING!
SO TODAY'S THE DAY. POOH.
I WONDER WHAT SHE'S LIKE?
IS SHE PRETTIER THAN ME?
WH-WHAT?! YOU MEAN THAT GIRL?!
THE ONE WHO'S SUPPOSED TO PLAY "SHINOBI"?! BUT WHY?!
SHE SAYS SHE'S SICK! HER STOMACH'S UPSET!
SHE USED OUR MONEY TO BUY PIZZA, AND A BURGER, AND SOME CANDY, AND ICE CREAM, AND RAMEN, AND FRIES, AND...
WE HIRED A MONSTER!
NOW WHAT DO WE DO?!
SO THAT'S IT!

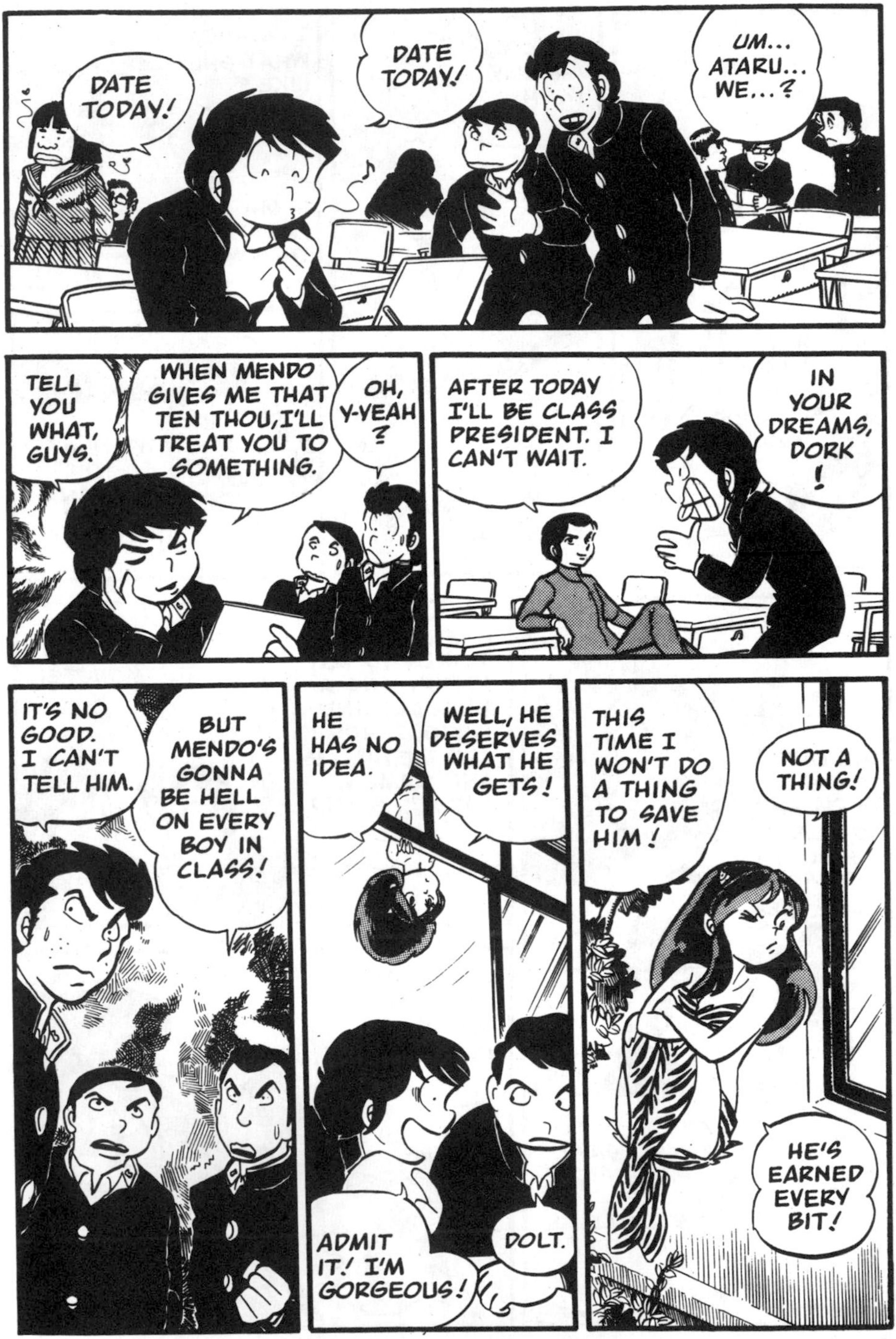
DATE TODAY!
DATE TODAY!
UM... ATARU... WE...?
TELL YOU WHAT, GUYS.
WHEN MENDO GIVES ME THAT TEN THOU, I'LL TREAT YOU TO SOMETHING.
OH, Y-YEAH?
AFTER TODAY I'LL BE CLASS PRESIDENT. I CAN'T WAIT.
IN YOUR DREAMS, DORK!
IT'S NO GOOD. I CAN'T TELL HIM.
BUT MENDO'S GONNA BE HELL ON EVERY BOY IN CLASS!
HE HAS NO IDEA.
WELL, HE DESERVES WHAT HE GETS!
ADMIT IT! I'M GORGEOUS!
DOLT.
THIS TIME I WON'T DO A THING TO SAVE HIM!
NOT A THING!
HE'S EARNED EVERY BIT!

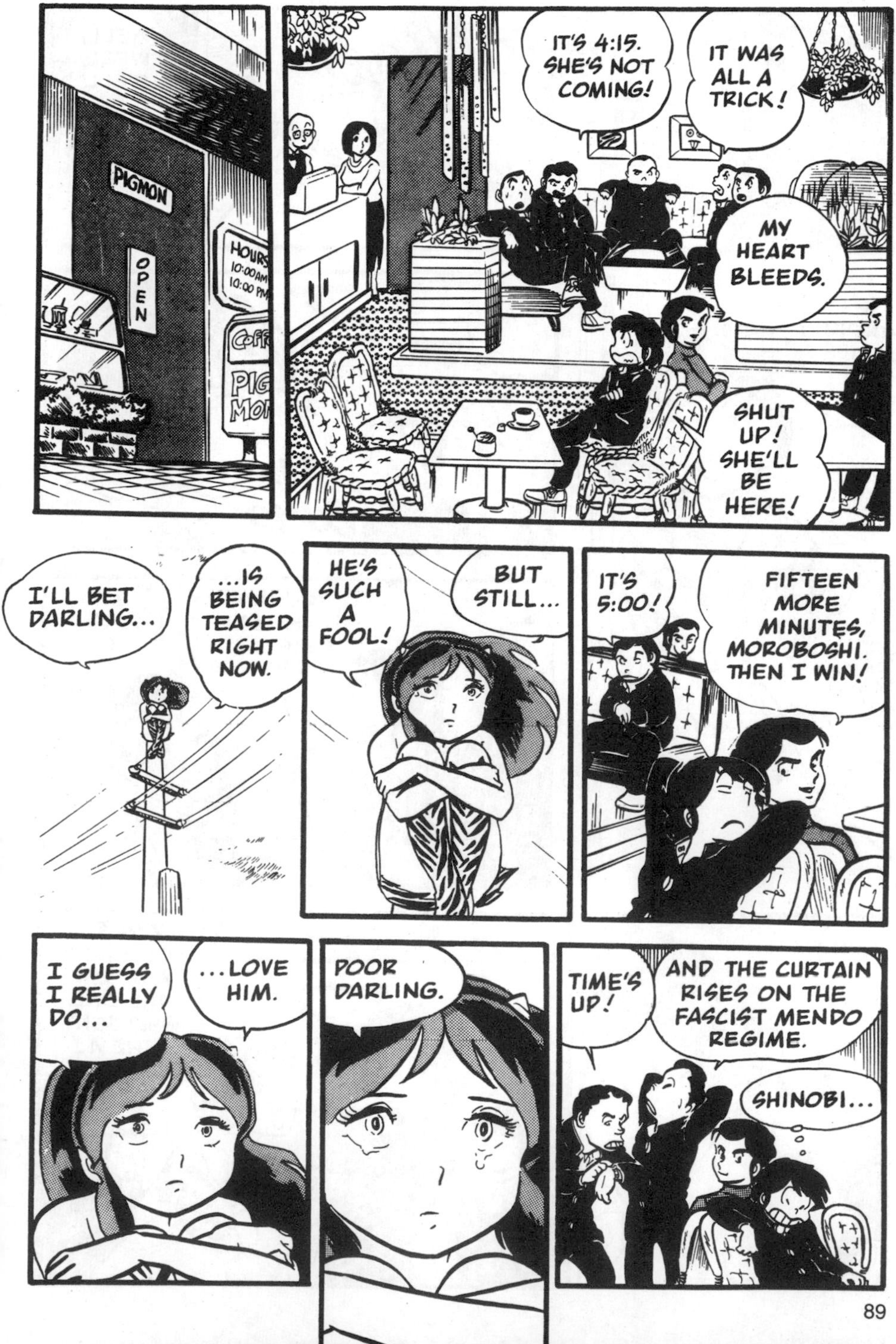
PIGMON
OPEN
HOURS 10:00AM 10:00PM
IT'S 4:15. SHE'S NOT COMING!
IT WAS ALL A TRICK!
MY HEART BLEEDS.
SHUT UP! SHE'LL BE HERE!
I'LL BET DARLING...
...IS BEING TEASED RIGHT NOW.
HE'S SUCH A FOOL!
BUT STILL...
IT'S 5:00!
FIFTEEN MORE MINUTES, MOROBOSHI. THEN I WIN!
I GUESS I REALLY DO...
...LOVE HIM.
POOR DARLING.
TIME'S UP!
AND THE CURTAIN RISES ON THE FASCIST MENDO REGIME.
SHINOBI...

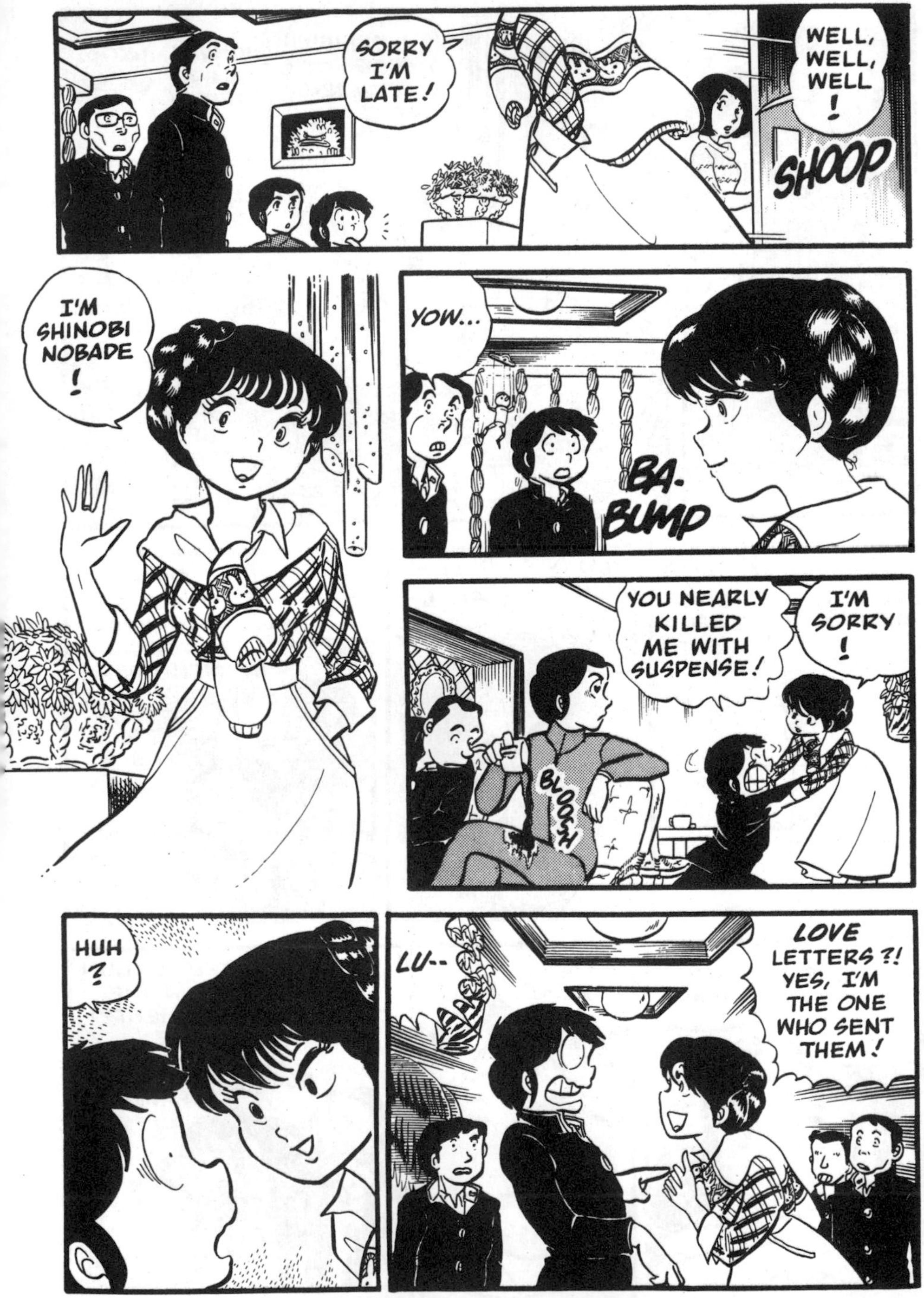
SORRY I'M LATE!
WELL, WELL, WELL!
SHOOP
I'M SHINOBI NOBADE!
YOW...
BA-BUMP
YOU NEARLY KILLED ME WITH SUSPENSE!
I'M SORRY!
BLOOSH
HUH?
LU--
LOVE LETTERS?! YES, I'M THE ONE WHO SENT THEM!

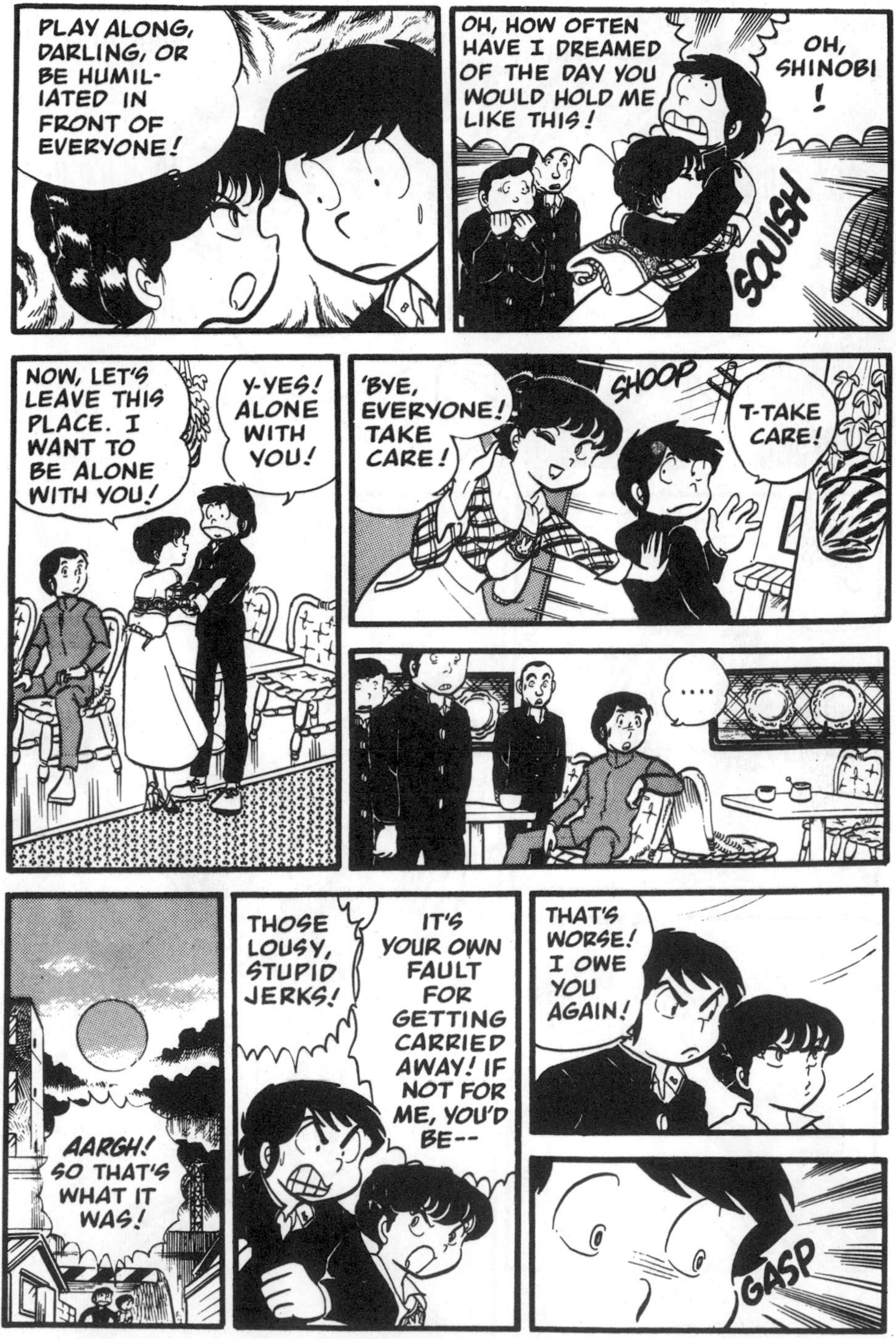
PLAY ALONG, DARLING, OR BE HUMIL- IATED IN FRONT OF EVERYONE!
OH, HOW OFTEN HAVE I DREAMED OF THE DAY YOU WOULD HOLD ME LIKE THIS!
OH, SHINOBI!
SQUISH
NOW, LET'S LEAVE THIS PLACE. I WANT TO BE ALONE WITH YOU!
Y-YES! ALONE WITH YOU!
'BYE, EVERYONE! TAKE CARE!
SHOOP
T-TAKE CARE!
.....
AARGH! SO THAT'S WHAT IT WAS!
THOSE LOUSY, STUPID JERKS!
IT'S YOUR OWN FAULT FOR GETTING CARRIED AWAY! IF NOT FOR ME, YOU'D BE--
THAT'S WORSE! I OWE YOU AGAIN!
GASP

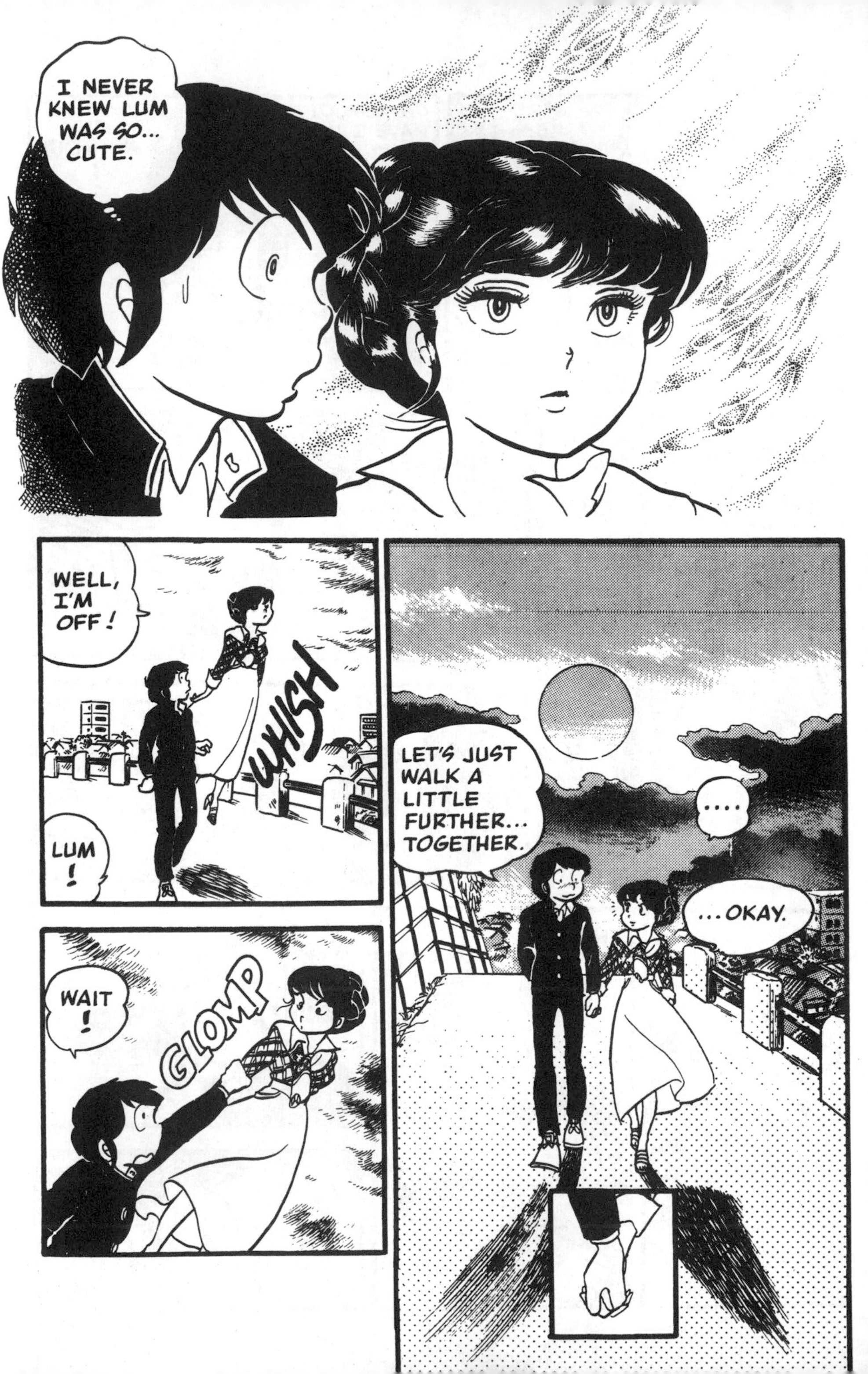
I NEVER KNEW LUM WAS SO... CUTE.
WELL, I'M OFF!
WHISH
LUM!
WAIT!
GLOMP
LET'S JUST WALK A LITTLE FURTHER... TOGETHER.
....
...OKAY.

Part 6
Diary of Tears

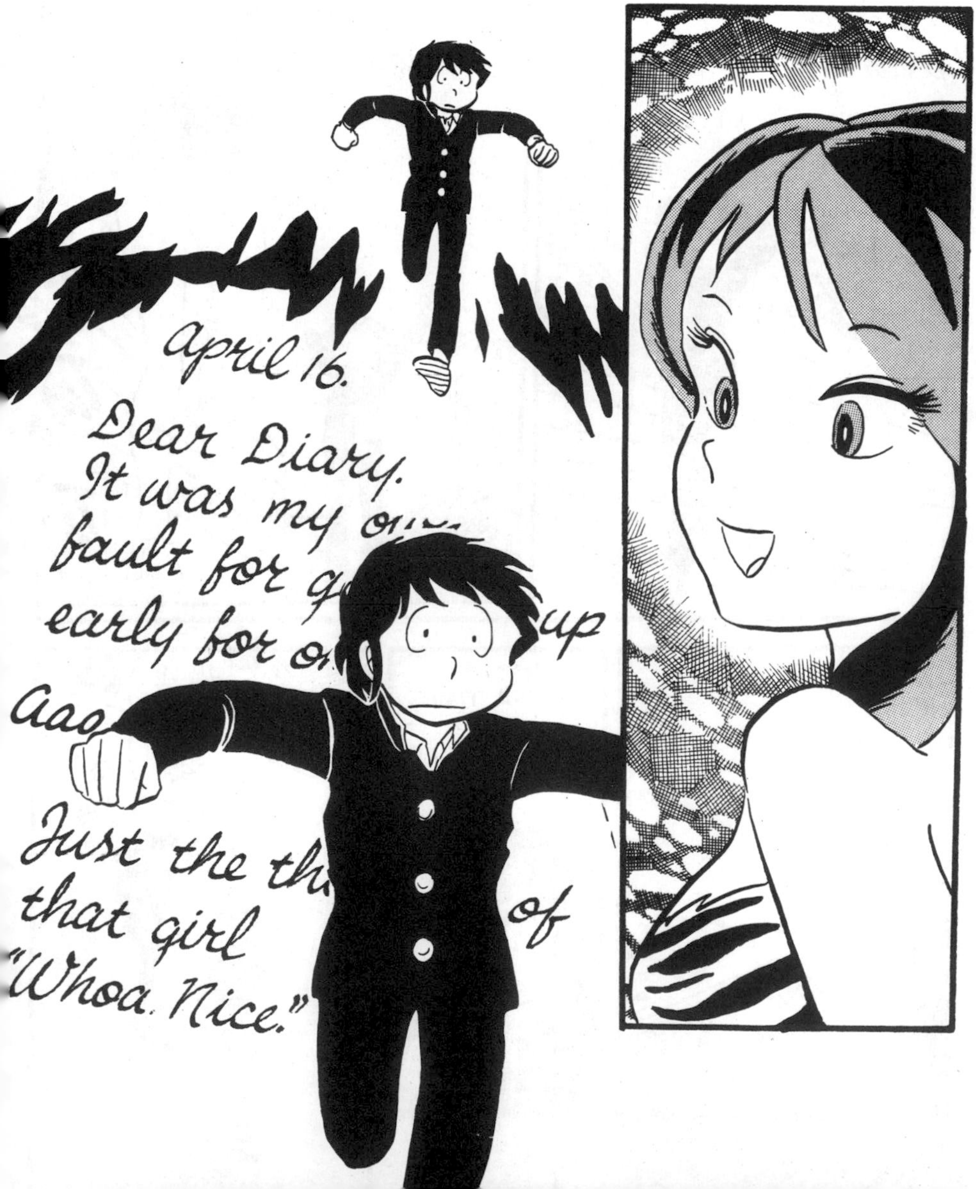
april 16.
Dear Diary.
It was my
fault for
early for
up
Just the
that girl
of
"Whoa. Nice."

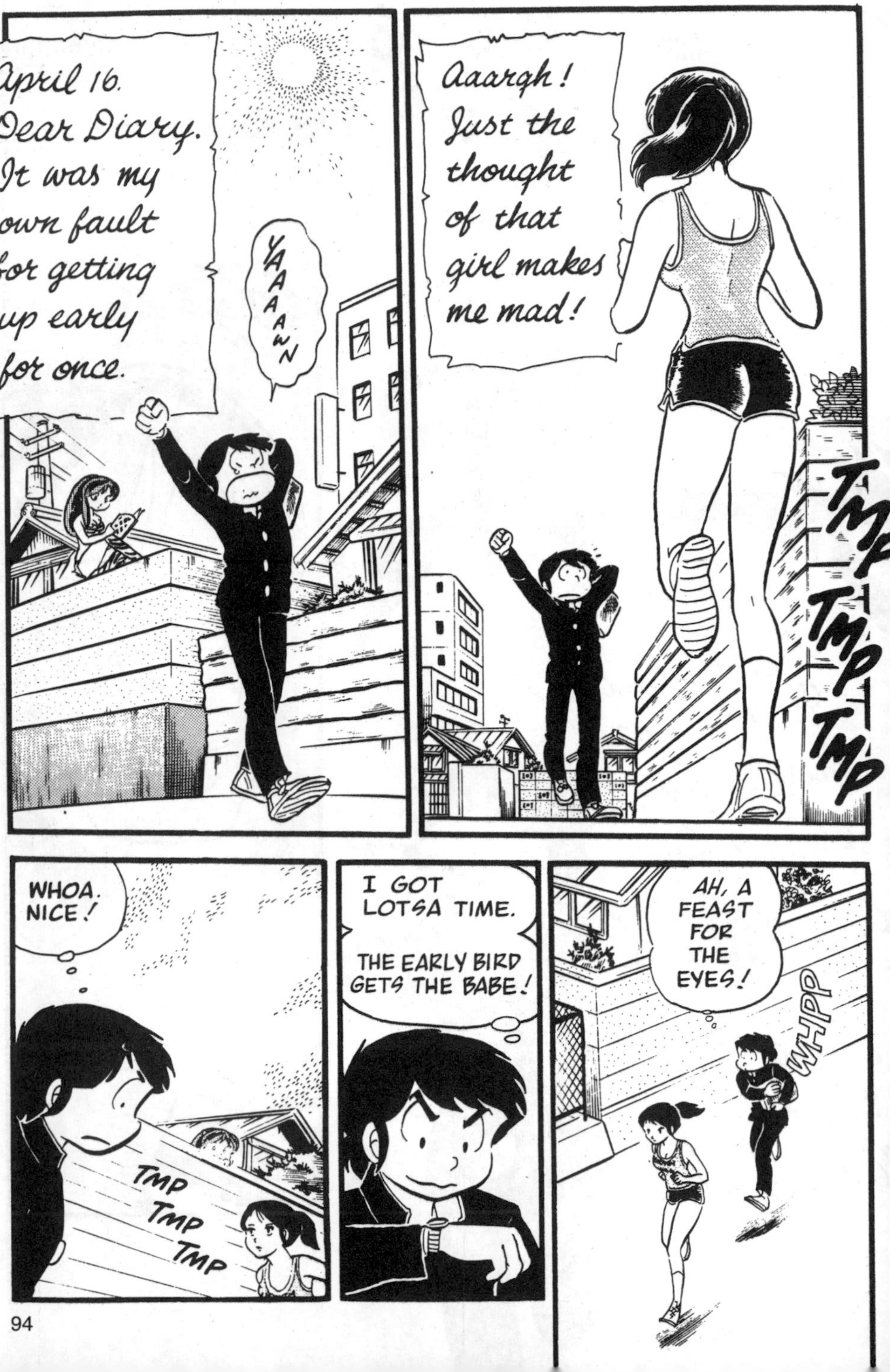
April 16. Dear Diary. It was my own fault for getting up early for once.
YAAAAAWN
Aaargh! Just the thought of that girl makes me mad!
TMP TMP TMP TMP
WHOA. NICE!
TMP TMP TMP
I GOT LOTSA TIME.
THE EARLY BIRD GETS THE BABE!
AH, A FEAST FOR THE EYES!
WHPP

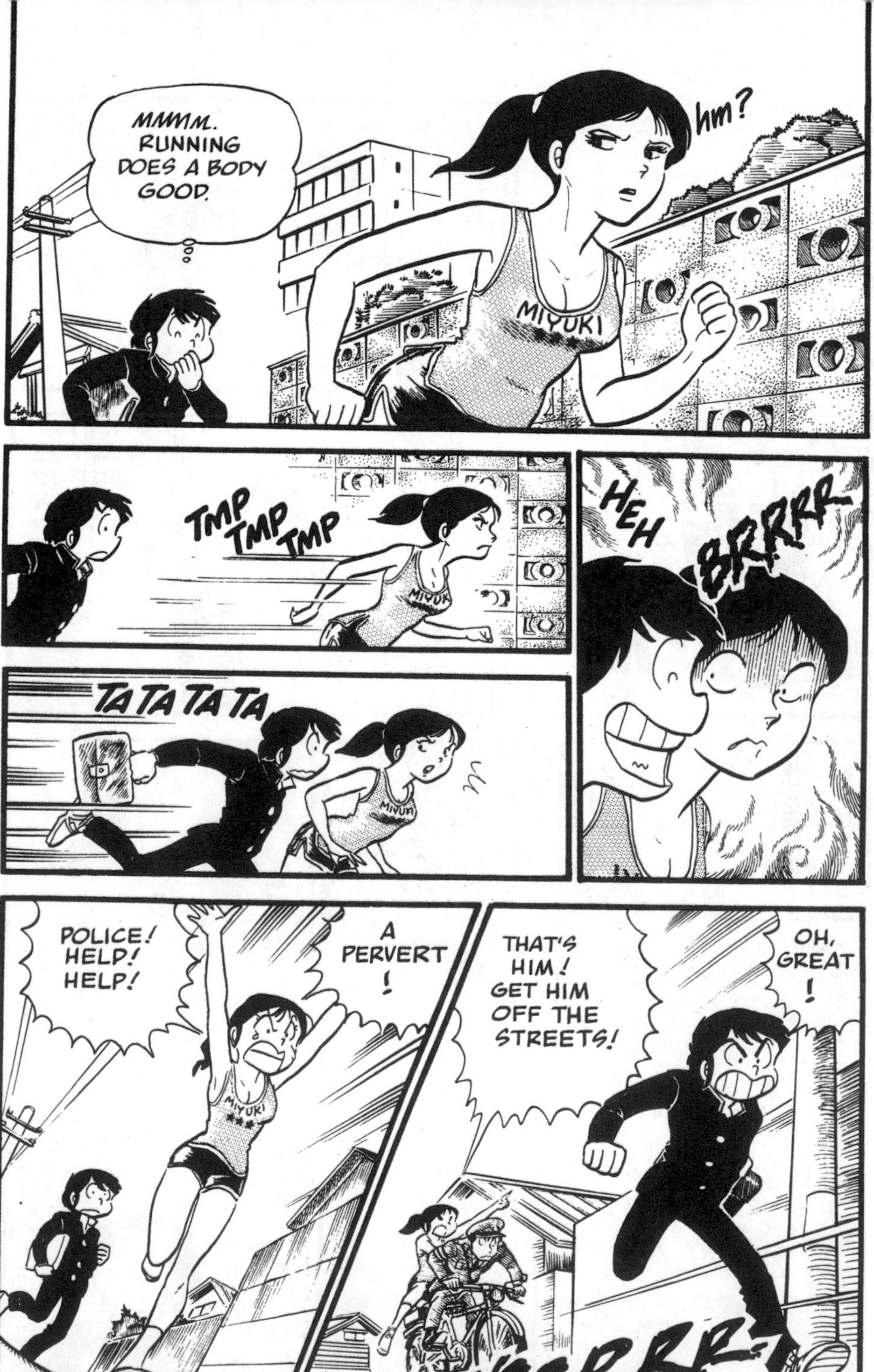

MMMM. RUNNING DOES A BODY GOOD.
hm?
MIYUKI
TMP TMP TMP
MIYUKI
HEH
BRRRR
TA TA TA TA
MIYUKI
POLICE! HELP! HELP!
A PERVERT!
MIYUKI
THAT'S HIM! GET HIM OFF THE STREETS!
OH, GREAT!
VRRRRR

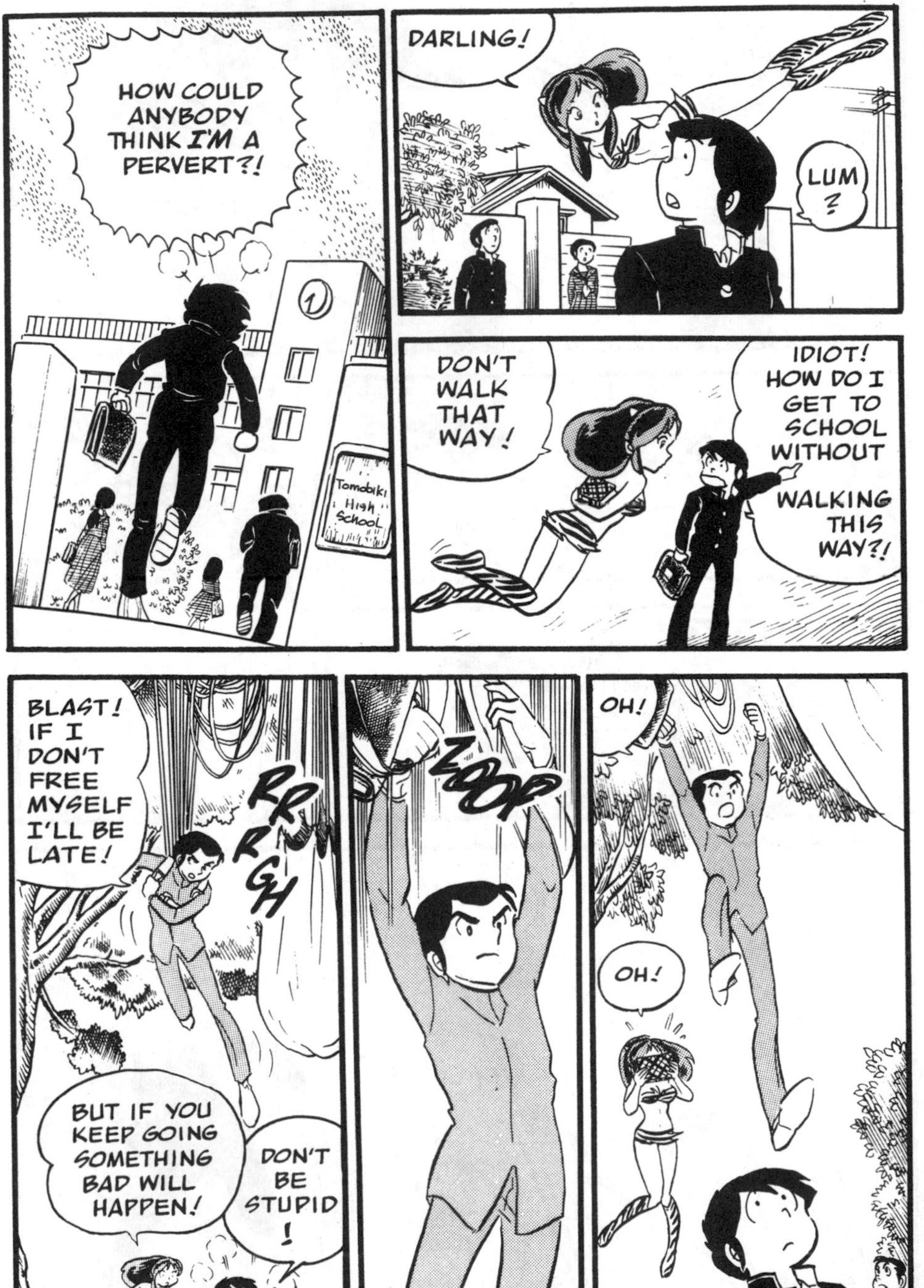
HOW COULD ANYBODY THINK I'M A PERVERT?!
Tomobiki High School
DARLING!
LUM?
DON'T WALK THAT WAY!
IDIOT! HOW DO I GET TO SCHOOL WITHOUT WALKING THIS WAY?!
BLAST! IF I DON'T FREE MYSELF I'LL BE LATE!
RRRGH
BUT IF YOU KEEP GOING SOMETHING BAD WILL HAPPEN!
DON'T BE STUPID!
ZOOP
OH!
OH!

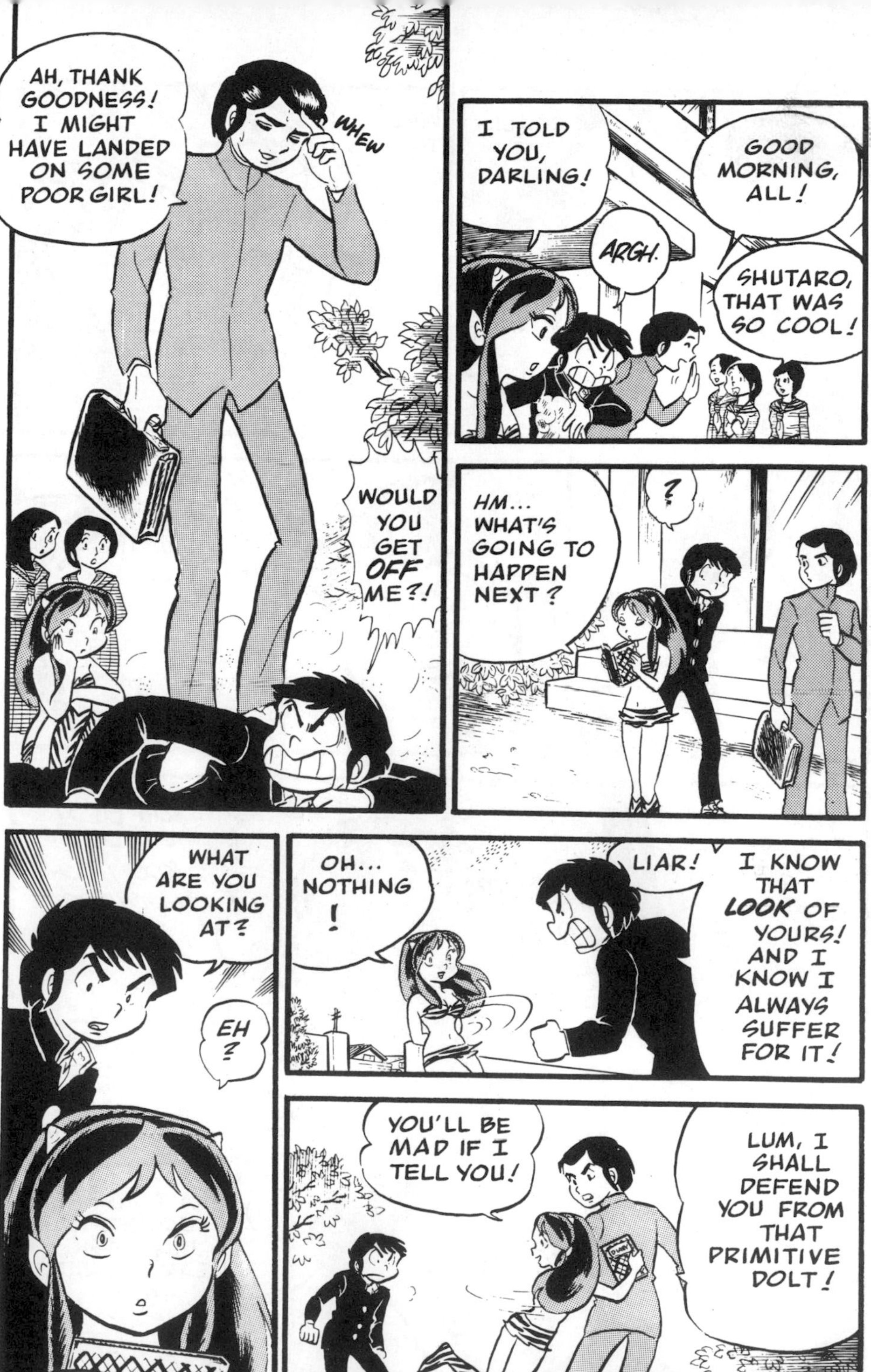
AH, THANK GOODNESS! I MIGHT HAVE LANDED ON SOME POOR GIRL!
WHEW
WOULD YOU GET OFF ME?!
I TOLD YOU, DARLING!
ARGH!
GOOD MORNING, ALL!
SHUTARO, THAT WAS SO COOL!
HM... WHAT'S GOING TO HAPPEN NEXT?
?
WHAT ARE YOU LOOKING AT?
EH?
OH... NOTHING!
LIAR!
I KNOW THAT LOOK OF YOURS! AND I KNOW I ALWAYS SUFFER FOR IT!
YOU'LL BE MAD IF I TELL YOU!
LUM, I SHALL DEFEND YOU FROM THAT PRIMITIVE DOLT!

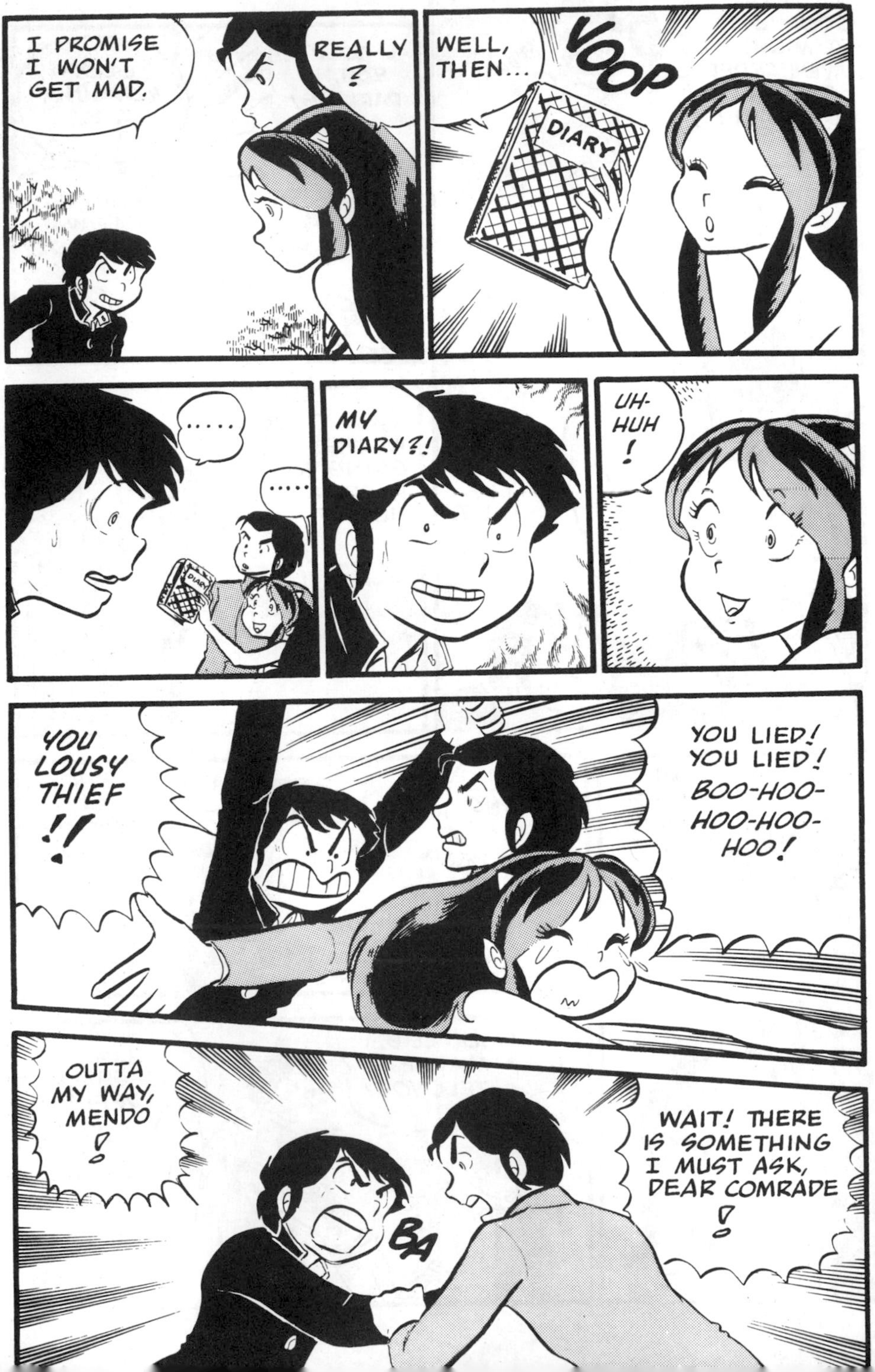
I PROMISE I WON'T GET MAD.
REALLY ?
WELL, THEN...
VOOP
DIARY
......
......
DIARY
MY DIARY?!
UH-HUH !
YOU LOUSY THIEF !!
YOU LIED! YOU LIED! BOO-HOO-HOO-HOO-HOO!
OUTTA MY WAY, MENDO !
BA
WAIT! THERE IS SOMETHING I MUST ASK, DEAR COMRADE !

WHAT GOT INTO YOU ALL OF A SUDDEN?

MOROBOSHI, ARE YOU TRULY...

...KEEPING A DIARY?

YEAH! SO WHAT?!

A BOY KEEPING A DIARY?!

THAT IS KIND OF... STRANGE, ISN'T IT?

KIND OF... ABNORMAL!

MOROBOSHI KEEPS A DIARY! A-HA-HA-HA-HA!

BAH! JUST BECAUSE I'M HONEST WITH MY FEELINGS!

DARLING'S GOING TO TRIP...

WHOMP

FATE JUST CAN'T BE BEATEN!

HEE HEE HEE HEE

A-HA HA HA HA

HOLD IT.

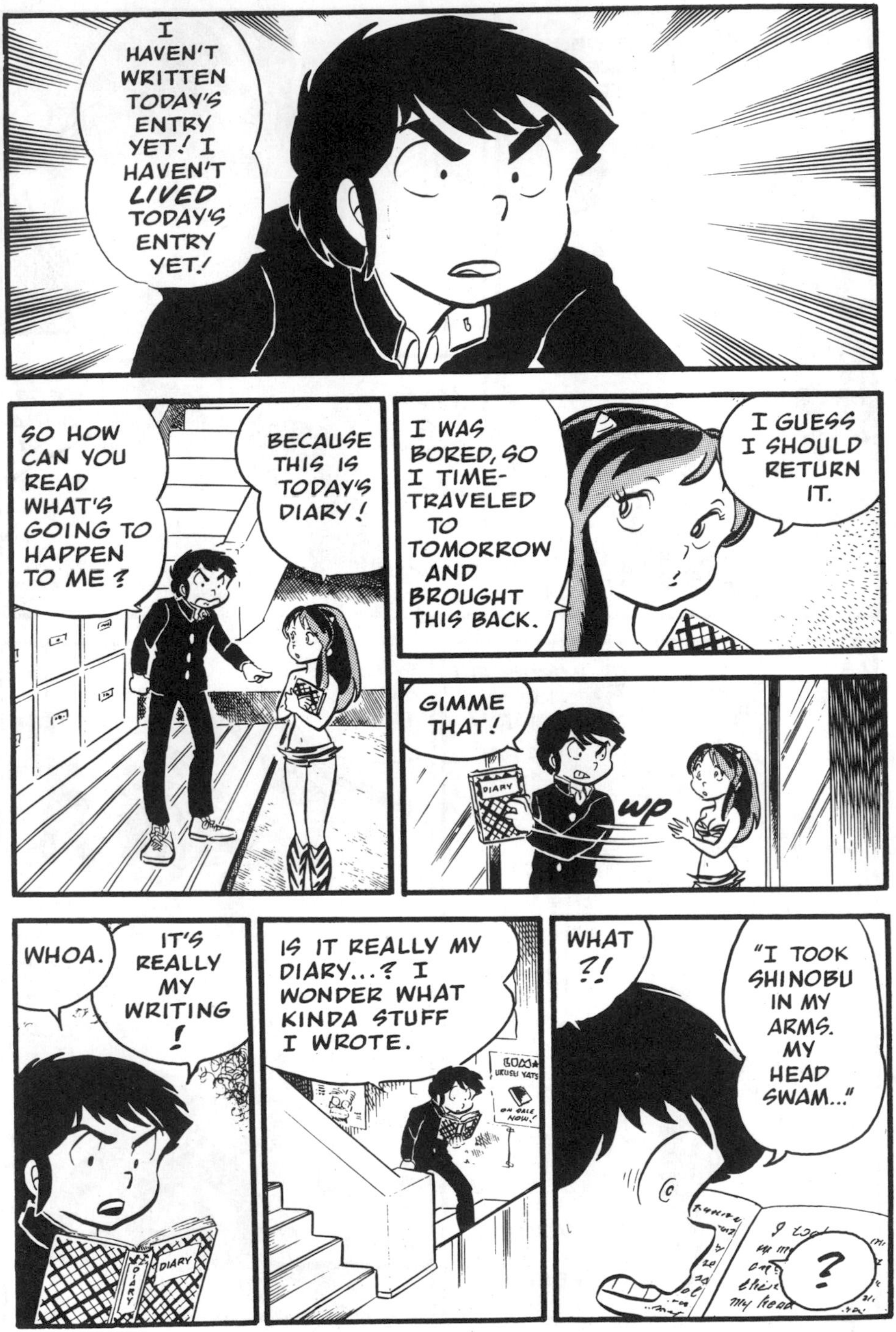

I HAVEN'T WRITTEN TODAY'S ENTRY YET! I HAVEN'T *LIVED* TODAY'S ENTRY YET!
SO HOW CAN YOU READ WHAT'S GOING TO HAPPEN TO ME?
BECAUSE THIS IS TODAY'S DIARY!
I WAS BORED, SO I TIME-TRAVELED TO TOMORROW AND BROUGHT THIS BACK.
I GUESS I SHOULD RETURN IT.
GIMME THAT!
DIARY
WP
WHOA.
IT'S REALLY MY WRITING!
DIARY
IS IT REALLY MY DIARY...? I WONDER WHAT KINDA STUFF I WROTE.
WHAT?!
"I TOOK SHINOBU IN MY ARMS. MY HEAD SWAM..."
?

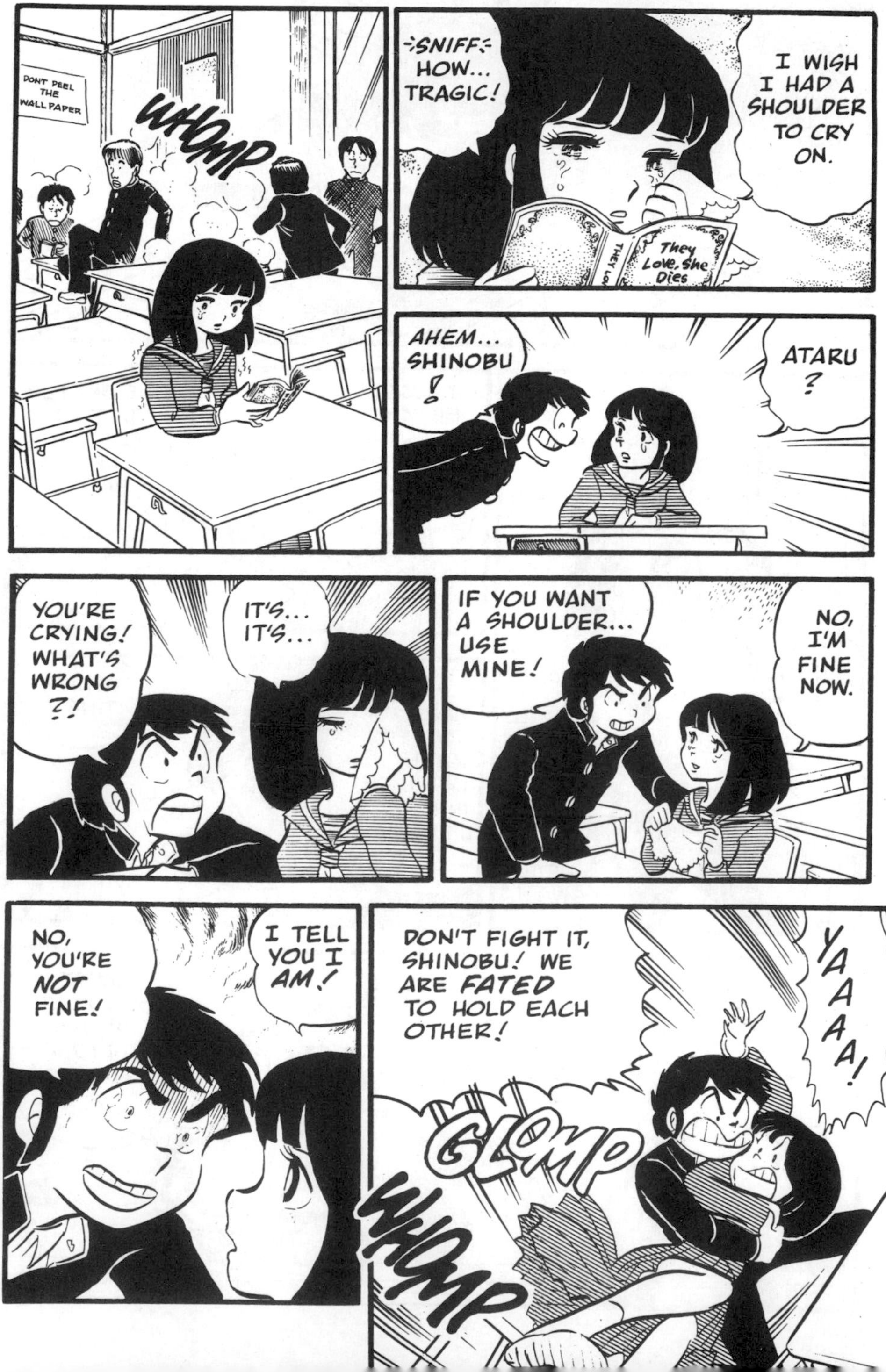
DON'T PEEL THE WALL PAPER
WHOMP
-SNIFF- HOW... TRAGIC!
THEY LO...
They Love, She Dies
I WISH I HAD A SHOULDER TO CRY ON.
AHEM... SHINOBU!
ATARU?
YOU'RE CRYING! WHAT'S WRONG?!
IT'S... IT'S...
IF YOU WANT A SHOULDER... USE MINE!
NO, I'M FINE NOW.
NO, YOU'RE *NOT* FINE!
I TELL YOU I *AM*!
DON'T FIGHT IT, SHINOBU! WE ARE *FATED* TO HOLD EACH OTHER!
YAAAAA!
GLOMP
WHOMP

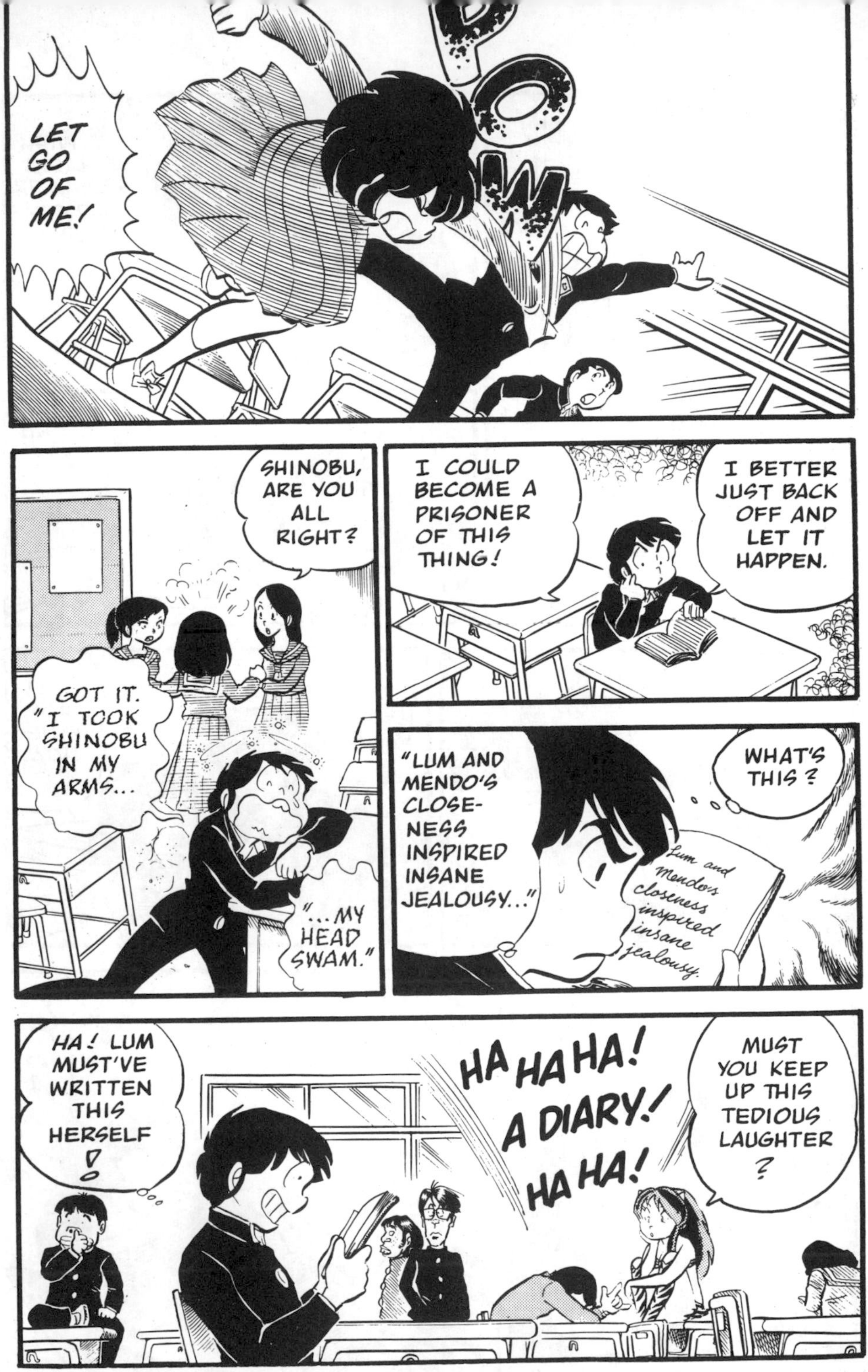
POW
LET GO OF ME!
SHINOBU, ARE YOU ALL RIGHT?
GOT IT. "I TOOK SHINOBU IN MY ARMS...
"...MY HEAD SWAM."
I COULD BECOME A PRISONER OF THIS THING!
I BETTER JUST BACK OFF AND LET IT HAPPEN.
"LUM AND MENDO'S CLOSENESS INSPIRED INSANE JEALOUSY..."
WHAT'S THIS?
Lum and Mendo's closeness inspired insane jealousy.
HA! LUM MUST'VE WRITTEN THIS HERSELF!
HA HA HA! A DIARY! HA HA!
MUST YOU KEEP UP THIS TEDIOUS LAUGHTER?

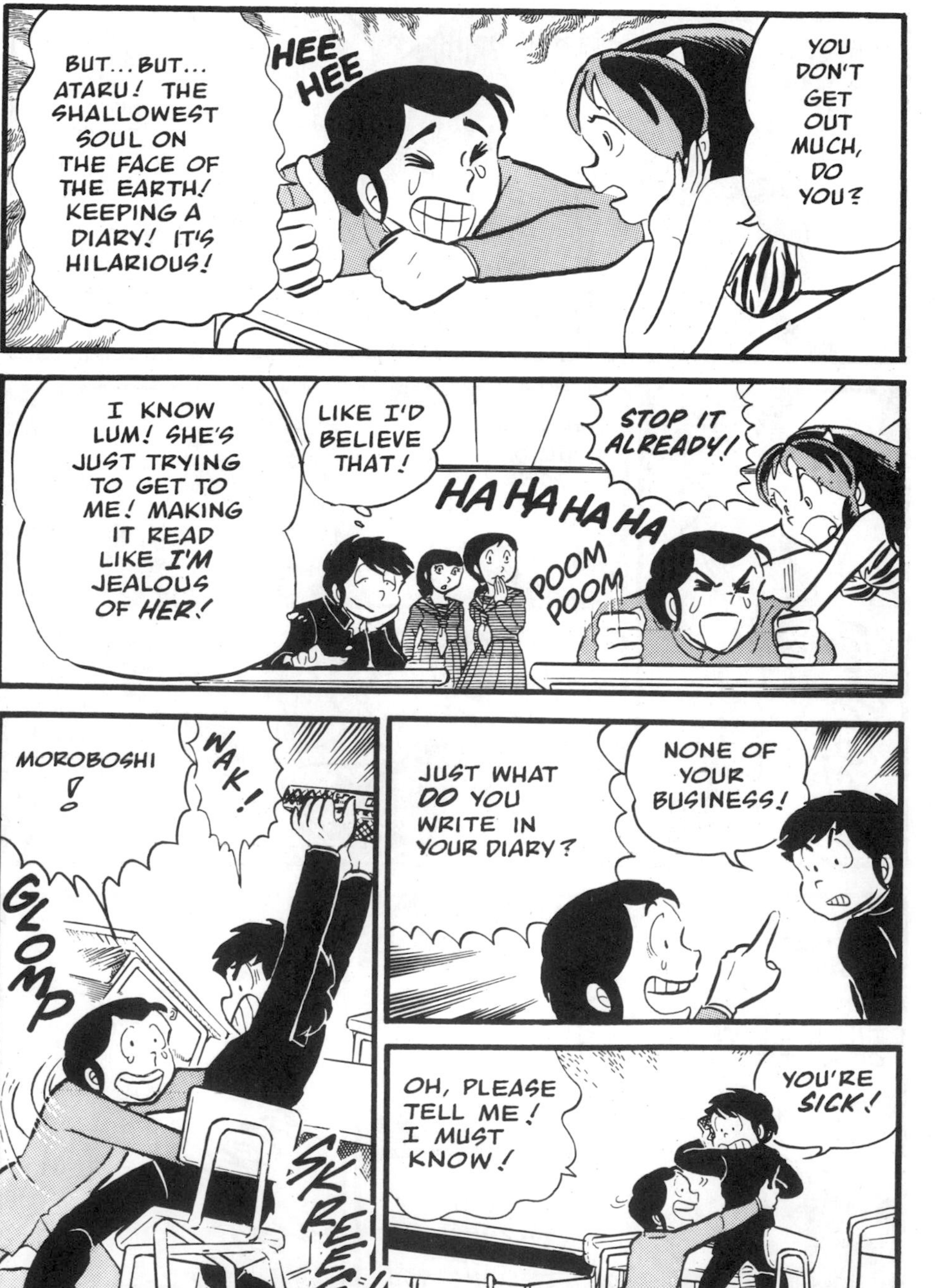
BUT... BUT... ATARU! THE SHALLOWEST SOUL ON THE FACE OF THE EARTH! KEEPING A DIARY! IT'S HILARIOUS!
HEE HEE
YOU DON'T GET OUT MUCH, DO YOU?
I KNOW LUM! SHE'S JUST TRYING TO GET TO ME! MAKING IT READ LIKE I'M JEALOUS OF HER!
LIKE I'D BELIEVE THAT!
STOP IT ALREADY!
HA HA HA HA HA
POOM POOM
MOROBOSHI!
WAK!
GLOMP
SKREEECH
JUST WHAT DO YOU WRITE IN YOUR DIARY?
NONE OF YOUR BUSINESS!
OH, PLEASE TELL ME! I MUST KNOW!
YOU'RE SICK!

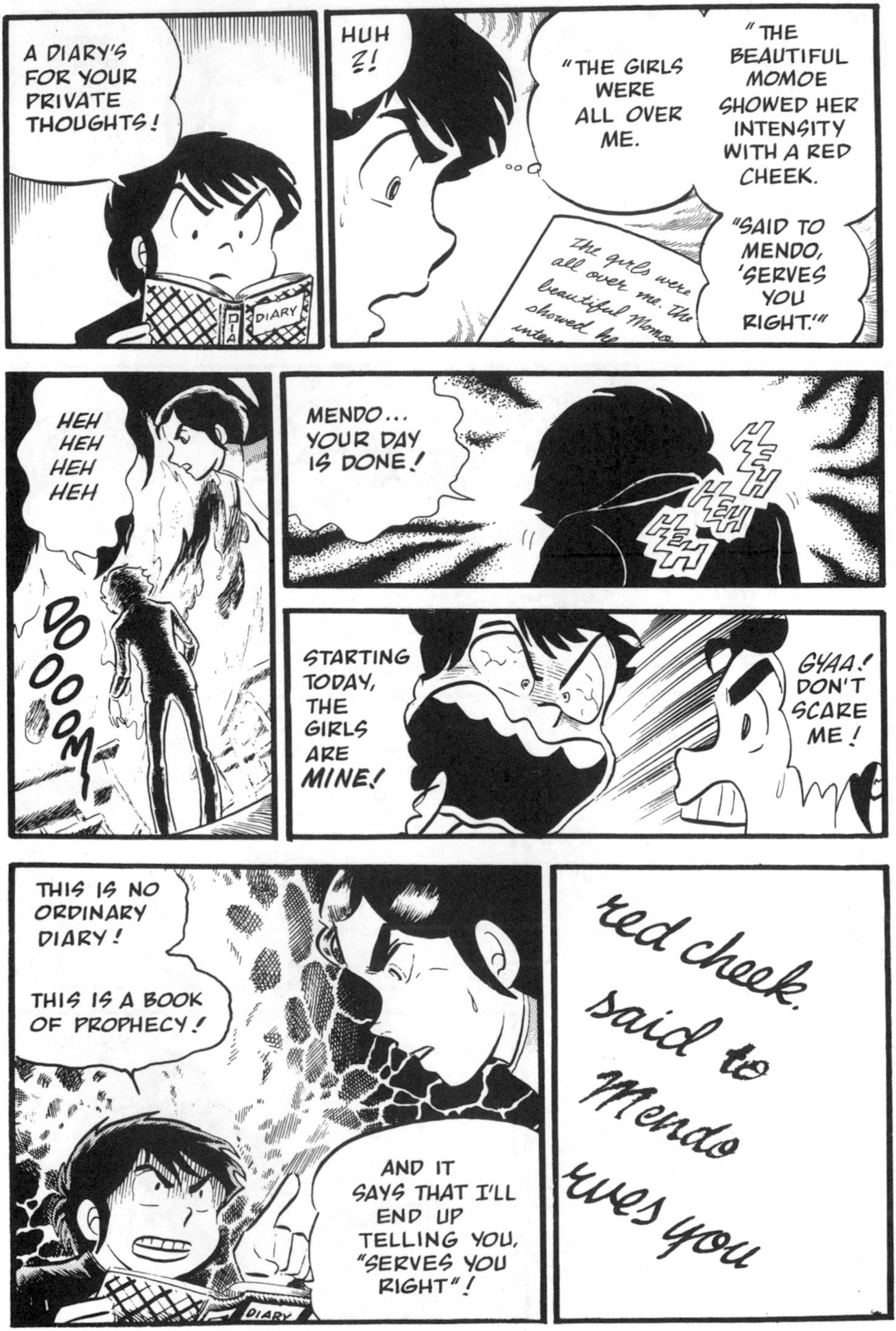

A DIARY'S FOR YOUR PRIVATE THOUGHTS!
HUH ?!
"THE GIRLS WERE ALL OVER ME.
"THE BEAUTIFUL MOMOE SHOWED HER INTENSITY WITH A RED CHEEK.
"SAID TO MENDO, 'SERVES YOU RIGHT.'"
The girls were all over me. The beautiful Momo showed he
HEH HEH HEH HEH
DOOOOM
MENDO... YOUR DAY IS DONE!
HEH HEH HEH
STARTING TODAY, THE GIRLS ARE MINE!
GYAA! DON'T SCARE ME!
THIS IS NO ORDINARY DIARY!
THIS IS A BOOK OF PROPHECY!
AND IT SAYS THAT I'LL END UP TELLING YOU, "SERVES YOU RIGHT"!
DIARY
red cheek. said to Mendo rves you

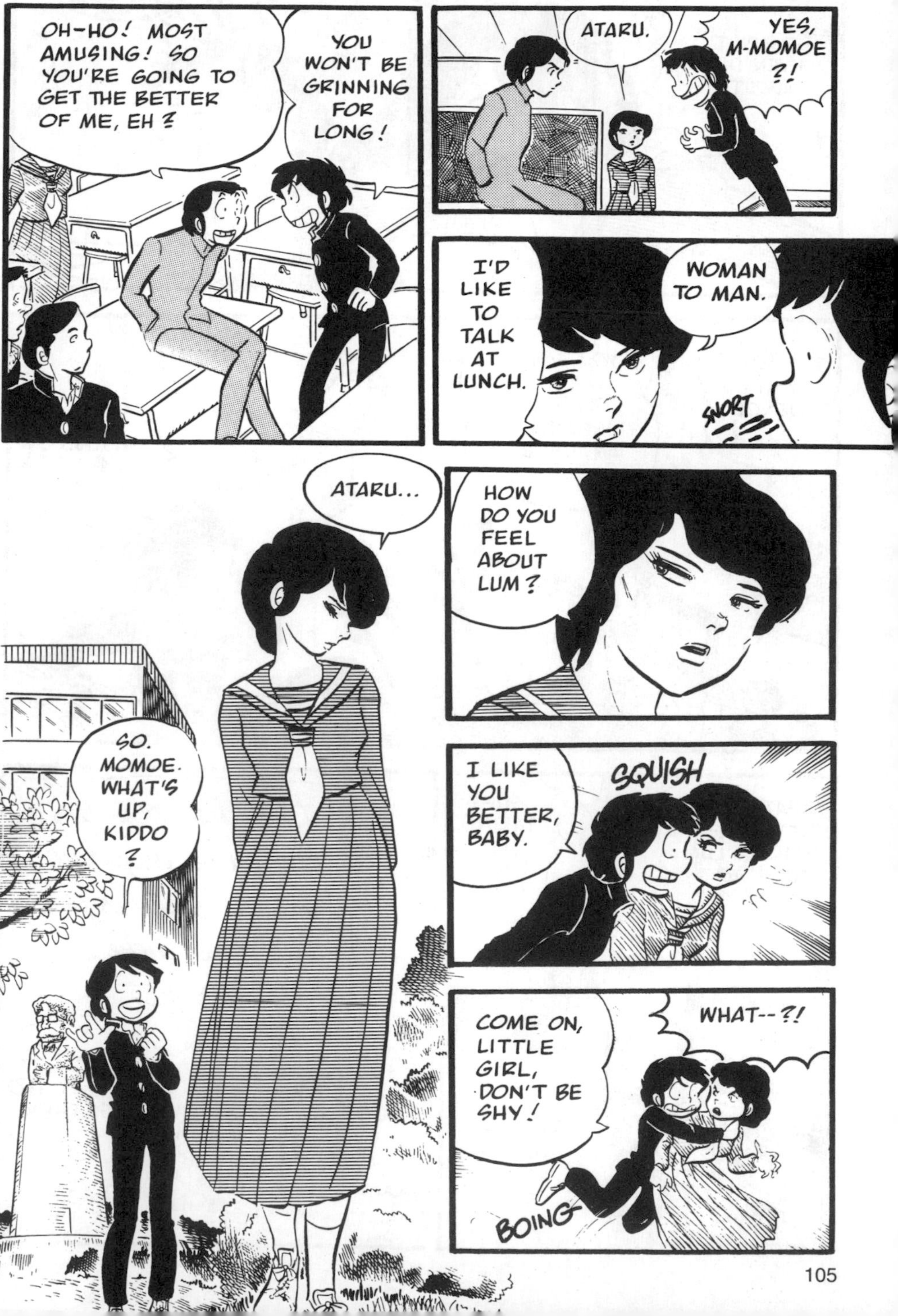
OH-HO! MOST AMUSING! SO YOU'RE GOING TO GET THE BETTER OF ME, EH?
YOU WON'T BE GRINNING FOR LONG!
ATARU.
YES, M-MOMOE?!
I'D LIKE TO TALK AT LUNCH.
WOMAN TO MAN.
SNORT
ATARU...
SO. MOMOE. WHAT'S UP, KIDDO?
HOW DO YOU FEEL ABOUT LUM?
I LIKE YOU BETTER, BABY.
SQUISH
COME ON, LITTLE GIRL, DON'T BE SHY!
WHAT--?!
BOING

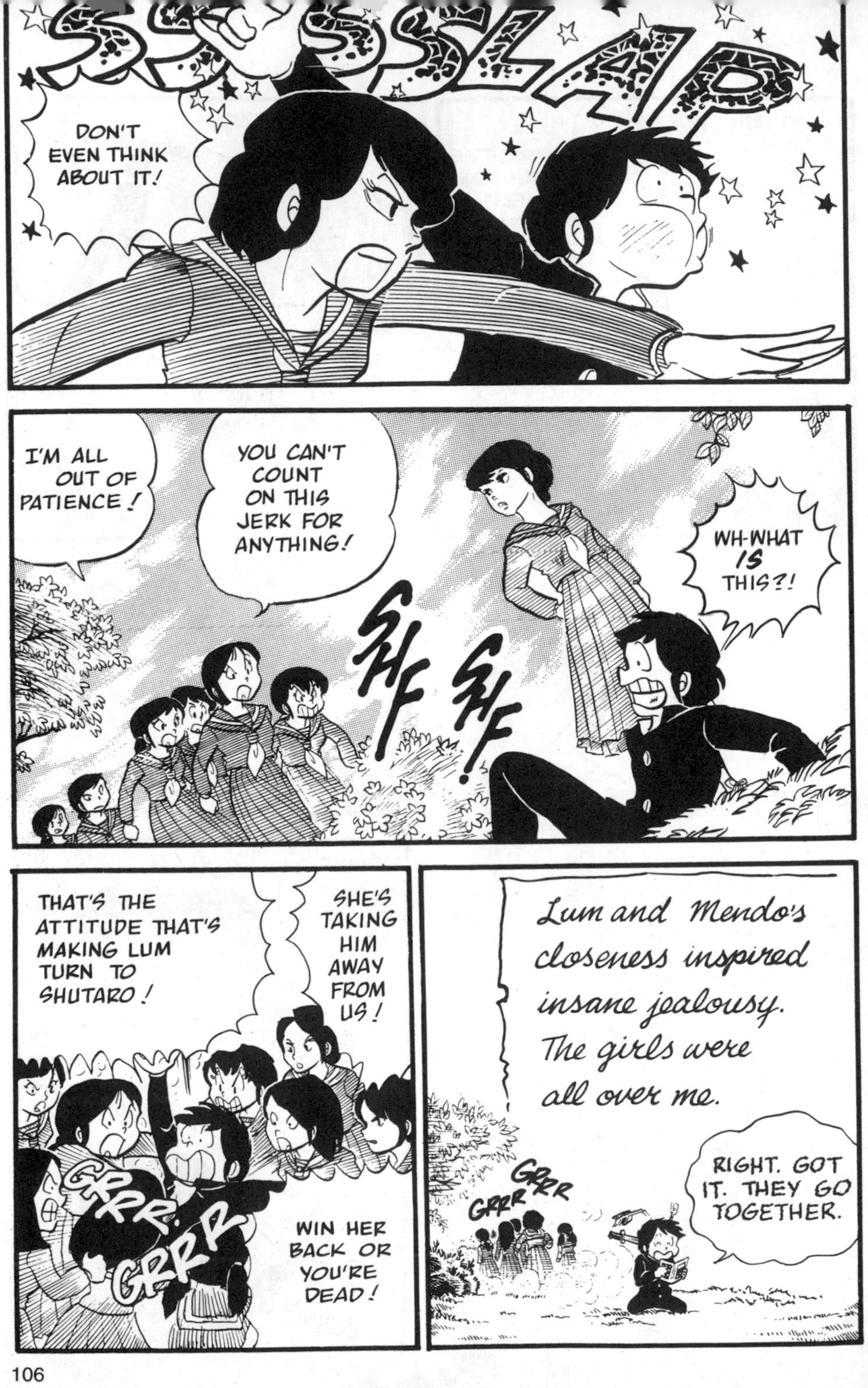
SSSSLAP
DON'T EVEN THINK ABOUT IT!
I'M ALL OUT OF PATIENCE!
YOU CAN'T COUNT ON THIS JERK FOR ANYTHING!
SHF SHF!
WH-WHAT IS THIS?!
THAT'S THE ATTITUDE THAT'S MAKING LUM TURN TO SHUTARO!
SHE'S TAKING HIM AWAY FROM US!
GRRR. GRRR
WIN HER BACK OR YOU'RE DEAD!
Lum and Mendo's closeness inspired insane jealousy. The girls were all over me.
GRRR GRRR
RIGHT. GOT IT. THEY GO TOGETHER.

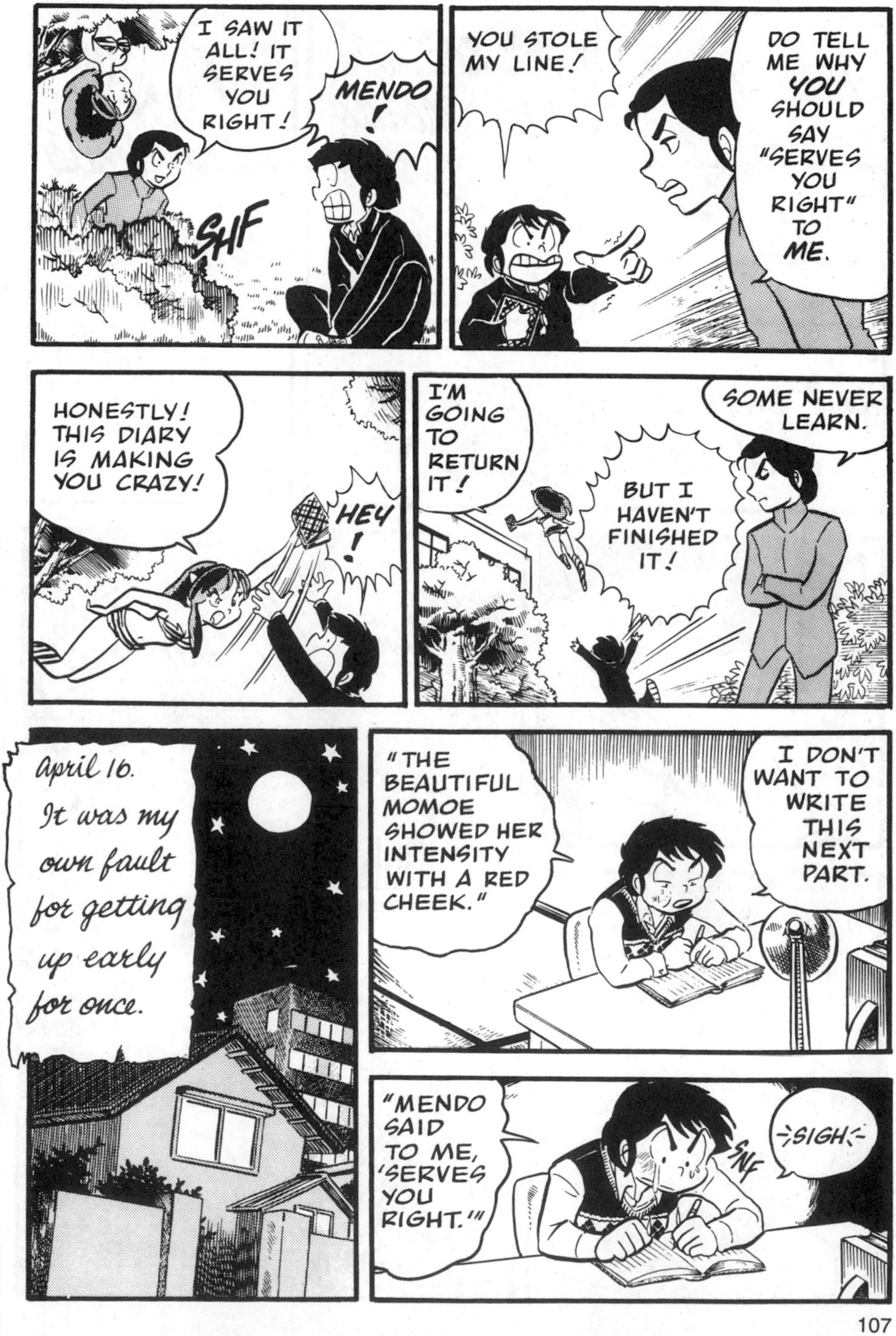
I SAW IT ALL! IT SERVES YOU RIGHT!
SHF
MENDO!
YOU STOLE MY LINE!
DO TELL ME WHY YOU SHOULD SAY "SERVES YOU RIGHT" TO ME.
HONESTLY! THIS DIARY IS MAKING YOU CRAZY!
HEY!
I'M GOING TO RETURN IT!
SOME NEVER LEARN.
BUT I HAVEN'T FINISHED IT!
April 16.
It was my own fault for getting up early for once.
"THE BEAUTIFUL MOMOE SHOWED HER INTENSITY WITH A RED CHEEK."
I DON'T WANT TO WRITE THIS NEXT PART.
"MENDO SAID TO ME, 'SERVES YOU RIGHT.'"
SNF
SIGH

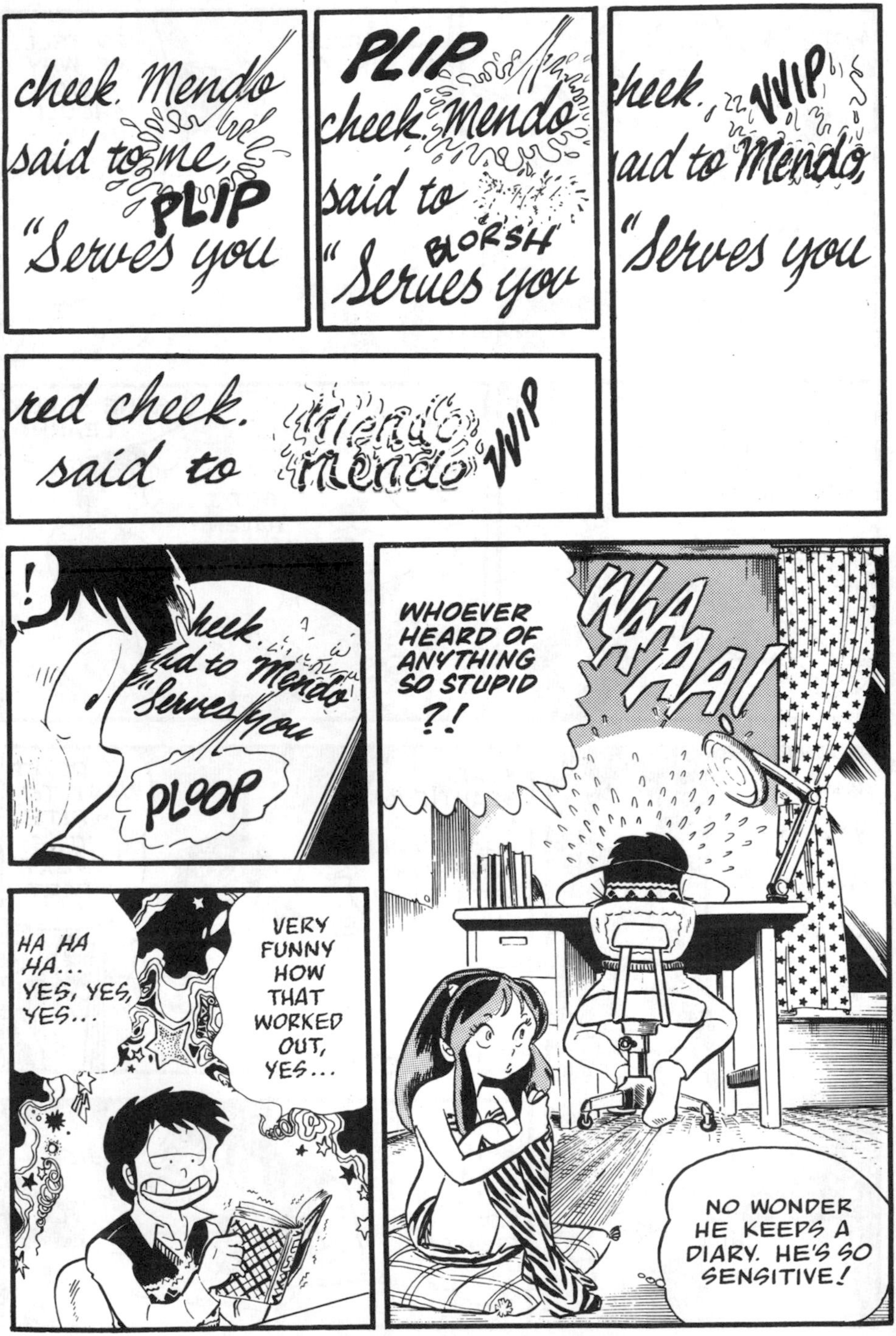
cheek. Mendo
said to me,
PLIP
"Serves you
PLIP
cheek. Mendo
said to
BLORSH
"Serves you
cheek.
VVIP
said to Mendo,
"Serves you
red cheek.
said to
VVIP
!
cheek.
said to Mendo
"Serves you
PLOOP
WHOEVER HEARD OF ANYTHING SO STUPID ?!
WAAAA!
HA HA HA... YES, YES, YES...
VERY FUNNY HOW THAT WORKED OUT, YES...
NO WONDER HE KEEPS A DIARY. HE'S SO SENSITIVE!

Part 7
What Child Is This?

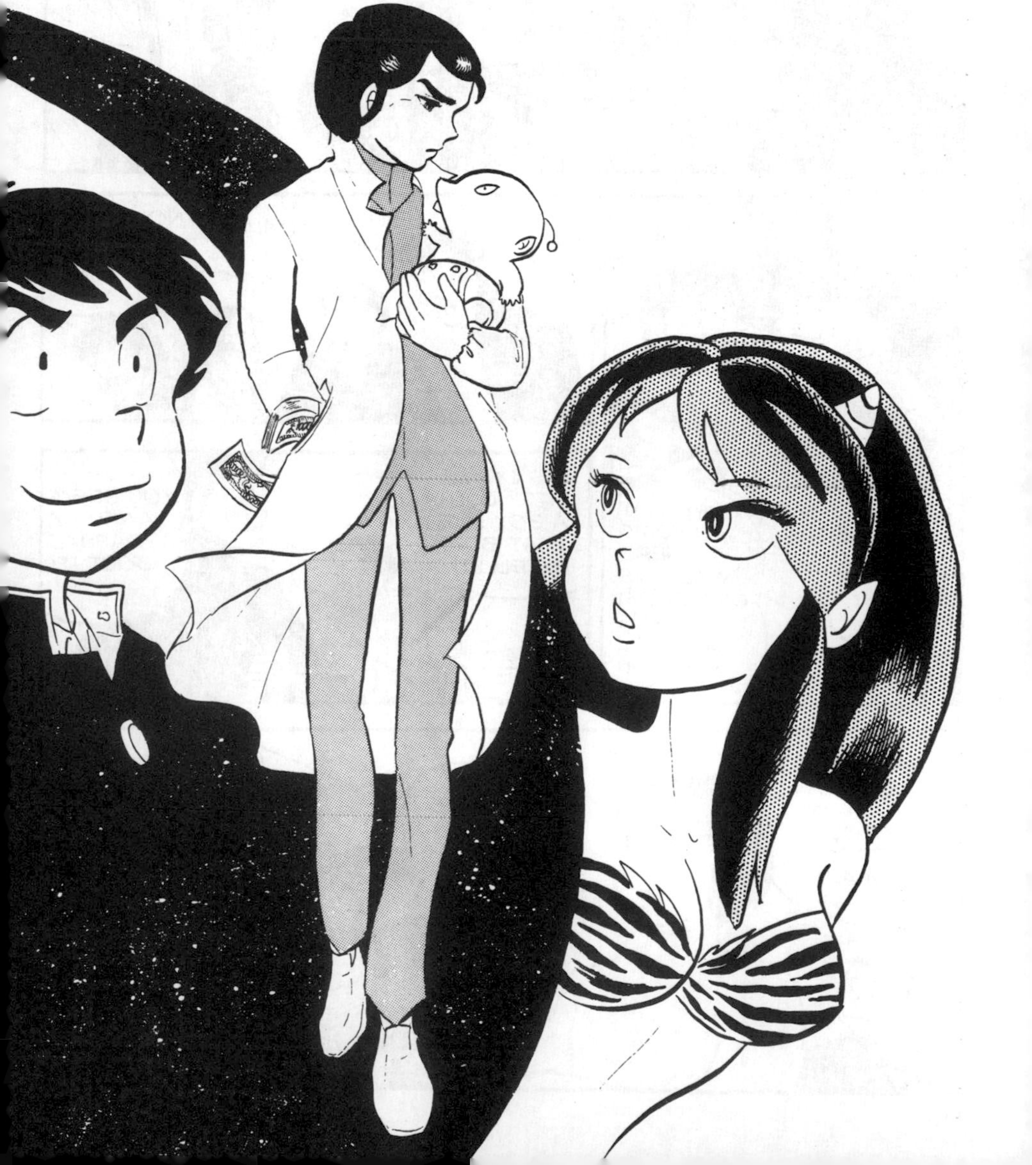

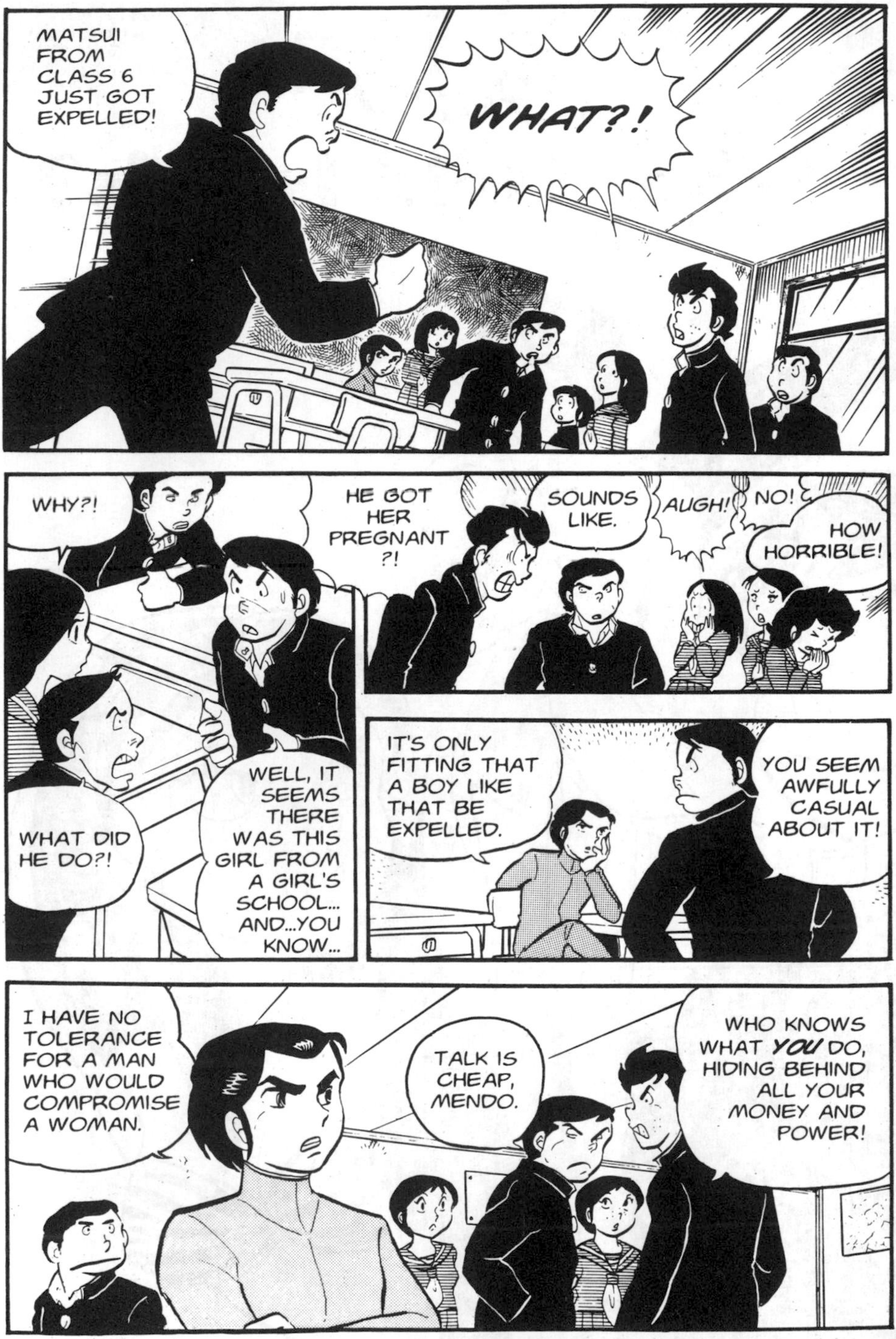
MATSUI FROM CLASS 6 JUST GOT EXPELLED!
WHAT?!
WHY?!
WHAT DID HE DO?!
WELL, IT SEEMS THERE WAS THIS GIRL FROM A GIRL'S SCHOOL... AND...YOU KNOW...
HE GOT HER PREGNANT?!
SOUNDS LIKE.
AUGH!
NO!
HOW HORRIBLE!
IT'S ONLY FITTING THAT A BOY LIKE THAT BE EXPELLED.
YOU SEEM AWFULLY CASUAL ABOUT IT!
I HAVE NO TOLERANCE FOR A MAN WHO WOULD COMPROMISE A WOMAN.
TALK IS CHEAP, MENDO.
WHO KNOWS WHAT *YOU* DO, HIDING BEHIND ALL YOUR MONEY AND POWER!

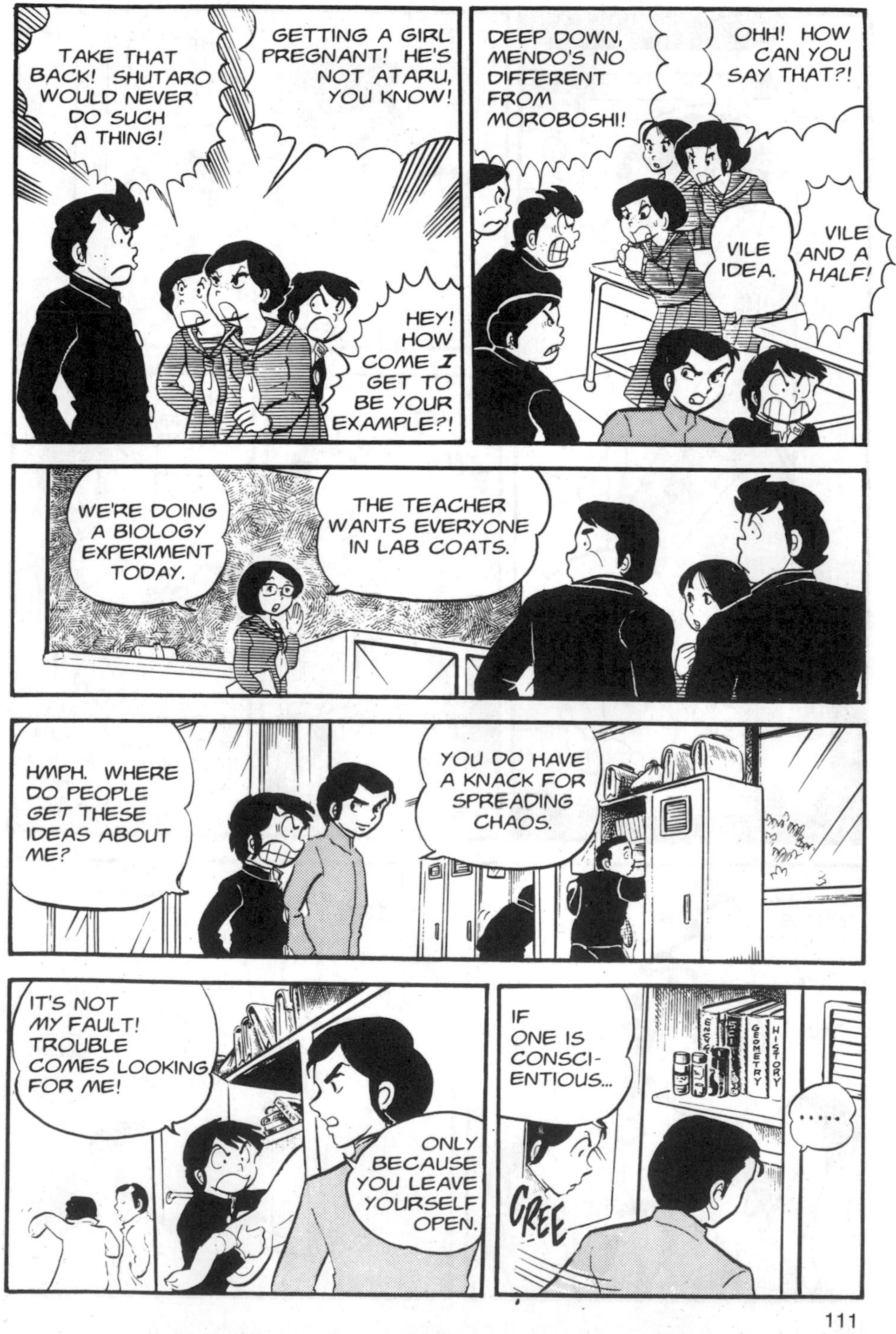
TAKE THAT BACK! SHUTARO WOULD NEVER DO SUCH A THING!
GETTING A GIRL PREGNANT! HE'S NOT ATARU, YOU KNOW!
HEY! HOW COME I GET TO BE YOUR EXAMPLE?!
DEEP DOWN, MENDO'S NO DIFFERENT FROM MOROBOSHI!
OHH! HOW CAN YOU SAY THAT?!
VILE IDEA.
VILE AND A HALF!
WE'RE DOING A BIOLOGY EXPERIMENT TODAY.
THE TEACHER WANTS EVERYONE IN LAB COATS.
HMPH. WHERE DO PEOPLE GET THESE IDEAS ABOUT ME?
YOU DO HAVE A KNACK FOR SPREADING CHAOS.
IT'S NOT MY FAULT! TROUBLE COMES LOOKING FOR ME!
ONLY BECAUSE YOU LEAVE YOURSELF OPEN.
IF ONE IS CONSCI-ENTIOUS...
GEOMETRY
HISTORY
CREE
......

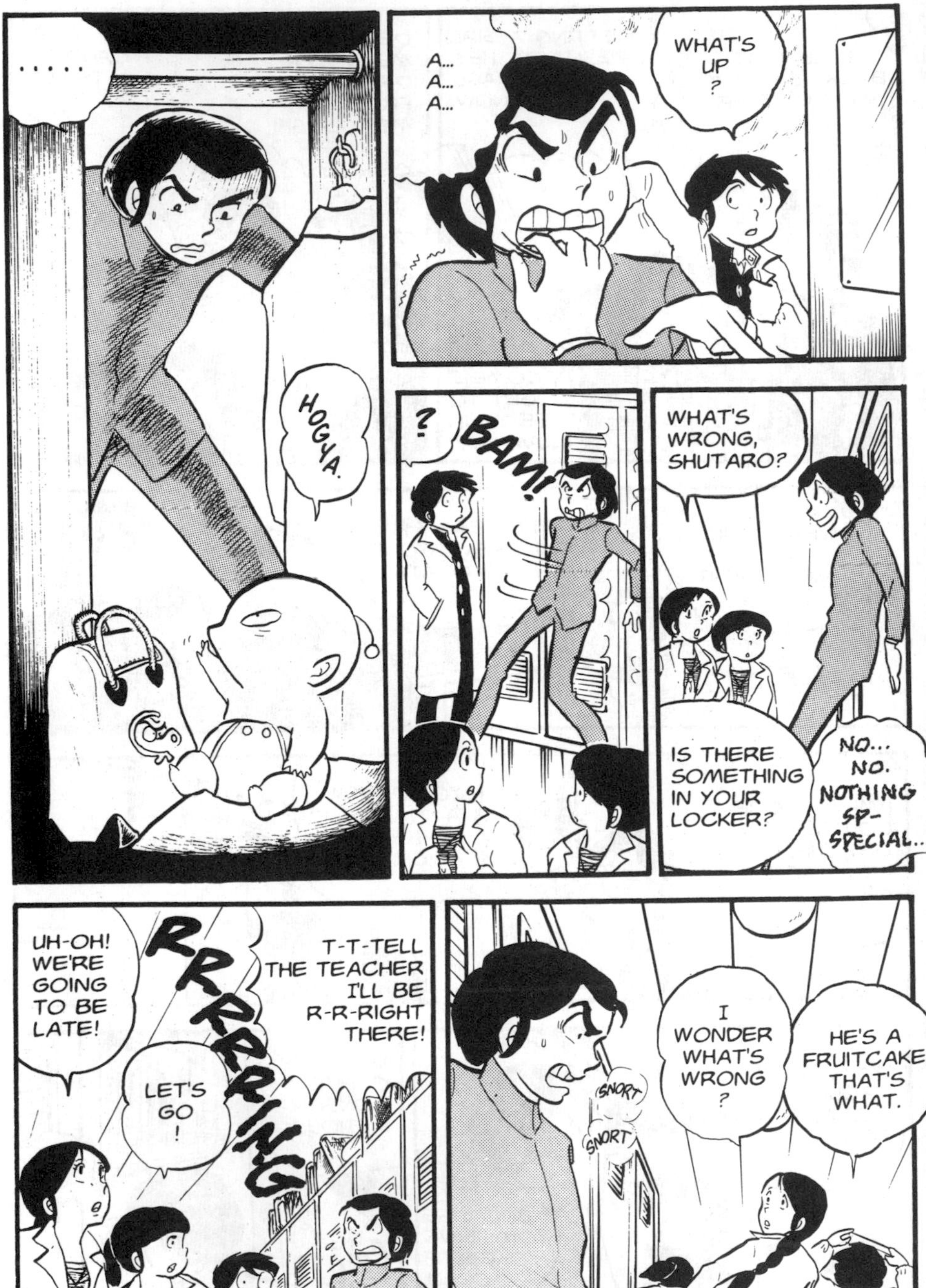
.....
HOGYA.
A...
A...
A...
WHAT'S UP ?
?
BAM!
WHAT'S WRONG, SHUTARO?
IS THERE SOMETHING IN YOUR LOCKER?
NO... NO. NOTHING SP- SPECIAL...
UH-OH! WE'RE GOING TO BE LATE!
RRRRRING
T-T-TELL THE TEACHER I'LL BE R-R-RIGHT THERE!
LET'S GO !
SNORT
SNORT
I WONDER WHAT'S WRONG ?
HE'S A FRUITCAKE, THAT'S WHAT.

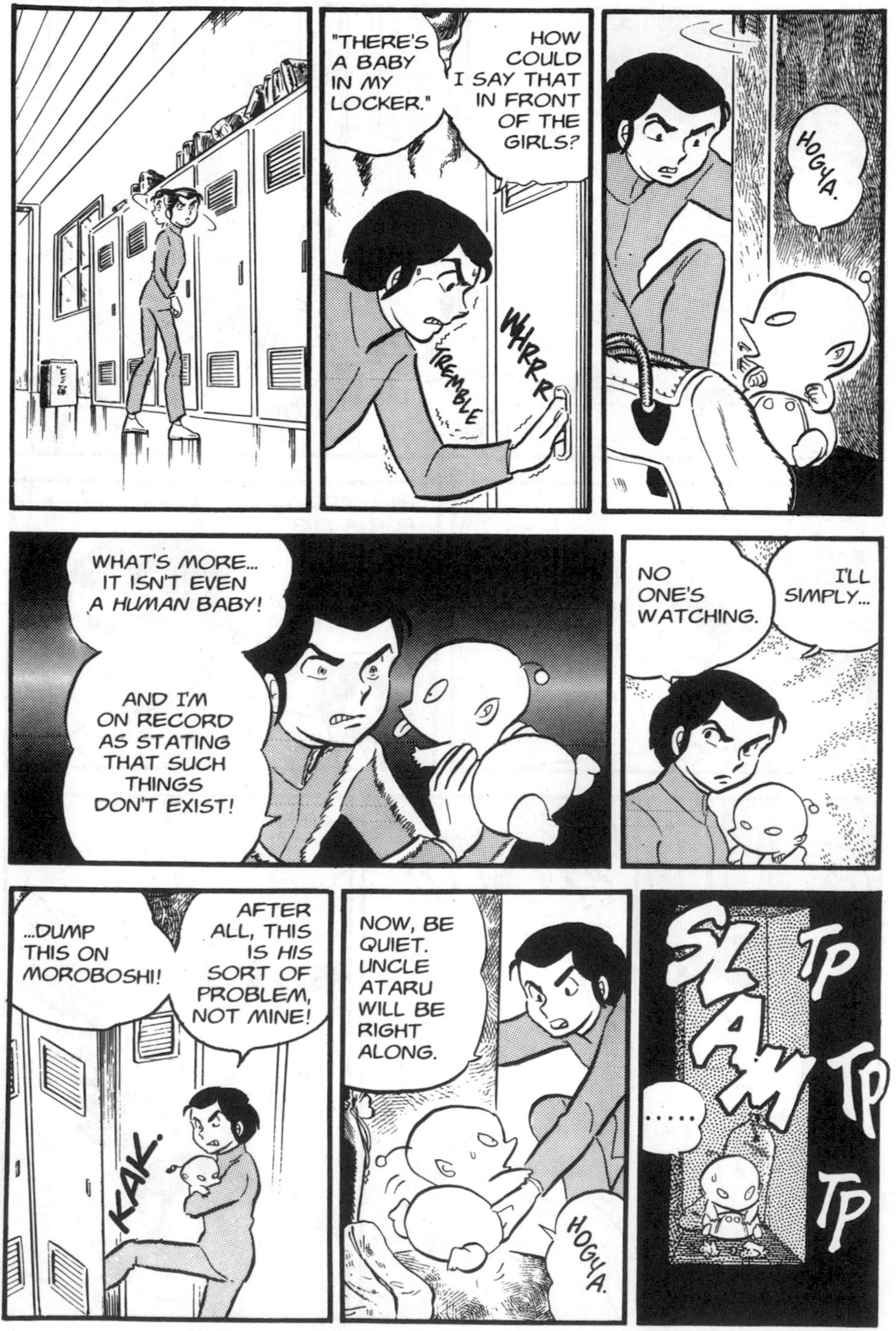
"THERE'S A BABY IN MY LOCKER."
HOW COULD I SAY THAT IN FRONT OF THE GIRLS?
TREMBLE
WHRRR
HOGYA.
WHAT'S MORE... IT ISN'T EVEN A *HUMAN* BABY!
AND I'M ON RECORD AS STATING THAT SUCH THINGS DON'T EXIST!
NO ONE'S WATCHING.
I'LL SIMPLY...
...DUMP THIS ON MOROBOSHI!
AFTER ALL, THIS IS *HIS* SORT OF PROBLEM, NOT MINE!
KAK
NOW, BE QUIET. UNCLE ATARU WILL BE RIGHT ALONG.
HOGYA.
SLAM
TP TP TP TP
......

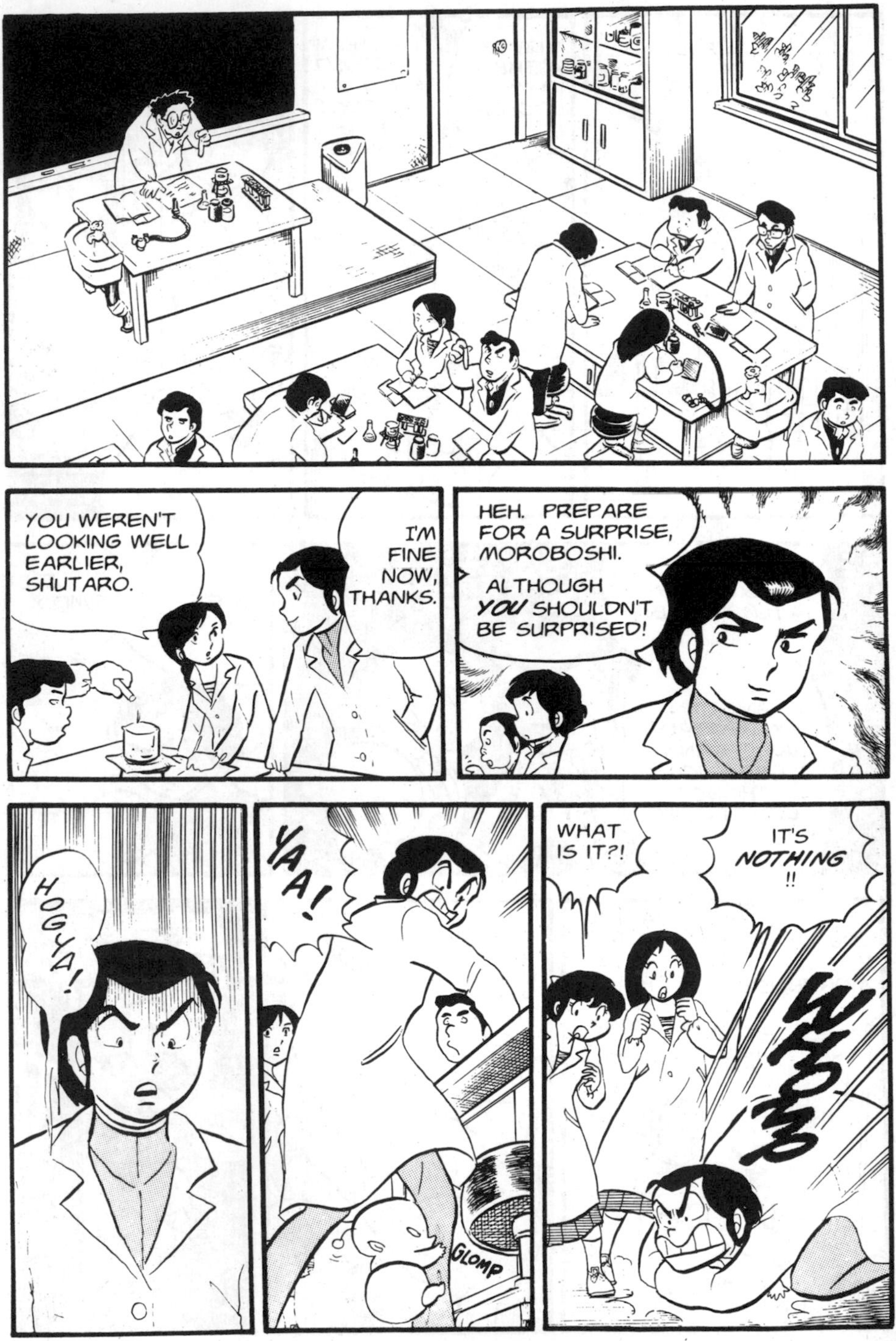

YOU WEREN'T LOOKING WELL EARLIER, SHUTARO.
I'M FINE NOW, THANKS.
HEH. PREPARE FOR A SURPRISE, MOROBOSHI.
ALTHOUGH *YOU* SHOULDN'T BE SURPRISED!
HOGYA!
YAAA!
GLOMP
WHAT IS IT?!
IT'S *NOTHING* !!
WHOMP

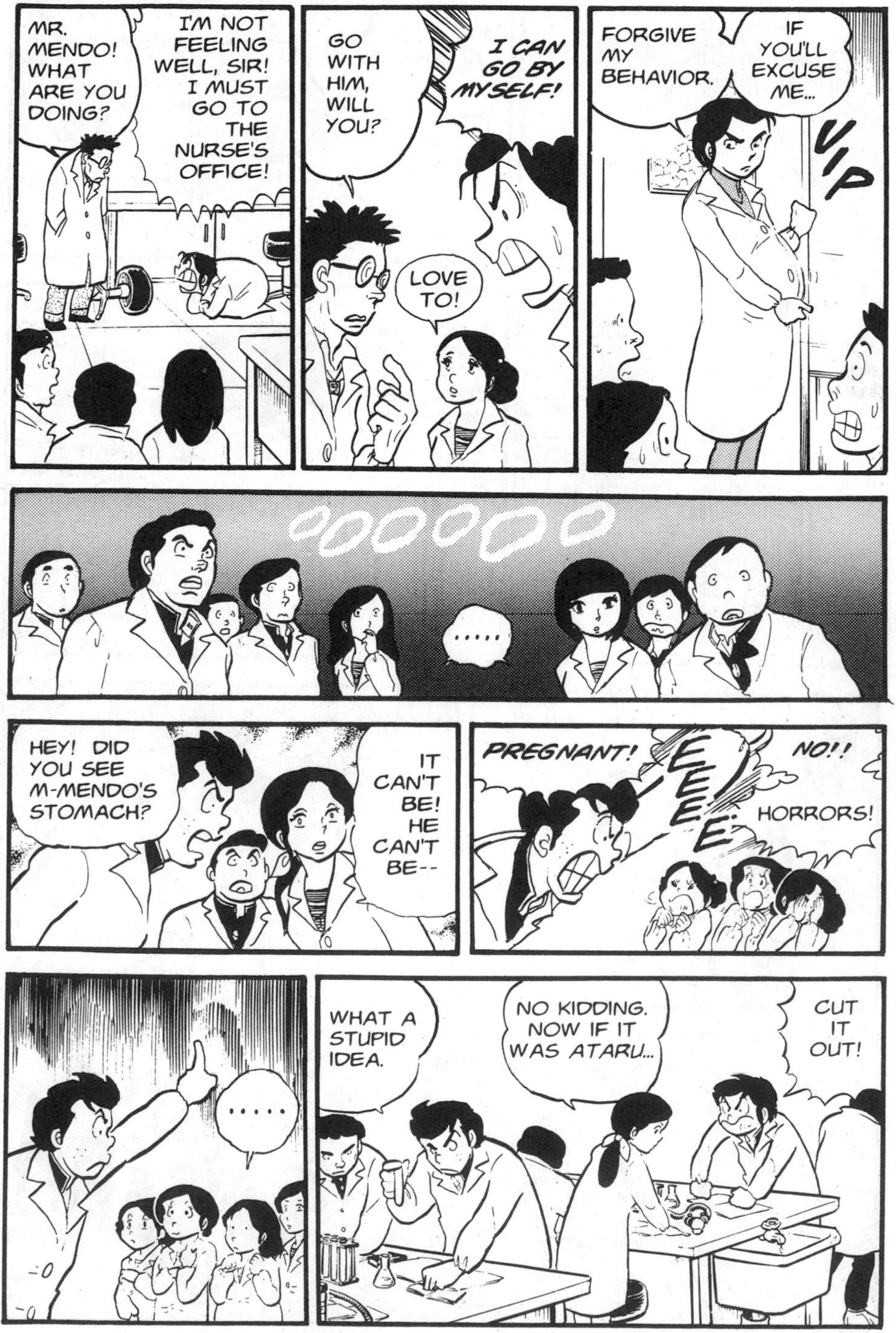
MR. MENDO! WHAT ARE YOU DOING?
I'M NOT FEELING WELL, SIR! I MUST GO TO THE NURSE'S OFFICE!
GO WITH HIM, WILL YOU?
I CAN GO BY MYSELF!
LOVE TO!
FORGIVE MY BEHAVIOR.
IF YOU'LL EXCUSE ME...
VIP
.....
HEY! DID YOU SEE M-MENDO'S STOMACH?
IT CAN'T BE! HE CAN'T BE--
PREGNANT!
EEEE
NO!!
HORRORS!
.....
WHAT A STUPID IDEA.
NO KIDDING. NOW IF IT WAS ATARU...
CUT IT OUT!

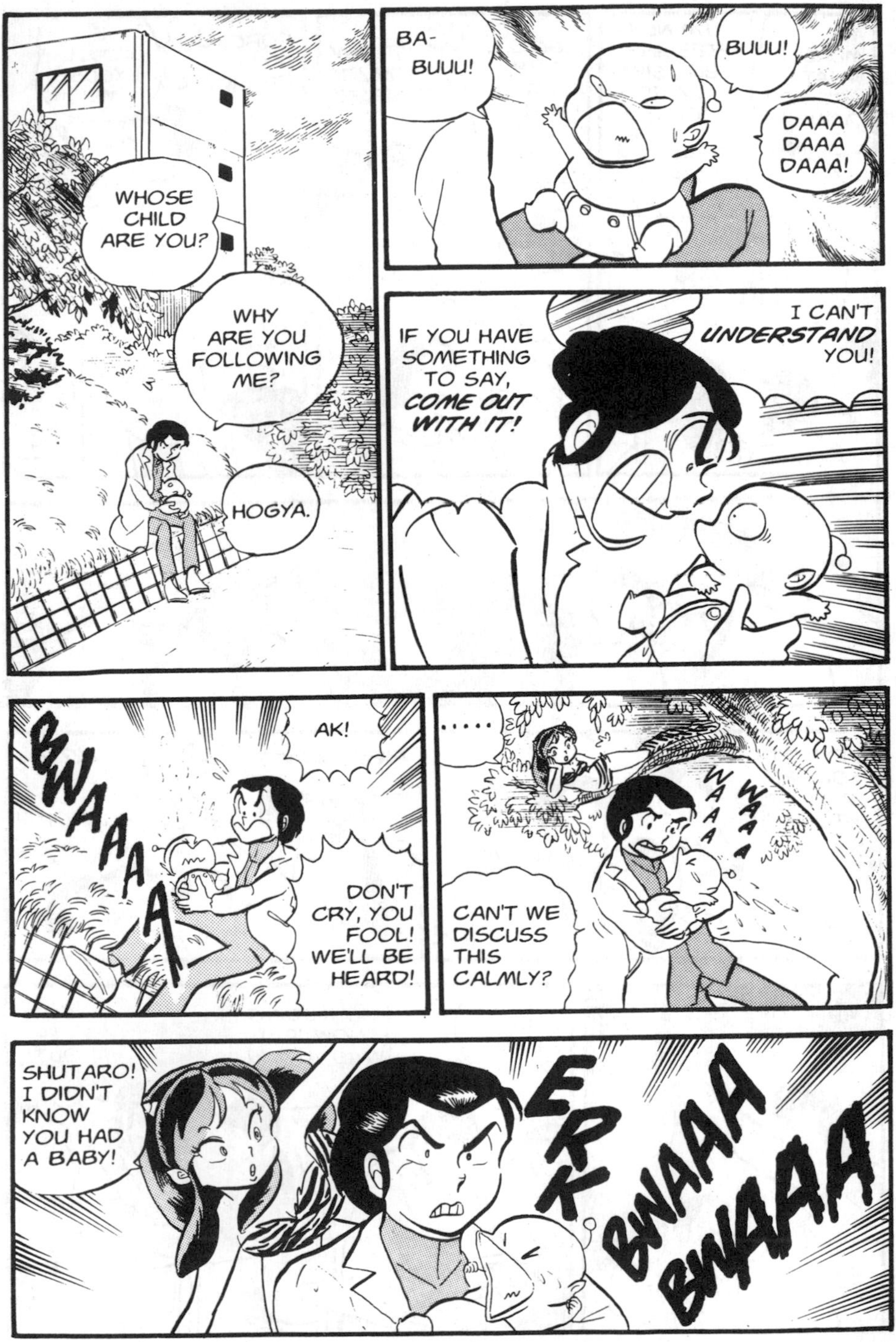
WHOSE CHILD ARE YOU?
WHY ARE YOU FOLLOWING ME?
HOGYA.
BA-BUUU!
BUUU!
DAAA DAAA DAAA!
IF YOU HAVE SOMETHING TO SAY, COME OUT WITH IT!
I CAN'T UNDERSTAND YOU!
BWAAAA
AK!
DON'T CRY, YOU FOOL! WE'LL BE HEARD!
.....
WAAA
WAAA
CAN'T WE DISCUSS THIS CALMLY?
SHUTARO! I DIDN'T KNOW YOU HAD A BABY!
ERK
BWAAA
BWAAA

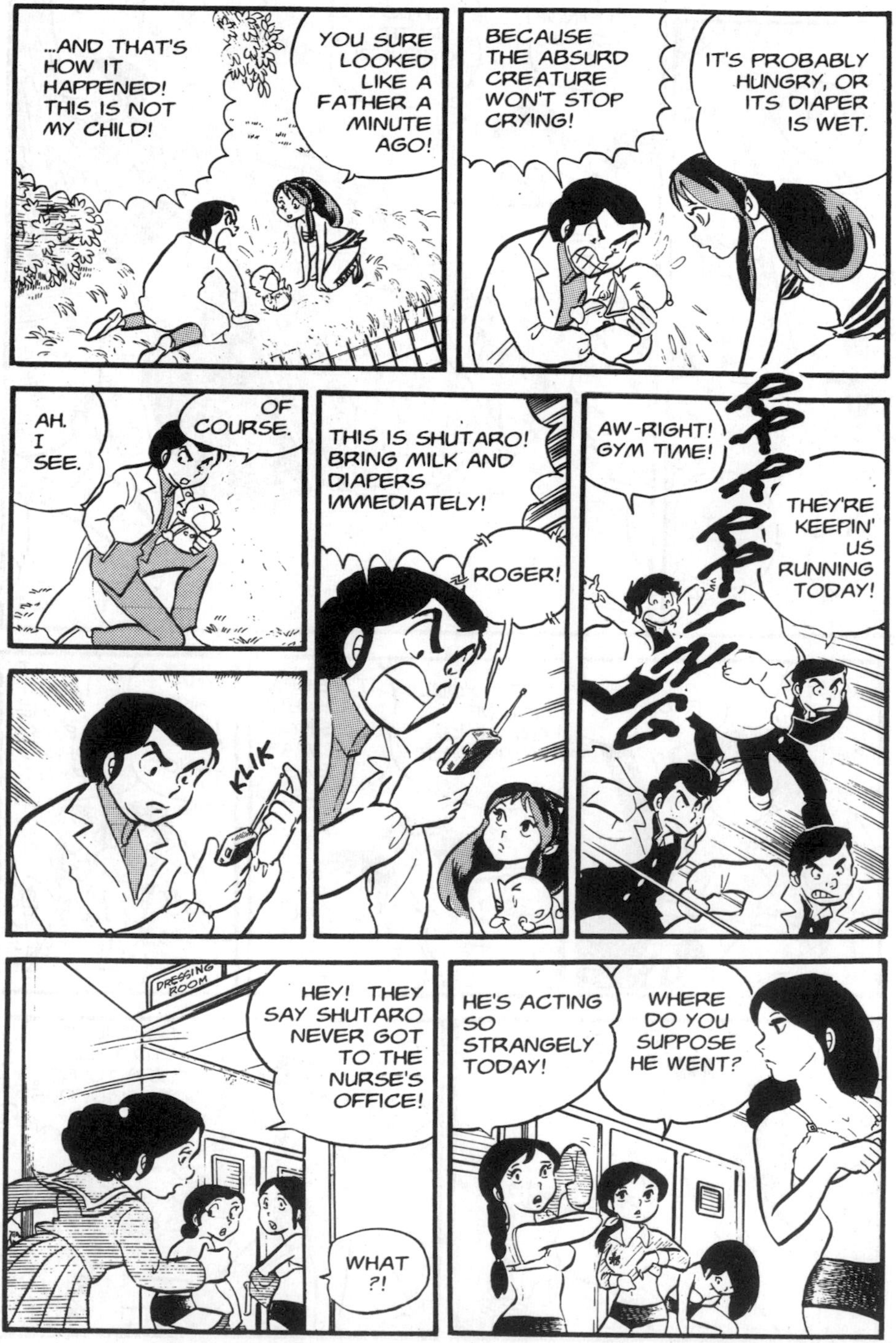

...AND THAT'S HOW IT HAPPENED! THIS IS NOT MY CHILD!
YOU SURE LOOKED LIKE A FATHER A MINUTE AGO!
BECAUSE THE ABSURD CREATURE WON'T STOP CRYING!
IT'S PROBABLY HUNGRY, OR ITS DIAPER IS WET.
AH. I SEE.
OF COURSE.
THIS IS SHUTARO! BRING MILK AND DIAPERS IMMEDIATELY!
ROGER!
AW-RIGHT! GYM TIME!
RRRRIIING
THEY'RE KEEPIN' US RUNNING TODAY!
KLIK
DRESSING ROOM
HEY! THEY SAY SHUTARO NEVER GOT TO THE NURSE'S OFFICE!
WHAT ?!
HE'S ACTING SO STRANGELY TODAY!
WHERE DO YOU SUPPOSE HE WENT?

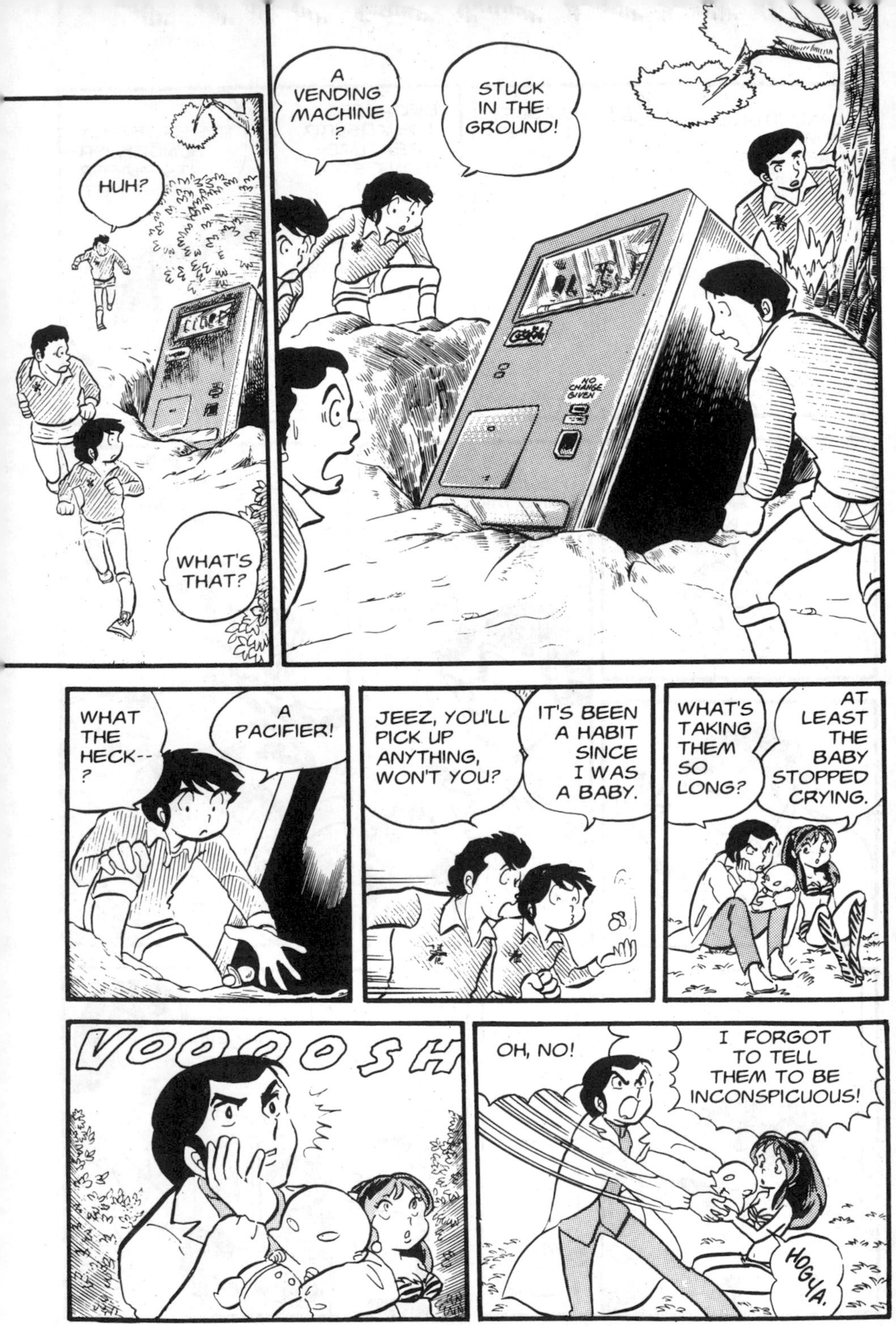
HUH?
WHAT'S THAT?
A VENDING MACHINE?
STUCK IN THE GROUND!
NO CHANGE GIVEN
WHAT THE HECK--?
A PACIFIER!
JEEZ, YOU'LL PICK UP ANYTHING, WON'T YOU?
IT'S BEEN A HABIT SINCE I WAS A BABY.
WHAT'S TAKING THEM SO LONG?
AT LEAST THE BABY STOPPED CRYING.
VOOOOSH
OH, NO!
I FORGOT TO TELL THEM TO BE INCONSPICUOUS!
HOGYA.

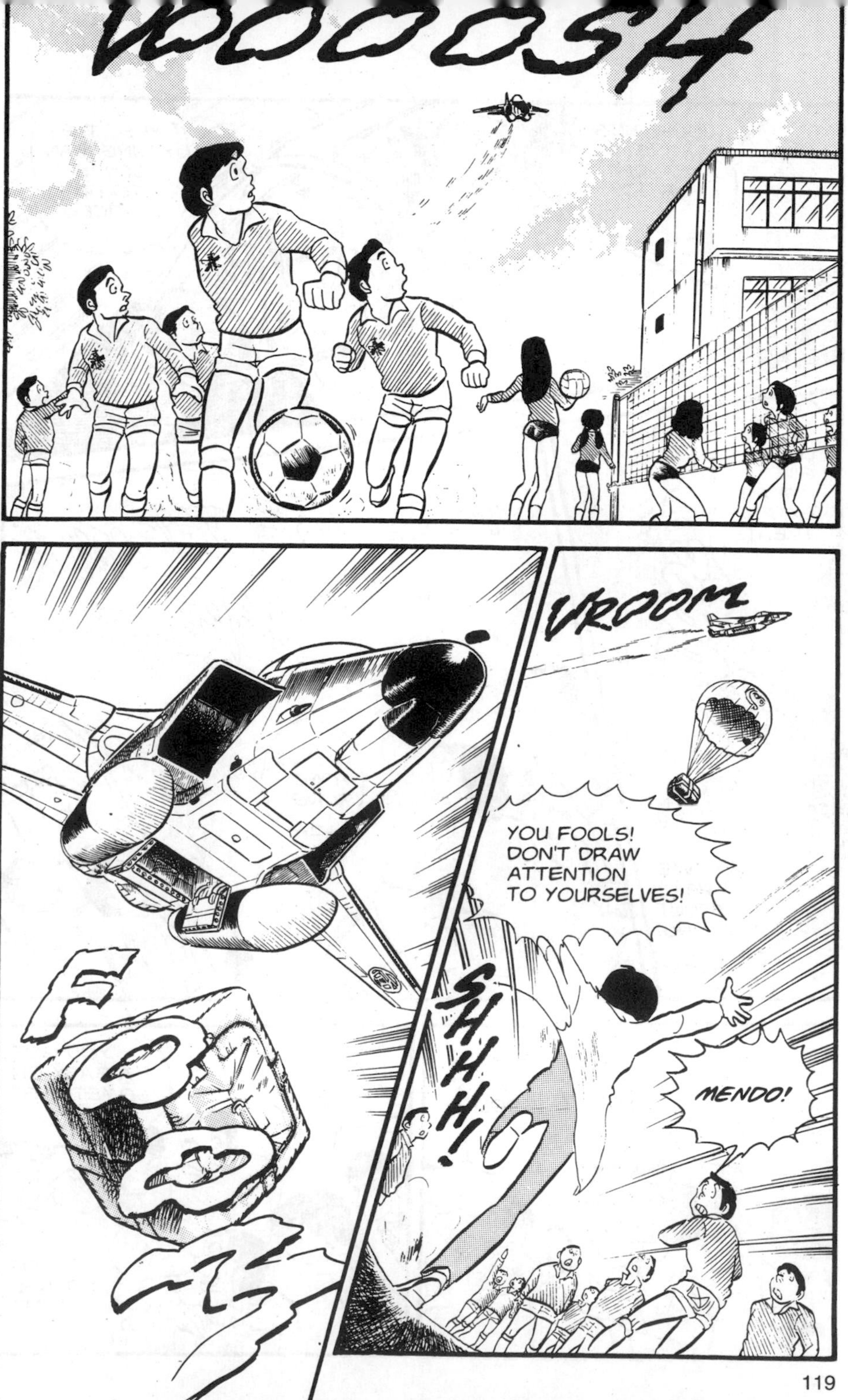
VOOOOSH
VROOM
YOU FOOLS! DON'T DRAW ATTENTION TO YOURSELVES!
FOOM
SHHHH!
MENDO!

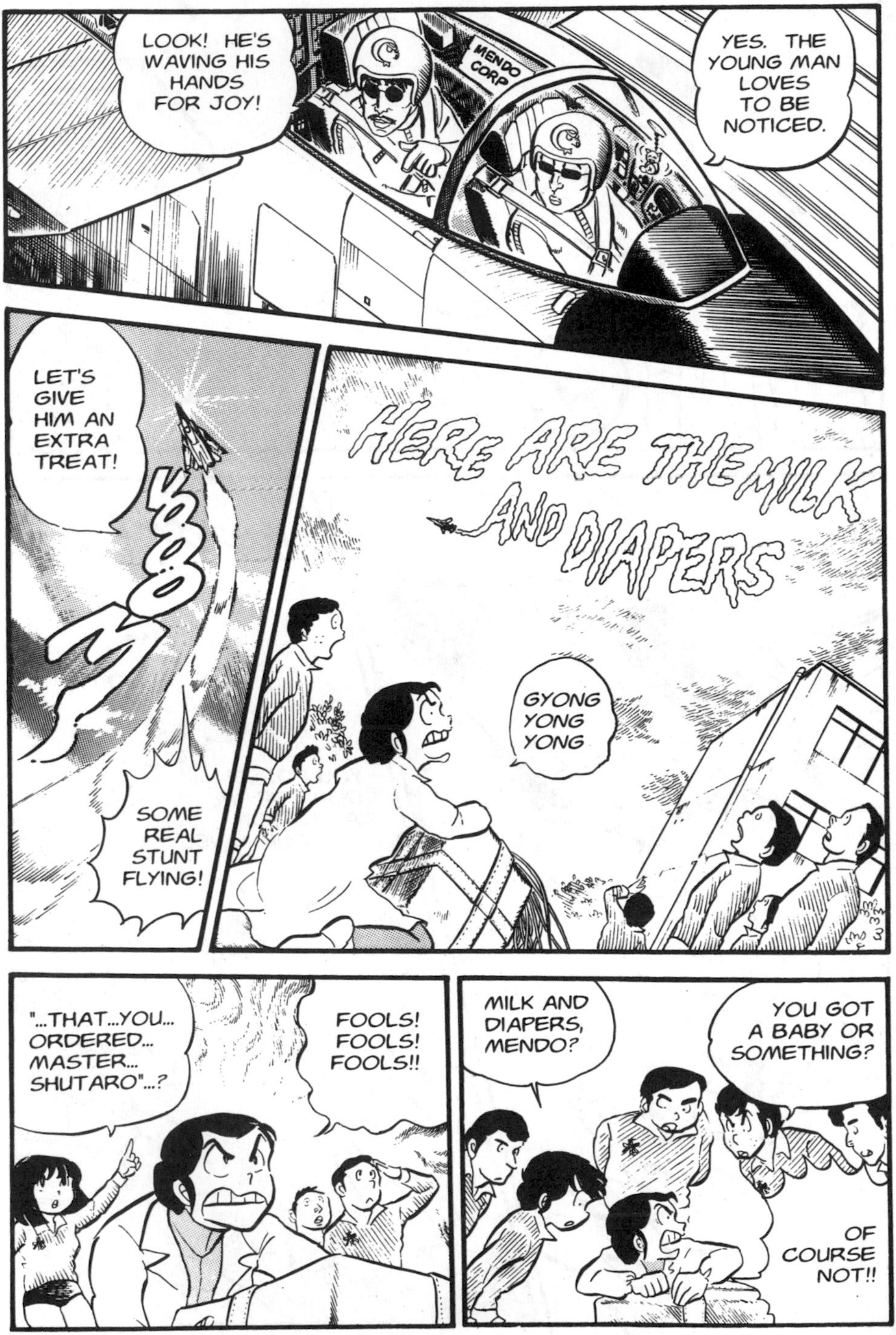

LOOK! HE'S WAVING HIS HANDS FOR JOY!
MENDO CORP
YES. THE YOUNG MAN LOVES TO BE NOTICED.
LET'S GIVE HIM AN EXTRA TREAT!
VOOOM
SOME REAL STUNT FLYING!
HERE ARE THE MILK AND DIAPERS
GYONG YONG YONG
"...THAT...YOU... ORDERED... MASTER... SHUTARO"...?
FOOLS! FOOLS! FOOLS!!
MILK AND DIAPERS, MENDO?
YOU GOT A BABY OR SOMETHING?
OF COURSE NOT!!

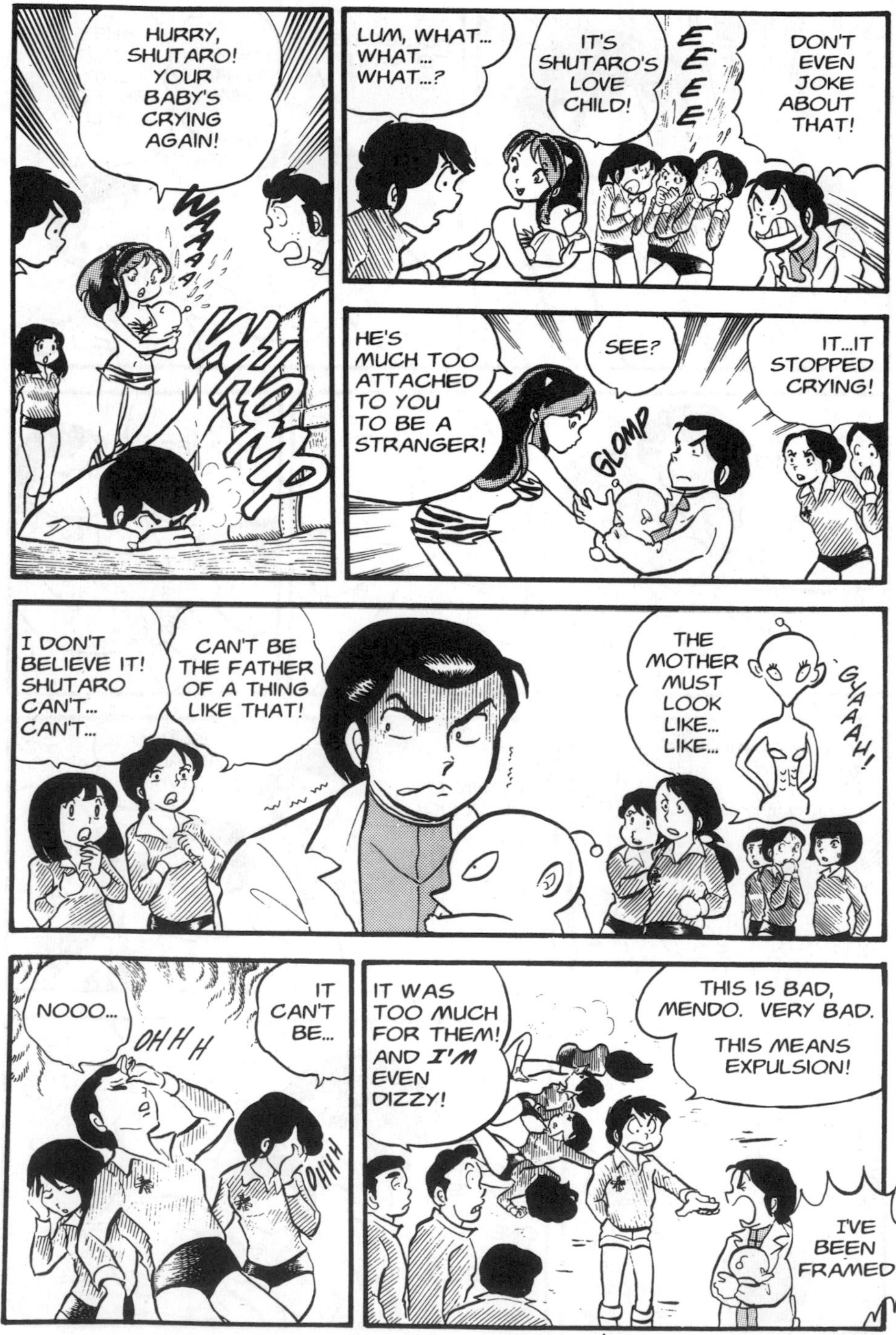
HURRY, SHUTARO! YOUR BABY'S CRYING AGAIN!
WAAAAA
WHOMP
LUM, WHAT... WHAT... WHAT...?
IT'S SHUTARO'S LOVE CHILD!
EEEE
DON'T EVEN JOKE ABOUT THAT!
HE'S MUCH TOO ATTACHED TO YOU TO BE A STRANGER!
SEE?
GLOMP
IT...IT STOPPED CRYING!
I DON'T BELIEVE IT! SHUTARO CAN'T... CAN'T...
CAN'T BE THE FATHER OF A THING LIKE THAT!
THE MOTHER MUST LOOK LIKE... LIKE...
GYAAAH!
NOOO...
OHHH
IT CAN'T BE...
OHHH
IT WAS TOO MUCH FOR THEM! AND *I'M* EVEN DIZZY!
THIS IS BAD, MENDO. VERY BAD.
THIS MEANS EXPULSION!
I'VE BEEN FRAMED!

EH?!

BABU.

HE SEEMS TO WANT YOU!

HERE! TAKE HIM!

HE'S NOT MY RESPONSIBILITY!

HEY! WHY DON'T YOU TEACH YOUR KID NOT TO--

IT ISN'T MY KID!

BABU.

THAT PACIFIER I FOUND!

PORP

AT LAST! I'VE RECOVERED MY TRANSLATOR!

GYAH! A FREAK!

YOW!

IT TALKS LIKE A GROWN-UP!

I AM A GROWN-UP, YOU CLOD!

IS THIS AN ALIEN, LUM?

IT'S NEW TO ME!

IF YOU'RE AN ALIEN, ACT LIKE ONE! GO AFTER MOROBOSHI!

NICE TRY, JERK!

YOU ARE THE ONLY ONE WHO CAN SERVE ME!

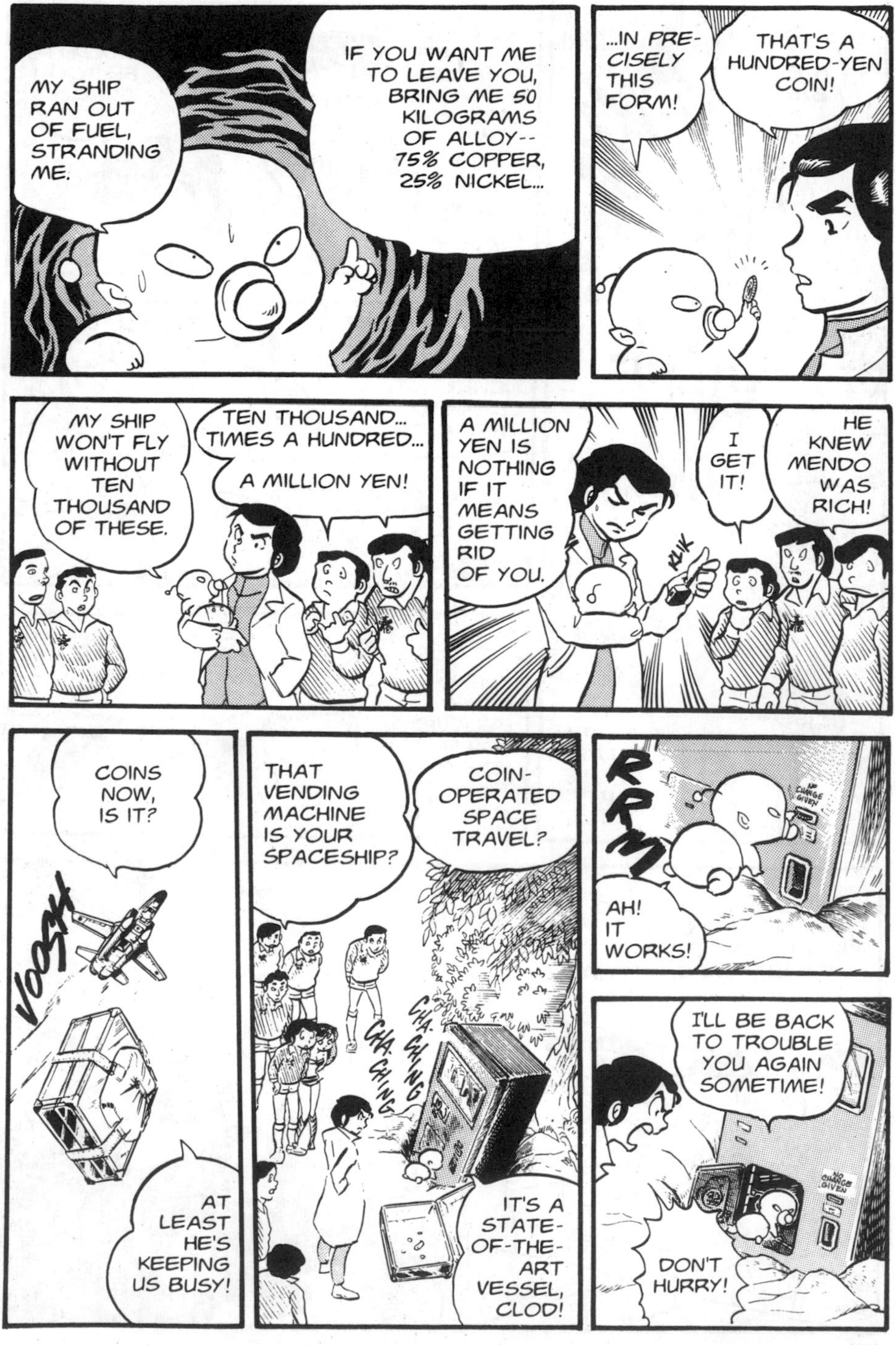
MY SHIP RAN OUT OF FUEL, STRANDING ME.
IF YOU WANT ME TO LEAVE YOU, BRING ME 50 KILOGRAMS OF ALLOY-- 75% COPPER, 25% NICKEL...
THAT'S A HUNDRED-YEN COIN!
...IN PRECISELY THIS FORM!
MY SHIP WON'T FLY WITHOUT TEN THOUSAND OF THESE.
TEN THOUSAND... TIMES A HUNDRED... A MILLION YEN!
A MILLION YEN IS NOTHING IF IT MEANS GETTING RID OF YOU.
KLIK
I GET IT!
HE KNEW MENDO WAS RICH!
COINS NOW, IS IT?
VOOSH
AT LEAST HE'S KEEPING US BUSY!
THAT VENDING MACHINE IS YOUR SPACESHIP?
COIN-OPERATED SPACE TRAVEL?
CHA-CHING CHA-CHING
IT'S A STATE-OF-THE-ART VESSEL, CLOD!
RRM
AH! IT WORKS!
I'LL BE BACK TO TROUBLE YOU AGAIN SOMETIME!
DON'T HURRY!

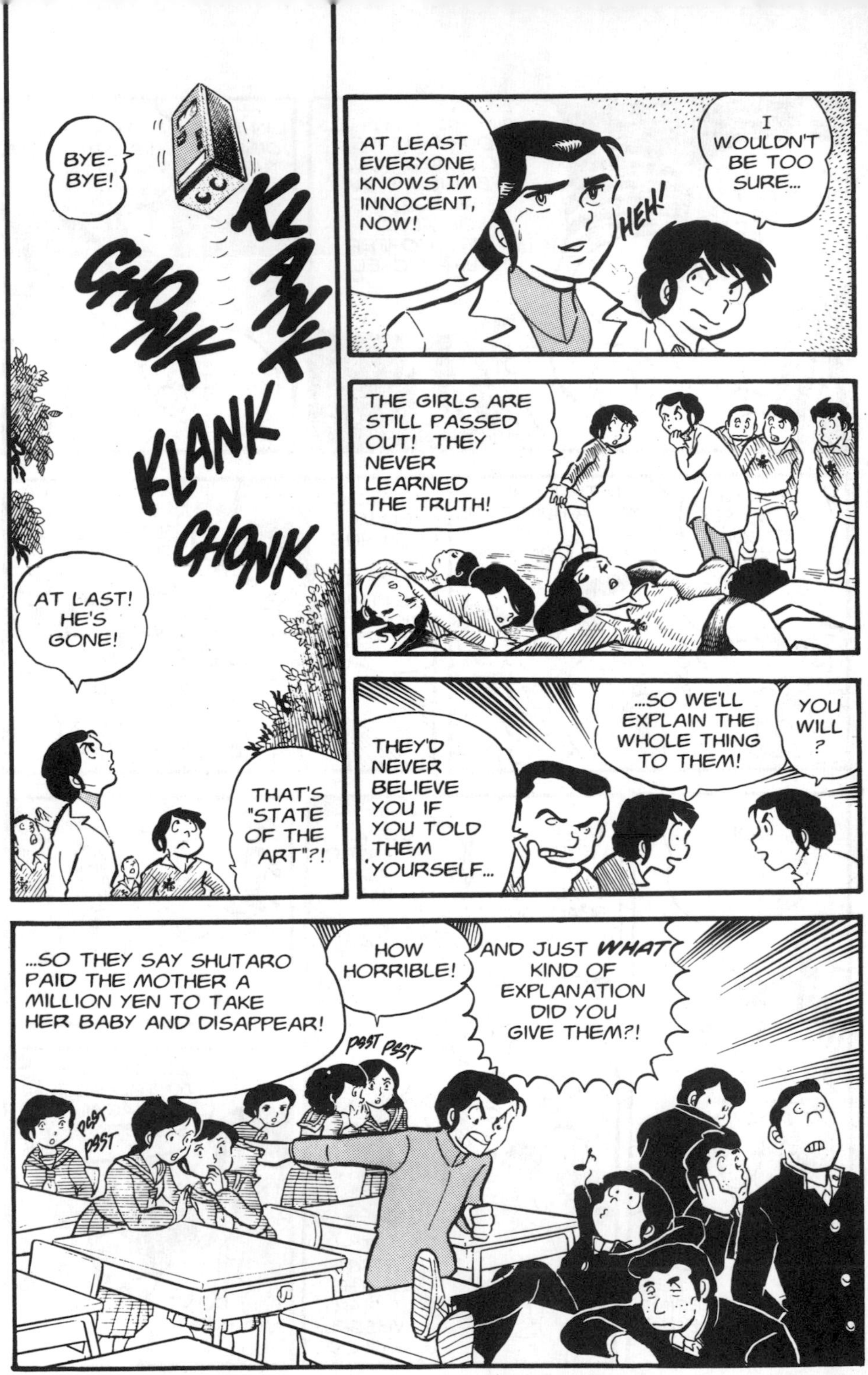
BYE-BYE!
KLANK
CHONK
KLANK
CHONK
AT LAST! HE'S GONE!
THAT'S "STATE OF THE ART"?!
AT LEAST EVERYONE KNOWS I'M INNOCENT, NOW!
HEH!
I WOULDN'T BE TOO SURE...
THE GIRLS ARE STILL PASSED OUT! THEY NEVER LEARNED THE TRUTH!
THEY'D NEVER BELIEVE YOU IF YOU TOLD THEM YOURSELF...
...SO WE'LL EXPLAIN THE WHOLE THING TO THEM!
YOU WILL ?
...SO THEY SAY SHUTARO PAID THE MOTHER A MILLION YEN TO TAKE HER BABY AND DISAPPEAR!
HOW HORRIBLE!
AND JUST WHAT KIND OF EXPLANATION DID YOU GIVE THEM?!
PSST PSST
PSST PSST

Part 8
A-Mazed!

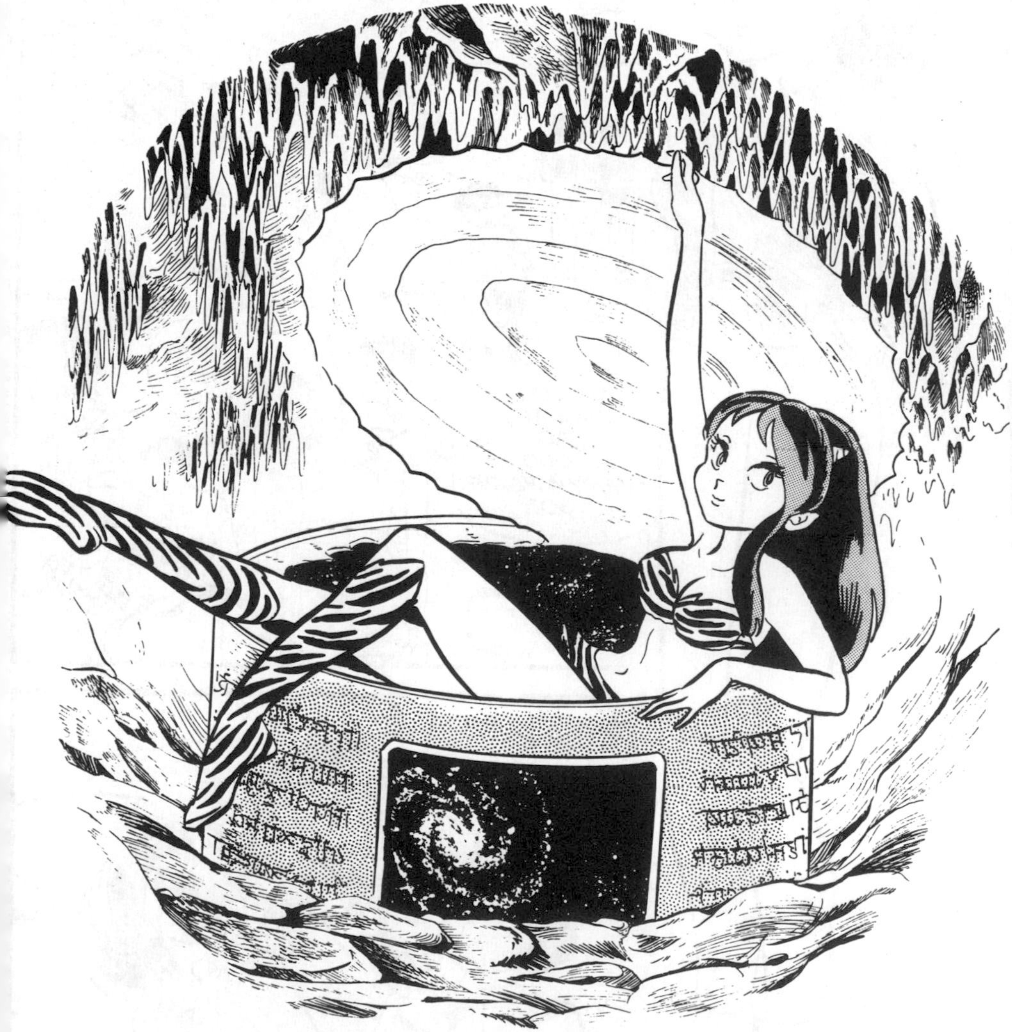

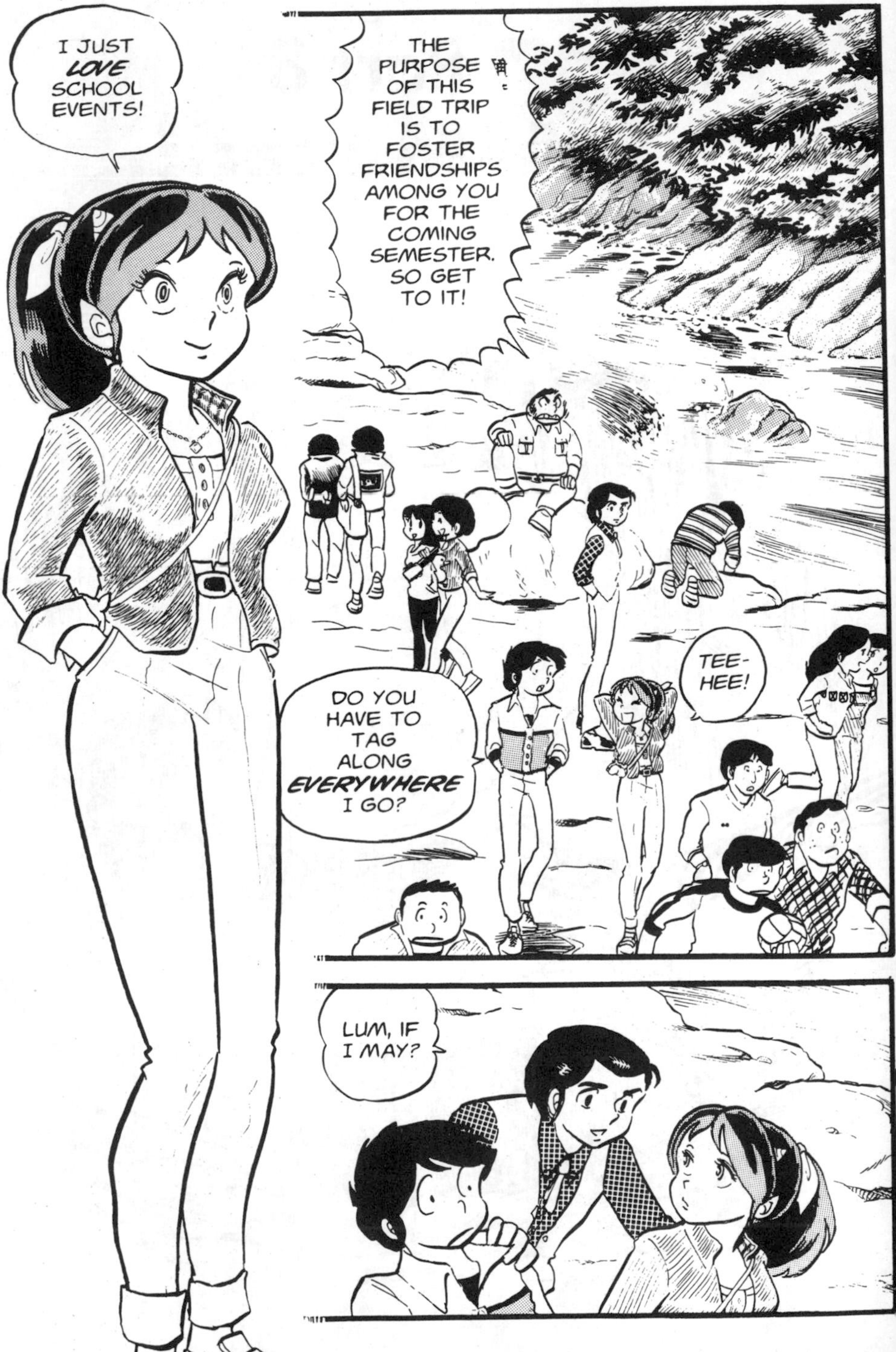
I JUST LOVE SCHOOL EVENTS!
THE PURPOSE OF THIS FIELD TRIP IS TO FOSTER FRIENDSHIPS AMONG YOU FOR THE COMING SEMESTER. SO GET TO IT!
DO YOU HAVE TO TAG ALONG EVERYWHERE I GO?
TEE-HEE!
LUM, IF I MAY?

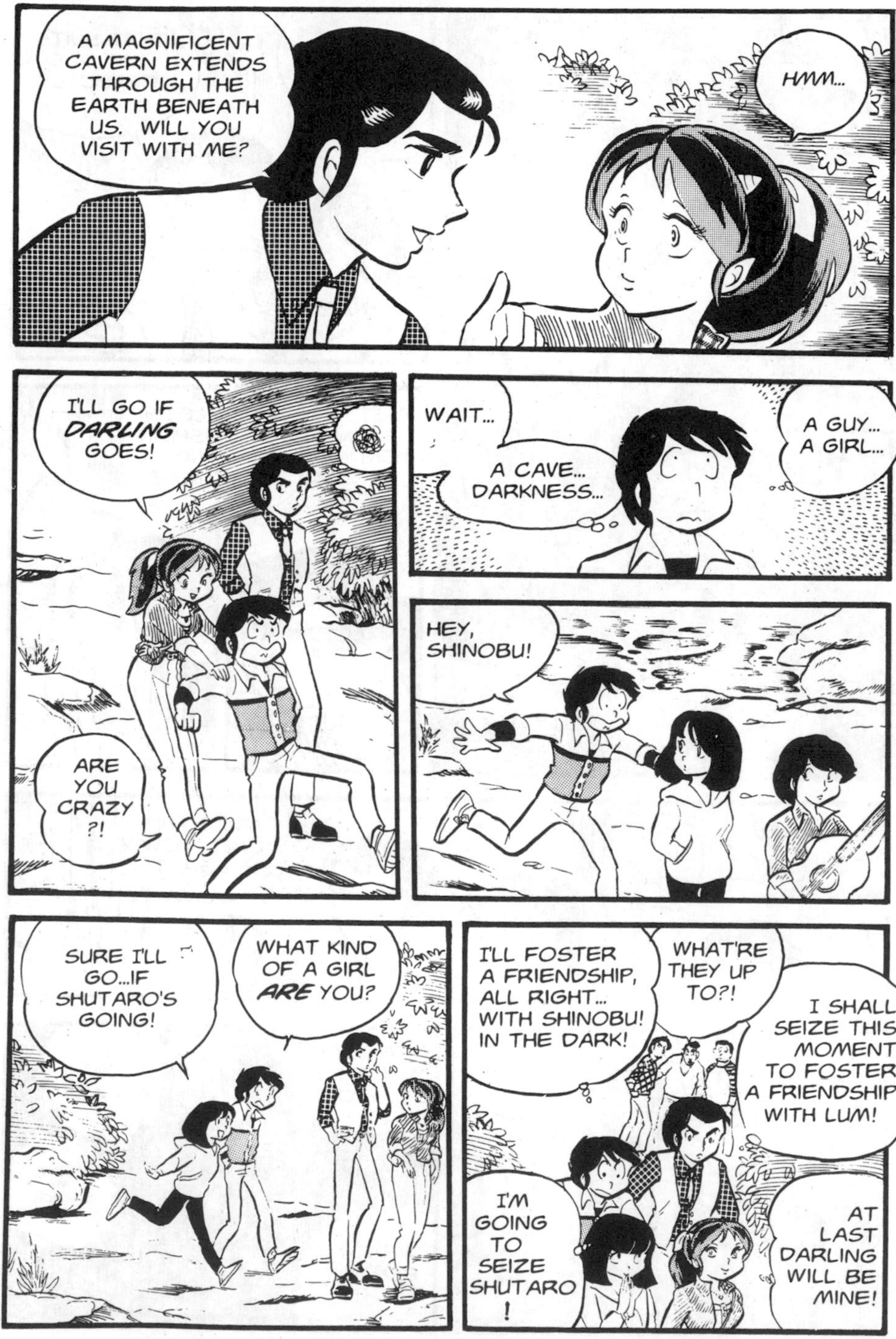
A MAGNIFICENT CAVERN EXTENDS THROUGH THE EARTH BENEATH US. WILL YOU VISIT WITH ME?
HMM...
I'LL GO IF DARLING GOES!
ARE YOU CRAZY?!
WAIT...
A CAVE... DARKNESS...
A GUY... A GIRL...
HEY, SHINOBU!
SURE I'LL GO...IF SHUTARO'S GOING!
WHAT KIND OF A GIRL ARE YOU?
I'LL FOSTER A FRIENDSHIP, ALL RIGHT... WITH SHINOBU! IN THE DARK!
WHAT'RE THEY UP TO?!
I SHALL SEIZE THIS MOMENT TO FOSTER A FRIENDSHIP WITH LUM!
I'M GOING TO SEIZE SHUTARO!
AT LAST DARLING WILL BE MINE!

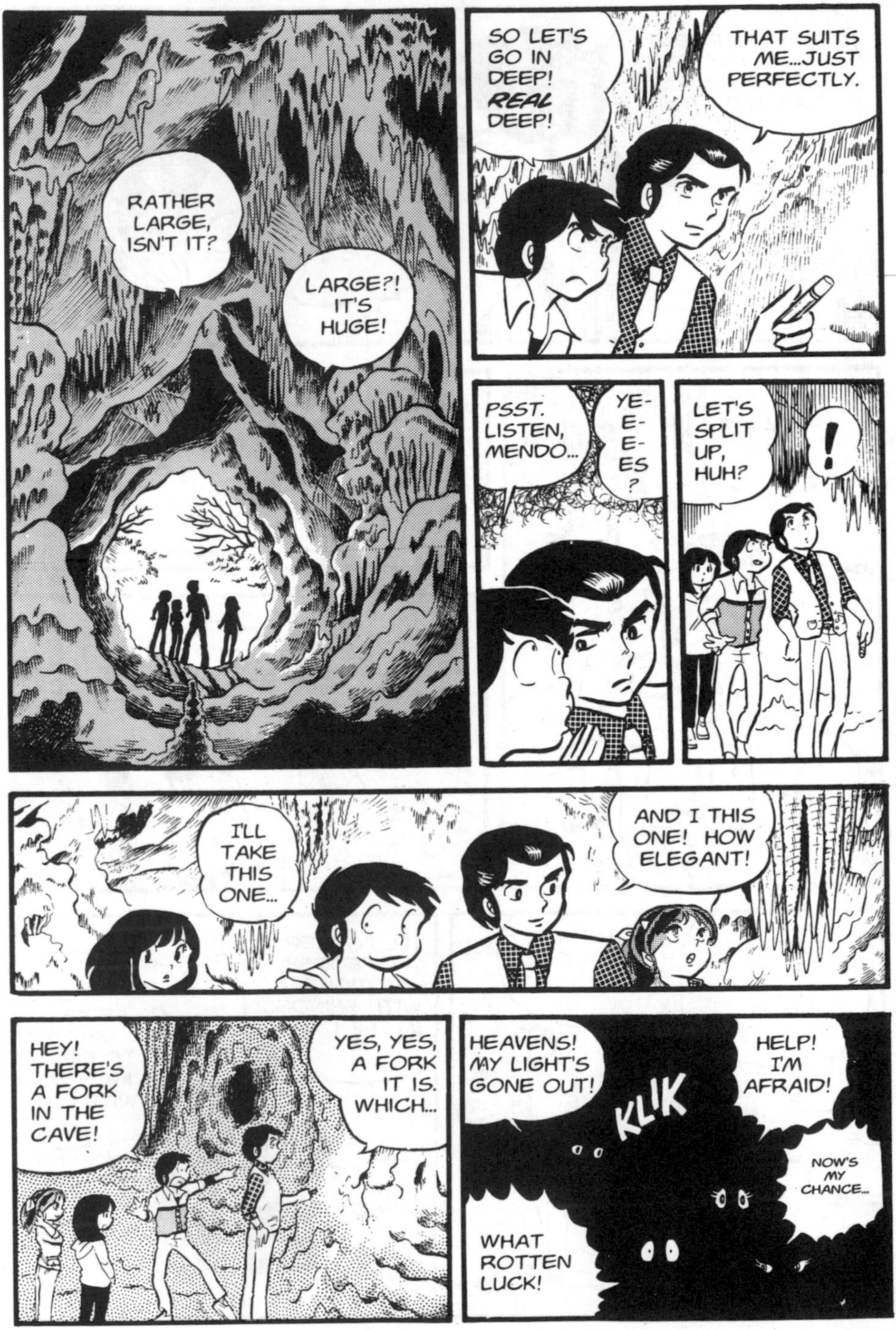
RATHER LARGE, ISN'T IT?
LARGE?! IT'S HUGE!
SO LET'S GO IN DEEP! REAL DEEP!
THAT SUITS ME...JUST PERFECTLY.
PSST. LISTEN, MENDO...
YE-E-E-ES?
LET'S SPLIT UP, HUH?
!
I'LL TAKE THIS ONE...
AND I THIS ONE! HOW ELEGANT!
HEY! THERE'S A FORK IN THE CAVE!
YES, YES, A FORK IT IS. WHICH...
HEAVENS! MY LIGHT'S GONE OUT!
KLIK
HELP! I'M AFRAID!
NOW'S MY CHANCE...
WHAT ROTTEN LUCK!

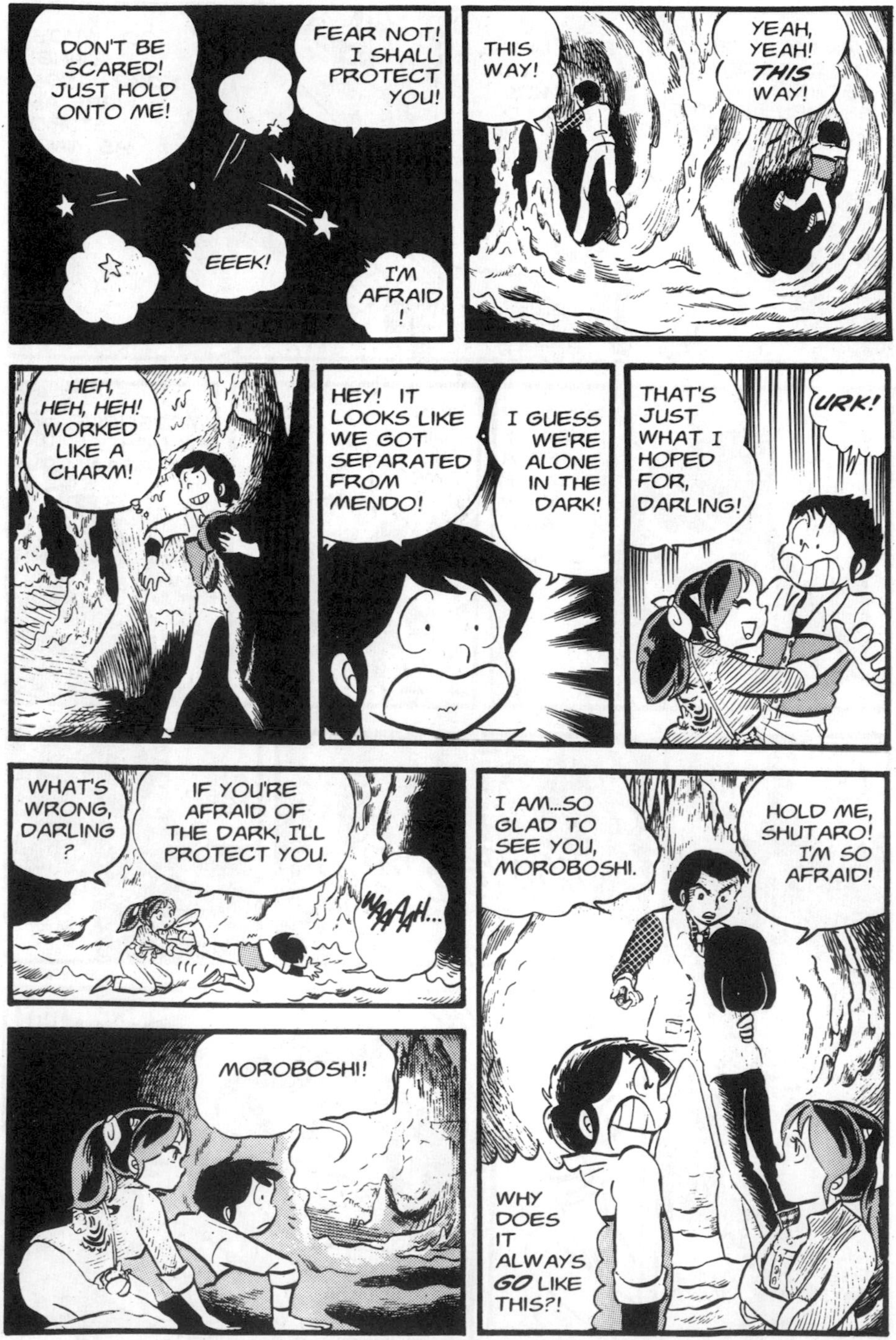
DON'T BE SCARED! JUST HOLD ONTO ME!
FEAR NOT! I SHALL PROTECT YOU!
EEEK!
I'M AFRAID!
THIS WAY!
YEAH, YEAH! THIS WAY!
HEH, HEH, HEH! WORKED LIKE A CHARM!
HEY! IT LOOKS LIKE WE GOT SEPARATED FROM MENDO!
I GUESS WE'RE ALONE IN THE DARK!
THAT'S JUST WHAT I HOPED FOR, DARLING!
URK!
WHAT'S WRONG, DARLING?
IF YOU'RE AFRAID OF THE DARK, I'LL PROTECT YOU.
WAAAAH...
MOROBOSHI!
I AM...SO GLAD TO SEE YOU, MOROBOSHI.
HOLD ME, SHUTARO! I'M SO AFRAID!
WHY DOES IT ALWAYS GO LIKE THIS?!

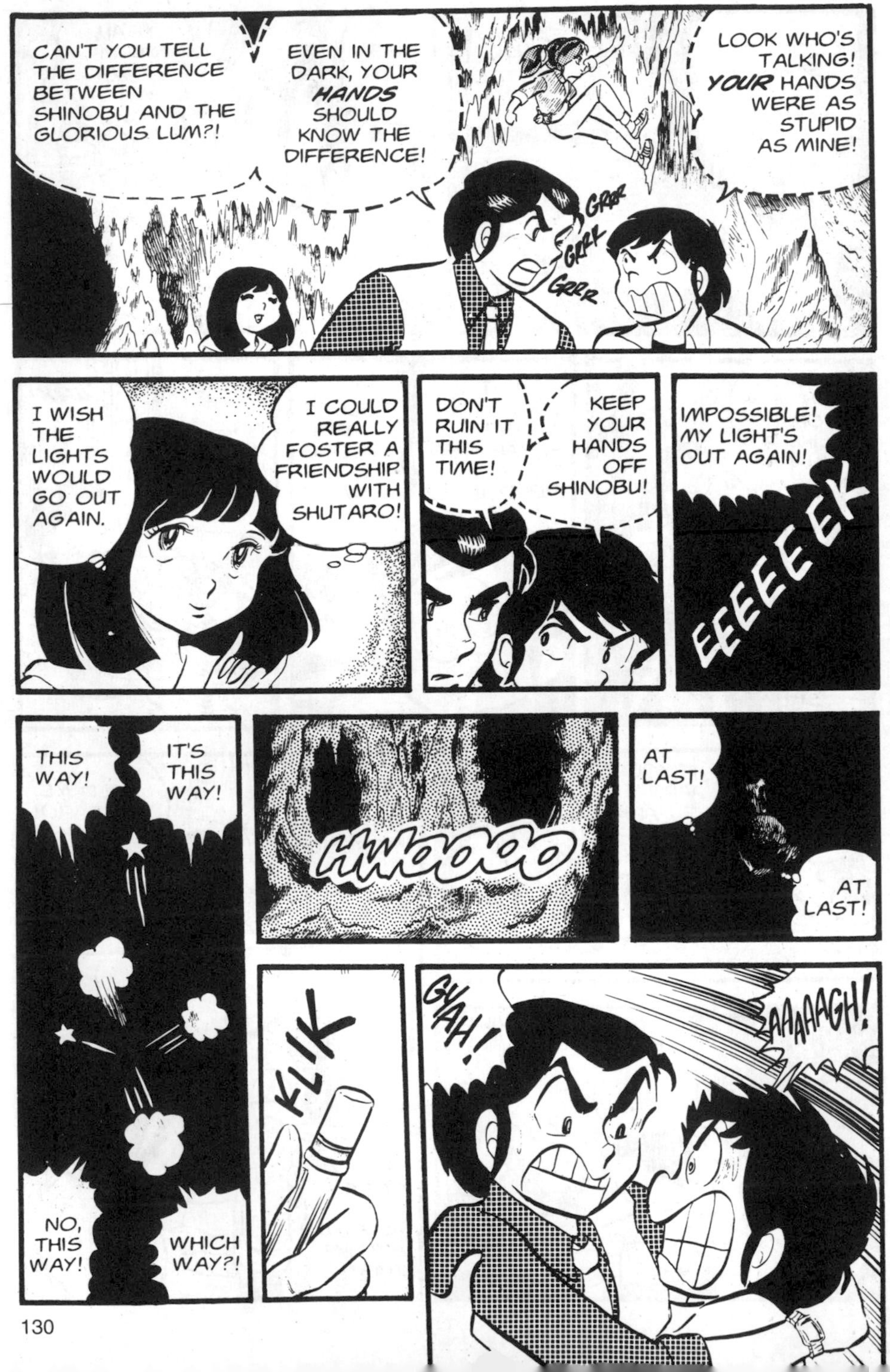
CAN'T YOU TELL THE DIFFERENCE BETWEEN SHINOBU AND THE GLORIOUS LUM?!
EVEN IN THE DARK, YOUR HANDS SHOULD KNOW THE DIFFERENCE!
LOOK WHO'S TALKING! YOUR HANDS WERE AS STUPID AS MINE!
GRRR
GRRR
GRRR
I WISH THE LIGHTS WOULD GO OUT AGAIN.
I COULD REALLY FOSTER A FRIENDSHIP WITH SHUTARO!
DON'T RUIN IT THIS TIME!
KEEP YOUR HANDS OFF SHINOBU!
IMPOSSIBLE! MY LIGHT'S OUT AGAIN!
EEEEEEK
THIS WAY!
IT'S THIS WAY!
NO, THIS WAY!
WHICH WAY?!
HWOOOOO
AT LAST!
AT LAST!
KLIK
GYAH!
AAAAAGH!

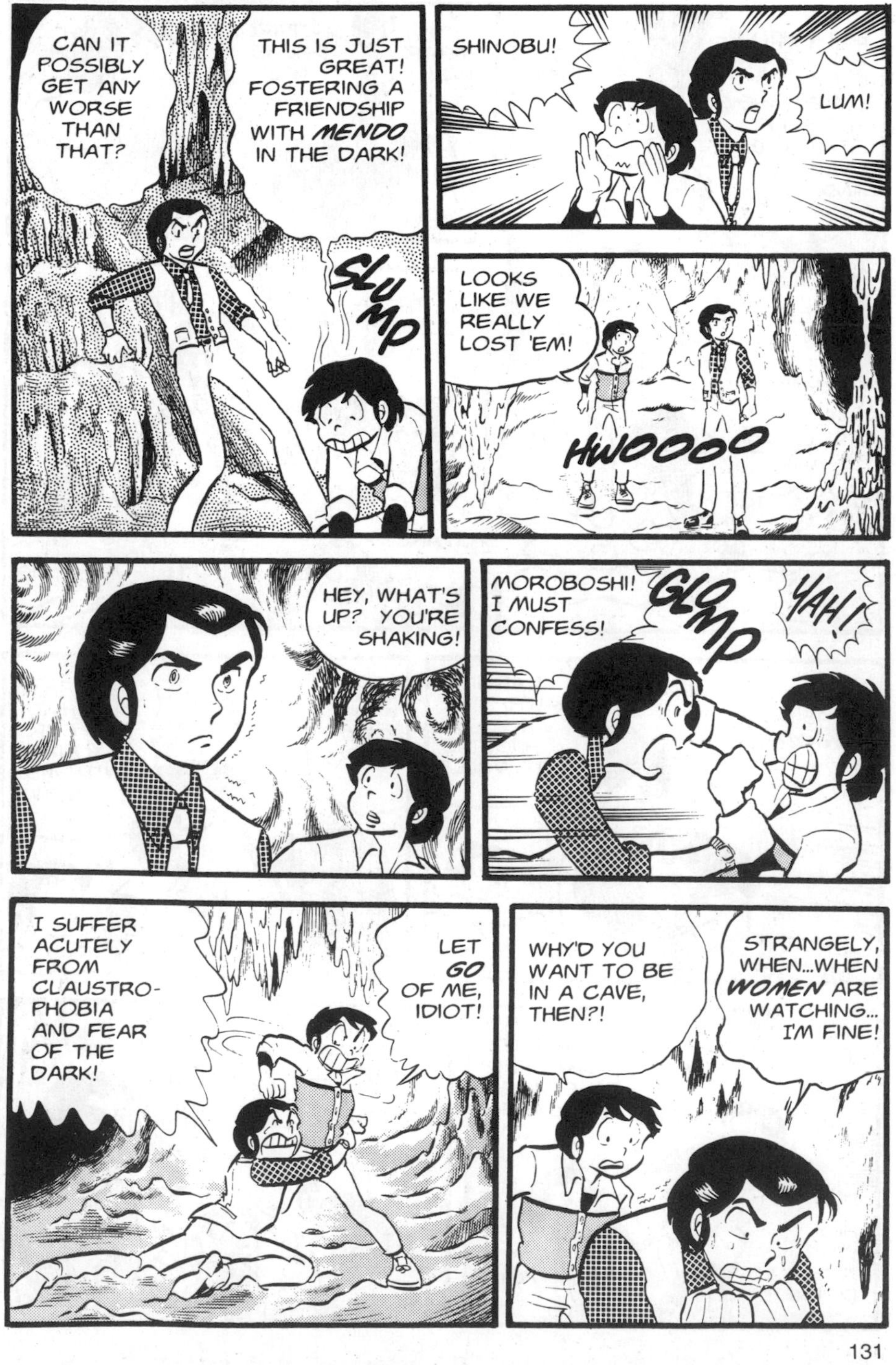
CAN IT POSSIBLY GET ANY WORSE THAN THAT?
THIS IS JUST GREAT! FOSTERING A FRIENDSHIP WITH *MENDO* IN THE DARK!
SLUMP
SHINOBU!
LUM!
LOOKS LIKE WE REALLY LOST 'EM!
HWOOOOO
HEY, WHAT'S UP? YOU'RE SHAKING!
MOROBOSHI! I MUST CONFESS!
GLOMP
YAH!
I SUFFER ACUTELY FROM CLAUSTRO-PHOBIA AND FEAR OF THE DARK!
LET *GO* OF ME, IDIOT!
WHY'D YOU WANT TO BE IN A CAVE, THEN?!
STRANGELY, WHEN...WHEN *WOMEN* ARE WATCHING... I'M FINE!

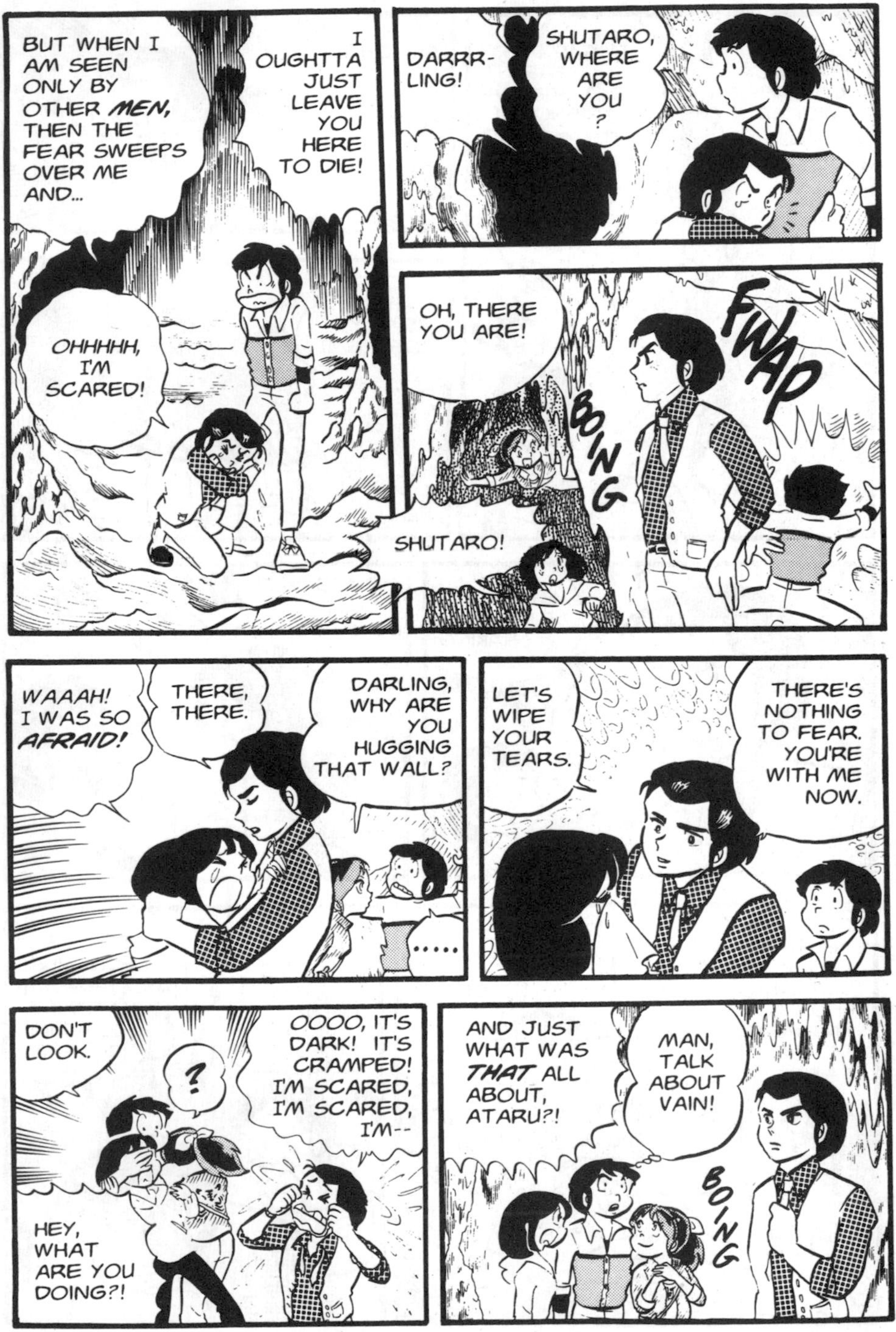
BUT WHEN I AM SEEN ONLY BY OTHER *MEN*, THEN THE FEAR SWEEPS OVER ME AND...
I OUGHTTA JUST LEAVE YOU HERE TO DIE!
OHHHHH, I'M SCARED!
DARRR-LING!
SHUTARO, WHERE ARE YOU?
OH, THERE YOU ARE!
FWAP
BOING
SHUTARO!
WAAAH! I WAS SO *AFRAID!*
THERE, THERE.
DARLING, WHY ARE YOU HUGGING THAT WALL?
.....
LET'S WIPE YOUR TEARS.
THERE'S NOTHING TO FEAR. YOU'RE WITH ME NOW.
DON'T LOOK.
?
OOOO, IT'S DARK! IT'S CRAMPED! I'M SCARED, I'M SCARED, I'M--
HEY, WHAT ARE YOU DOING?!
AND JUST WHAT WAS *THAT* ALL ABOUT, ATARU?!
MAN, TALK ABOUT VAIN!
BOING

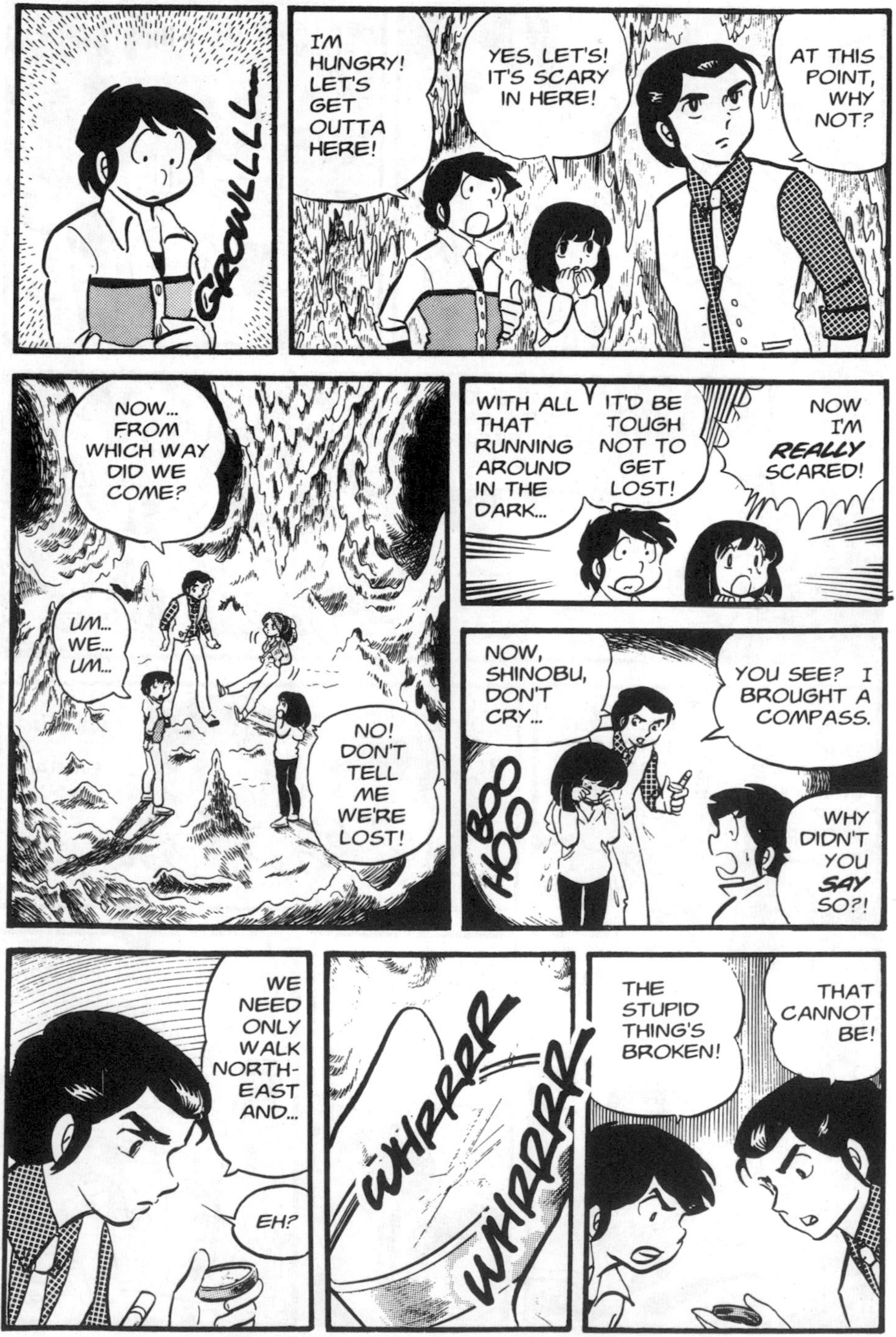
GROWLLLL...
I'M HUNGRY! LET'S GET OUTTA HERE!
YES, LET'S! IT'S SCARY IN HERE!
AT THIS POINT, WHY NOT?
NOW... FROM WHICH WAY DID WE COME?
UM... WE... UM...
NO! DON'T TELL ME WE'RE LOST!
WITH ALL THAT RUNNING AROUND IN THE DARK...
IT'D BE TOUGH NOT TO GET LOST!
NOW I'M REALLY SCARED!
NOW, SHINOBU, DON'T CRY...
YOU SEE? I BROUGHT A COMPASS.
BOO HOO
WHY DIDN'T YOU SAY SO?!
WE NEED ONLY WALK NORTH-EAST AND...
EH?
WHRRRR
WHRRRR
THE STUPID THING'S BROKEN!
THAT CANNOT BE!

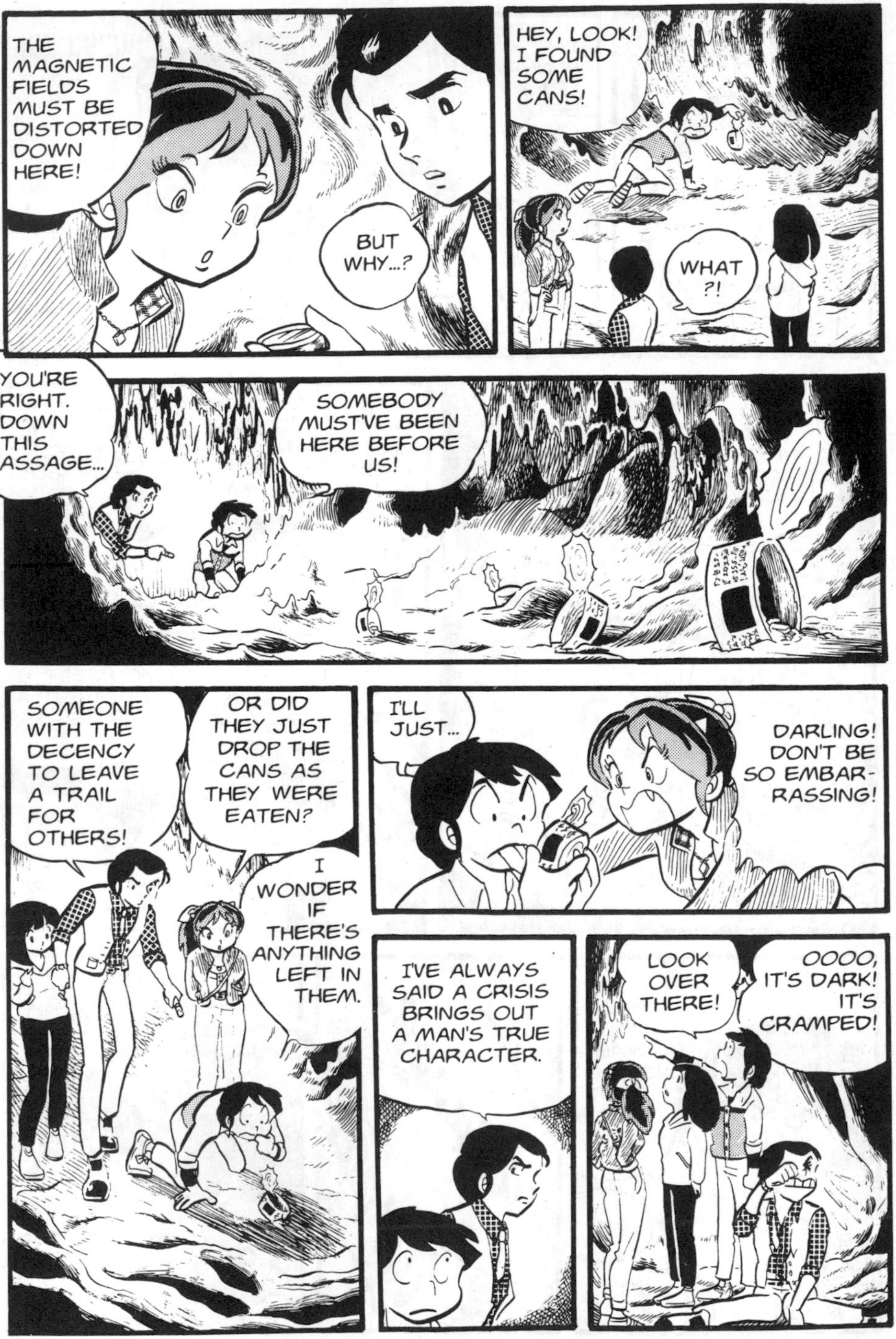
THE MAGNETIC FIELDS MUST BE DISTORTED DOWN HERE!
BUT WHY...?
HEY, LOOK! I FOUND SOME CANS!
WHAT ?!
YOU'RE RIGHT. DOWN THIS PASSAGE...
SOMEBODY MUST'VE BEEN HERE BEFORE US!
SOMEONE WITH THE DECENCY TO LEAVE A TRAIL FOR OTHERS!
OR DID THEY JUST DROP THE CANS AS THEY WERE EATEN?
I WONDER IF THERE'S ANYTHING LEFT IN THEM.
I'LL JUST...
DARLING! DON'T BE SO EMBAR-RASSING!
I'VE ALWAYS SAID A CRISIS BRINGS OUT A MAN'S TRUE CHARACTER.
LOOK OVER THERE!
OOOO, IT'S DARK! IT'S CRAMPED!

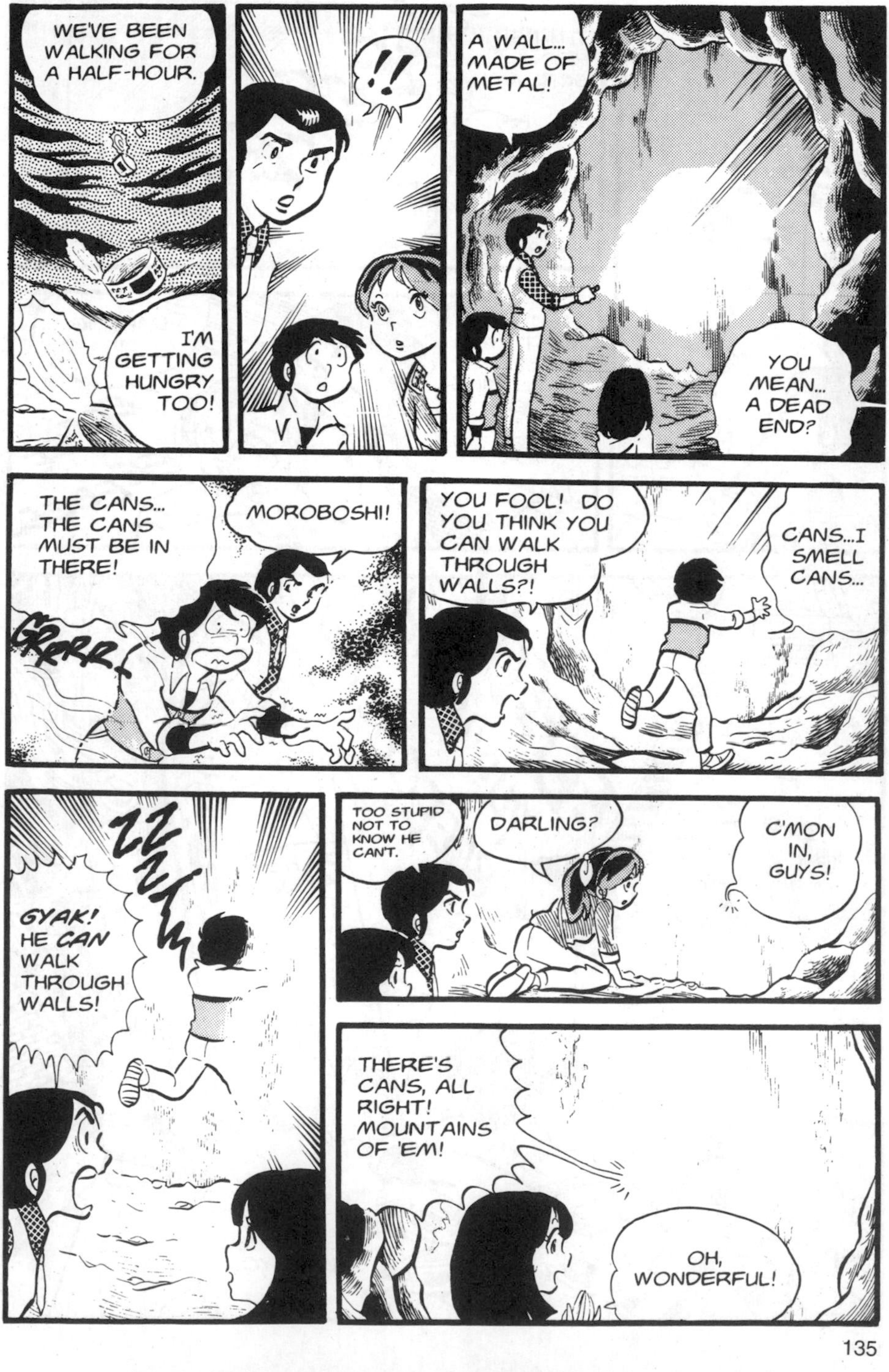
WE'VE BEEN WALKING FOR A HALF-HOUR.
I'M GETTING HUNGRY TOO!
!!
A WALL... MADE OF METAL!
YOU MEAN... A DEAD END?
THE CANS... THE CANS MUST BE IN THERE!
GRRRR
MOROBOSHI!
YOU FOOL! DO YOU THINK YOU CAN WALK THROUGH WALLS?!
CANS...I SMELL CANS...
ZZZZM
GYAK! HE *CAN* WALK THROUGH WALLS!
TOO STUPID NOT TO KNOW HE CAN'T.
DARLING?
C'MON IN, GUYS!
THERE'S CANS, ALL RIGHT! MOUNTAINS OF 'EM!
OH, WONDERFUL!

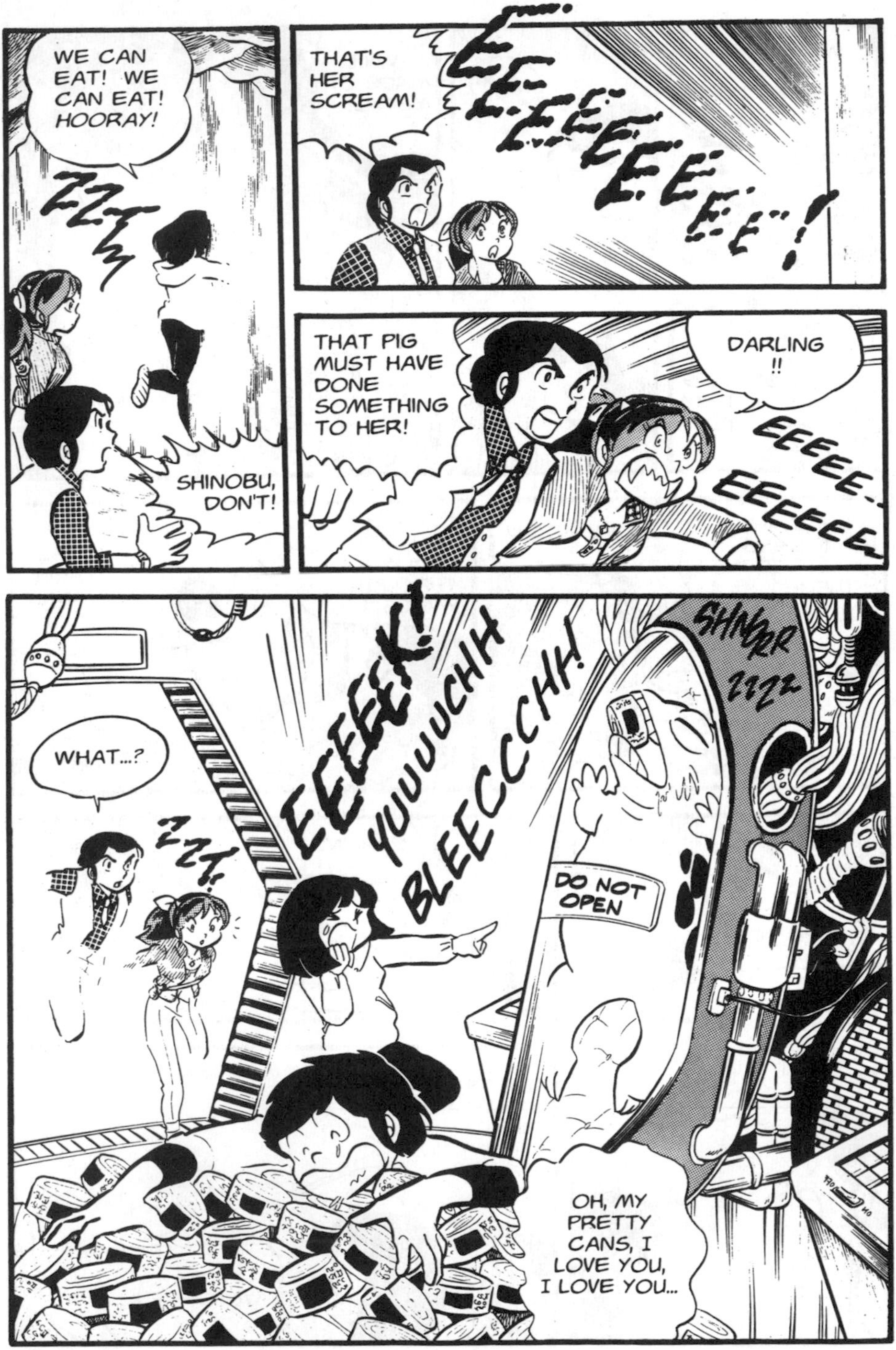

WE CAN EAT! WE CAN EAT! HOORAY!
ZZZ
SHINOBU, DON'T!
THAT'S HER SCREAM!
EEEEEEEEEE...!
THAT PIG MUST HAVE DONE SOMETHING TO HER!
DARLING !!
EEEEE... EEEEEE
WHAT...?
ZZZ
EEEEEK!
YUUUUUCHH
BLEECCCHH!
SHNORR ZZZZ
DO NOT OPEN
OH, MY PRETTY CANS, I LOVE YOU, I LOVE YOU...

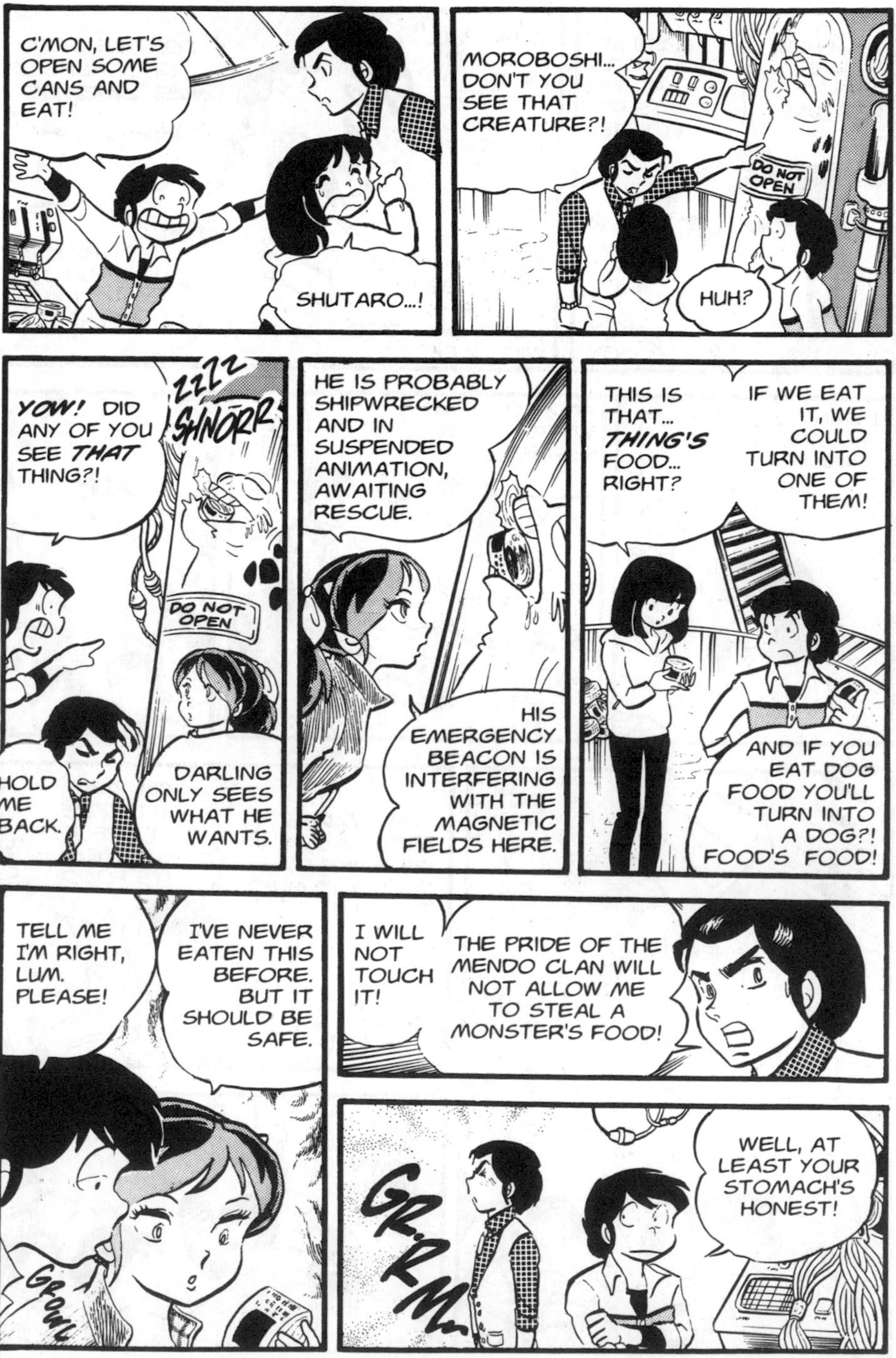

C'MON, LET'S OPEN SOME CANS AND EAT!
SHUTARO...!
MOROBOSHI... DON'T YOU SEE THAT CREATURE?!
DO NOT OPEN
HUH?
ZZZZ
SHNORR
YOW! DID ANY OF YOU SEE THAT THING?!
DO NOT OPEN
HOLD ME BACK.
DARLING ONLY SEES WHAT HE WANTS.
HE IS PROBABLY SHIPWRECKED AND IN SUSPENDED ANIMATION, AWAITING RESCUE.
HIS EMERGENCY BEACON IS INTERFERING WITH THE MAGNETIC FIELDS HERE.
THIS IS THAT... THING'S FOOD... RIGHT?
IF WE EAT IT, WE COULD TURN INTO ONE OF THEM!
AND IF YOU EAT DOG FOOD YOU'LL TURN INTO A DOG?! FOOD'S FOOD!
TELL ME I'M RIGHT, LUM. PLEASE!
I'VE NEVER EATEN THIS BEFORE. BUT IT SHOULD BE SAFE.
GROWL
I WILL NOT TOUCH IT!
THE PRIDE OF THE MENDO CLAN WILL NOT ALLOW ME TO STEAL A MONSTER'S FOOD!
GRRM
WELL, AT LEAST YOUR STOMACH'S HONEST!

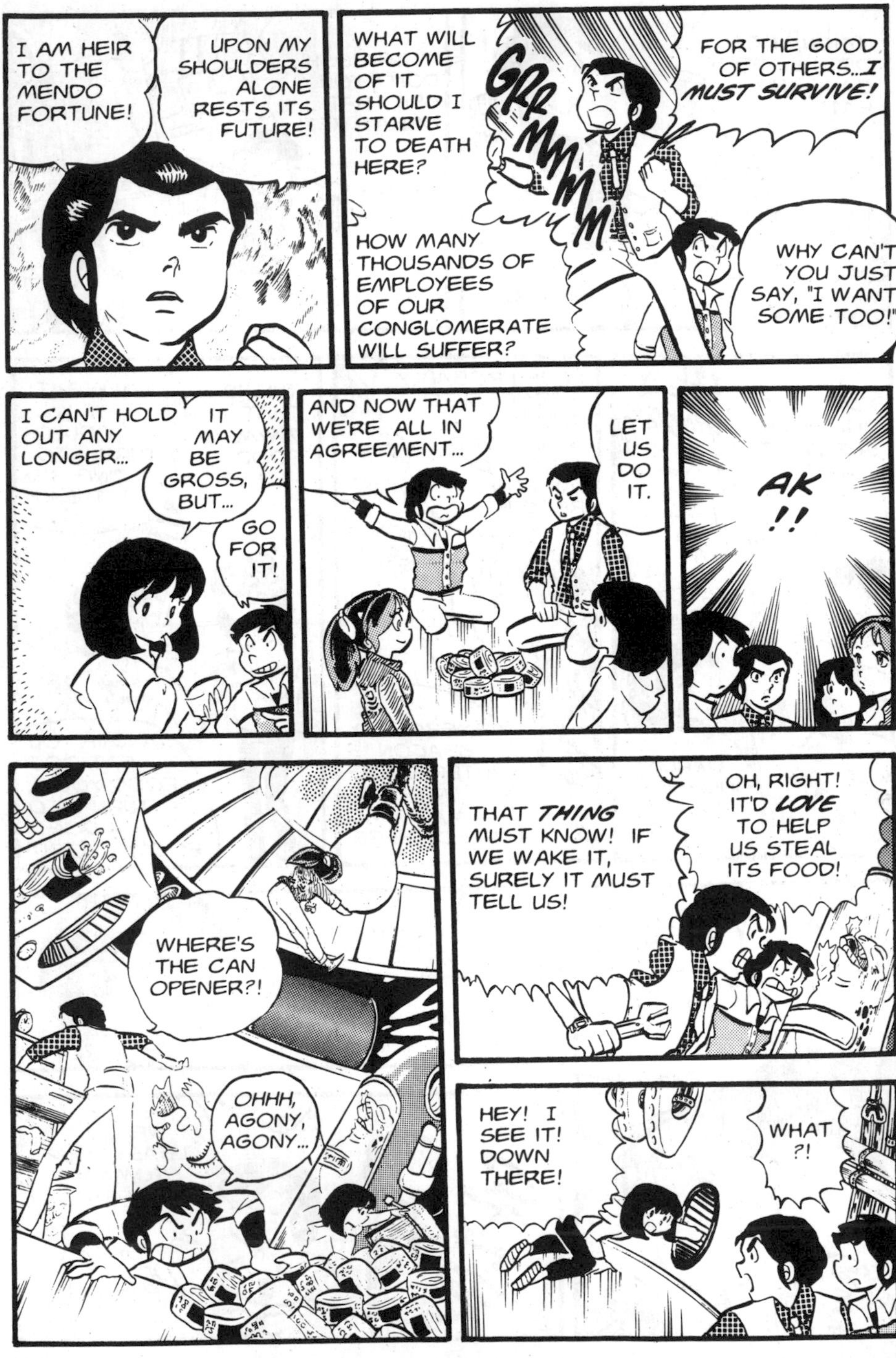

I AM HEIR TO THE MENDO FORTUNE!
UPON MY SHOULDERS ALONE RESTS ITS FUTURE!
WHAT WILL BECOME OF IT SHOULD I STARVE TO DEATH HERE?
HOW MANY THOUSANDS OF EMPLOYEES OF OUR CONGLOMERATE WILL SUFFER?
GRRMMMMM
FOR THE GOOD OF OTHERS...I MUST SURVIVE!
WHY CAN'T YOU JUST SAY, "I WANT SOME TOO!"
I CAN'T HOLD OUT ANY LONGER...
IT MAY BE GROSS, BUT...
GO FOR IT!
AND NOW THAT WE'RE ALL IN AGREEMENT...
LET US DO IT.
AK !!
WHERE'S THE CAN OPENER?!
OHHH, AGONY, AGONY...
THAT THING MUST KNOW! IF WE WAKE IT, SURELY IT MUST TELL US!
OH, RIGHT! IT'D LOVE TO HELP US STEAL ITS FOOD!
HEY! I SEE IT! DOWN THERE!
WHAT ?!

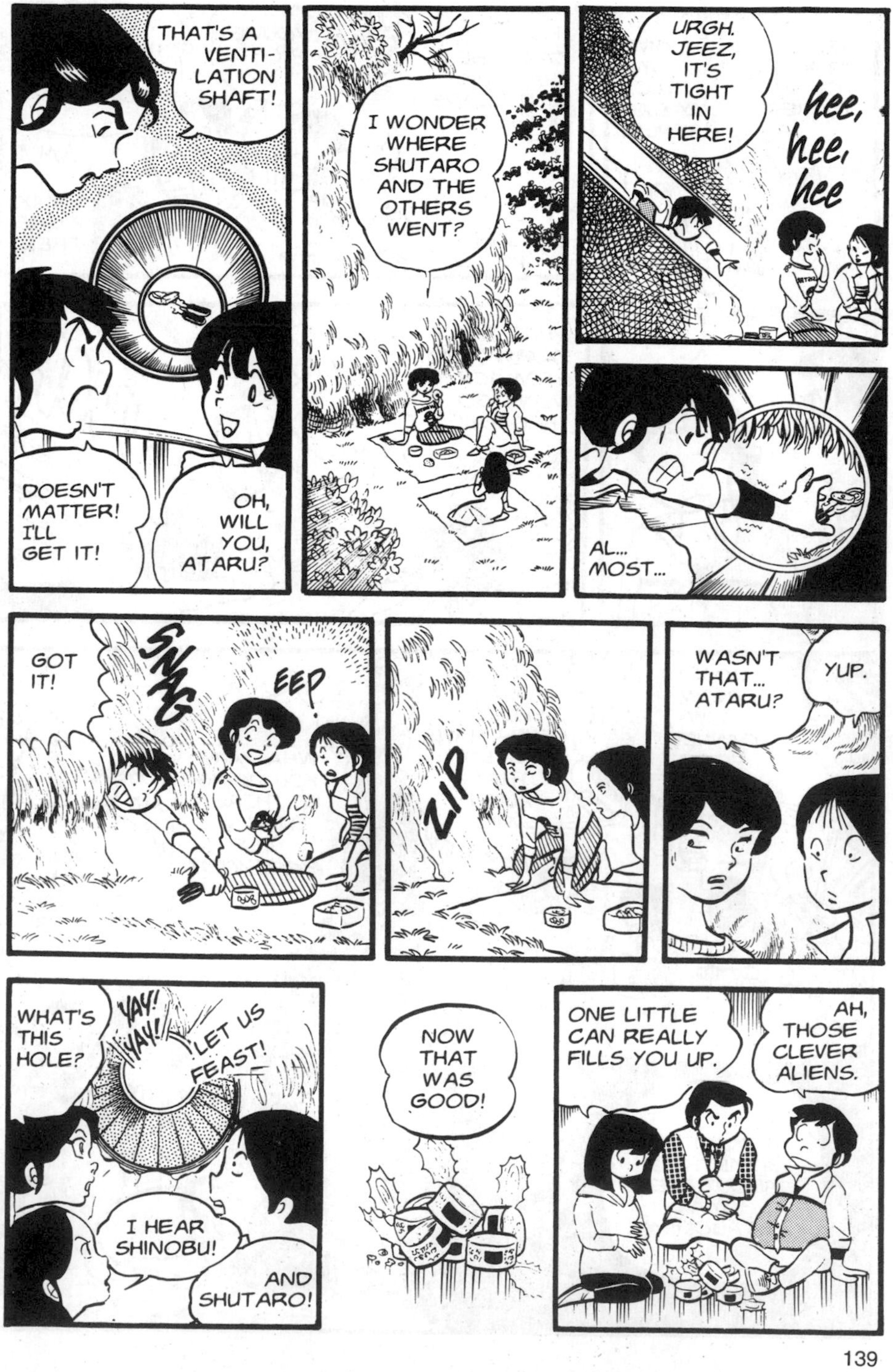
THAT'S A VENTI-LATION SHAFT!
DOESN'T MATTER! I'LL GET IT!
OH, WILL YOU, ATARU?
I WONDER WHERE SHUTARO AND THE OTHERS WENT?
URGH. JEEZ, IT'S TIGHT IN HERE!
hee, hee, hee
AL... MOST...
GOT IT!
SNAG
EEP!
ZIP
WASN'T THAT... ATARU?
YUP.
WHAT'S THIS HOLE?
YAY! YAY!
LET US FEAST!
I HEAR SHINOBU!
AND SHUTARO!
NOW THAT WAS GOOD!
ONE LITTLE CAN REALLY FILLS YOU UP.
AH, THOSE CLEVER ALIENS.

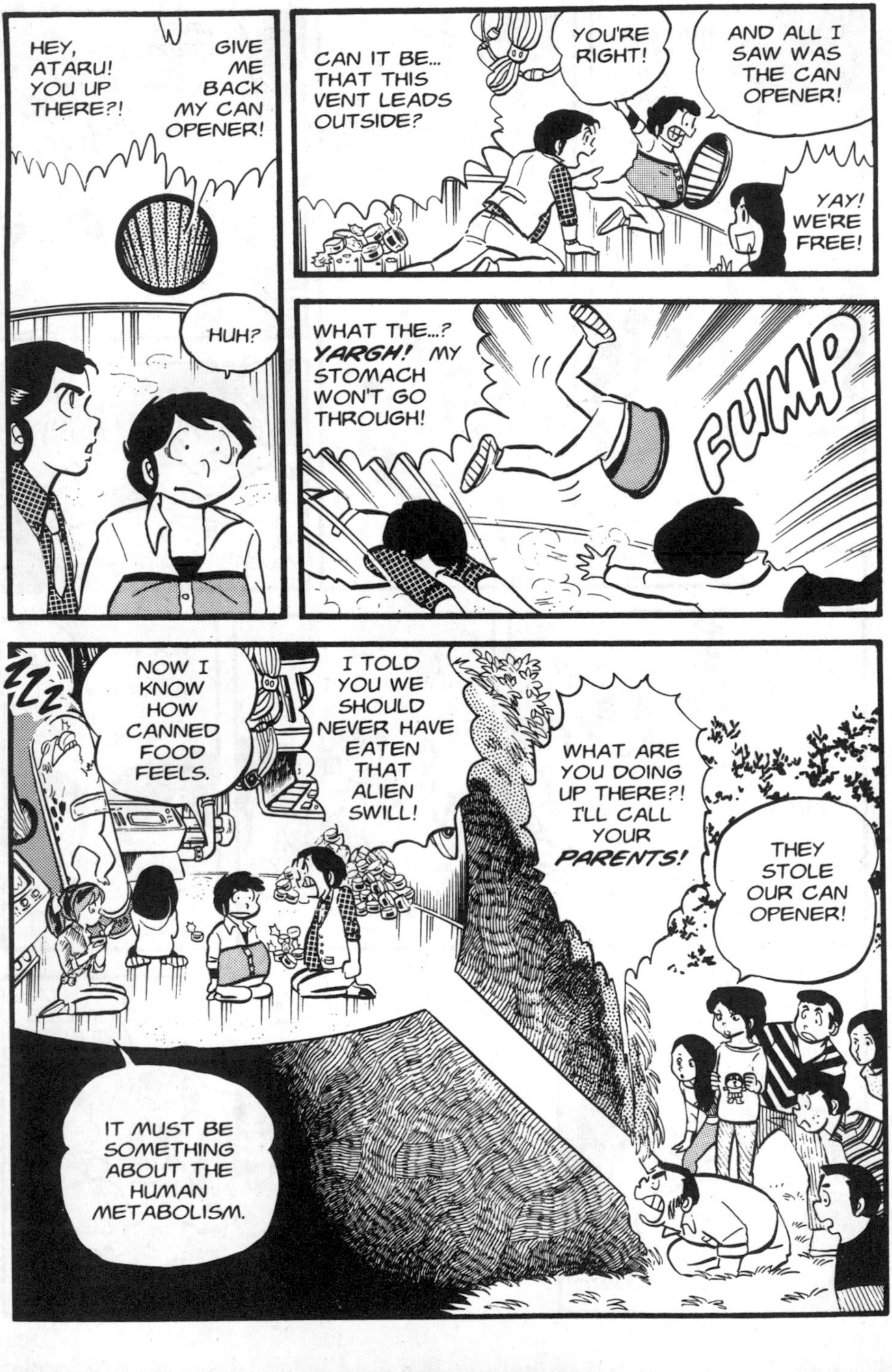
HEY, ATARU! YOU UP THERE?!
GIVE ME BACK MY CAN OPENER!
CAN IT BE... THAT THIS VENT LEADS OUTSIDE?
YOU'RE RIGHT!
AND ALL I SAW WAS THE CAN OPENER!
YAY! WE'RE FREE!
HUH?
WHAT THE...? YARGH! MY STOMACH WON'T GO THROUGH!
FUMP
ZZZ
NOW I KNOW HOW CANNED FOOD FEELS.
I TOLD YOU WE SHOULD NEVER HAVE EATEN THAT ALIEN SWILL!
WHAT ARE YOU DOING UP THERE?! I'LL CALL YOUR PARENTS!
THEY STOLE OUR CAN OPENER!
IT MUST BE SOMETHING ABOUT THE HUMAN METABOLISM.

Part 9 Waking to a Nightmare

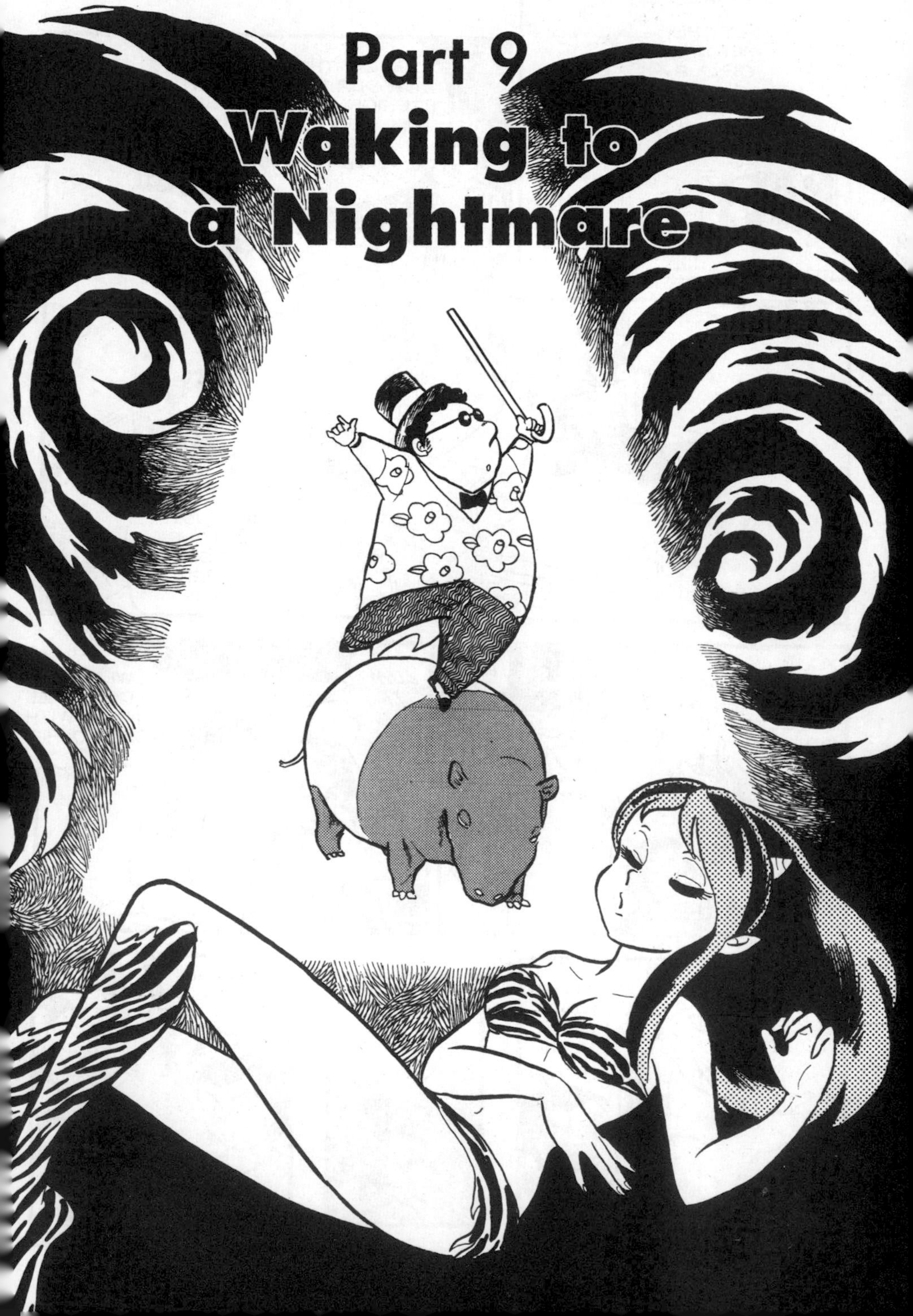

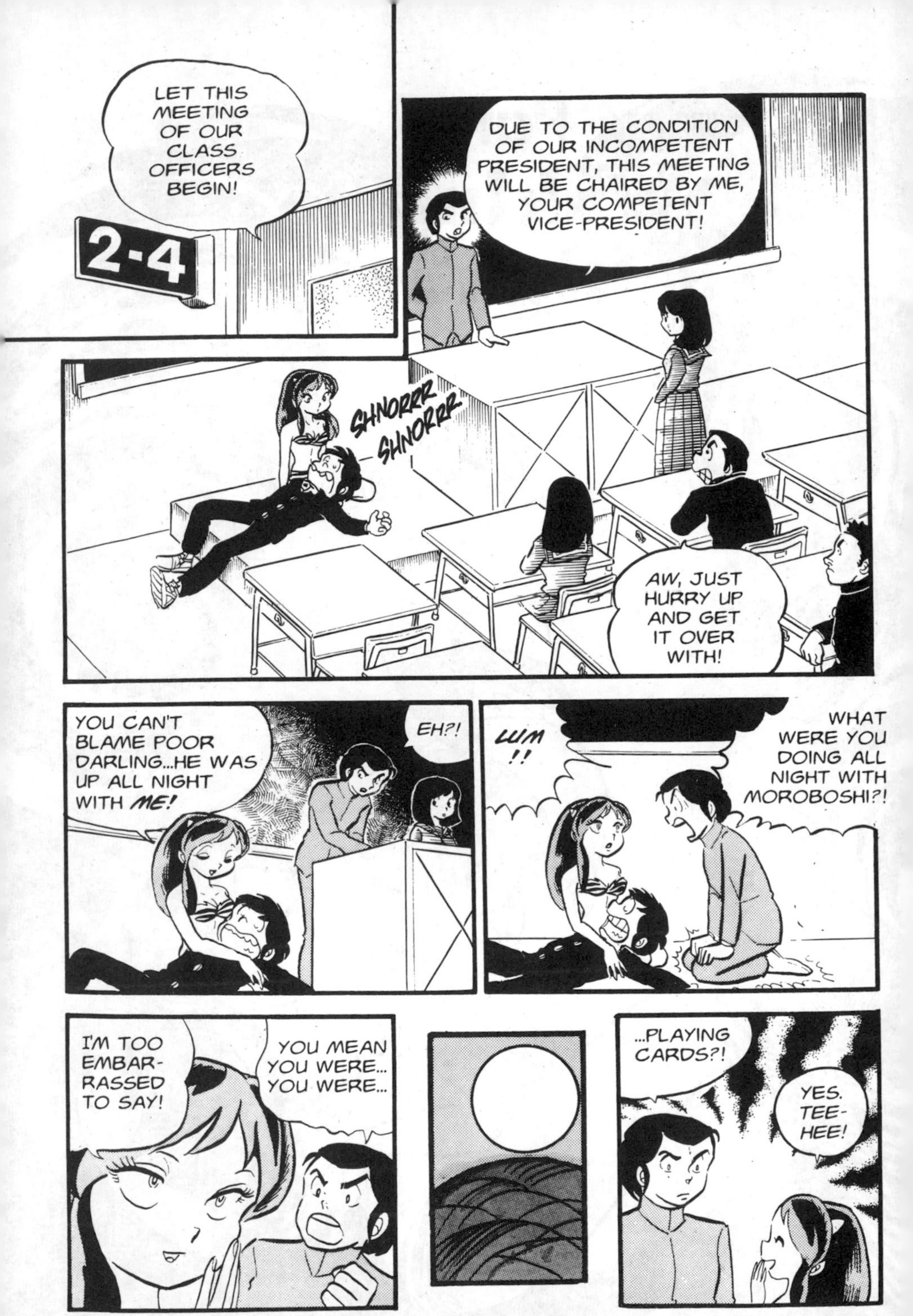
LET THIS MEETING OF OUR CLASS OFFICERS BEGIN!
2-4
DUE TO THE CONDITION OF OUR INCOMPETENT PRESIDENT, THIS MEETING WILL BE CHAIRED BY ME, YOUR COMPETENT VICE-PRESIDENT!
SHNORRR SHNORRR
AW, JUST HURRY UP AND GET IT OVER WITH!
YOU CAN'T BLAME POOR DARLING...HE WAS UP ALL NIGHT WITH ME!
EH?!
LUM !!
WHAT WERE YOU DOING ALL NIGHT WITH MOROBOSHI?!
I'M TOO EMBARRASSED TO SAY!
YOU MEAN YOU WERE... YOU WERE...
...PLAYING CARDS?!
YES. TEE-HEE!

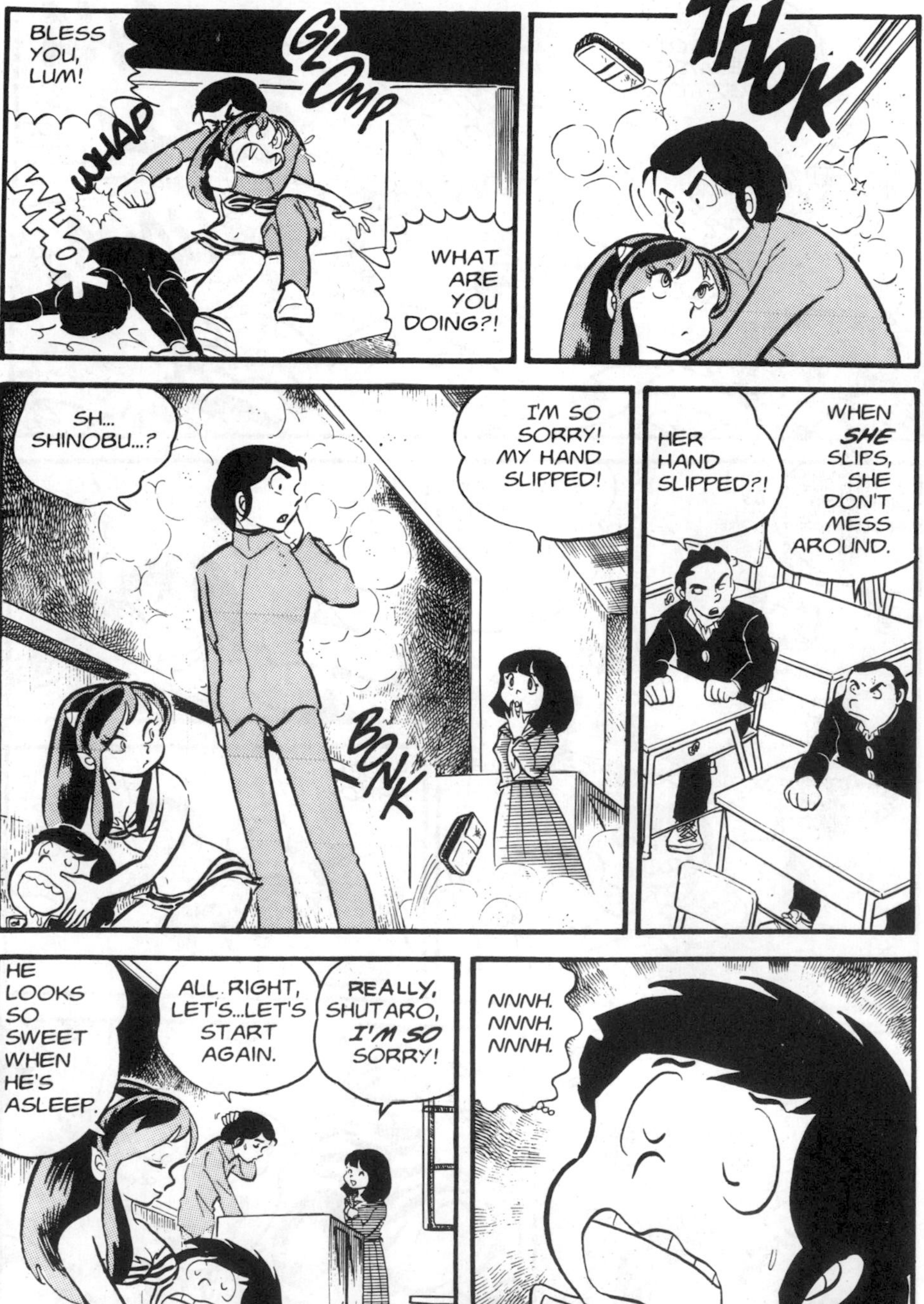

BLESS YOU, LUM!
GLOMP
WHAP
WHOK
WHAT ARE YOU DOING?!
THOK
SH... SHINOBU...?
I'M SO SORRY! MY HAND SLIPPED!
BONK
HER HAND SLIPPED?!
WHEN *SHE* SLIPS, SHE DON'T MESS AROUND.
HE LOOKS SO SWEET WHEN HE'S ASLEEP.
ALL RIGHT, LET'S...LET'S START AGAIN.
REALLY, SHUTARO, *I'M SO* SORRY!
NNNH. NNNH. NNNH.

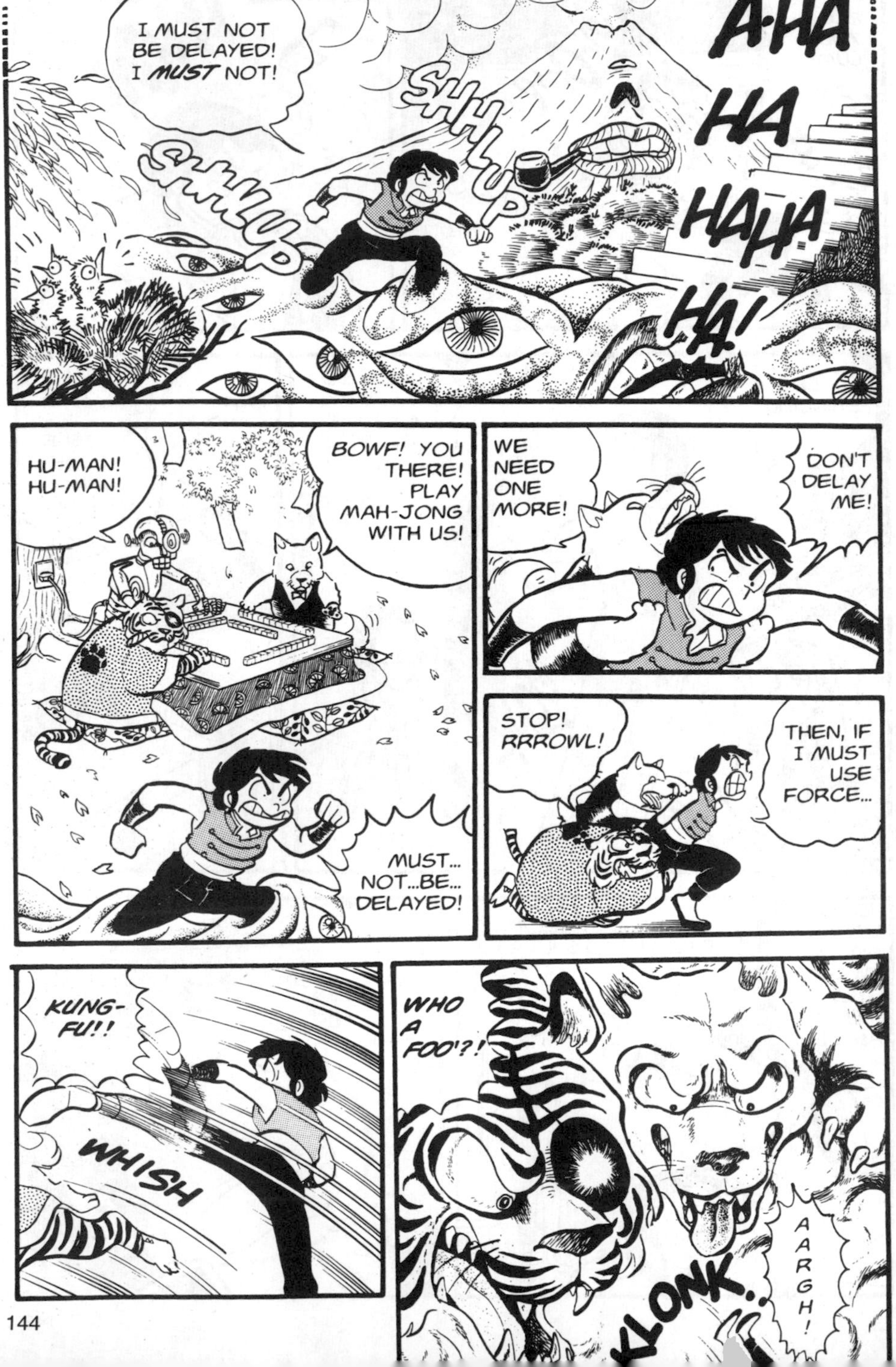

I MUST NOT BE DELAYED! I MUST NOT!
SHHLUP
SHHLUP
A-HA HA HAHA HA!
HU-MAN! HU-MAN!
BOWF! YOU THERE! PLAY MAH-JONG WITH US!
MUST... NOT...BE... DELAYED!
WE NEED ONE MORE!
DON'T DELAY ME!
STOP! RRROWL!
THEN, IF I MUST USE FORCE...
KUNG-FU!!
WHISH
WHO A FOO'?!
AARGH!
KLONK..

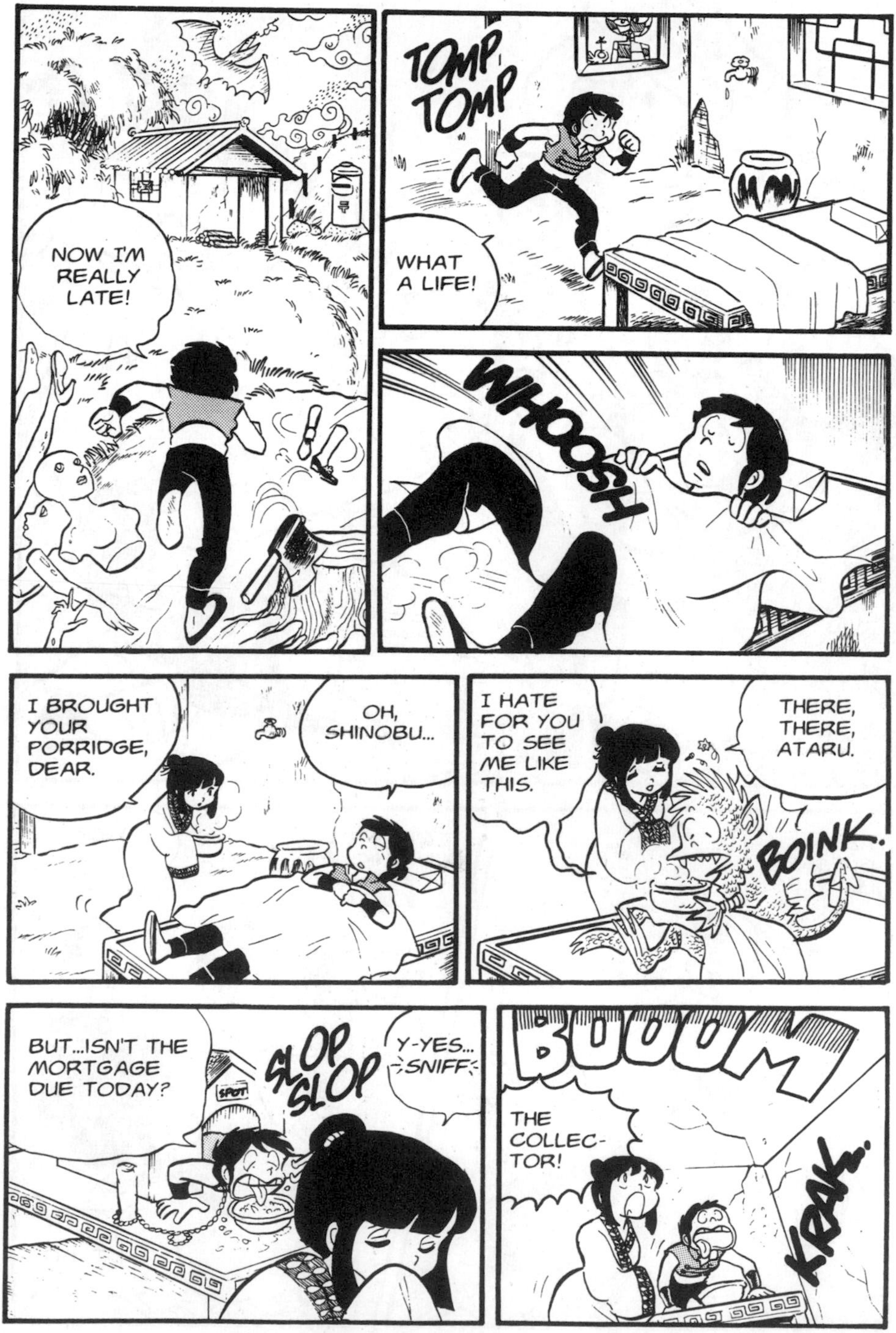
NOW I'M REALLY LATE!
TOMP TOMP
WHAT A LIFE!
WHOOSH
I BROUGHT YOUR PORRIDGE, DEAR.
OH, SHINOBU...
I HATE FOR YOU TO SEE ME LIKE THIS.
THERE, THERE, ATARU.
BOINK.
BUT...ISN'T THE MORTGAGE DUE TODAY?
SLOP SLOP
Y-YES... SNIFF
SPOT
BOOOM
THE COLLEC-TOR!
KRAK...

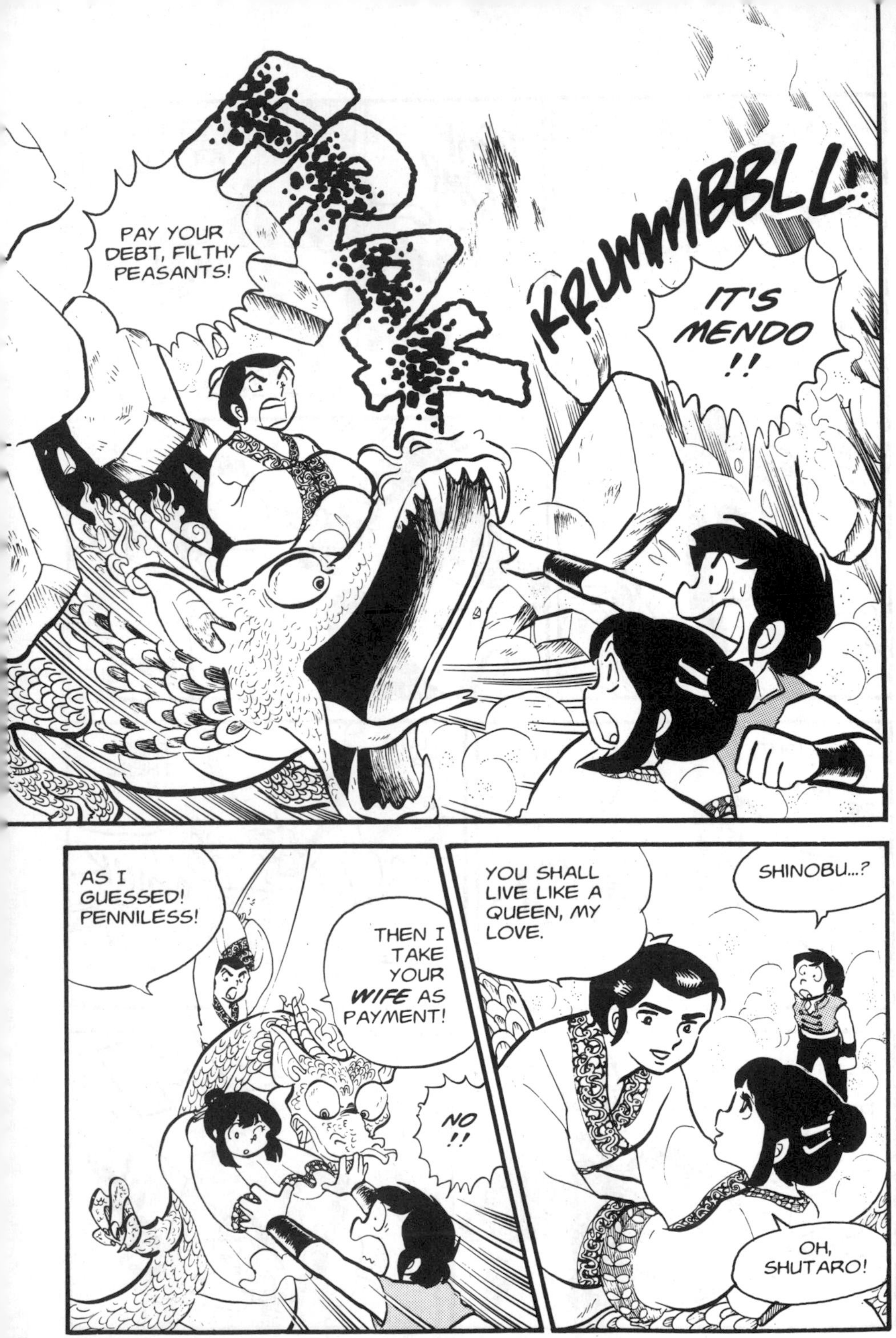
PAY YOUR DEBT, FILTHY PEASANTS!
KRUMMBBLL!
IT'S MENDO !!
AS I GUESSED! PENNILESS!
THEN I TAKE YOUR *WIFE* AS PAYMENT!
NO !!
YOU SHALL LIVE LIKE A QUEEN, MY LOVE.
SHINOBU...?
OH, SHUTARO!

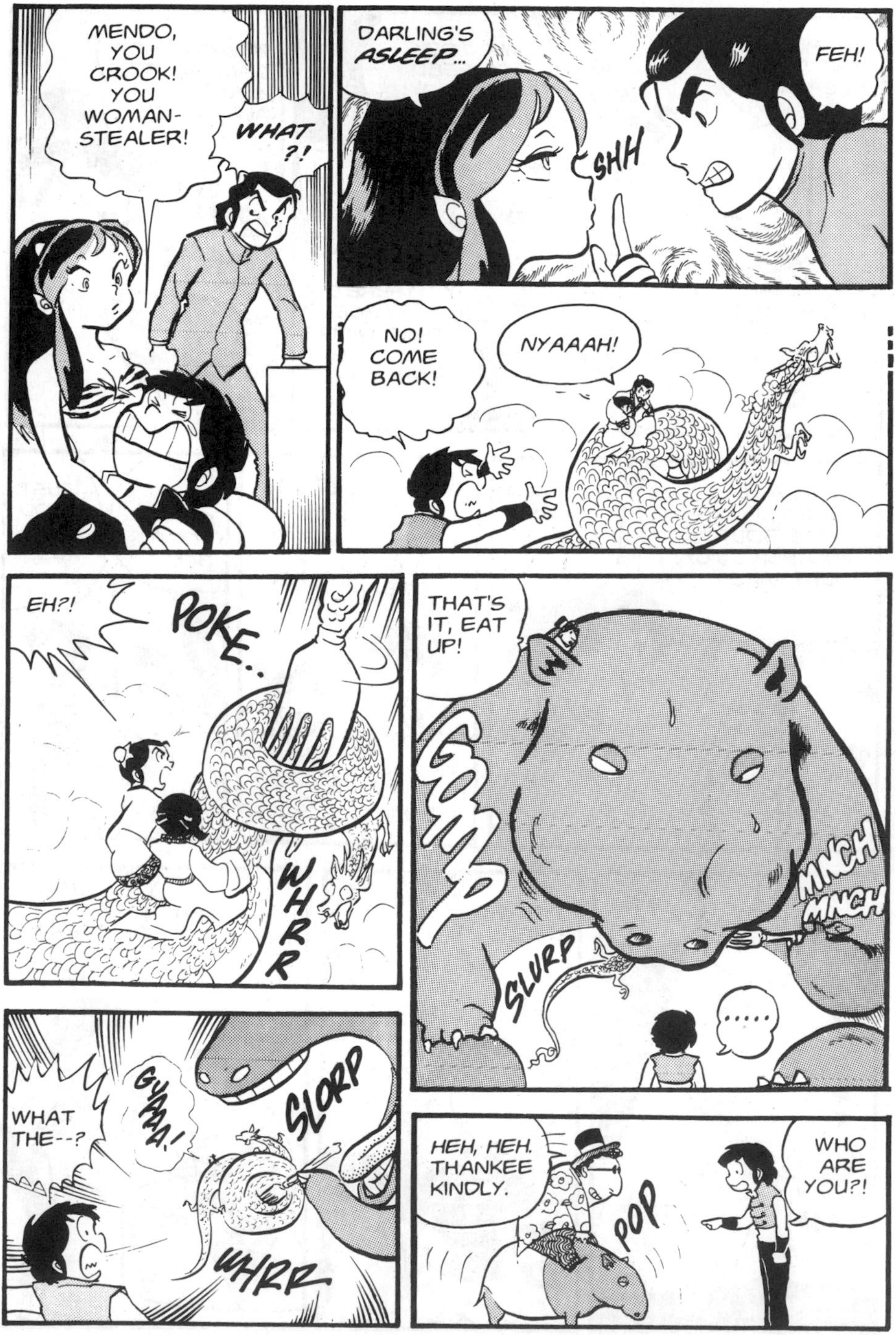

MENDO, YOU CROOK! YOU WOMAN-STEALER!
WHAT ?!
DARLING'S ASLEEP...
SHH
FEH!
NO! COME BACK!
NYAAAH!
EH?!
POKE...
WHRR
THAT'S IT, EAT UP!
GOMP
MNCH MNCH
SLURP
.....
WHAT THE--?
GYAAA!
SLORP
WHRR
HEH, HEH. THANKEE KINDLY.
POP
WHO ARE YOU?!

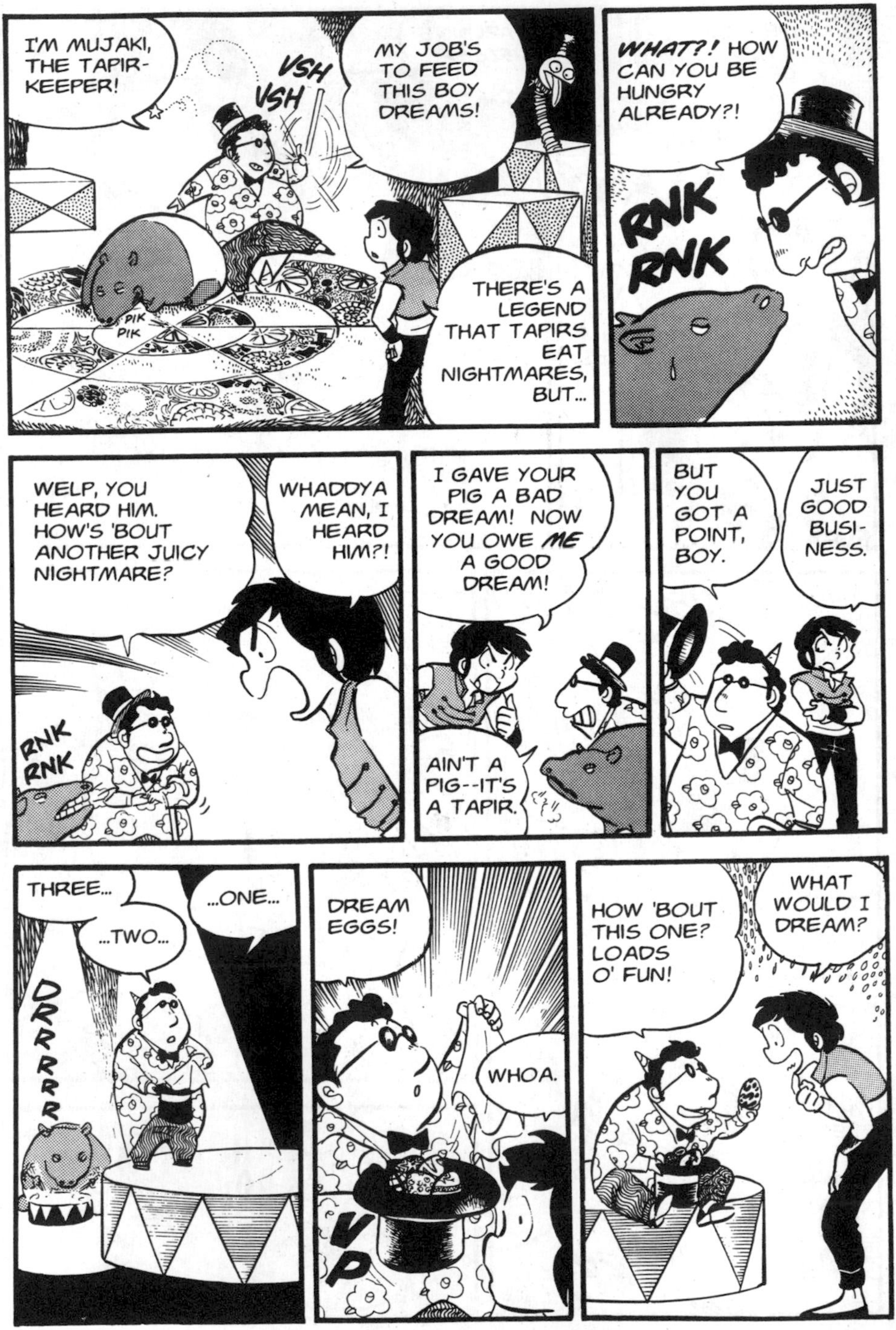
I'M MUJAKI, THE TAPIR-KEEPER!
VSH VSH
PIK PIK
MY JOB'S TO FEED THIS BOY DREAMS!
THERE'S A LEGEND THAT TAPIRS EAT NIGHTMARES, BUT...
WHAT?! HOW CAN YOU BE HUNGRY ALREADY?!
RNK RNK
WELP, YOU HEARD HIM. HOW'S 'BOUT ANOTHER JUICY NIGHTMARE?
WHADDYA MEAN, I HEARD HIM?!
RNK RNK
I GAVE YOUR PIG A BAD DREAM! NOW YOU OWE ME A GOOD DREAM!
AIN'T A PIG--IT'S A TAPIR.
BUT YOU GOT A POINT, BOY.
JUST GOOD BUSI-NESS.
THREE...
...TWO...
...ONE...
ORRRRRR
DREAM EGGS!
WHOA.
VP
HOW 'BOUT THIS ONE? LOADS O' FUN!
WHAT WOULD I DREAM?

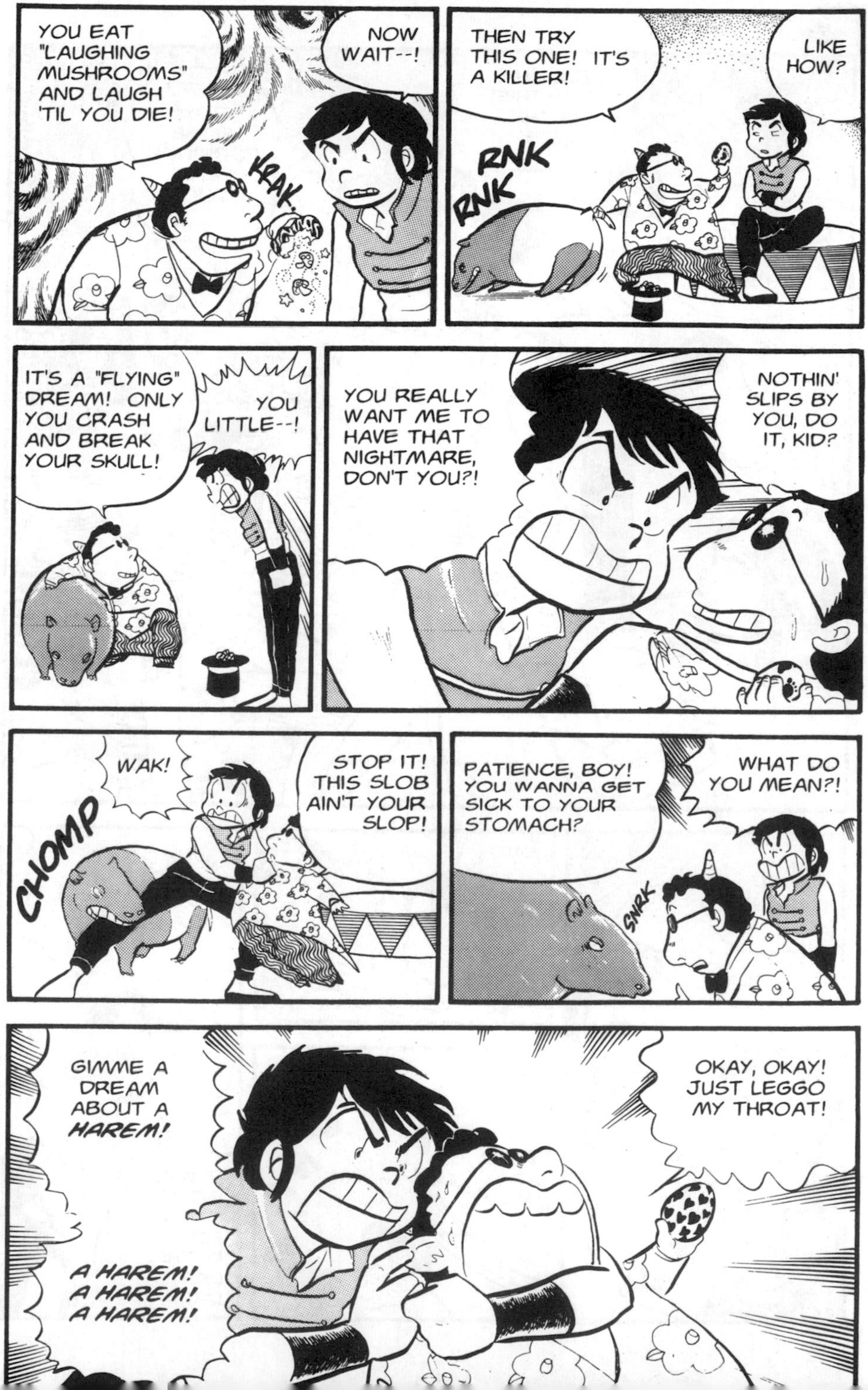
YOU EAT "LAUGHING MUSHROOMS" AND LAUGH 'TIL YOU DIE!
NOW WAIT--!
KRAK.
THEN TRY THIS ONE! IT'S A KILLER!
LIKE HOW?
RNK RNK
IT'S A "FLYING" DREAM! ONLY YOU CRASH AND BREAK YOUR SKULL!
YOU LITTLE--!
YOU REALLY WANT ME TO HAVE THAT NIGHTMARE, DON'T YOU?!
NOTHIN' SLIPS BY YOU, DO IT, KID?
WAK!
CHOMP
STOP IT! THIS SLOB AIN'T YOUR SLOP!
PATIENCE, BOY! YOU WANNA GET SICK TO YOUR STOMACH?
WHAT DO YOU MEAN?!
SNRK
GIMME A DREAM ABOUT A HAREM!
OKAY, OKAY! JUST LEGGO MY THROAT!
A HAREM! A HAREM! A HAREM!

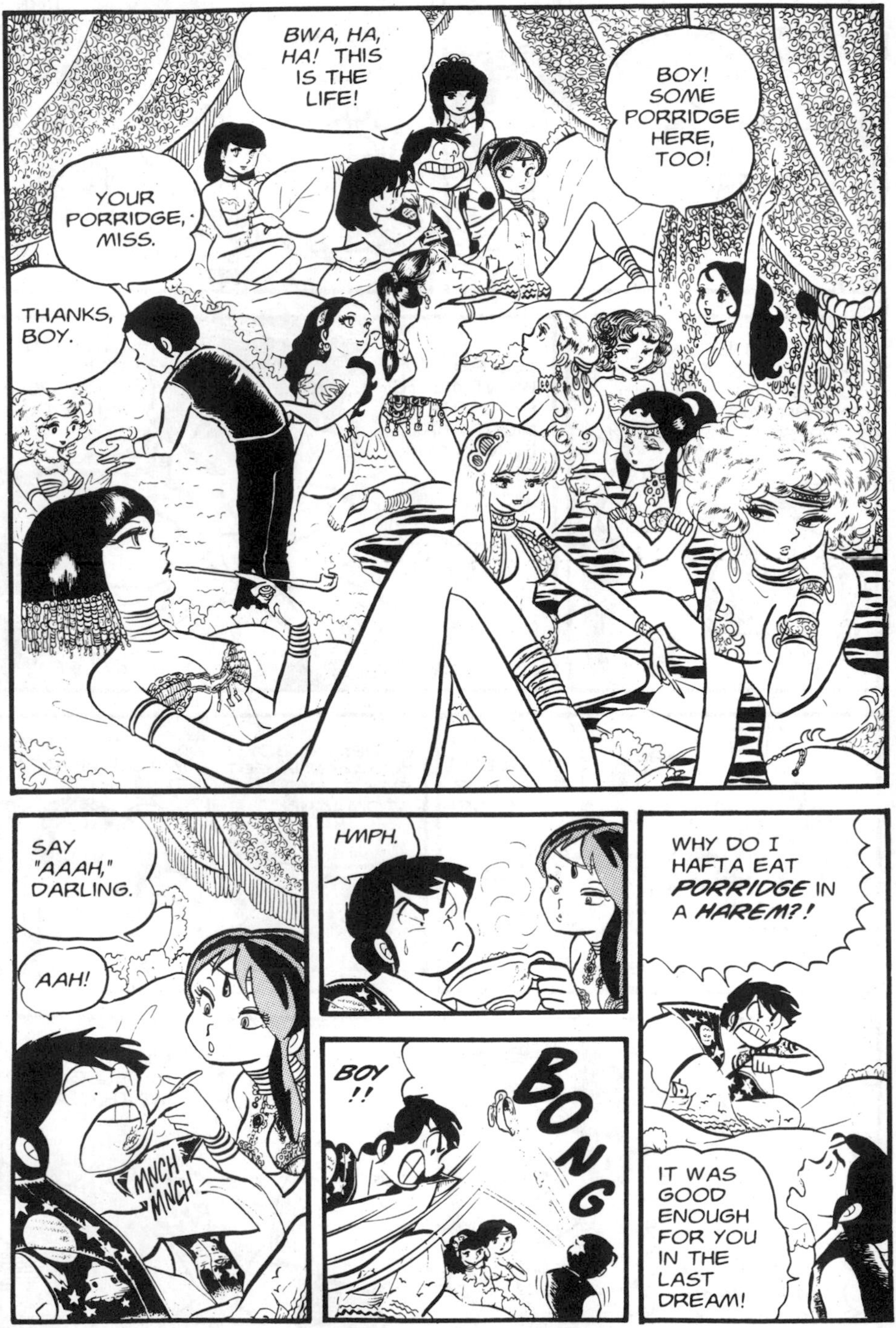
BWA, HA, HA! THIS IS THE LIFE!
BOY! SOME PORRIDGE HERE, TOO!
YOUR PORRIDGE, MISS.
THANKS, BOY.
SAY "AAAH," DARLING.
AAH!
MNCH MNCH
HMPH.
WHY DO I HAFTA EAT PORRIDGE IN A HAREM?!
BOY!!
BONG
IT WAS GOOD ENOUGH FOR YOU IN THE LAST DREAM!

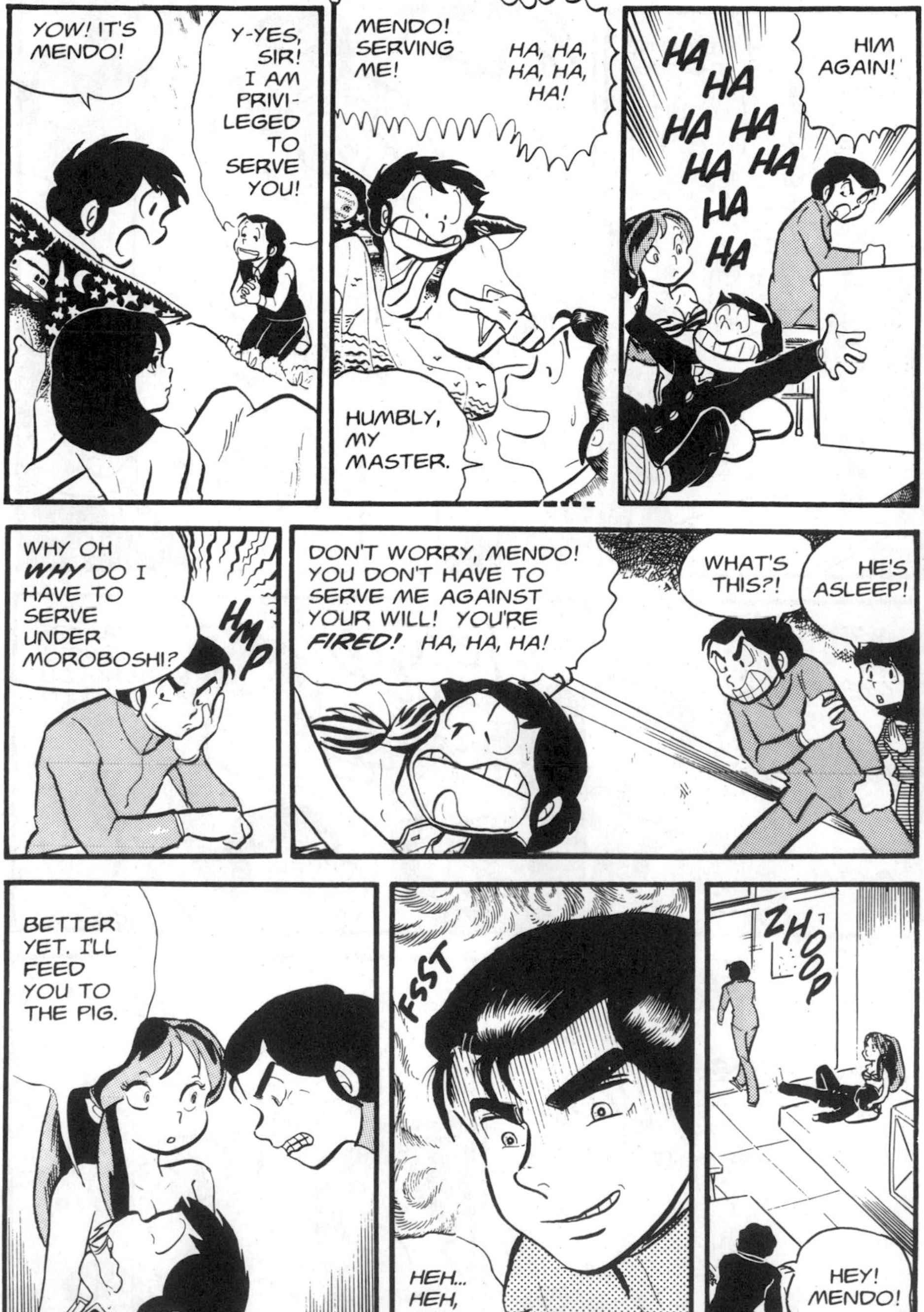
YOW! IT'S MENDO!
Y-YES, SIR! I AM PRIVI-LEGED TO SERVE YOU!
MENDO! SERVING ME!
HA, HA, HA, HA, HA!
HUMBLY, MY MASTER.
HA HA HA HA HA HA HA HA HA
HIM AGAIN!
WHY OH WHY DO I HAVE TO SERVE UNDER MOROBOSHI?
HMP
DON'T WORRY, MENDO! YOU DON'T HAVE TO SERVE ME AGAINST YOUR WILL! YOU'RE FIRED! HA, HA, HA!
WHAT'S THIS?!
HE'S ASLEEP!
BETTER YET. I'LL FEED YOU TO THE PIG.
FSST
HEH... HEH, HEH...
ZHOOP
HEY! MENDO!

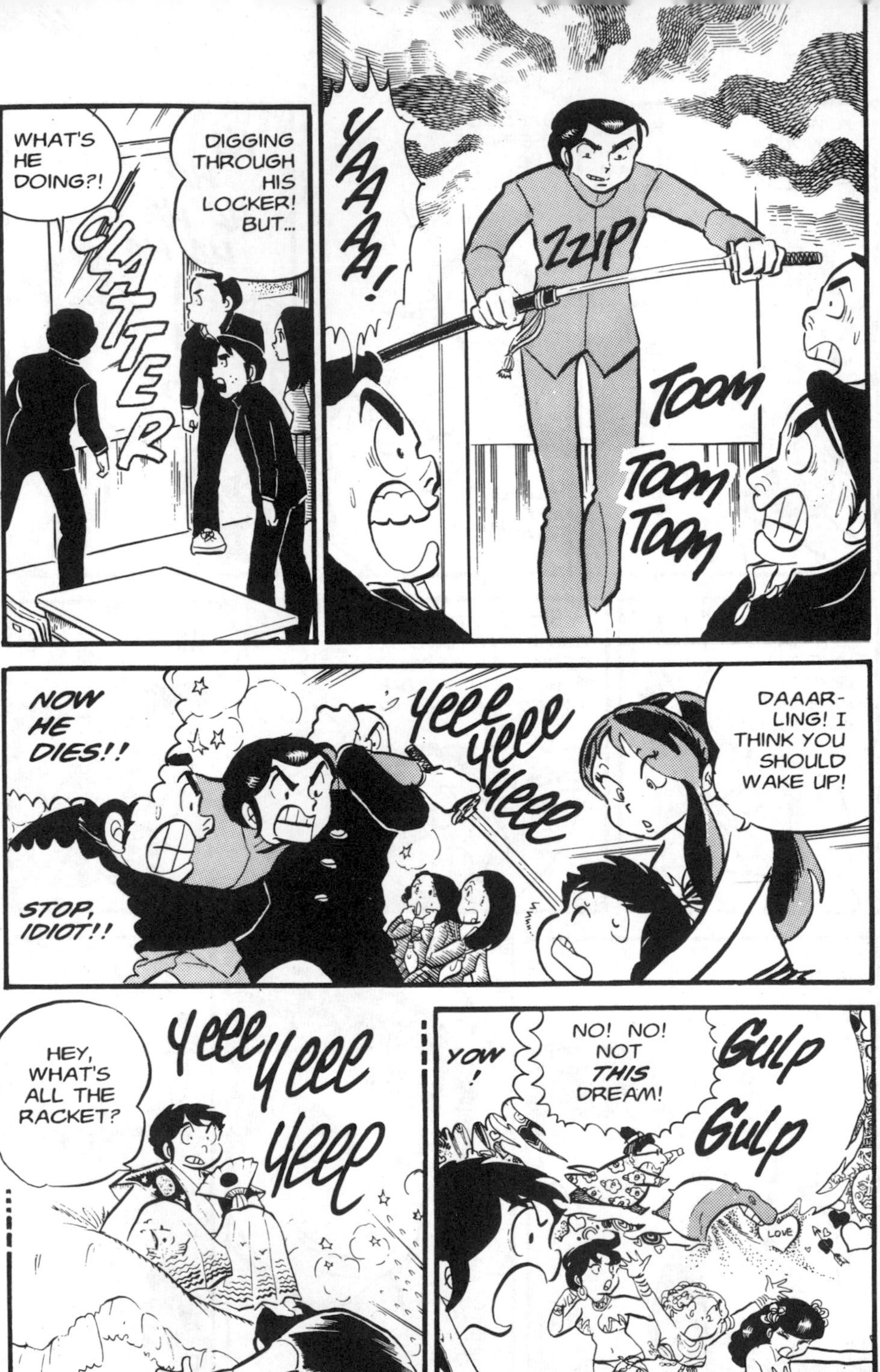
WHAT'S HE DOING?!
DIGGING THROUGH HIS LOCKER! BUT...
CLATTER
YAAAAA!
ZZIP
TOOM
TOOM TOOM
NOW HE DIES!!
STOP, IDIOT!!
YEEE YEEE YEEE
DAAAR-LING! I THINK YOU SHOULD WAKE UP!
HEY, WHAT'S ALL THE RACKET?
YEEE YEEE YEEE
YOW!
NO! NO! NOT THIS DREAM!
GULP
GULP
LOVE

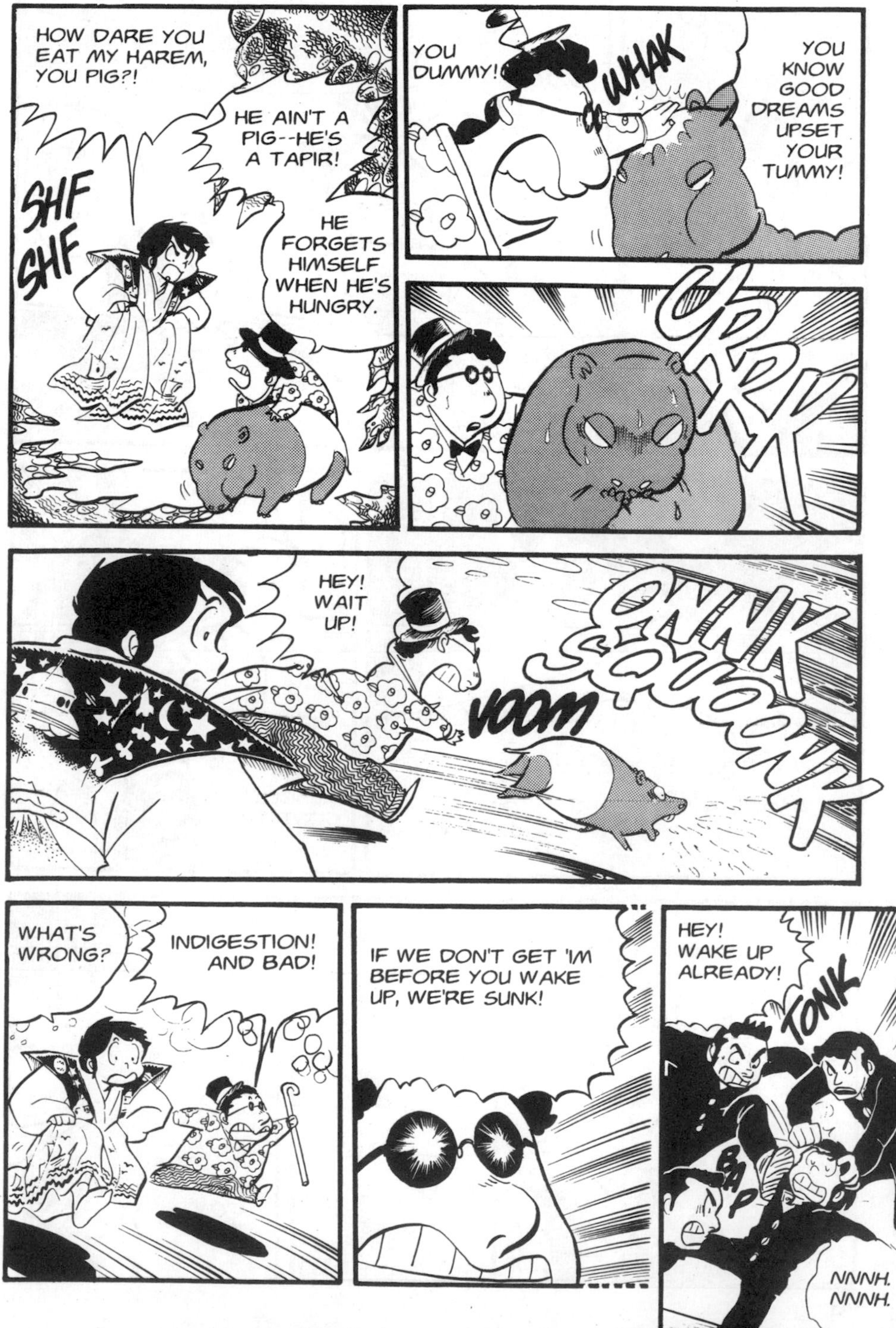
HOW DARE YOU EAT MY HAREM, YOU PIG?!
HE AIN'T A PIG--HE'S A TAPIR!
SHF SHF
HE FORGETS HIMSELF WHEN HE'S HUNGRY.
YOU DUMMY!
WHAK
YOU KNOW GOOD DREAMS UPSET YOUR TUMMY!
URRK
HEY! WAIT UP!
OINK SQUOONK
VOOM
WHAT'S WRONG?
INDIGESTION! AND BAD!
IF WE DON'T GET 'IM BEFORE YOU WAKE UP, WE'RE SUNK!
HEY! WAKE UP ALREADY!
TONK
NNNH. NNNH.

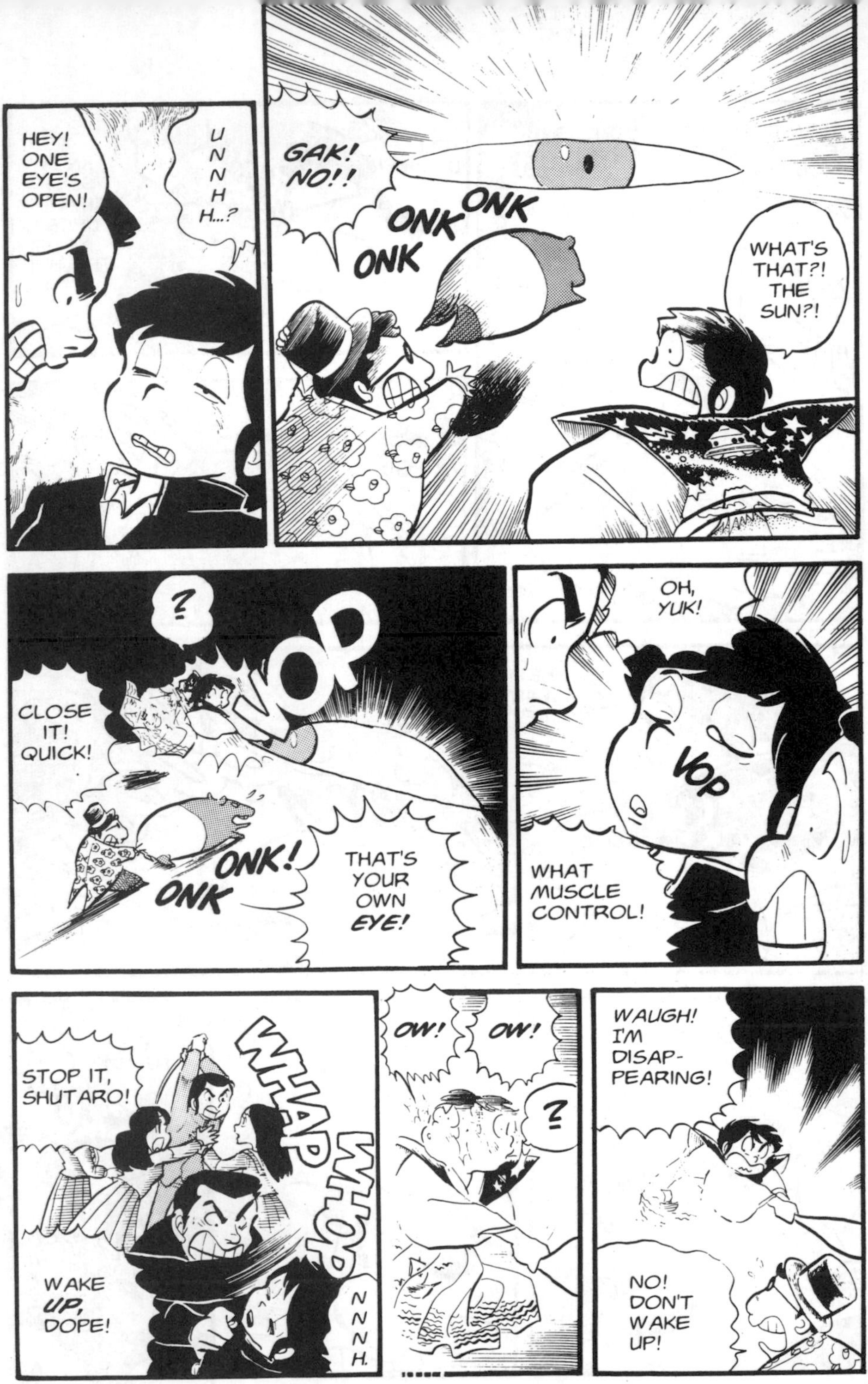
HEY! ONE EYE'S OPEN!
UNNHH...?
GAK! NO!!
ONK ONK ONK
WHAT'S THAT?! THE SUN?!
?
VOP
CLOSE IT! QUICK!
ONK ONK!
THAT'S YOUR OWN EYE!
OH, YUK!
VOP
WHAT MUSCLE CONTROL!
STOP IT, SHUTARO!
WHAP
WHOP
WAKE UP, DOPE!
NNNH.
OW! OW!
?
WAUGH! I'M DISAP-PEARING!
NO! DON'T WAKE UP!

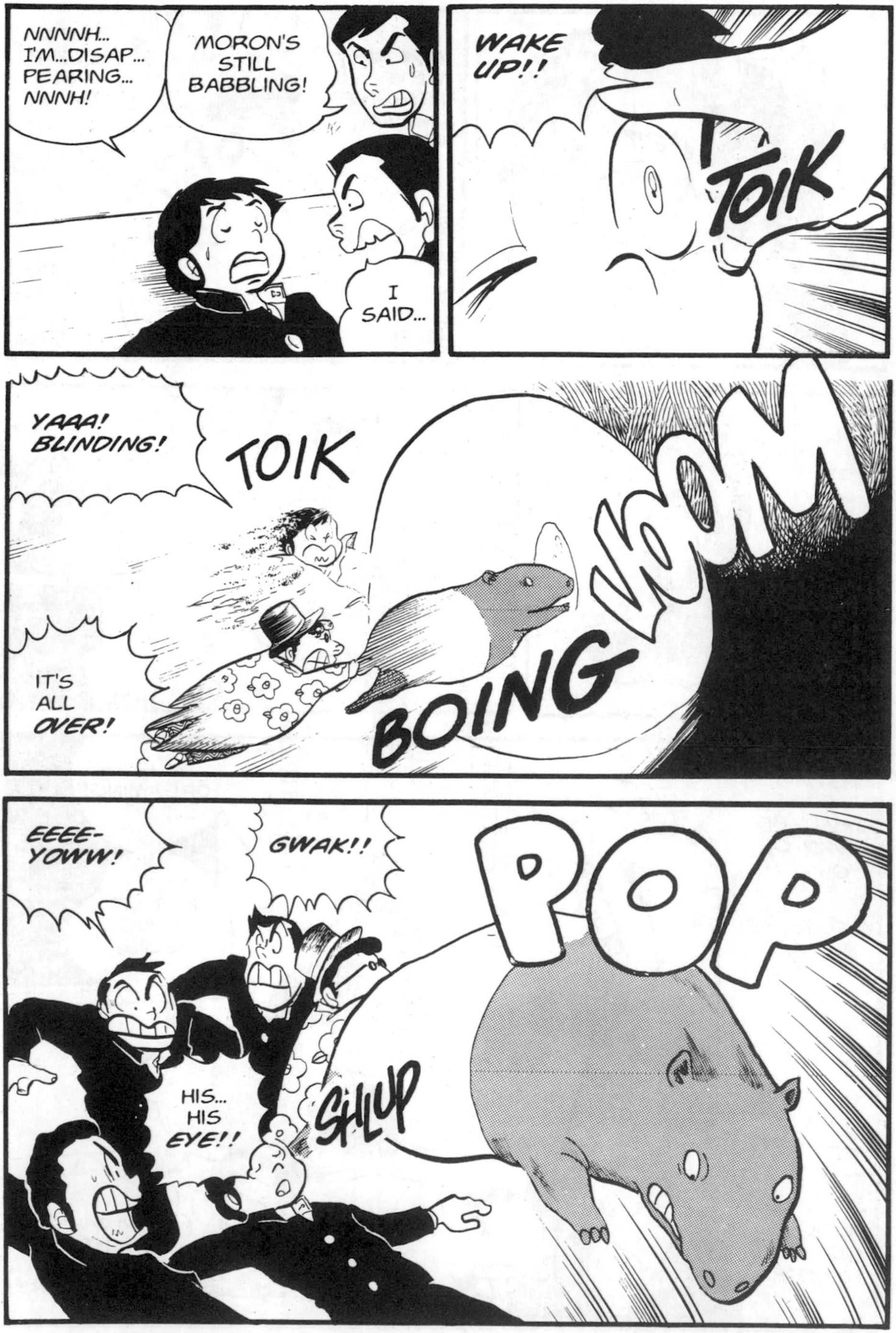
NNNNH... I'M...DISAP... PEARING... NNNH!
MORON'S STILL BABBLING!
I SAID...
WAKE UP!!
TOIK
YAAA! BLINDING!
TOIK
IT'S ALL OVER!
VOOOM
BOING
EEEE-YOWW!
GWAK!!
POP
HIS... HIS EYE!!
SHLUP

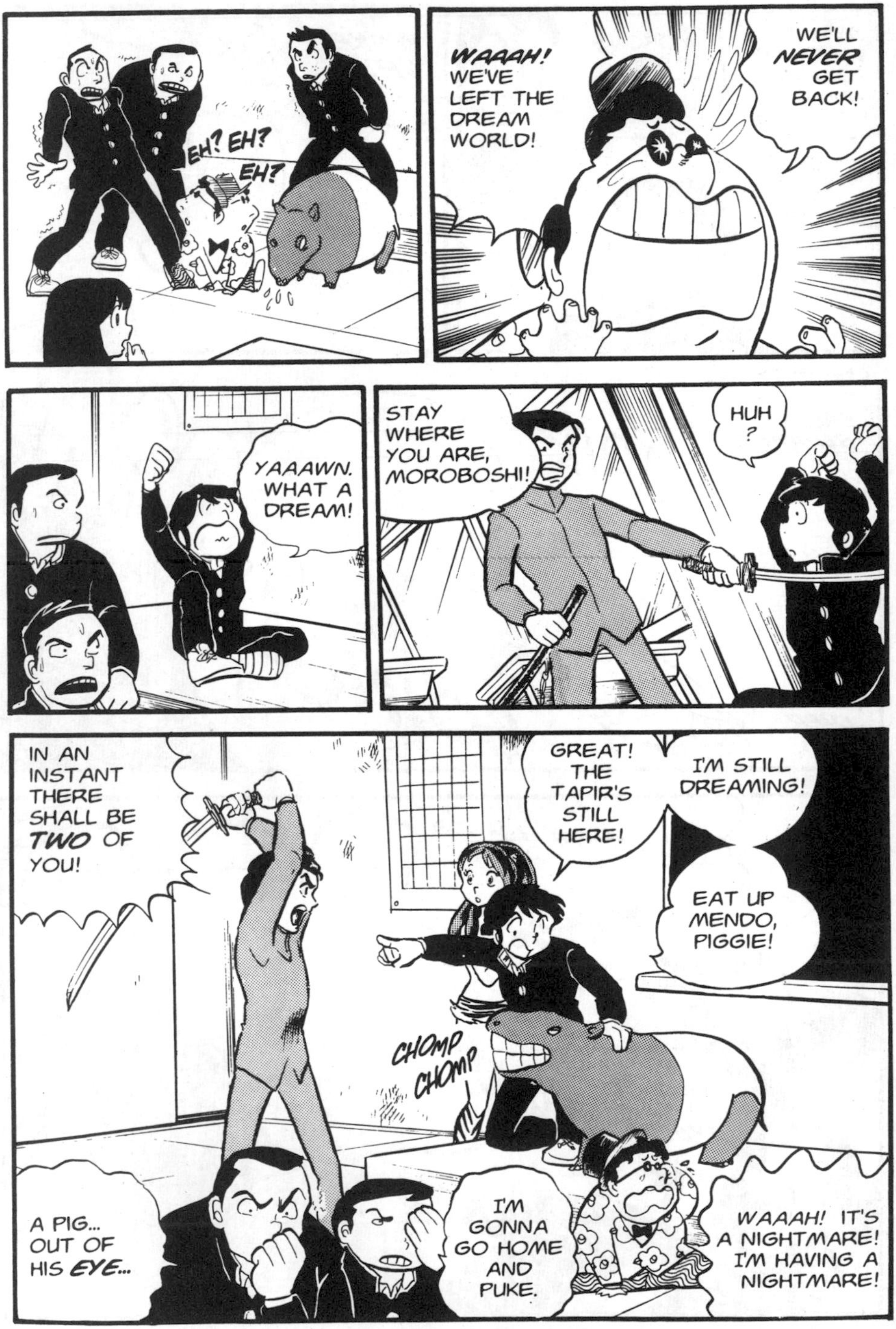
EH? EH?
EH?
WAAAH! WE'VE LEFT THE DREAM WORLD!
WE'LL NEVER GET BACK!
YAAAWN. WHAT A DREAM!
STAY WHERE YOU ARE, MOROBOSHI!
HUH ?
IN AN INSTANT THERE SHALL BE TWO OF YOU!
GREAT! THE TAPIR'S STILL HERE!
I'M STILL DREAMING!
EAT UP MENDO, PIGGIE!
CHOMP CHOMP
A PIG... OUT OF HIS EYE...
I'M GONNA GO HOME AND PUKE.
WAAAH! IT'S A NIGHTMARE! I'M HAVING A NIGHTMARE!

Part 10
Shooting the Fourth Dimension

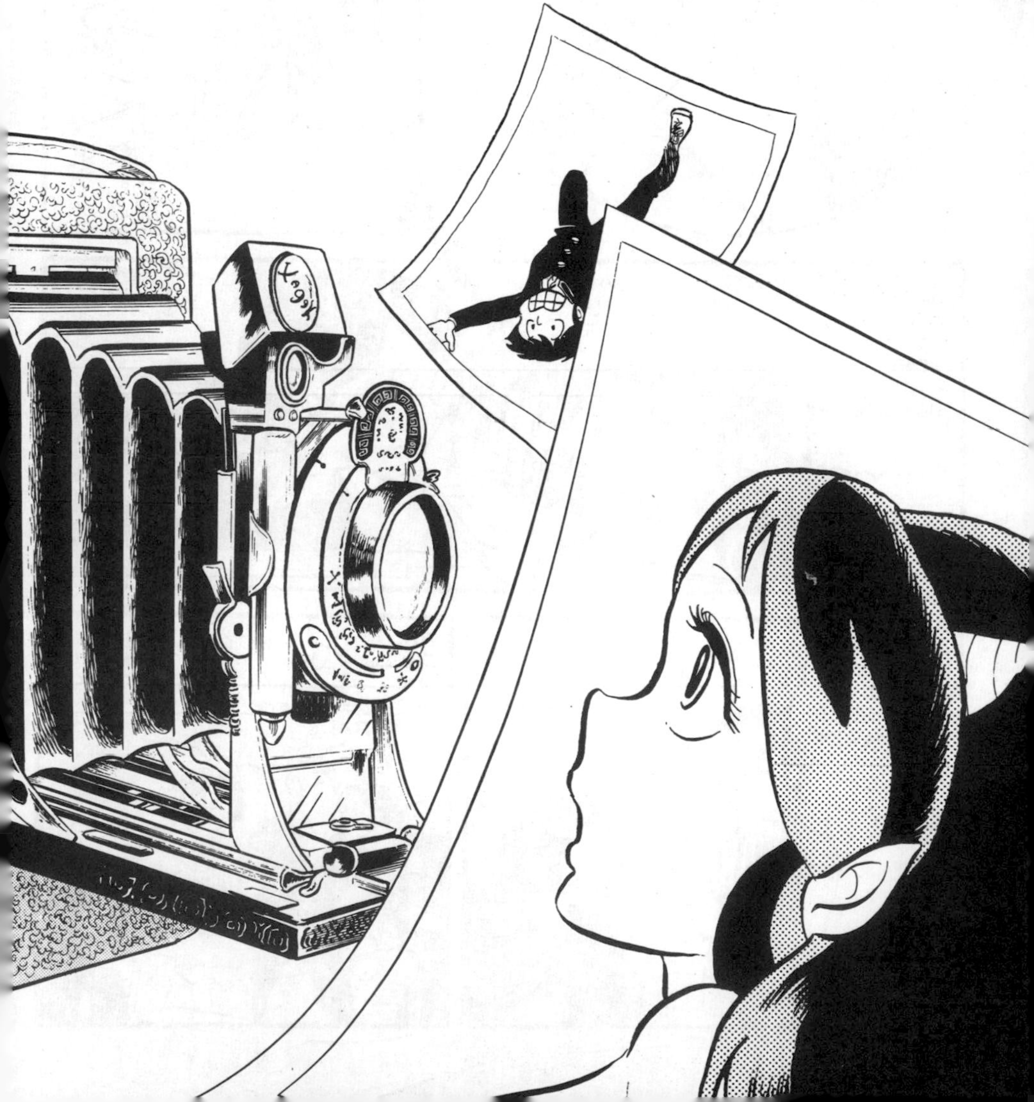

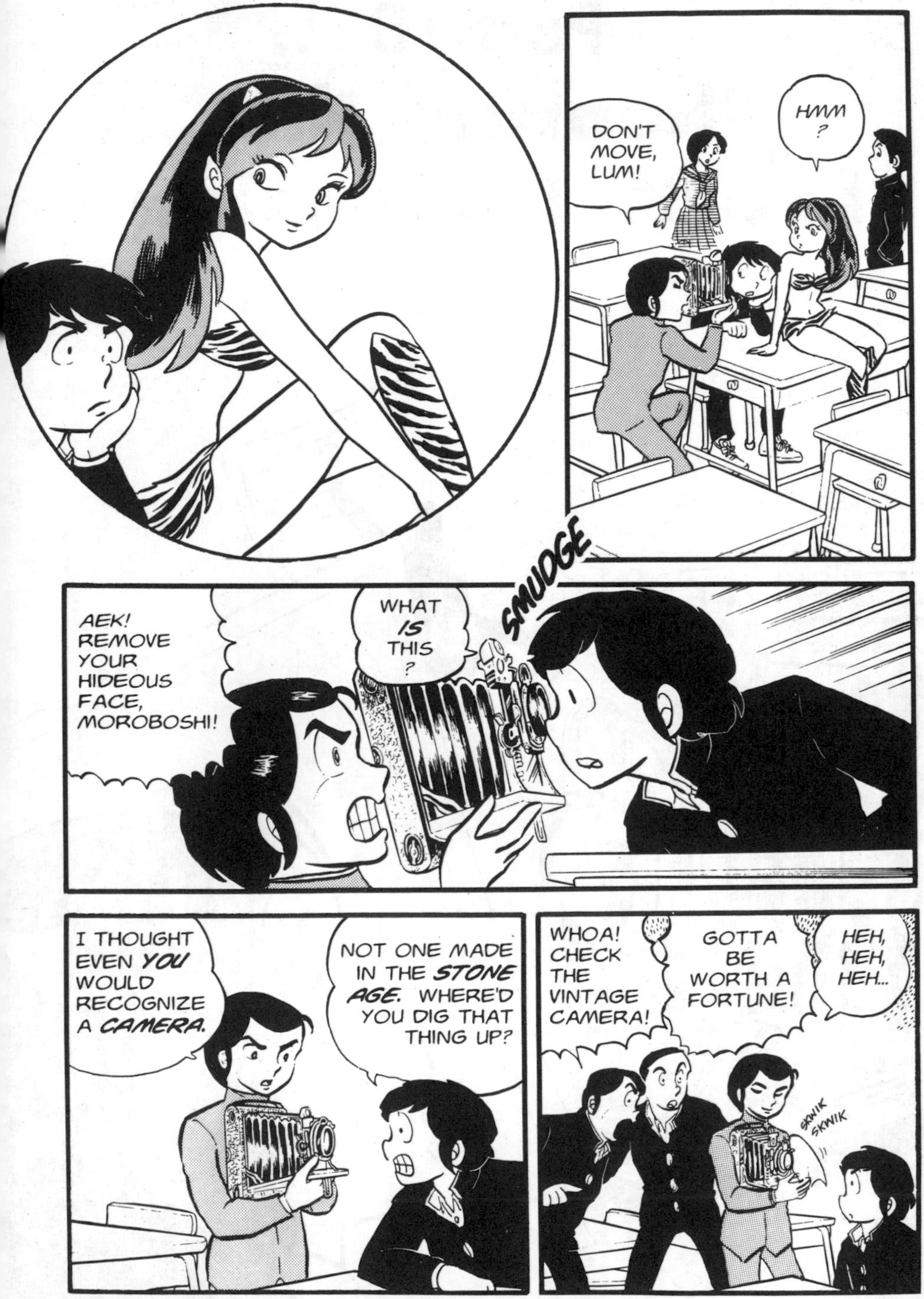
DON'T MOVE, LUM!
HMM?
SMUDGE
AEK! REMOVE YOUR HIDEOUS FACE, MOROBOSHI!
WHAT *IS* THIS?
I THOUGHT EVEN *YOU* WOULD RECOGNIZE A *CAMERA.*
NOT ONE MADE IN THE *STONE AGE.* WHERE'D YOU DIG THAT THING UP?
WHOA! CHECK THE VINTAGE CAMERA!
GOTTA BE WORTH A FORTUNE!
HEH, HEH, HEH...
SKWIK SKWIK

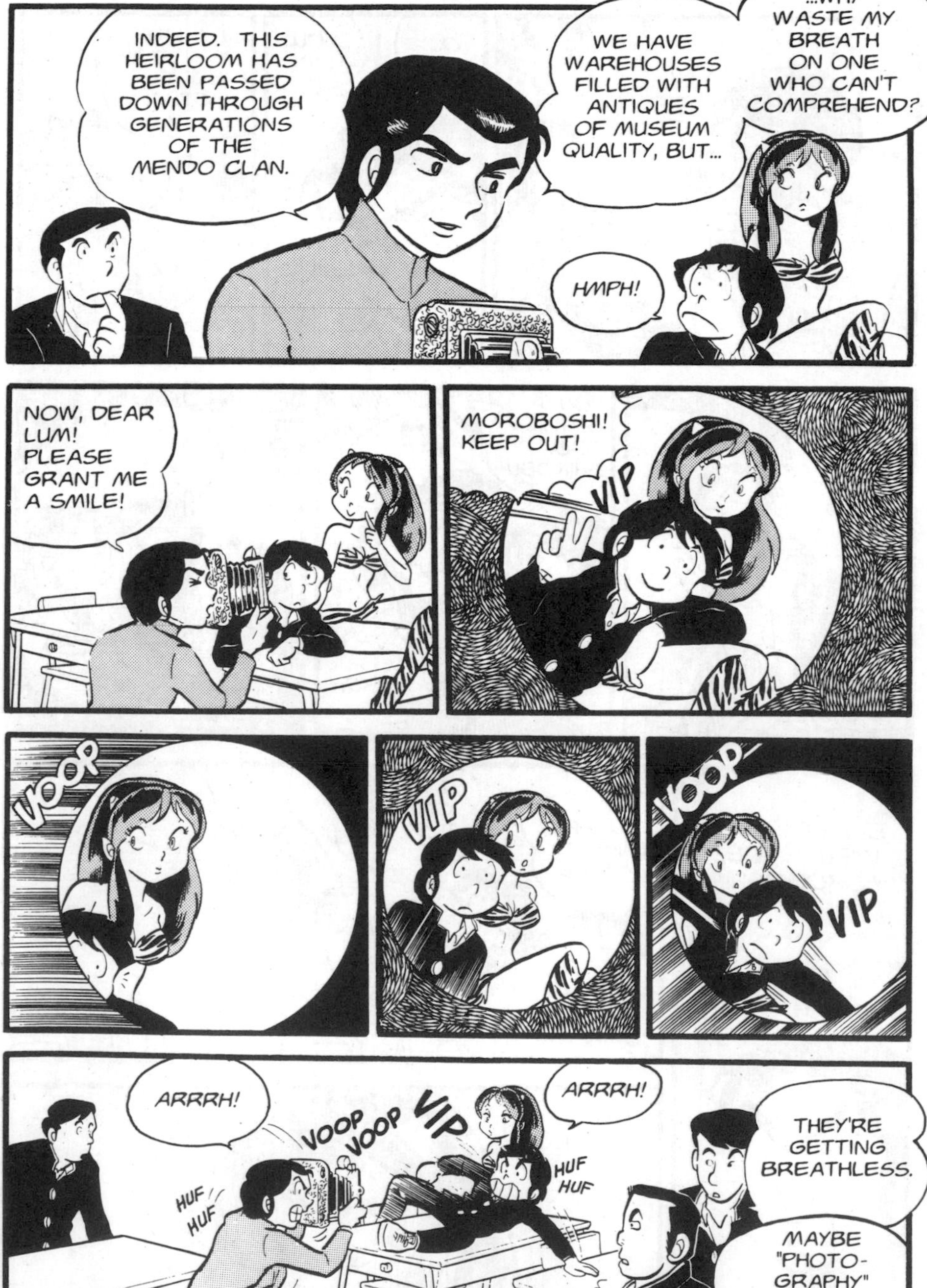
INDEED. THIS HEIRLOOM HAS BEEN PASSED DOWN THROUGH GENERATIONS OF THE MENDO CLAN.
WE HAVE WAREHOUSES FILLED WITH ANTIQUES OF MUSEUM QUALITY, BUT...
...WHY WASTE MY BREATH ON ONE WHO CAN'T COMPREHEND?
HMPH!
NOW, DEAR LUM! PLEASE GRANT ME A SMILE!
MOROBOSHI! KEEP OUT!
VIP
VOOP
VIP
VOOP
VIP
ARRRH!
VOOP
VOOP
VIP
ARRRH!
HUF HUF
HUF HUF
THEY'RE GETTING BREATHLESS.
MAYBE "PHOTOGRAPHY" SHOULD COUNT AS A SPORT.

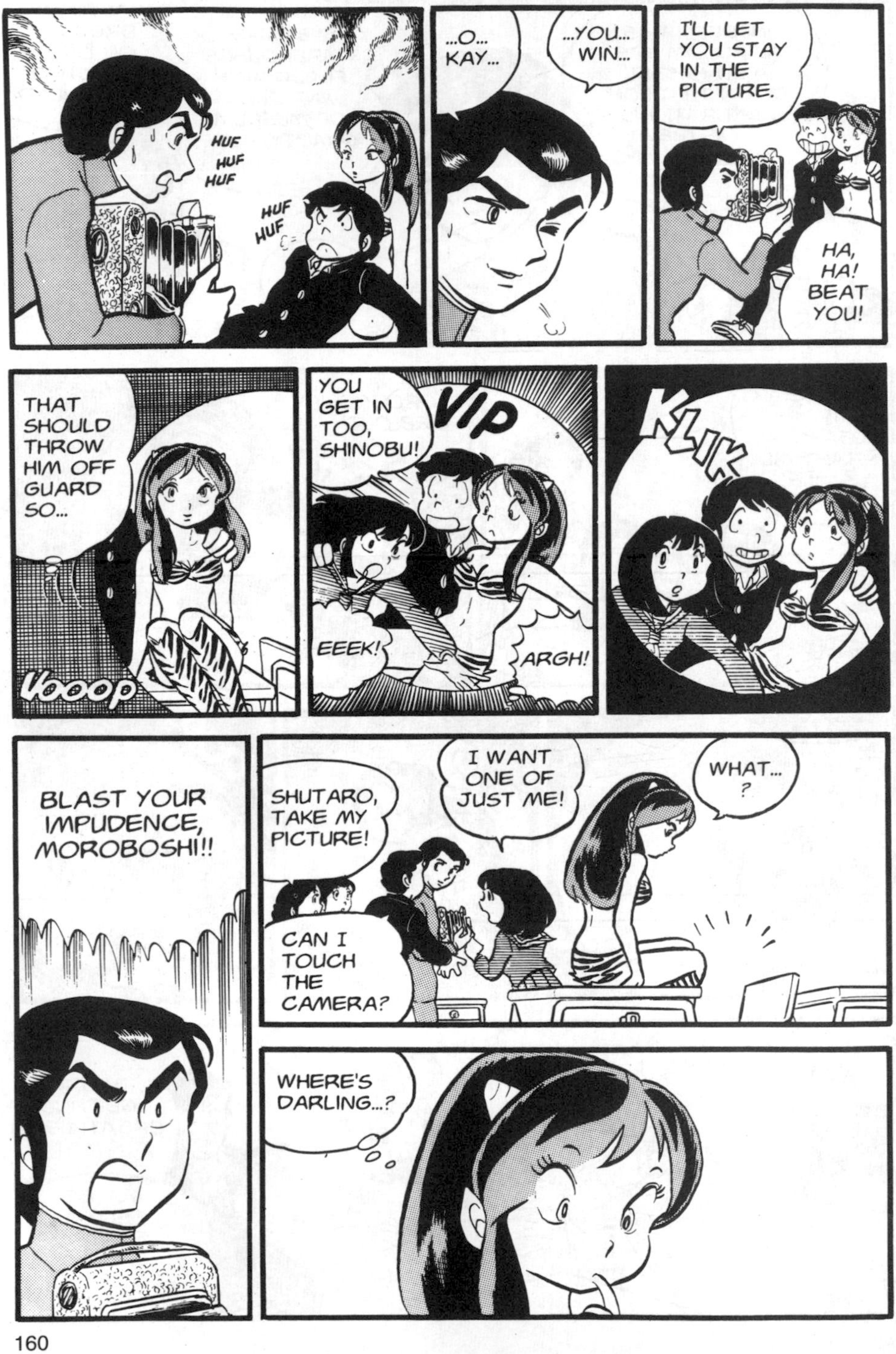
HUF
HUF
HUF
HUF
HUF
...O... KAY...
...YOU... WIN...
I'LL LET YOU STAY IN THE PICTURE.
HA, HA! BEAT YOU!
THAT SHOULD THROW HIM OFF GUARD SO...
VOOOP
YOU GET IN TOO, SHINOBU!
VIP
EEEK!
ARGH!
KLIK
BLAST YOUR IMPUDENCE, MOROBOSHI!!
SHUTARO, TAKE MY PICTURE!
I WANT ONE OF JUST ME!
WHAT... ?
CAN I TOUCH THE CAMERA?
WHERE'S DARLING...?

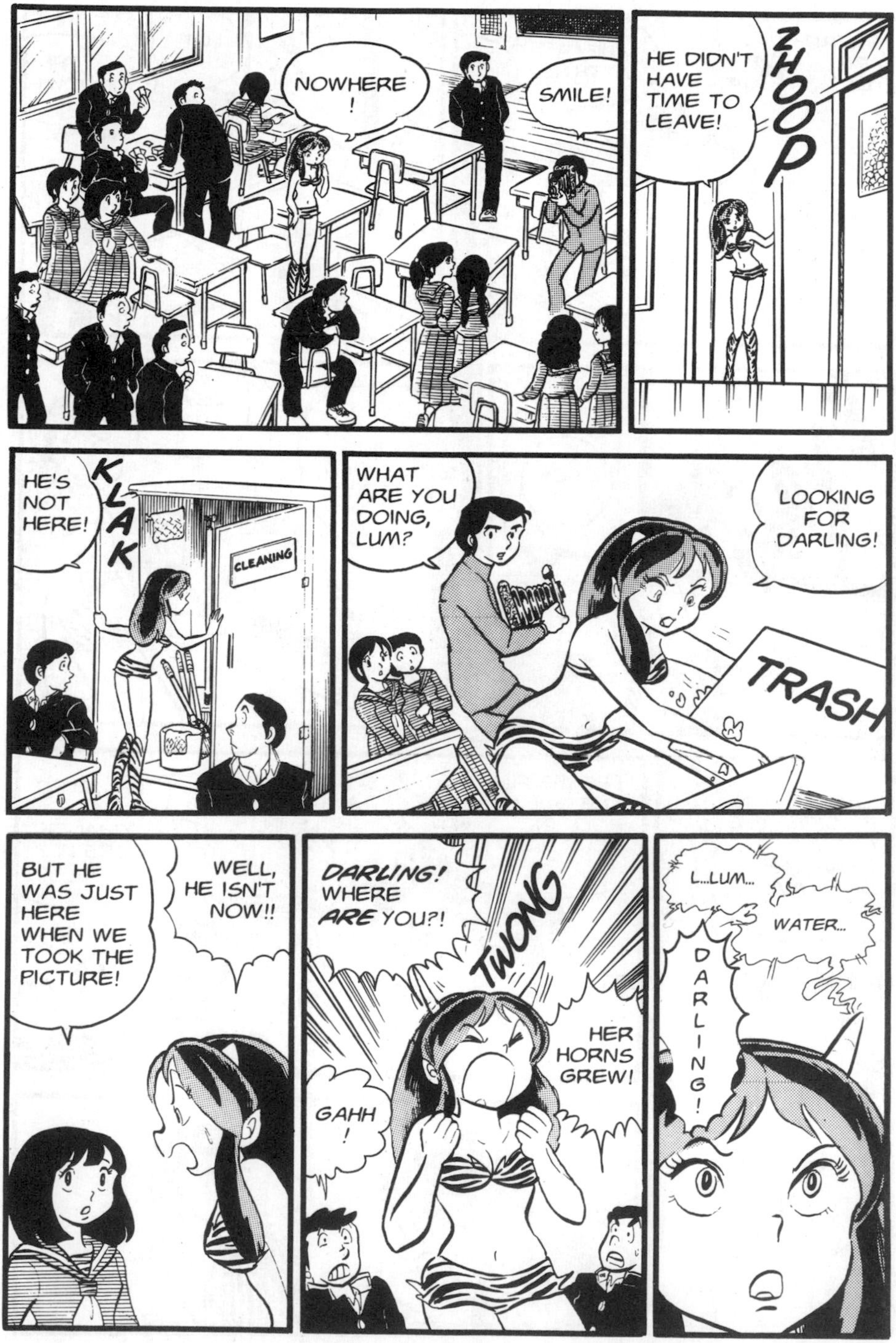
NOWHERE!
SMILE!
HE DIDN'T HAVE TIME TO LEAVE!
ZHOOP
HE'S NOT HERE!
KLAK
CLEANING
WHAT ARE YOU DOING, LUM?
LOOKING FOR DARLING!
TRASH
BUT HE WAS JUST HERE WHEN WE TOOK THE PICTURE!
WELL, HE ISN'T NOW!!
DARLING! WHERE ARE YOU?!
TWONG
HER HORNS GREW!
GAHH!
L...LUM...
WATER...
DARLING!

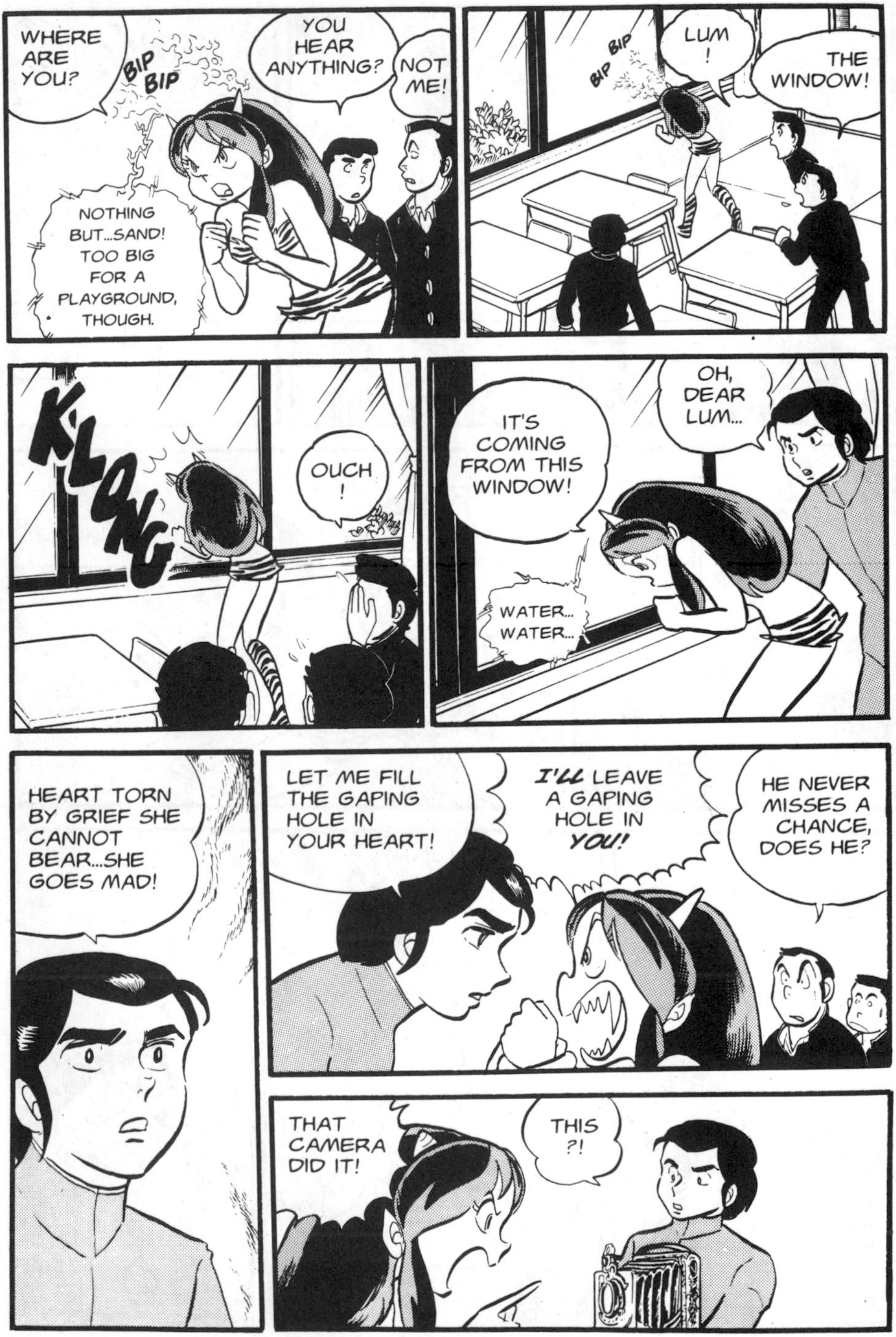
WHERE ARE YOU?
BIP BIP
YOU HEAR ANYTHING?
NOT ME!
NOTHING BUT...SAND! TOO BIG FOR A PLAYGROUND, THOUGH.
BIP BIP
LUM!
THE WINDOW!
K-LONG
OUCH!
OH, DEAR LUM...
IT'S COMING FROM THIS WINDOW!
WATER... WATER...
HEART TORN BY GRIEF SHE CANNOT BEAR...SHE GOES MAD!
LET ME FILL THE GAPING HOLE IN YOUR HEART!
I'LL LEAVE A GAPING HOLE IN YOU!
HE NEVER MISSES A CHANCE, DOES HE?
THAT CAMERA DID IT!
THIS?!

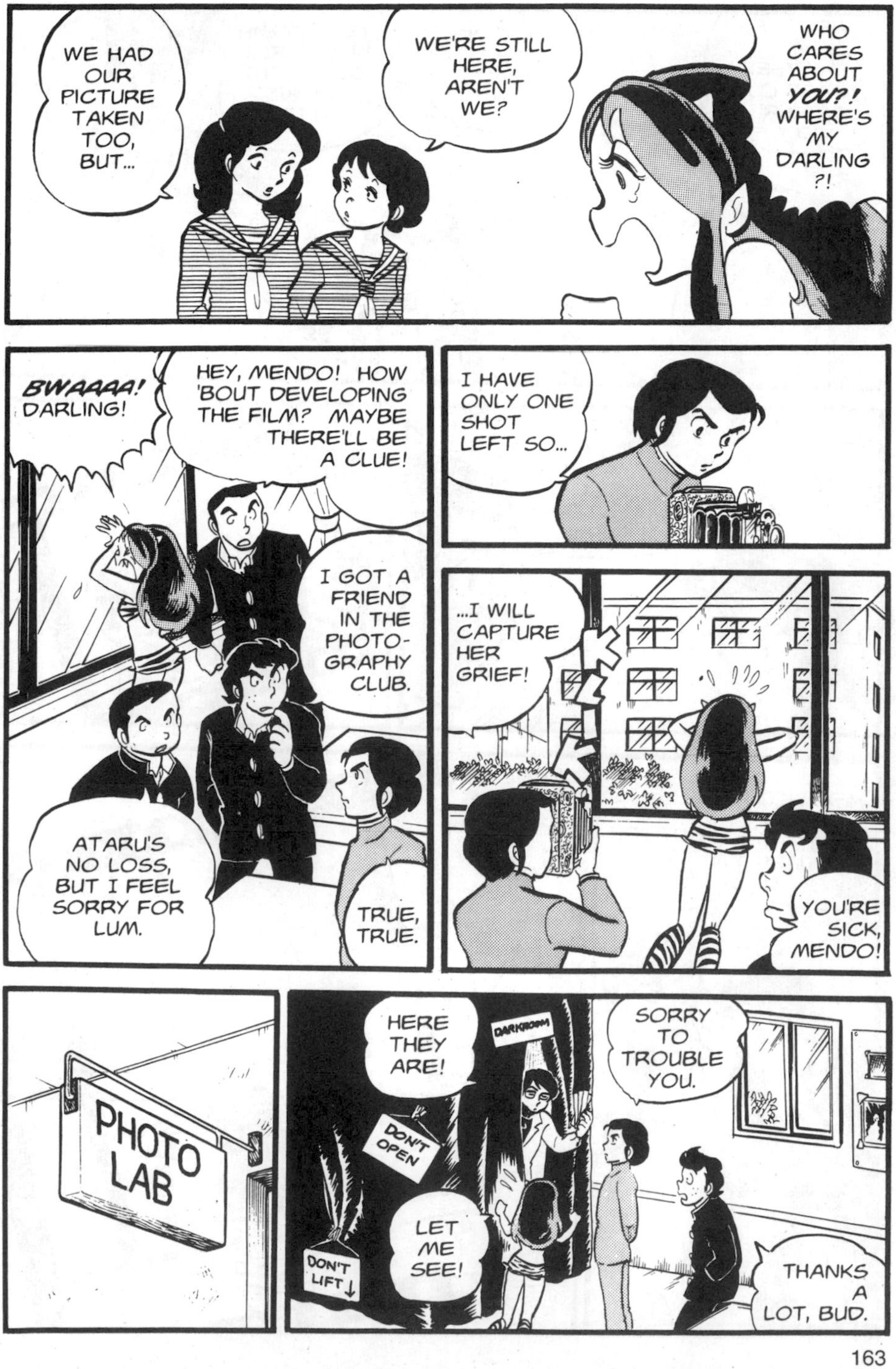

WE HAD OUR PICTURE TAKEN TOO, BUT...
WE'RE STILL HERE, AREN'T WE?
WHO CARES ABOUT YOU?! WHERE'S MY DARLING ?!
BWAAAA! DARLING!
HEY, MENDO! HOW 'BOUT DEVELOPING THE FILM? MAYBE THERE'LL BE A CLUE!
I GOT A FRIEND IN THE PHOTOGRAPHY CLUB.
ATARU'S NO LOSS, BUT I FEEL SORRY FOR LUM.
TRUE, TRUE.
I HAVE ONLY ONE SHOT LEFT SO...
...I WILL CAPTURE HER GRIEF!
YOU'RE SICK, MENDO!
PHOTO LAB
HERE THEY ARE!
DARKROOM
DON'T OPEN
SORRY TO TROUBLE YOU.
LET ME SEE!
DON'T LIFT ↓
THANKS A LOT, BUD.

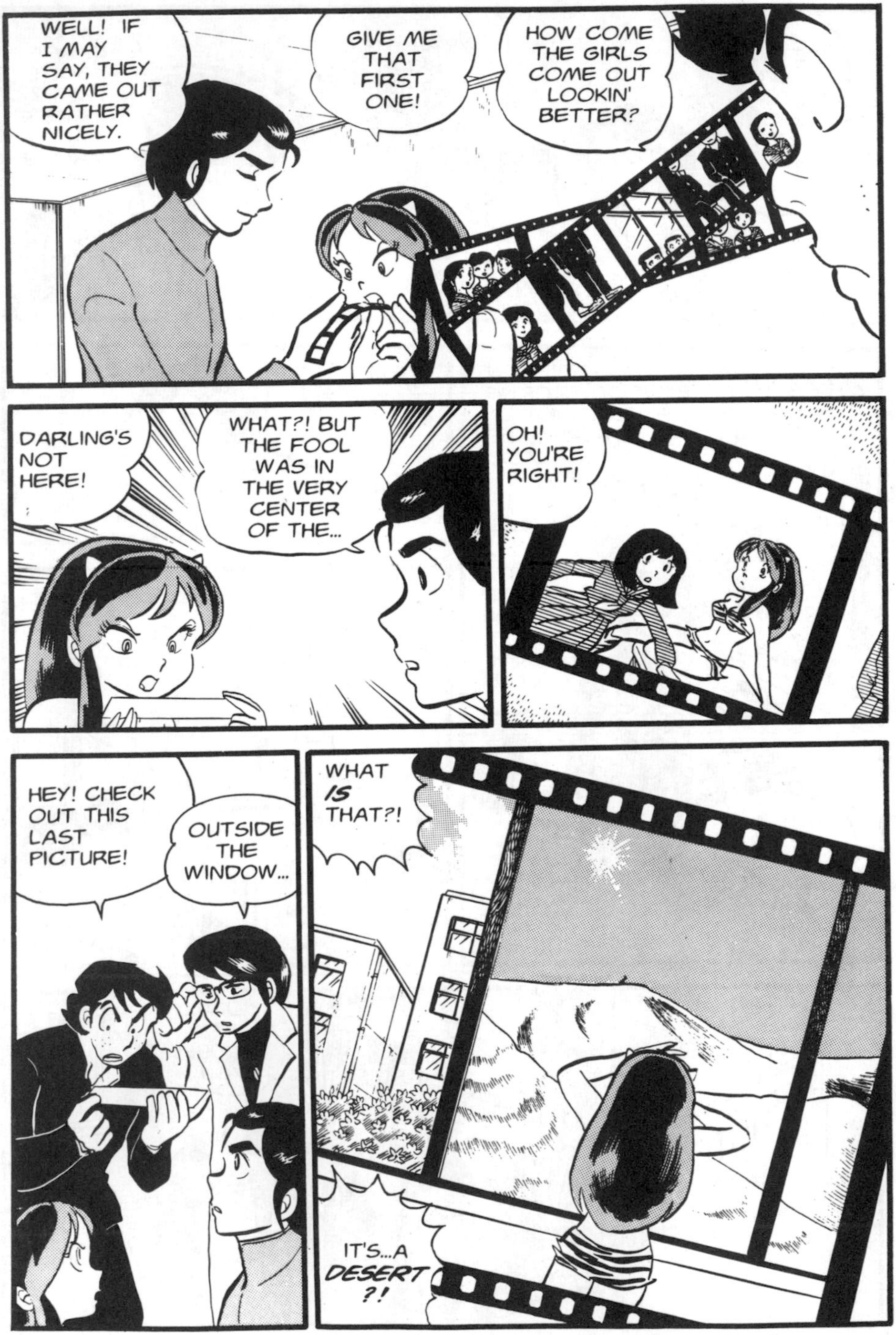

WELL! IF I MAY SAY, THEY CAME OUT RATHER NICELY.
GIVE ME THAT FIRST ONE!
HOW COME THE GIRLS COME OUT LOOKIN' BETTER?
DARLING'S NOT HERE!
WHAT?! BUT THE FOOL WAS IN THE VERY CENTER OF THE...
OH! YOU'RE RIGHT!
HEY! CHECK OUT THIS LAST PICTURE!
OUTSIDE THE WINDOW...
WHAT *IS* THAT?!
IT'S...A *DESERT* ?!

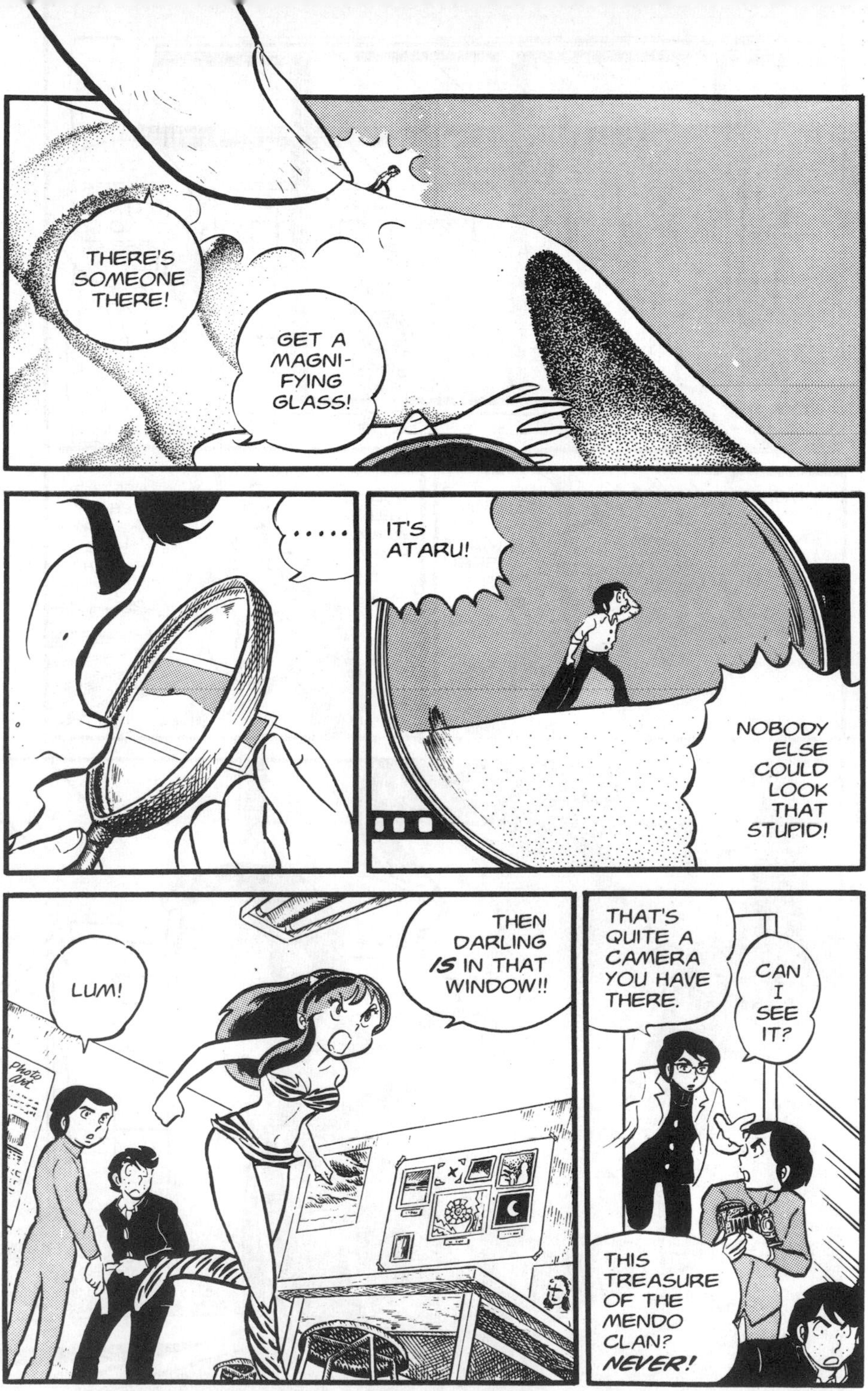
THERE'S SOMEONE THERE!
GET A MAGNI-FYING GLASS!
.....
IT'S ATARU!
NOBODY ELSE COULD LOOK THAT STUPID!
LUM!
THEN DARLING *IS* IN THAT WINDOW!!
THAT'S QUITE A CAMERA YOU HAVE THERE.
CAN I SEE IT?
THIS TREASURE OF THE MENDO CLAN? ***NEVER!***

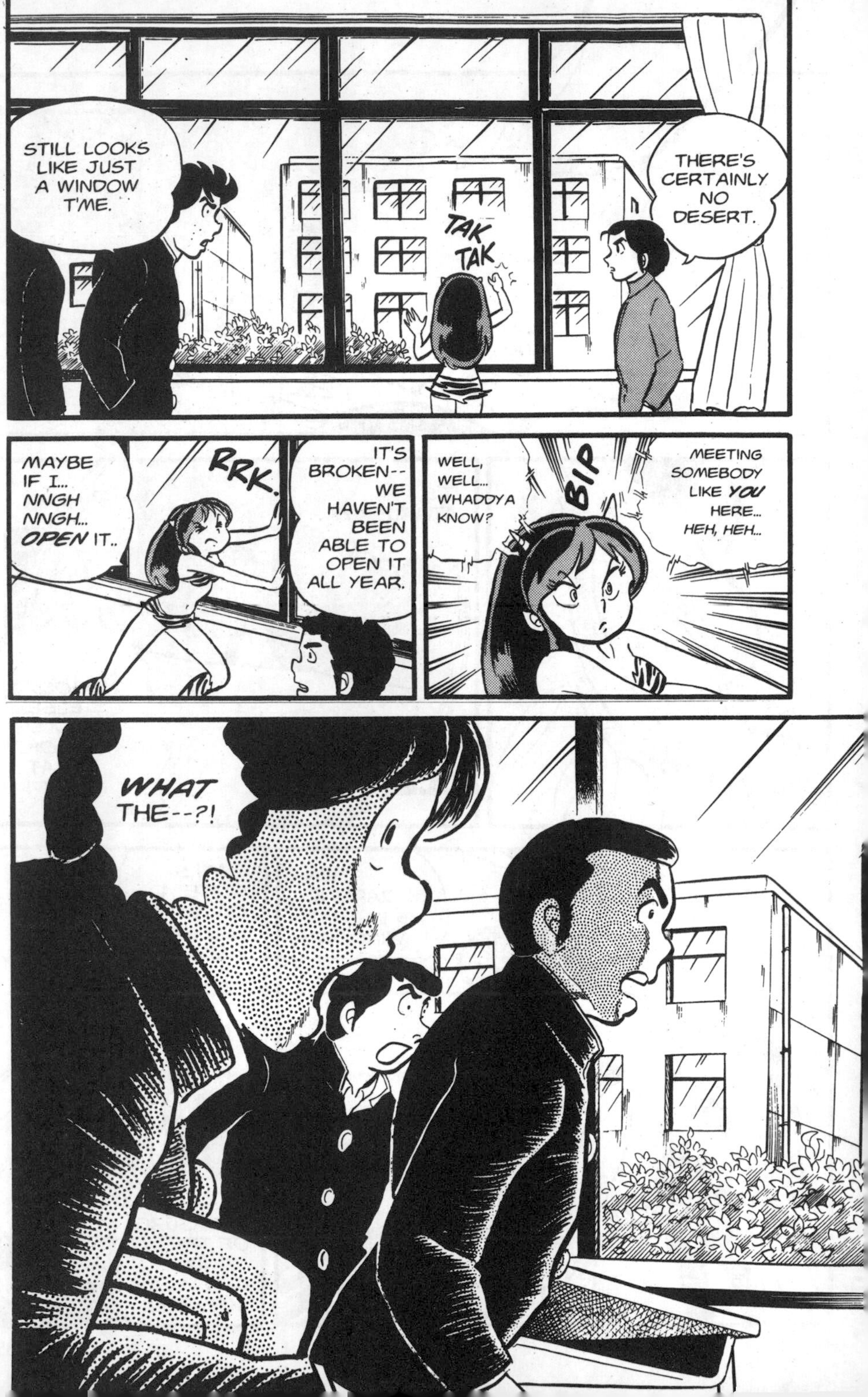
STILL LOOKS LIKE JUST A WINDOW T'ME.
TAK TAK
THERE'S CERTAINLY NO DESERT.
MAYBE IF I... NNGH NNGH... *OPEN* IT..
RRK.
IT'S BROKEN-- WE HAVEN'T BEEN ABLE TO OPEN IT ALL YEAR.
WELL, WELL... WHADDYA KNOW?
BIP
MEETING SOMEBODY LIKE *YOU* HERE... HEH, HEH...
WHAT THE--?!

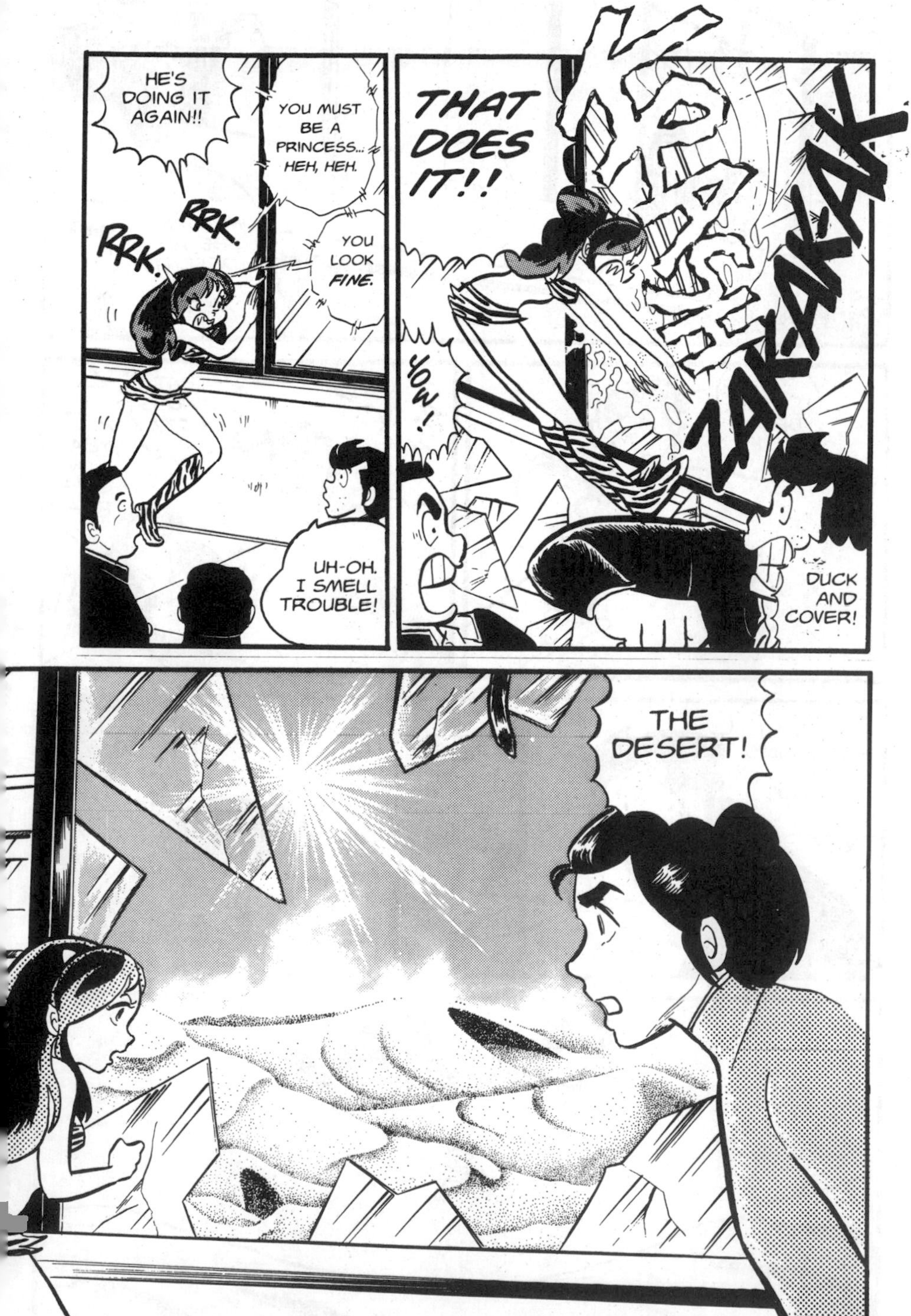
HE'S DOING IT AGAIN!!
YOU MUST BE A PRINCESS... HEH, HEH.
RRK.
RRK.
YOU LOOK *FINE*.
UH-OH. I SMELL TROUBLE!
THAT DOES IT!!
KSSHHH
ZAK-AK-AK
YOW!
DUCK AND COVER!
THE DESERT!

WE CAN'T SEE ANY DESERT FROM *HERE!*

IT MUST BE AN ILLU--

OUCH!

THAT SAND IS *HOT!*

YEAH. AN' IT'S REAL!

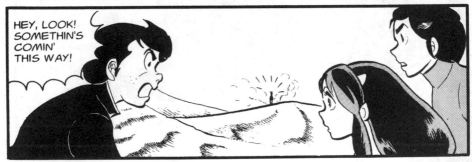

HEY, LOOK! SOMETHIN'S COMIN' THIS WAY!

YO! YO!

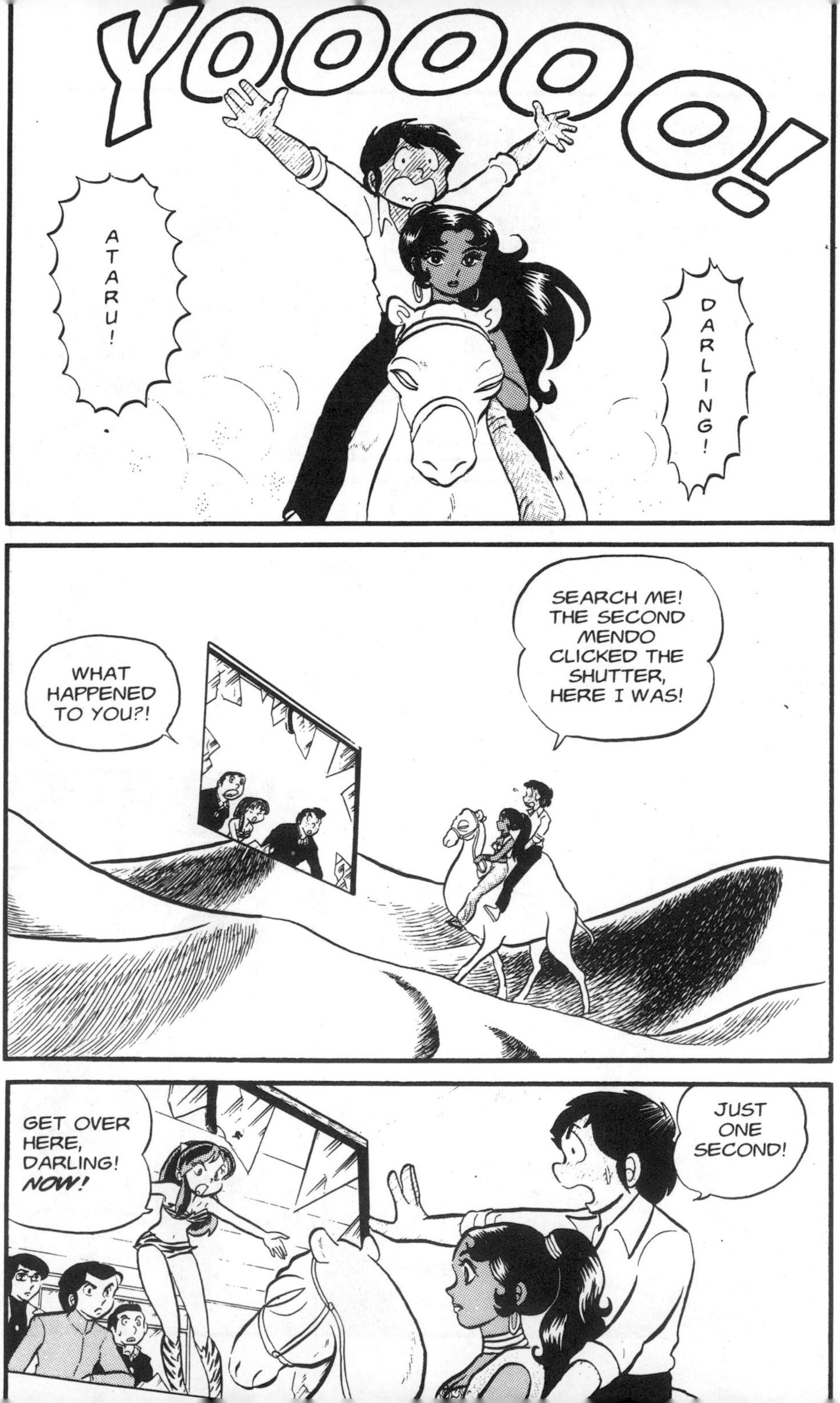
YOOOOOO!
ATARU!
DARLING!
WHAT HAPPENED TO YOU?!
SEARCH ME! THE SECOND MENDO CLICKED THE SHUTTER, HERE I WAS!
GET OVER HERE, DARLING! *NOW!*
JUST ONE SECOND!

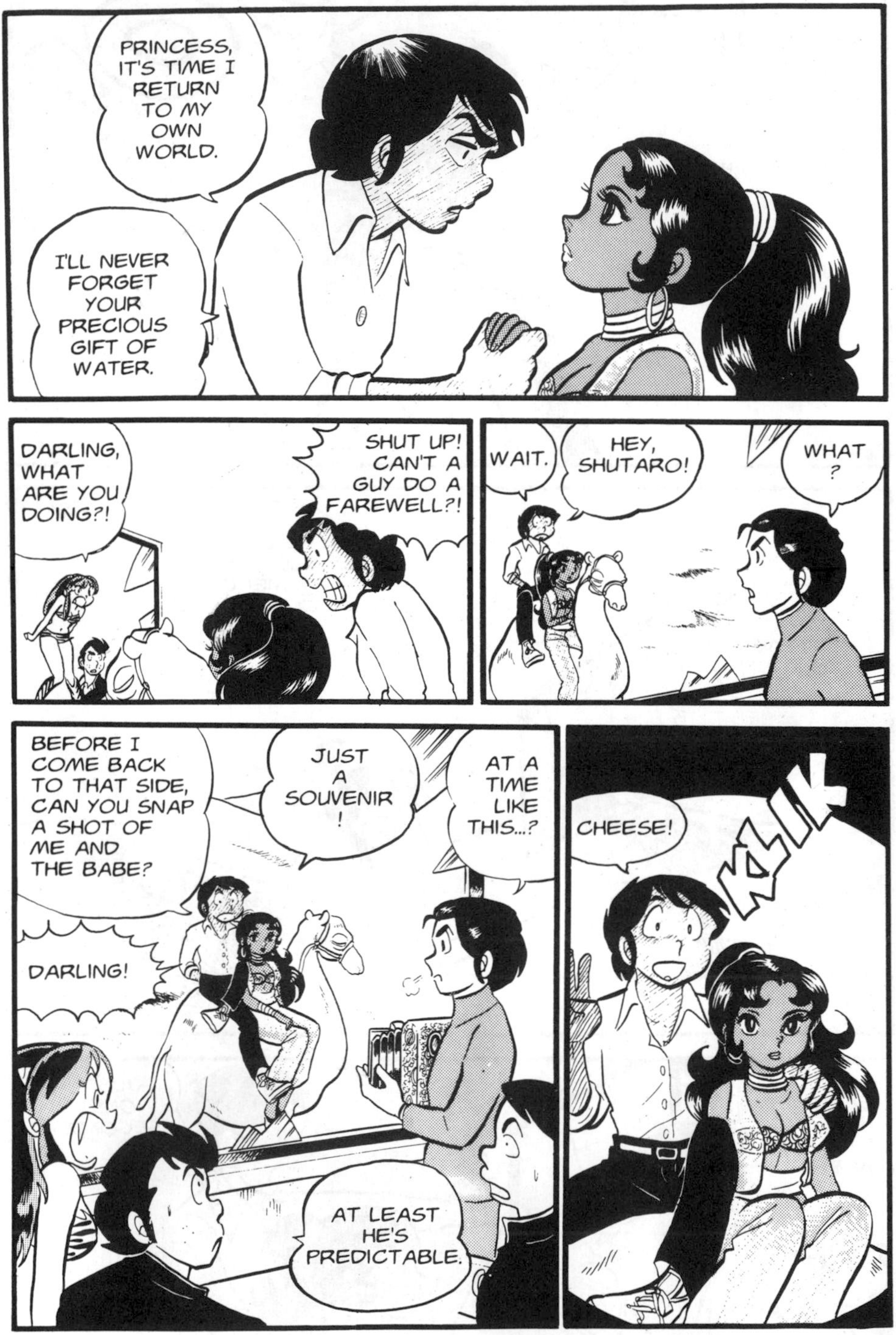
PRINCESS, IT'S TIME I RETURN TO MY OWN WORLD.
I'LL NEVER FORGET YOUR PRECIOUS GIFT OF WATER.
DARLING, WHAT ARE YOU DOING?!
SHUT UP! CAN'T A GUY DO A FAREWELL?!
WAIT.
HEY, SHUTARO!
WHAT?
BEFORE I COME BACK TO THAT SIDE, CAN YOU SNAP A SHOT OF ME AND THE BABE?
JUST A SOUVENIR!
AT A TIME LIKE THIS...?
DARLING!
AT LEAST HE'S PREDICTABLE.
CHEESE!
KLIK

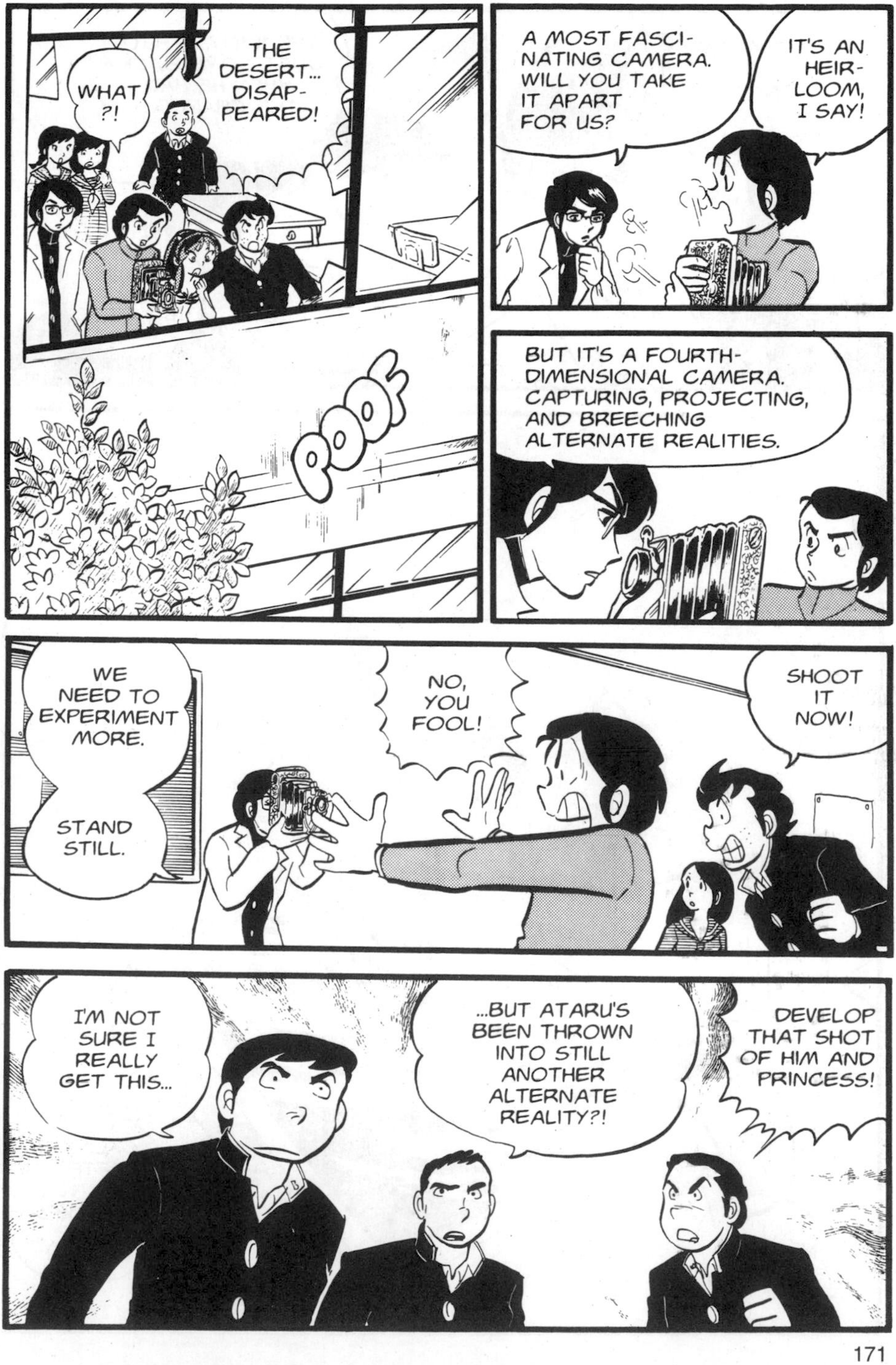
WHAT ?!
THE DESERT... DISAP-PEARED!
POOF
A MOST FASCI-NATING CAMERA. WILL YOU TAKE IT APART FOR US?
IT'S AN HEIR-LOOM, I SAY!
BUT IT'S A FOURTH-DIMENSIONAL CAMERA. CAPTURING, PROJECTING, AND BREECHING ALTERNATE REALITIES.
WE NEED TO EXPERIMENT MORE.
STAND STILL.
NO, YOU FOOL!
SHOOT IT NOW!
I'M NOT SURE I REALLY GET THIS...
...BUT ATARU'S BEEN THROWN INTO STILL ANOTHER ALTERNATE REALITY?!
DEVELOP THAT SHOT OF HIM AND PRINCESS!

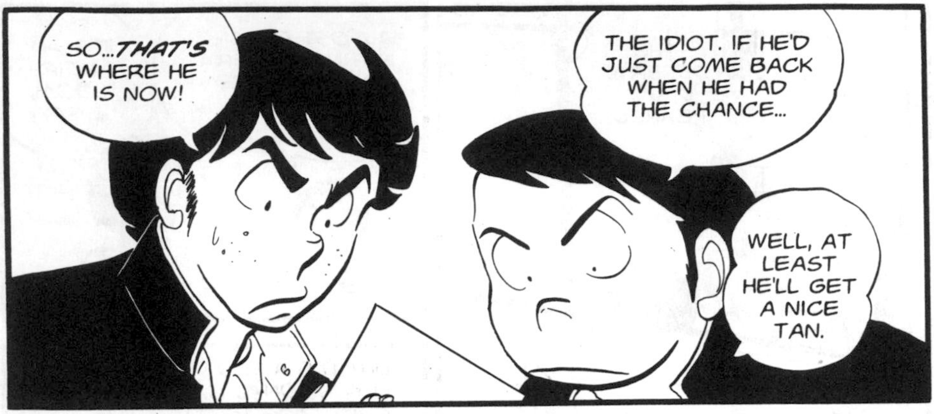
SO...THAT'S WHERE HE IS NOW!
THE IDIOT. IF HE'D JUST COME BACK WHEN HE HAD THE CHANCE...
WELL, AT LEAST HE'LL GET A NICE TAN.
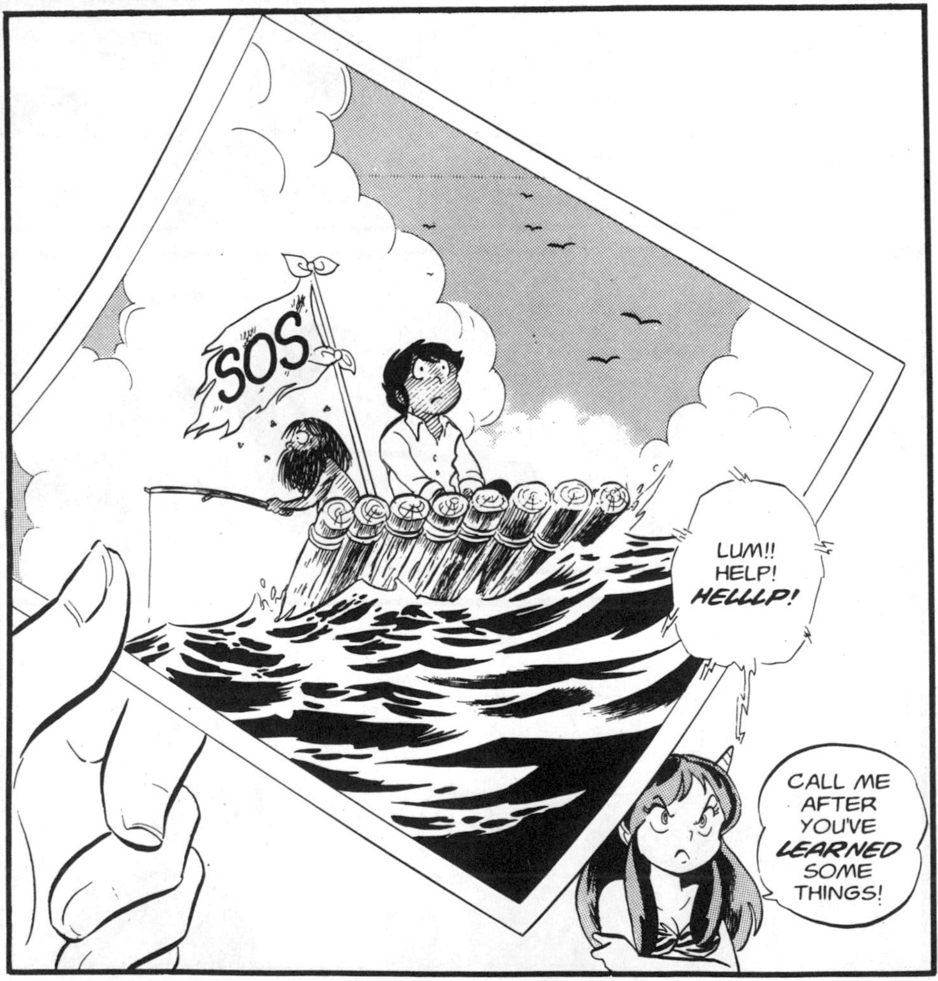
SOS
LUM!! HELP! HELLLP!
CALL ME AFTER YOU'VE LEARNED SOME THINGS!

Part 11
A Flying Start

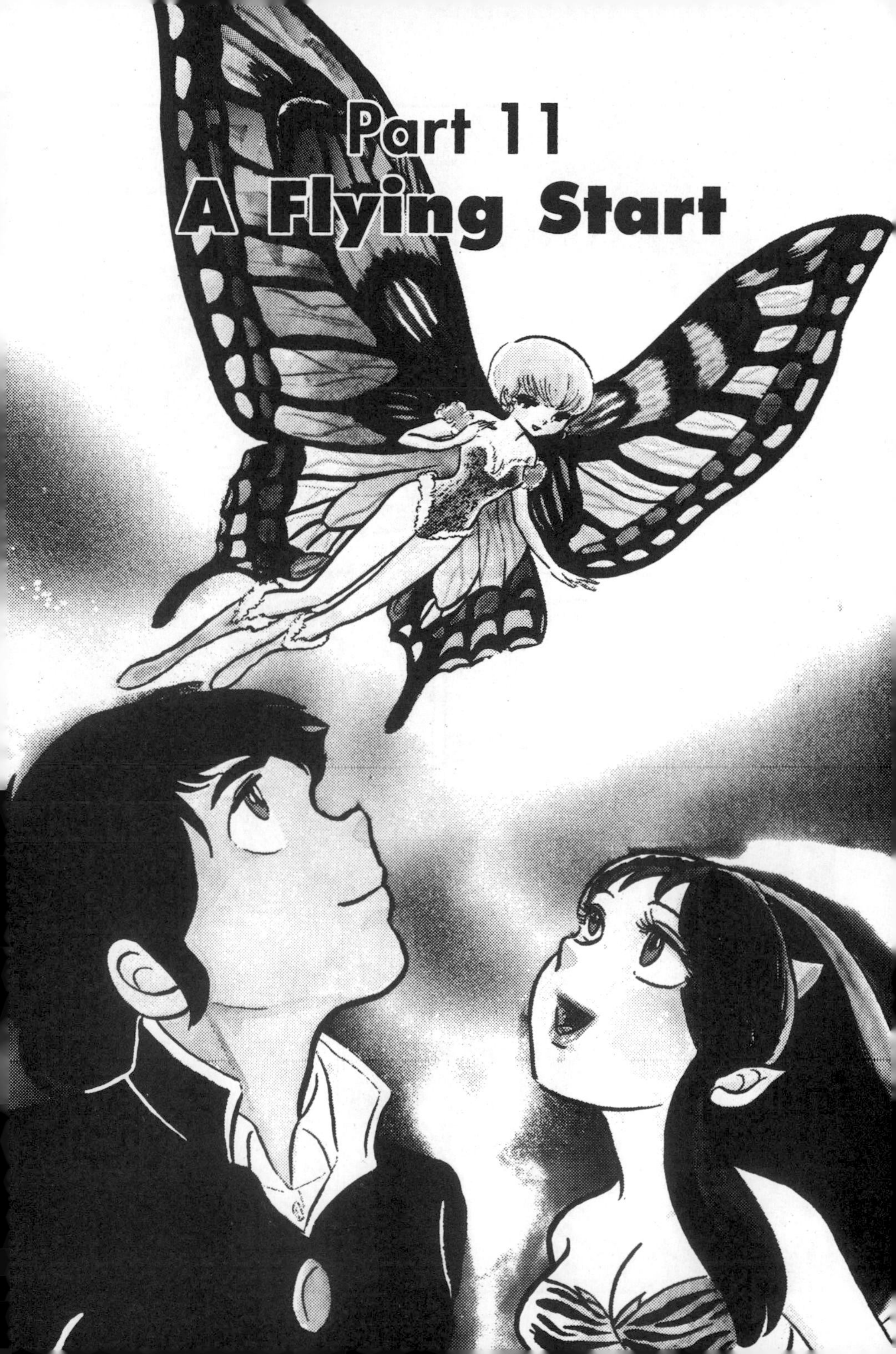

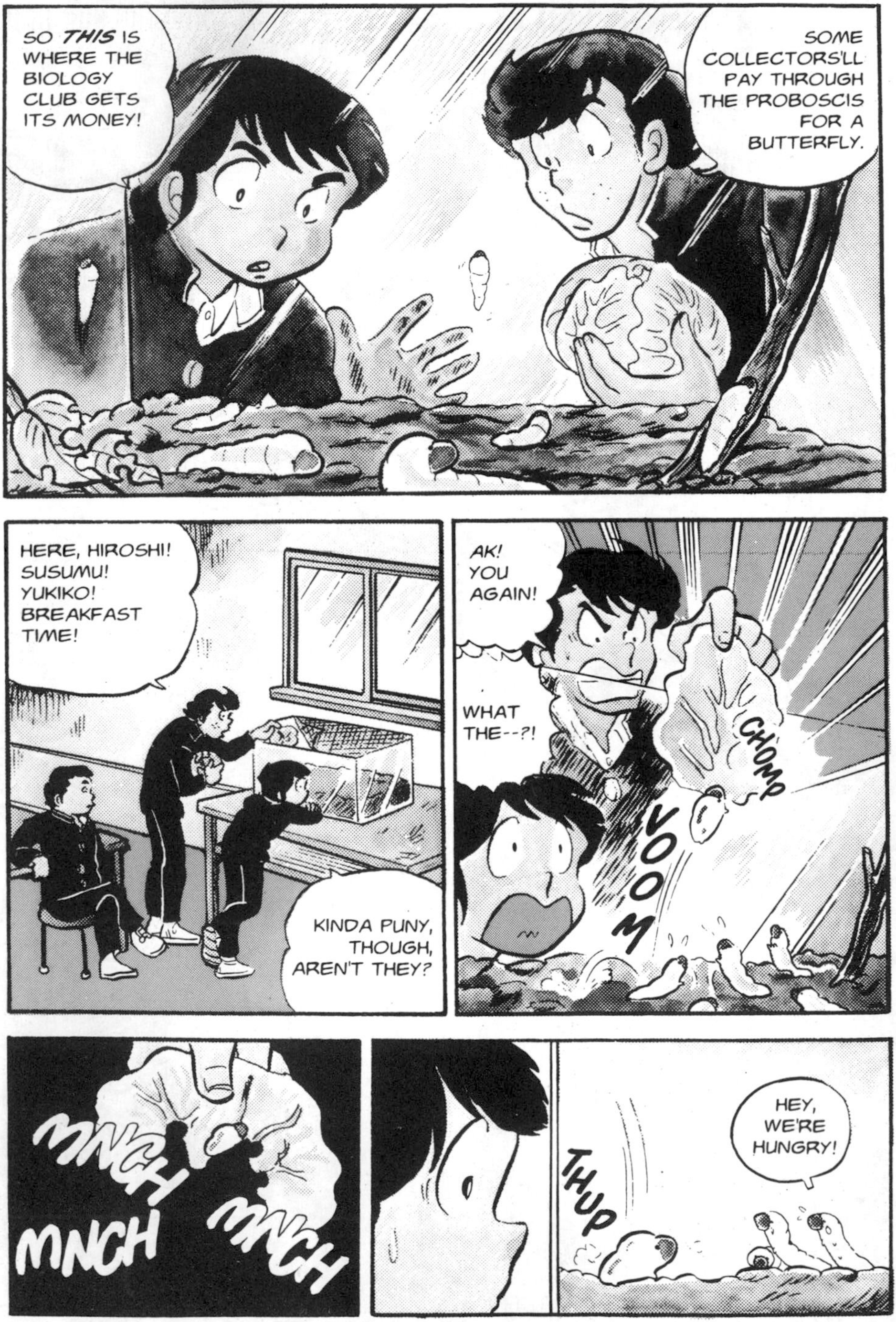
SO THIS IS WHERE THE BIOLOGY CLUB GETS ITS MONEY!
SOME COLLECTORS'LL PAY THROUGH THE PROBOSCIS FOR A BUTTERFLY.
HERE, HIROSHI! SUSUMU! YUKIKO! BREAKFAST TIME!
KINDA PUNY, THOUGH, AREN'T THEY?
AK! YOU AGAIN!
WHAT THE--?!
CHOMP
VOOOM
MNCH
MNCH
MNCH
THUP
HEY, WE'RE HUNGRY!

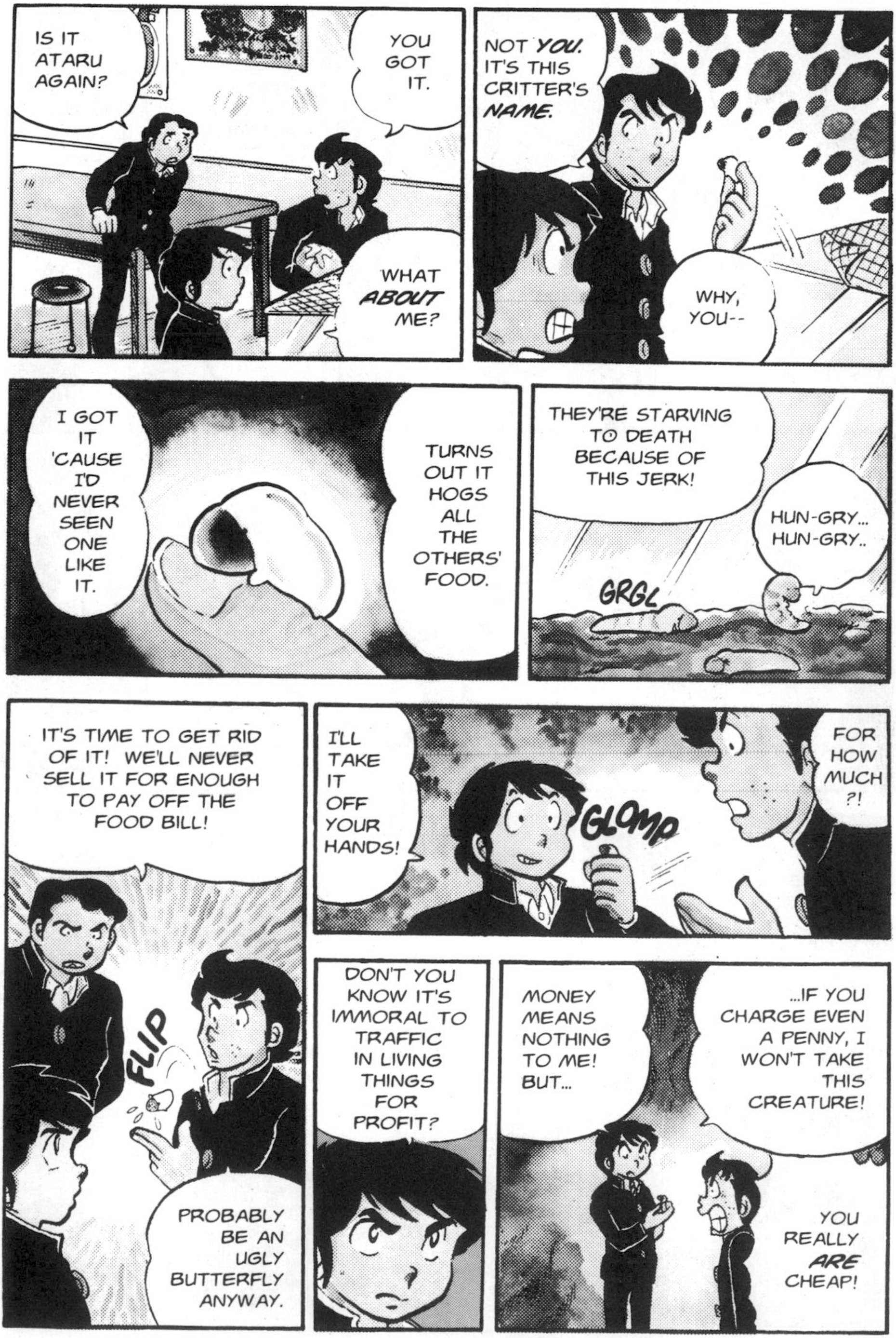
IS IT ATARU AGAIN?
YOU GOT IT.
WHAT ABOUT ME?
NOT YOU. IT'S THIS CRITTER'S NAME.
WHY, YOU--
I GOT IT 'CAUSE I'D NEVER SEEN ONE LIKE IT.
TURNS OUT IT HOGS ALL THE OTHERS' FOOD.
THEY'RE STARVING TO DEATH BECAUSE OF THIS JERK!
HUN-GRY... HUN-GRY..
GRGL
IT'S TIME TO GET RID OF IT! WE'LL NEVER SELL IT FOR ENOUGH TO PAY OFF THE FOOD BILL!
FLIP
PROBABLY BE AN UGLY BUTTERFLY ANYWAY.
I'LL TAKE IT OFF YOUR HANDS!
GLOMP
FOR HOW MUCH?!
DON'T YOU KNOW IT'S IMMORAL TO TRAFFIC IN LIVING THINGS FOR PROFIT?
MONEY MEANS NOTHING TO ME! BUT...
...IF YOU CHARGE EVEN A PENNY, I WON'T TAKE THIS CREATURE!
YOU REALLY ARE CHEAP!

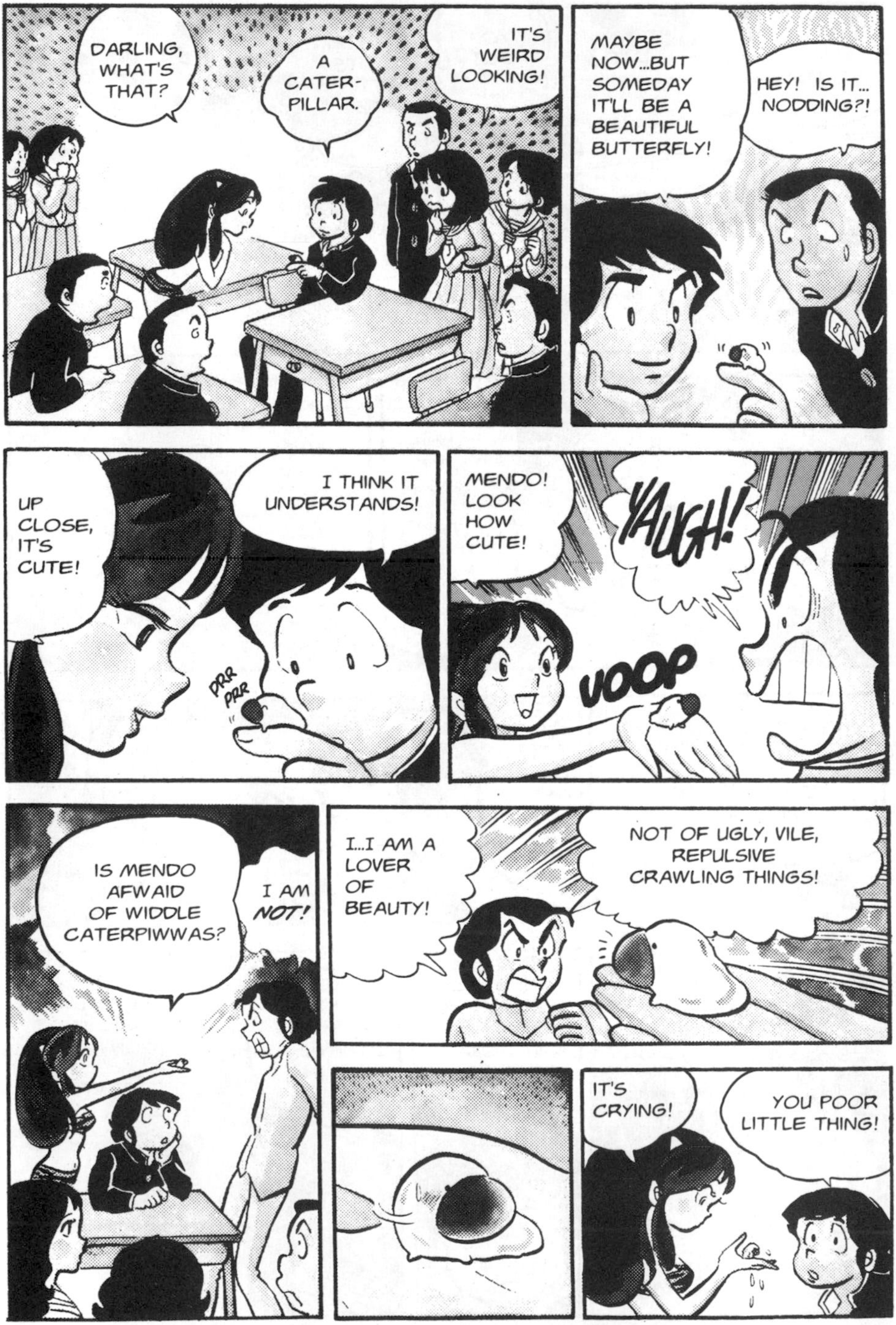
DARLING, WHAT'S THAT?
A CATER-PILLAR.
IT'S WEIRD LOOKING!
MAYBE NOW...BUT SOMEDAY IT'LL BE A BEAUTIFUL BUTTERFLY!
HEY! IS IT... NODDING?!
UP CLOSE, IT'S CUTE!
I THINK IT UNDERSTANDS!
PRR PRR
MENDO! LOOK HOW CUTE!
YAUGH!
VOOP
IS MENDO AFWAID OF WIDDLE CATERPIWWAS?
I AM *NOT!*
I...I AM A LOVER OF BEAUTY!
NOT OF UGLY, VILE, REPULSIVE CRAWLING THINGS!
IT'S CRYING!
YOU POOR LITTLE THING!

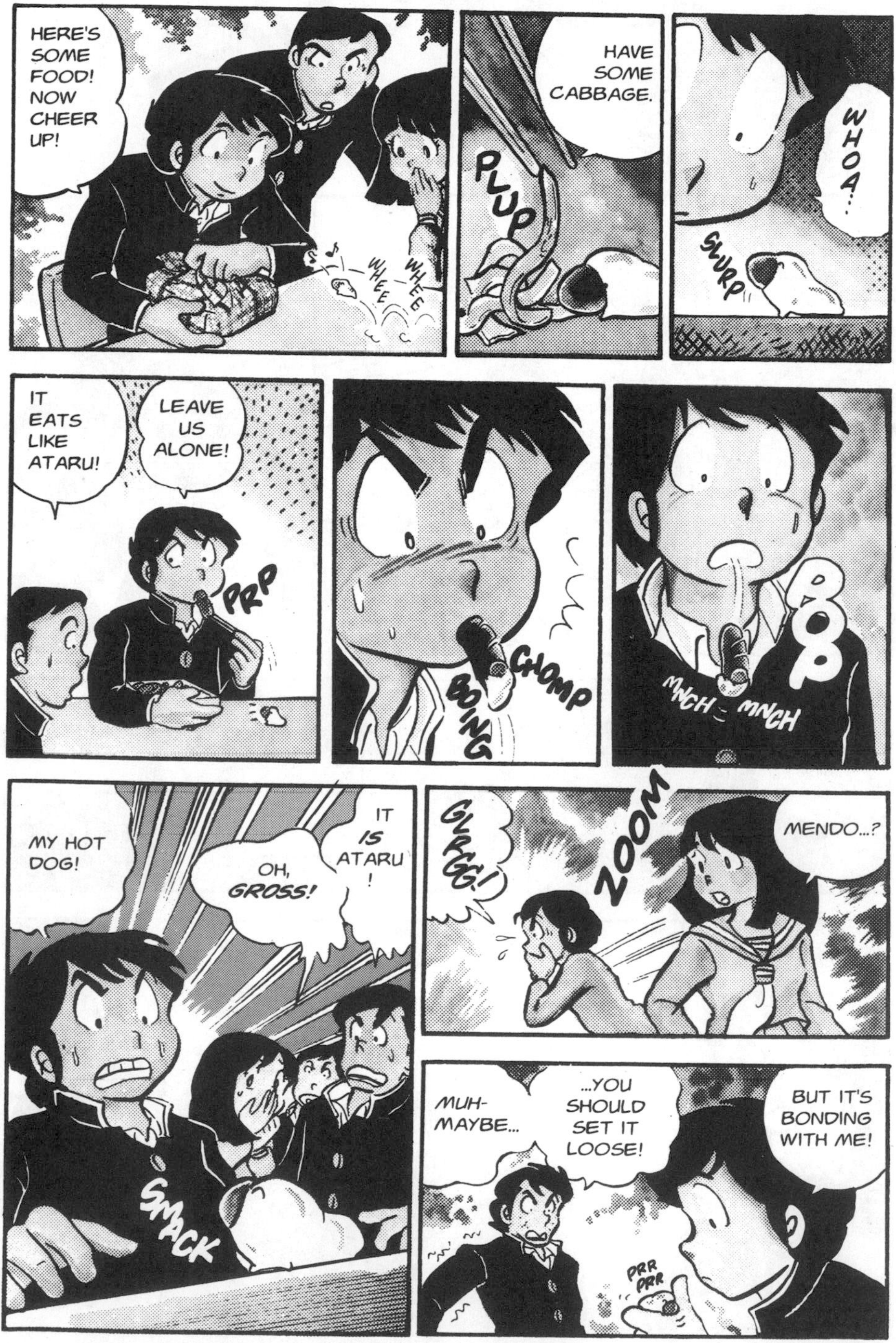
HERE'S SOME FOOD! NOW CHEER UP!
WHEE
WHEE
HAVE SOME CABBAGE.
PLUP
WHOA...
SLURP
IT EATS LIKE ATARU!
LEAVE US ALONE!
PRP
CHOMP
BOING
POP
MNCH MNCH
MY HOT DOG!
OH, GROSS!
IT IS ATARU!
SMACK
GLRGG!
ZOOM
MENDO...?
MUH-MAYBE...
...YOU SHOULD SET IT LOOSE!
BUT IT'S BONDING WITH ME!
PRR PRR

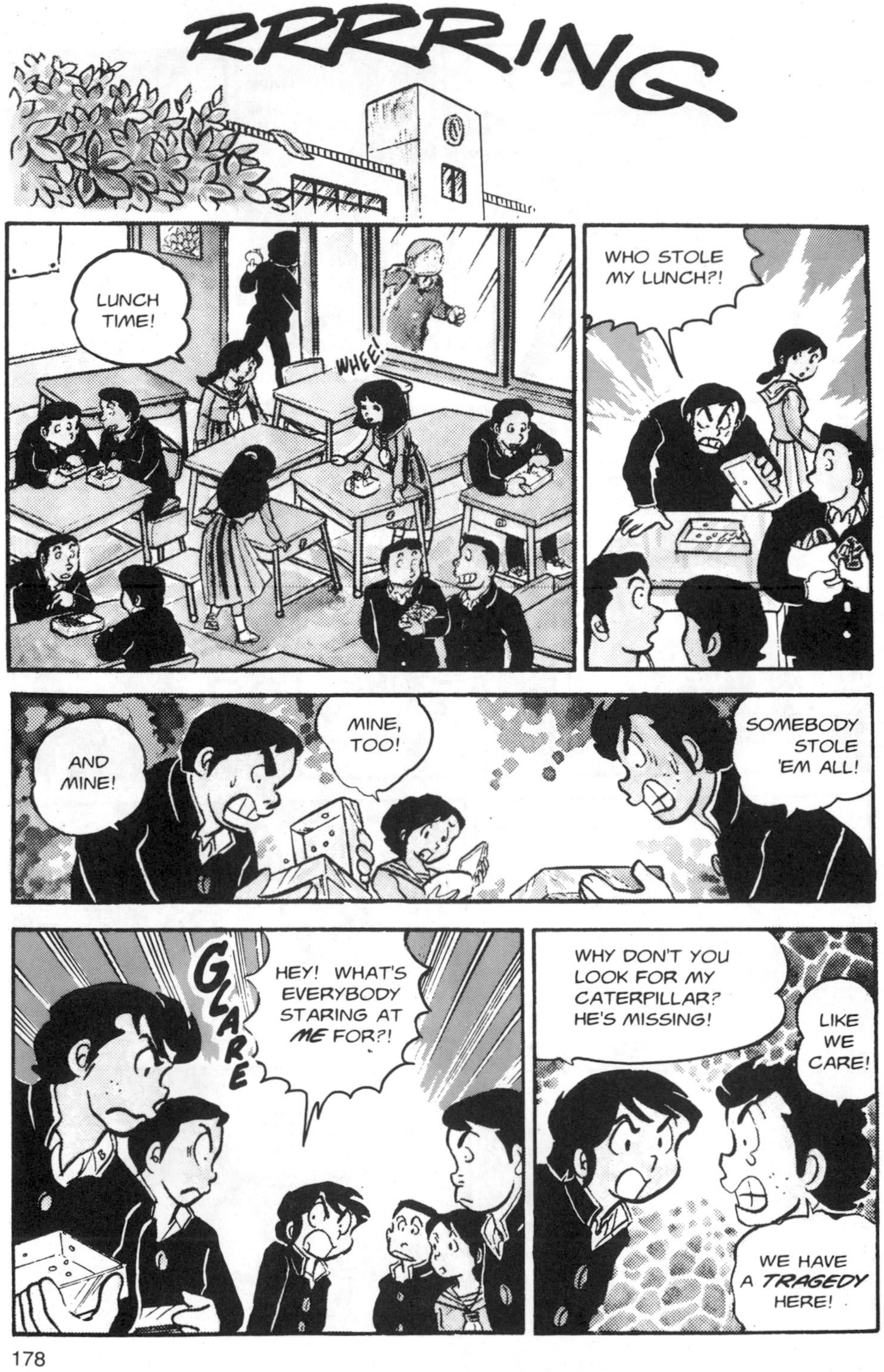
RRRRING
LUNCH TIME!
WHEE!
WHO STOLE MY LUNCH?!
AND MINE!
MINE, TOO!
SOMEBODY STOLE 'EM ALL!
GLARE
HEY! WHAT'S EVERYBODY STARING AT ME FOR?!
WHY DON'T YOU LOOK FOR MY CATERPILLAR? HE'S MISSING!
LIKE WE CARE!
WE HAVE A TRAGEDY HERE!

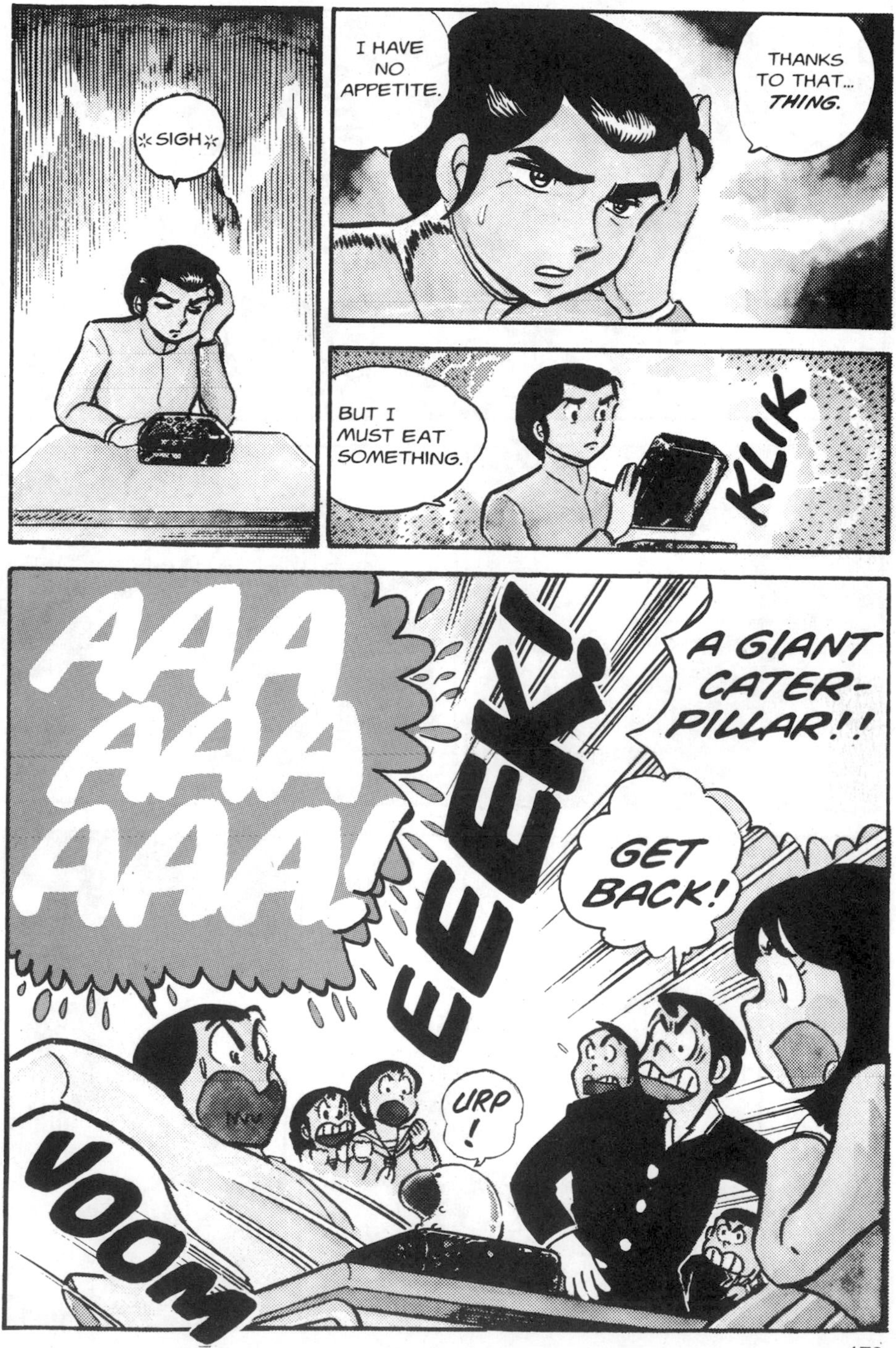

SIGH
I HAVE NO APPETITE.
THANKS TO THAT... *THING*.
BUT I MUST EAT SOMETHING.
KLIK
AAAAAAAAA!
EEEEK!
A GIANT CATER-PILLAR!!
GET BACK!
URP!
VOOM

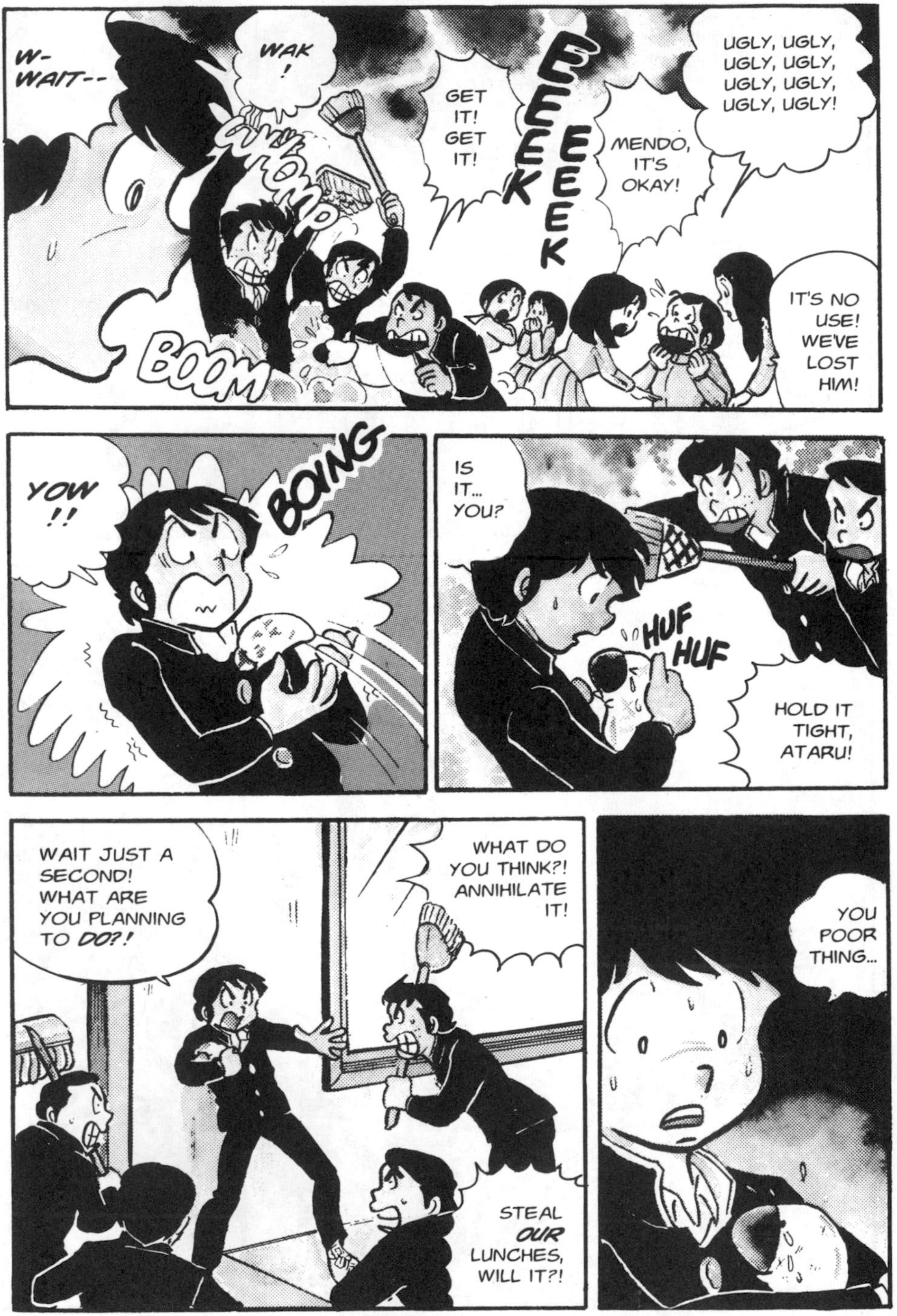
W-WAIT--
WAK!
CHOMP
BOOM
GET IT! GET IT!
EEEEK
EEEEK
MENDO, IT'S OKAY!
UGLY, UGLY, UGLY, UGLY, UGLY, UGLY, UGLY, UGLY!
IT'S NO USE! WE'VE LOST HIM!
YOW!!
BOING
IS IT... YOU?
HUF HUF
HOLD IT TIGHT, ATARU!
WAIT JUST A SECOND! WHAT ARE YOU PLANNING TO *DO?!*
WHAT DO YOU THINK?! ANNIHILATE IT!
STEAL *OUR* LUNCHES, WILL IT?!
YOU POOR THING...

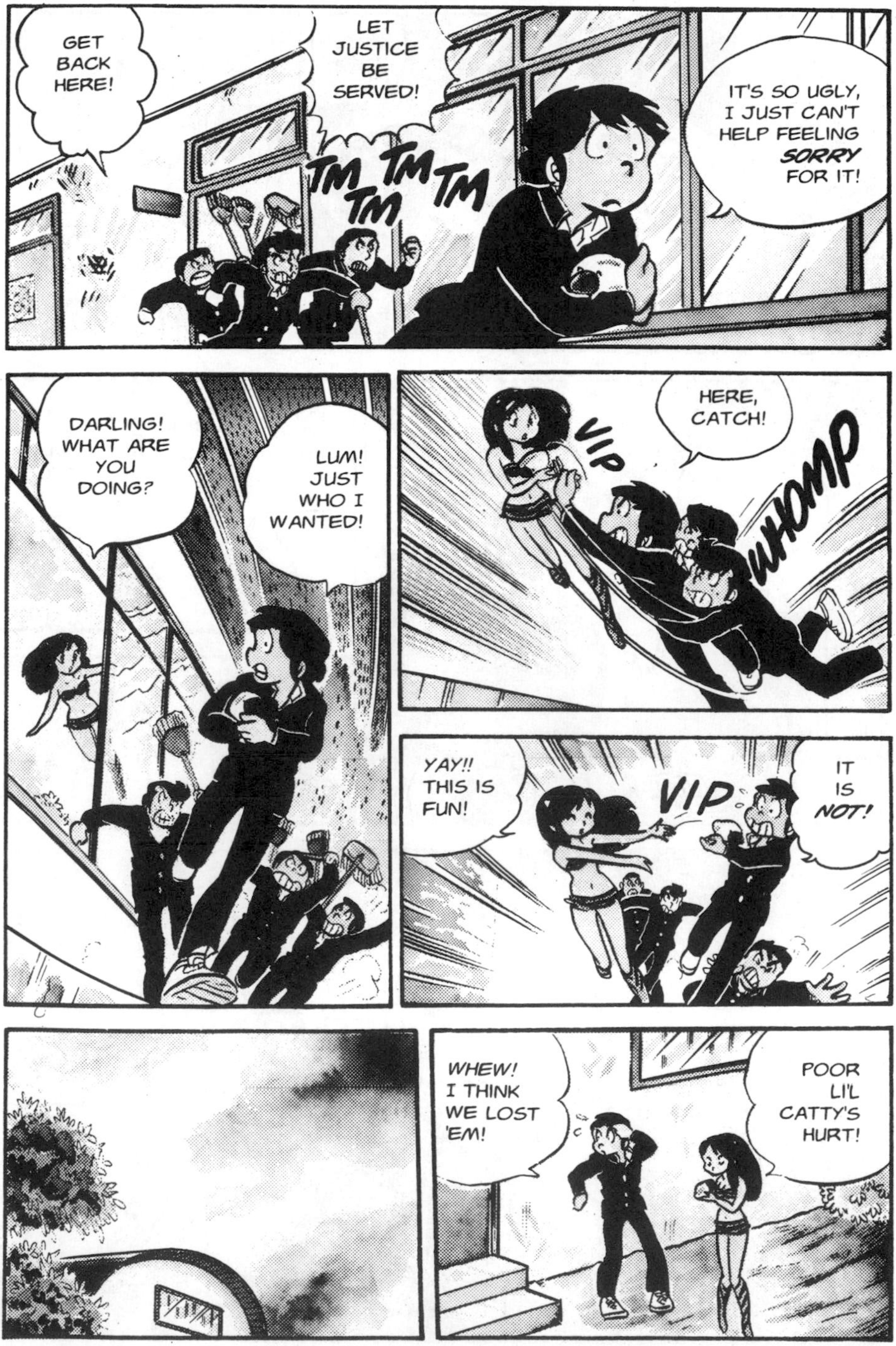
GET BACK HERE!
LET JUSTICE BE SERVED!
TM TM TM TM TM
IT'S SO UGLY, I JUST CAN'T HELP FEELING SORRY FOR IT!
DARLING! WHAT ARE YOU DOING?
LUM! JUST WHO I WANTED!
VIP
HERE, CATCH!
WHOMP
YAY!! THIS IS FUN!
VIP
IT IS NOT!
WHEW! I THINK WE LOST 'EM!
POOR LI'L CATTY'S HURT!

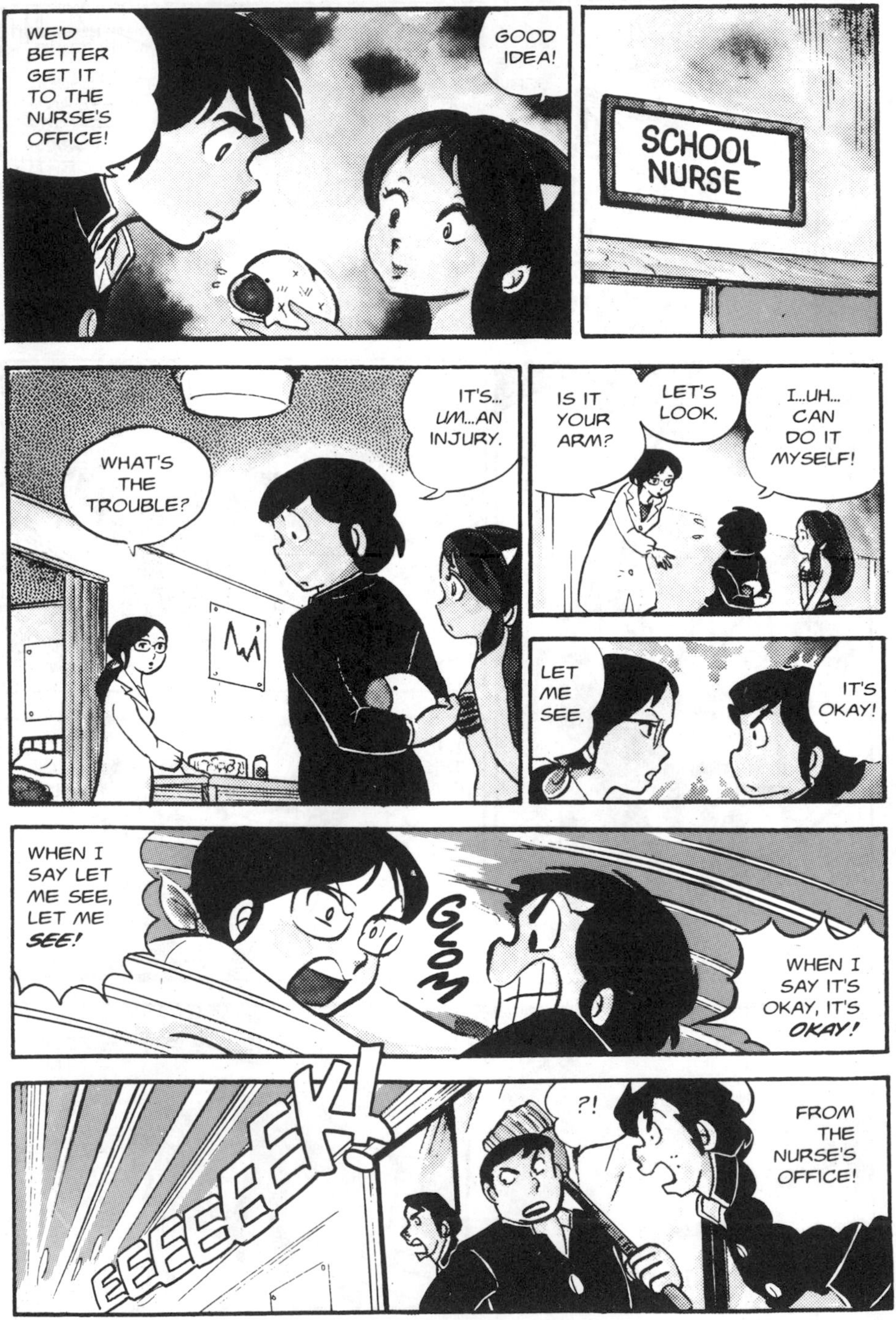
WE'D BETTER GET IT TO THE NURSE'S OFFICE!
GOOD IDEA!
SCHOOL NURSE
WHAT'S THE TROUBLE?
IT'S... UM...AN INJURY.
IS IT YOUR ARM?
LET'S LOOK.
I...UH... CAN DO IT MYSELF!
LET ME SEE.
IT'S OKAY!
WHEN I SAY LET ME SEE, LET ME SEE!
GLOM
WHEN I SAY IT'S OKAY, IT'S OKAY!
EEEEEEEK!
?!
FROM THE NURSE'S OFFICE!

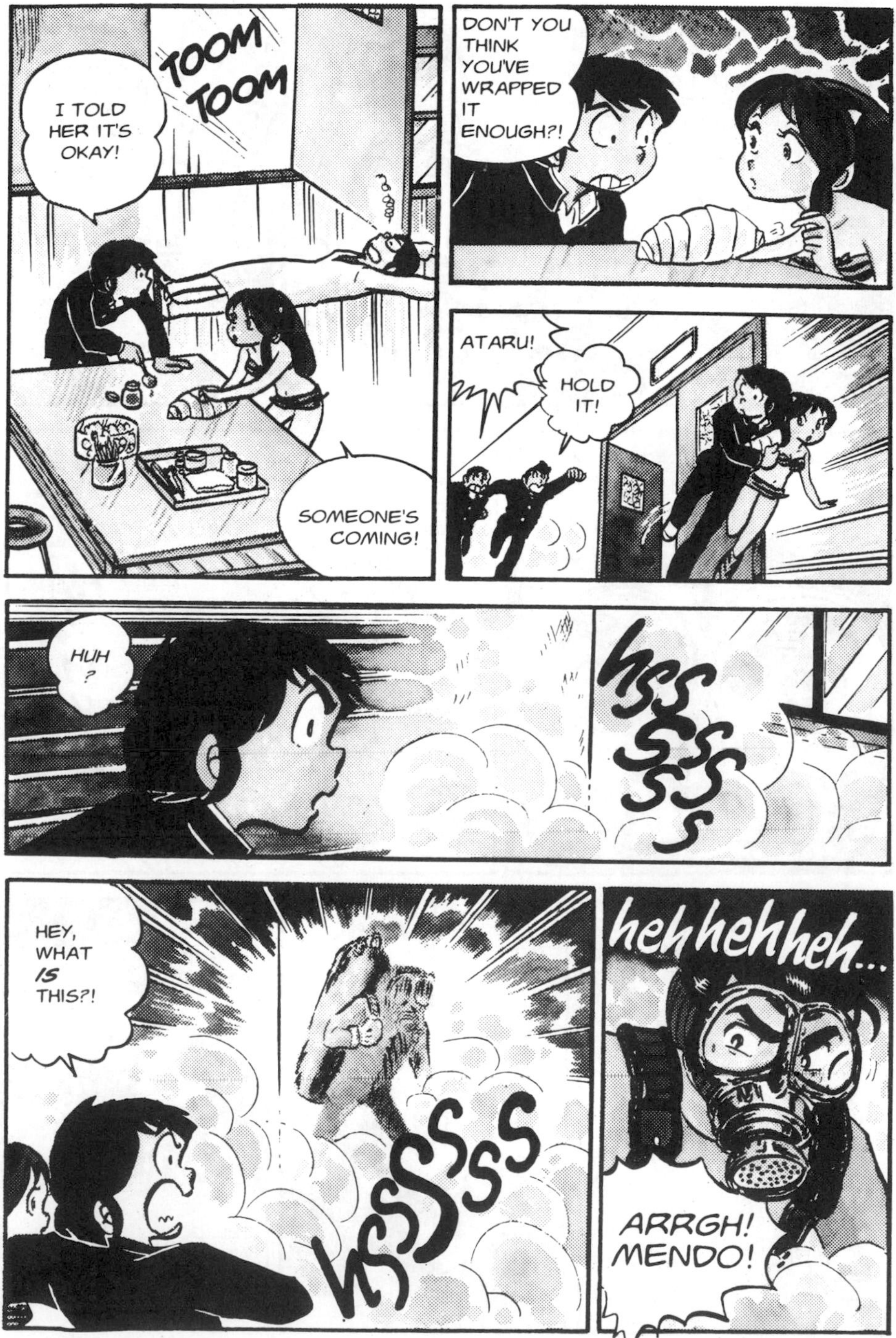
TOOM TOOM
I TOLD HER IT'S OKAY!
SOMEONE'S COMING!
DON'T YOU THINK YOU'VE WRAPPED IT ENOUGH?!
ATARU!
HOLD IT!
HUH?
hsssssss
HEY, WHAT *IS* THIS?!
hssssss
heh heh heh...
ARRGH! MENDO!

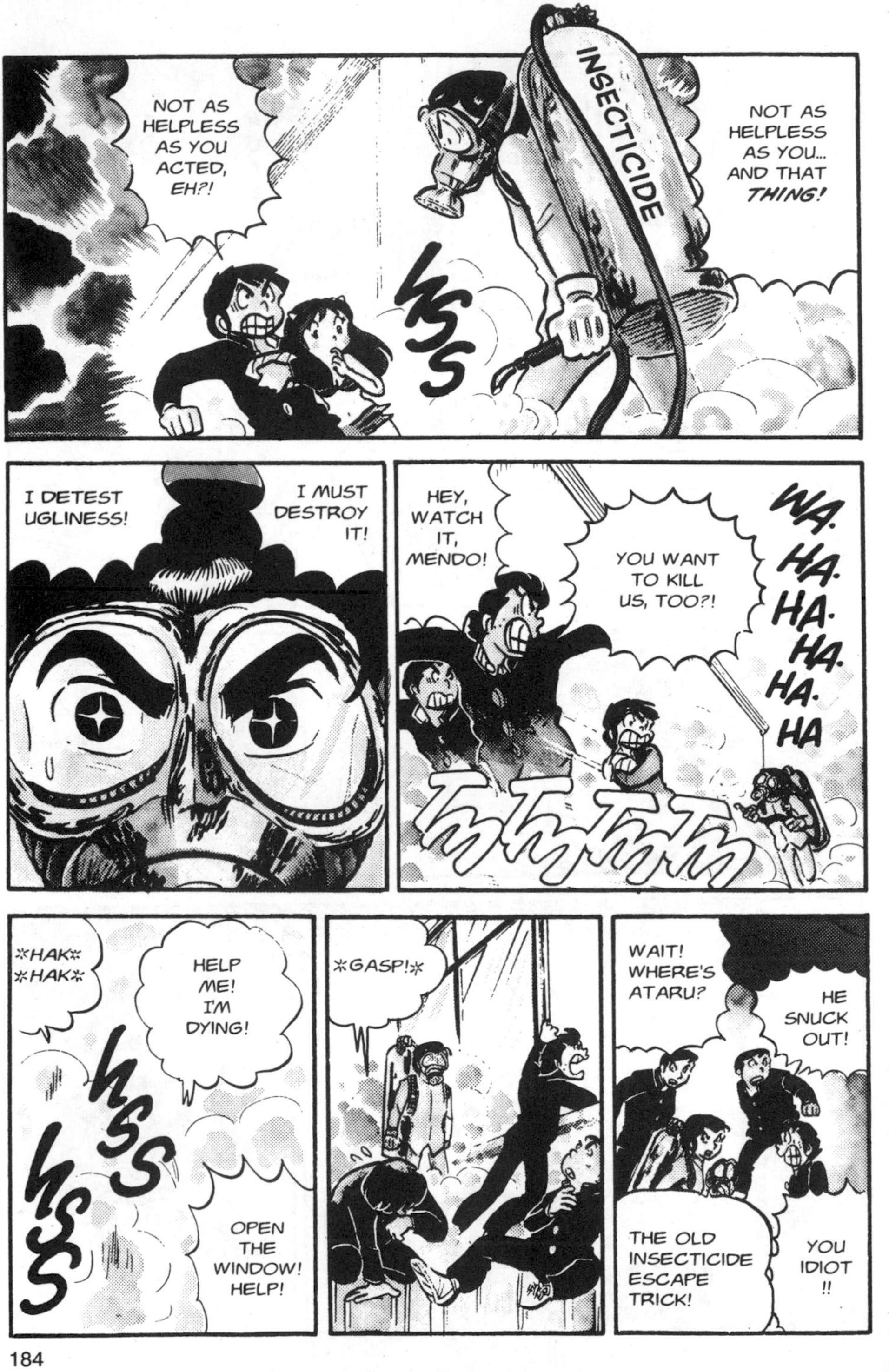
NOT AS HELPLESS AS YOU ACTED, EH?!
INSECTICIDE
HSS
NOT AS HELPLESS AS YOU... AND THAT *THING!*
I DETEST UGLINESS!
I MUST DESTROY IT!
HEY, WATCH IT, MENDO!
YOU WANT TO KILL US, TOO?!
WA. HA. HA. HA. HA. HA. HA
HAK *HAK*
HELP ME! I'M DYING!
HSS HSS
OPEN THE WINDOW! HELP!
GASP!
WAIT! WHERE'S ATARU?
HE SNUCK OUT!
THE OLD INSECTICIDE ESCAPE TRICK!
YOU IDIOT !!

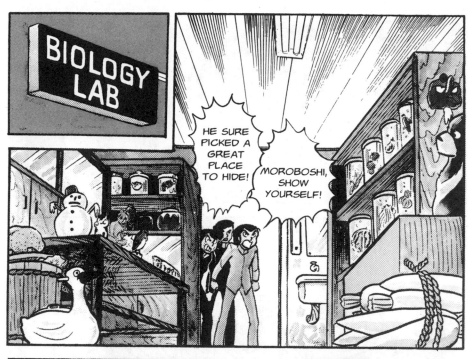

BIOLOGY LAB

HE SURE PICKED A GREAT PLACE TO HIDE!

MOROBOSHI, SHOW YOURSELF!

THERE YOU ARE!

NYAAH!

STUFFED

YOW!

AH! THE OLD BODY-SWITCHING TRICK!

KLATTER

HYAH!

BONG

BULL'S EYE!

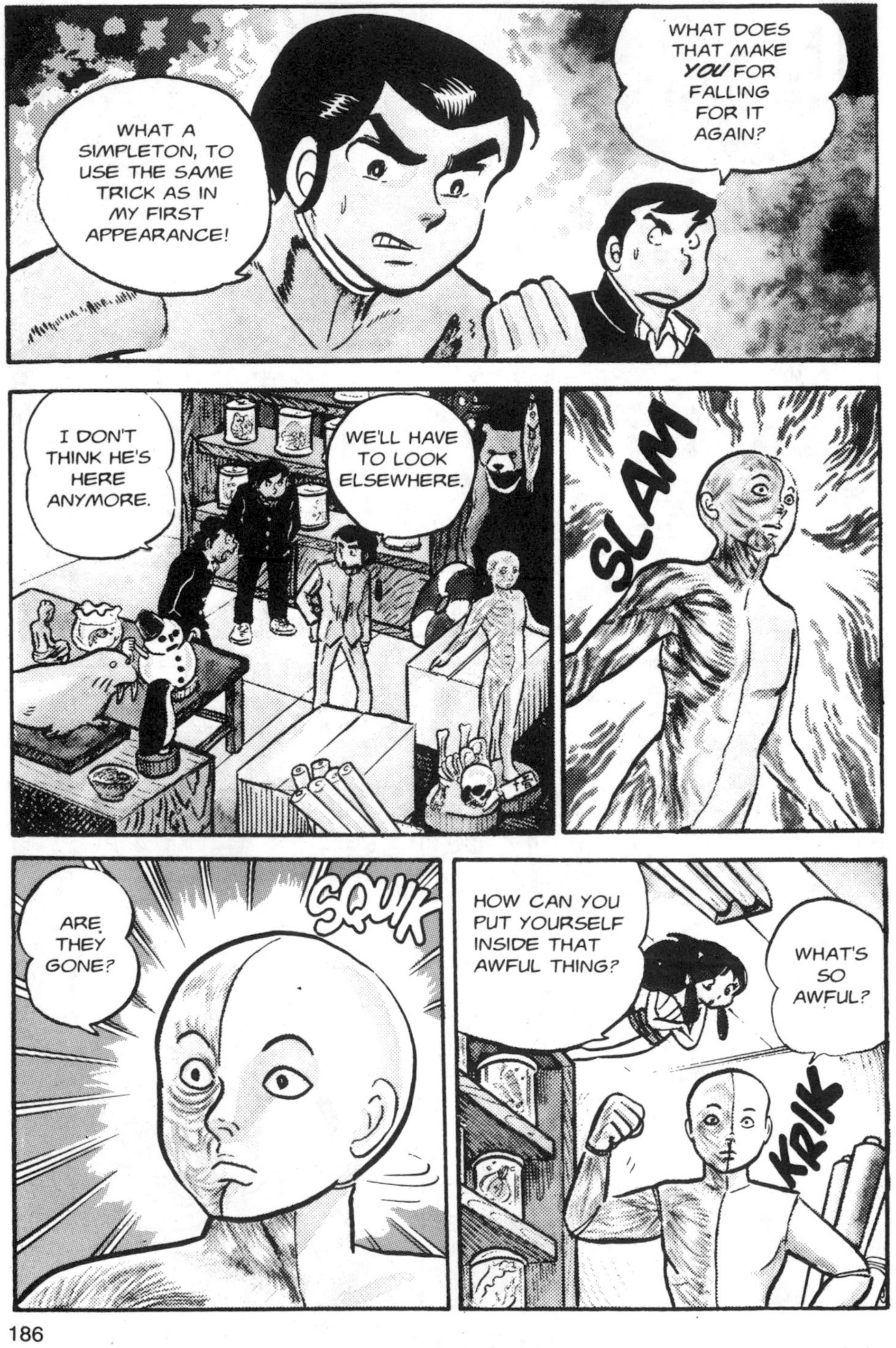
WHAT A SIMPLETON, TO USE THE SAME TRICK AS IN MY FIRST APPEARANCE!
WHAT DOES THAT MAKE YOU FOR FALLING FOR IT AGAIN?
I DON'T THINK HE'S HERE ANYMORE.
WE'LL HAVE TO LOOK ELSEWHERE.
SLAM
ARE THEY GONE?
SQUIK
HOW CAN YOU PUT YOURSELF INSIDE THAT AWFUL THING?
WHAT'S SO AWFUL?
KRIK

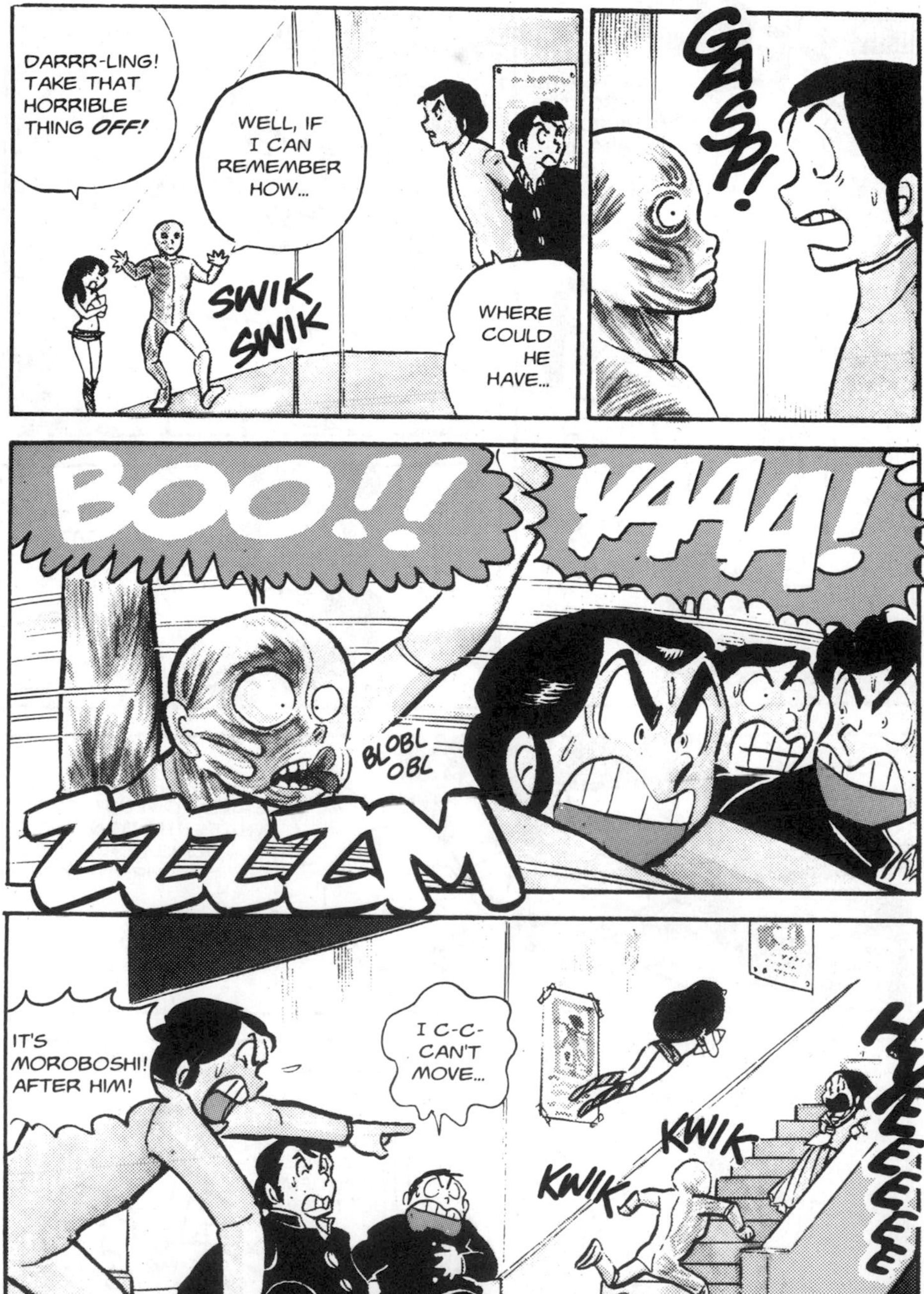

DARRR-LING! TAKE THAT HORRIBLE THING *OFF!*
WELL, IF I CAN REMEMBER HOW...
SWIK SWIK
WHERE COULD HE HAVE...
GASP!
BOO!!
YAAA!
BLOBL OBL
ZZZZM
IT'S MOROBOSHI! AFTER HIM!
I C-C-CAN'T MOVE...
KWIK
KWIK
HYEEEEEE

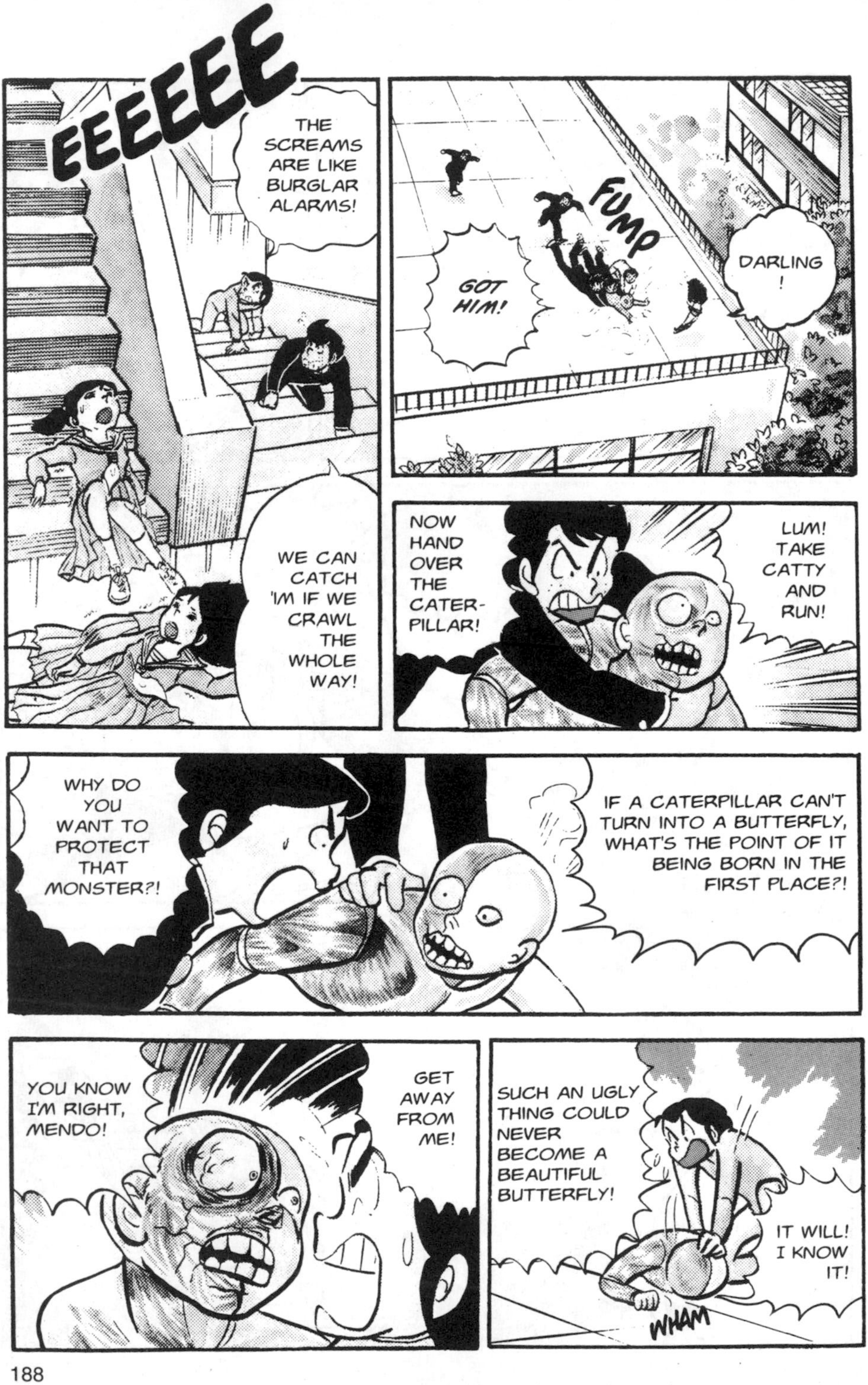
EEEEEE
THE SCREAMS ARE LIKE BURGLAR ALARMS!
WE CAN CATCH 'IM IF WE CRAWL THE WHOLE WAY!
GOT HIM!
FUMP
DARLING!
NOW HAND OVER THE CATER-PILLAR!
LUM! TAKE CATTY AND RUN!
WHY DO YOU WANT TO PROTECT THAT MONSTER?!
IF A CATERPILLAR CAN'T TURN INTO A BUTTERFLY, WHAT'S THE POINT OF IT BEING BORN IN THE FIRST PLACE?!
YOU KNOW I'M RIGHT, MENDO!
GET AWAY FROM ME!
SUCH AN UGLY THING COULD NEVER BECOME A BEAUTIFUL BUTTERFLY!
IT WILL! I KNOW IT!
WHAM

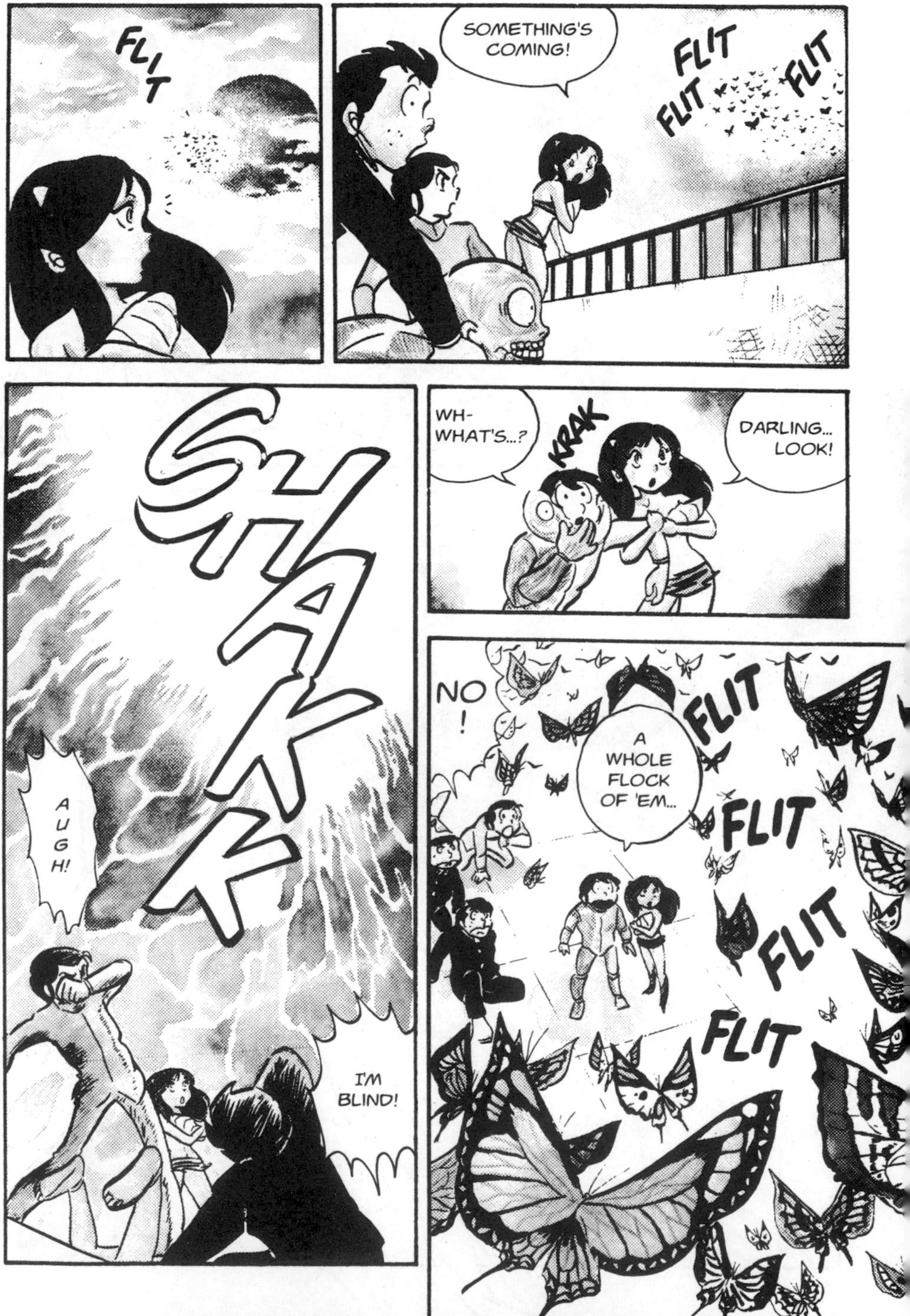
FLIT
SOMETHING'S COMING!
FLIT FLIT FLIT FLIT
SHAKK
AUGH!
I'M BLIND!
WH- WHAT'S...?
KRAK
DARLING... LOOK!
NO!
A WHOLE FLOCK OF 'EM...
FLIT
FLIT
FLIT
FLIT

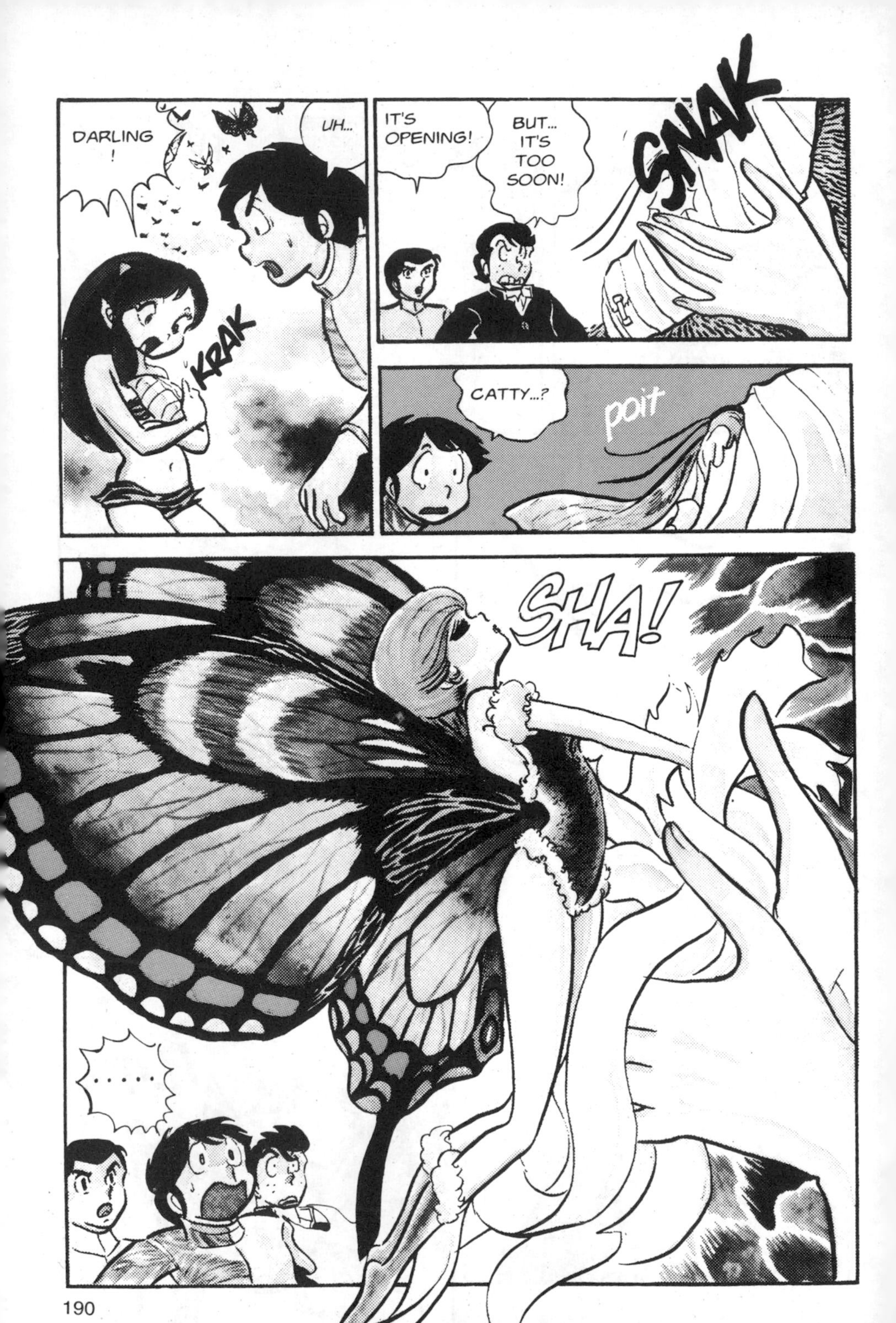

DARLING
!
UH...
KRAK
IT'S OPENING!
BUT... IT'S TOO SOON!
SNAK
CATTY...?
poit
SHA!
......

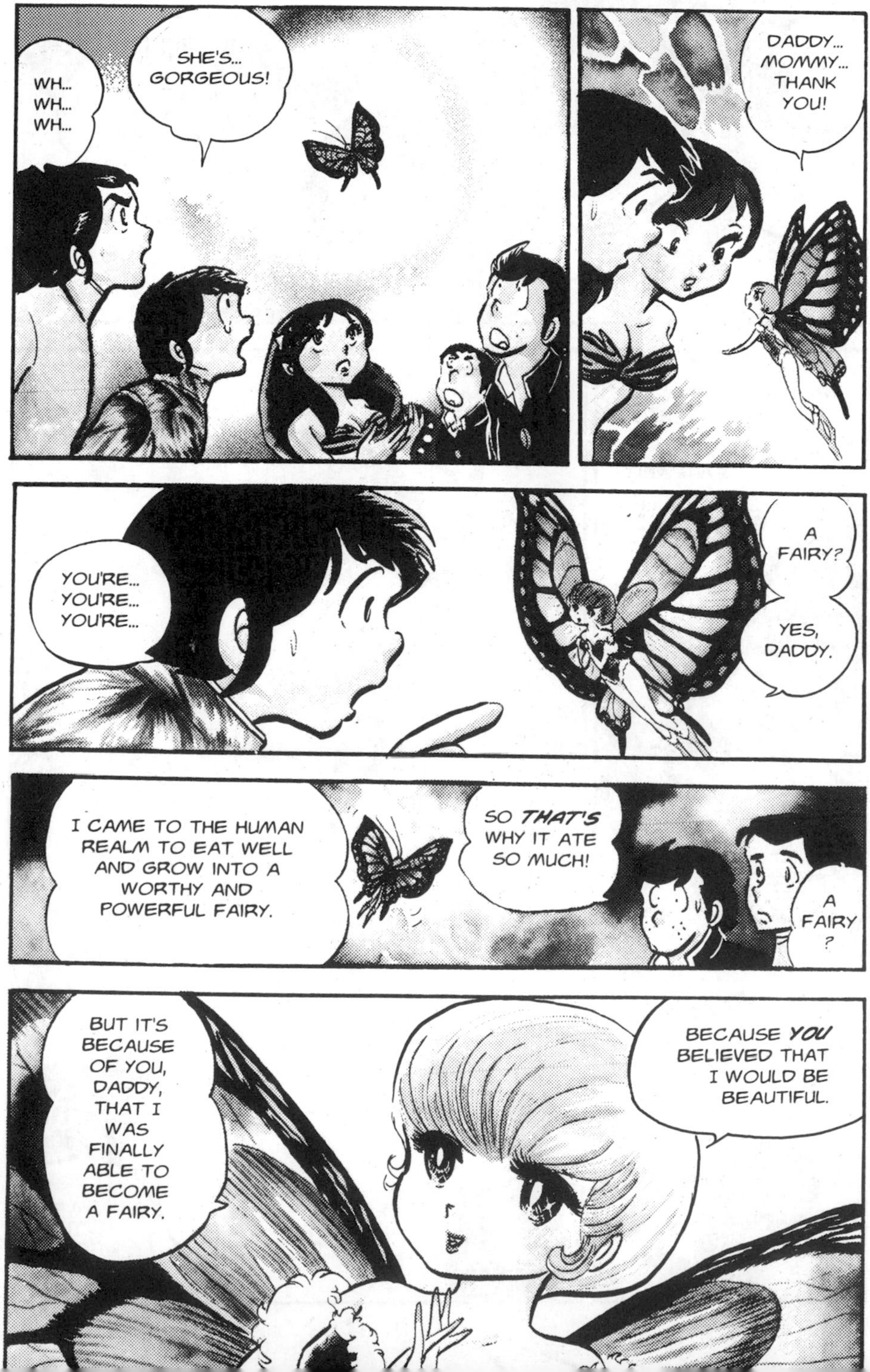
WH...
WH...
WH...
SHE'S... GORGEOUS!
DADDY... MOMMY... THANK YOU!
YOU'RE... YOU'RE... YOU'RE...
A FAIRY?
YES, DADDY.
I CAME TO THE HUMAN REALM TO EAT WELL AND GROW INTO A WORTHY AND POWERFUL FAIRY.
SO THAT'S WHY IT ATE SO MUCH!
A FAIRY ?
BUT IT'S BECAUSE OF YOU, DADDY, THAT I WAS FINALLY ABLE TO BECOME A FAIRY.
BECAUSE YOU BELIEVED THAT I WOULD BE BEAUTIFUL.

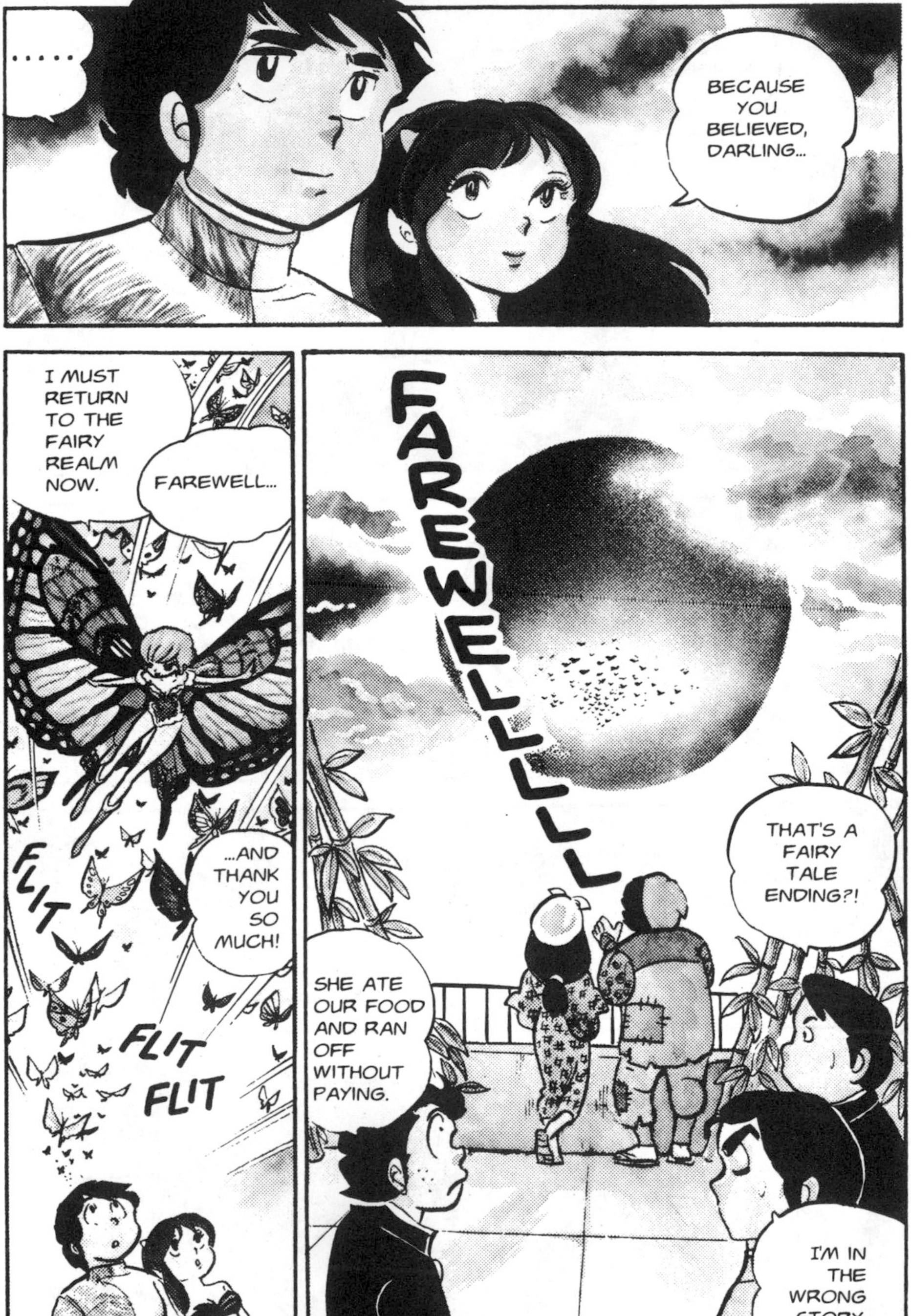
......
BECAUSE YOU BELIEVED, DARLING...
I MUST RETURN TO THE FAIRY REALM NOW.
FAREWELL...
...AND THANK YOU SO MUCH!
FLIT
FLIT
FLIT
FAREWELLLLL
THAT'S A FAIRY TALE ENDING?!
SHE ATE OUR FOOD AND RAN OFF WITHOUT PAYING.
I'M IN THE WRONG STORY.

Part 12
Since You Went Away

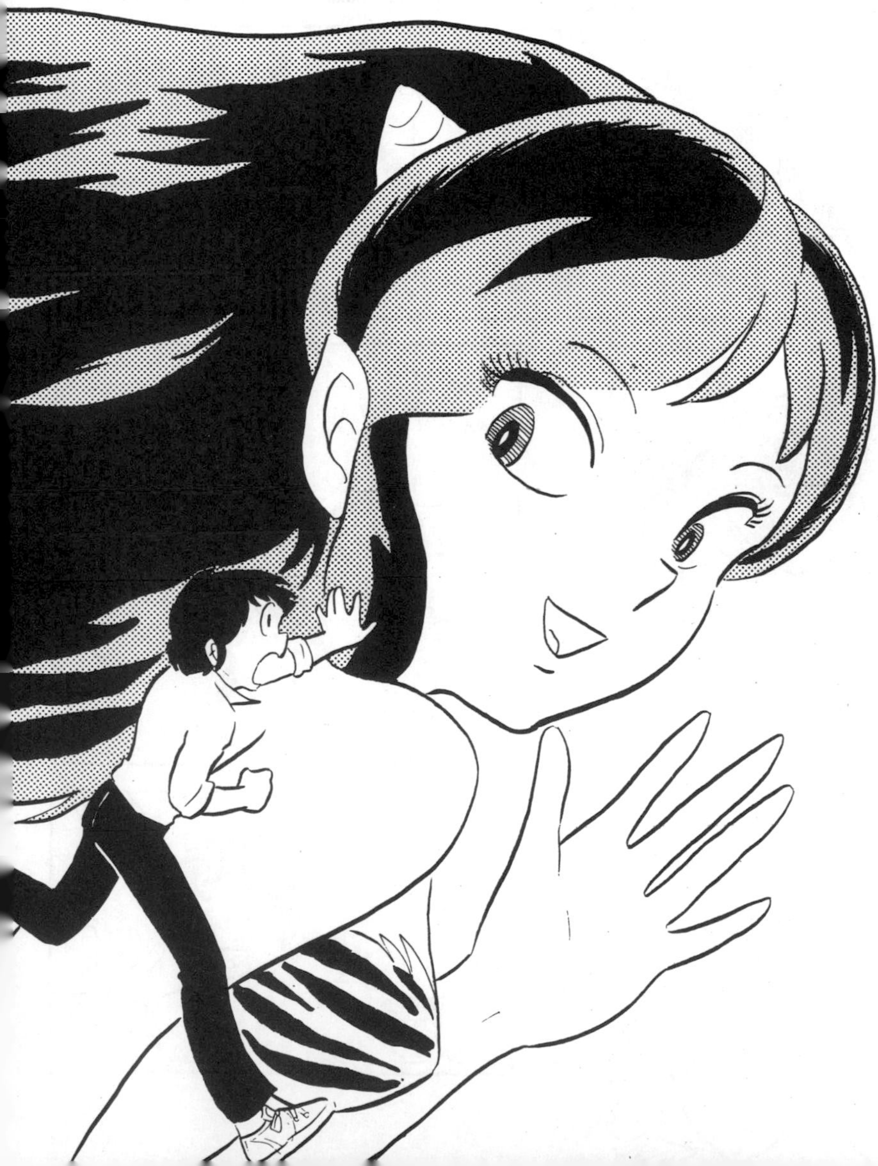

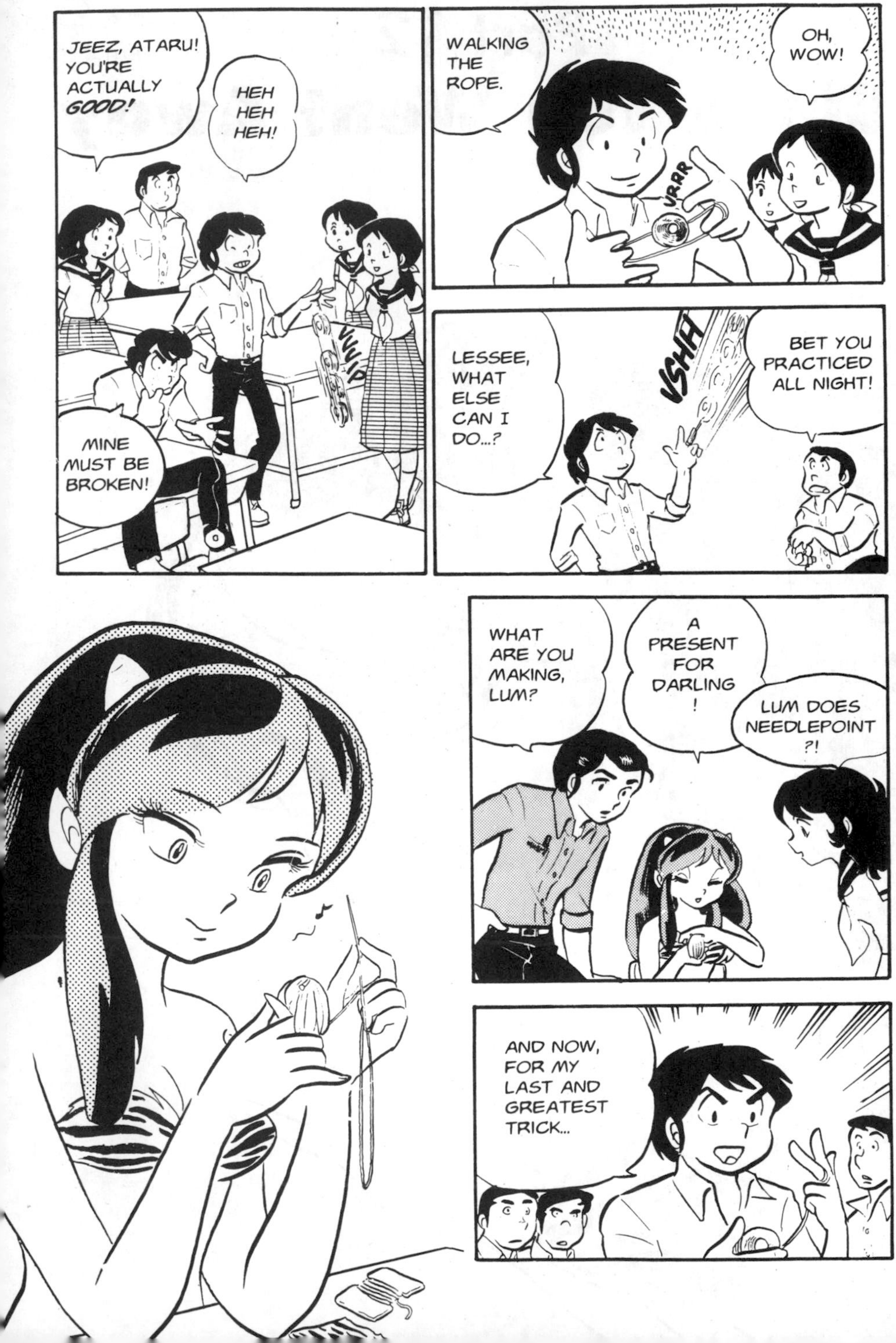
JEEZ, ATARU! YOU'RE ACTUALLY **GOOD!**
HEH HEH HEH!
VWIP
MINE MUST BE BROKEN!
WALKING THE ROPE.
OH, WOW!
URRR
LESSEE, WHAT ELSE CAN I DO...?
VSHA
BET YOU PRACTICED ALL NIGHT!
WHAT ARE YOU MAKING, LUM?
A PRESENT FOR DARLING!
LUM DOES NEEDLEPOINT?!
AND NOW, FOR MY LAST AND GREATEST TRICK...

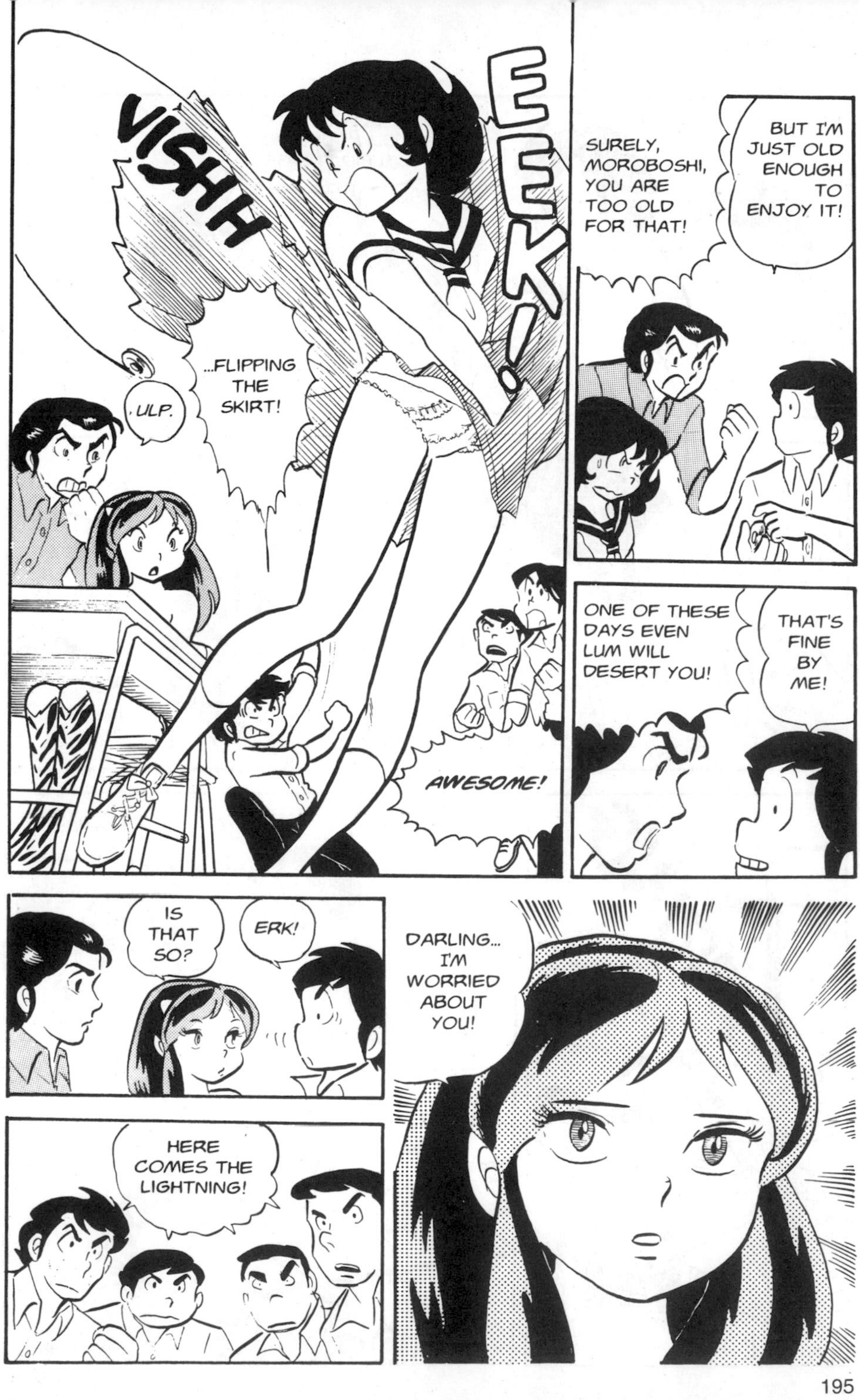
VISHH
EEK!
...FLIPPING THE SKIRT!
ULP.
AWESOME!
SURELY, MOROBOSHI, YOU ARE TOO OLD FOR THAT!
BUT I'M JUST OLD ENOUGH TO ENJOY IT!
ONE OF THESE DAYS EVEN LUM WILL DESERT YOU!
THAT'S FINE BY ME!
IS THAT SO?
ERK!
HERE COMES THE LIGHTNING!
DARLING... I'M WORRIED ABOUT YOU!

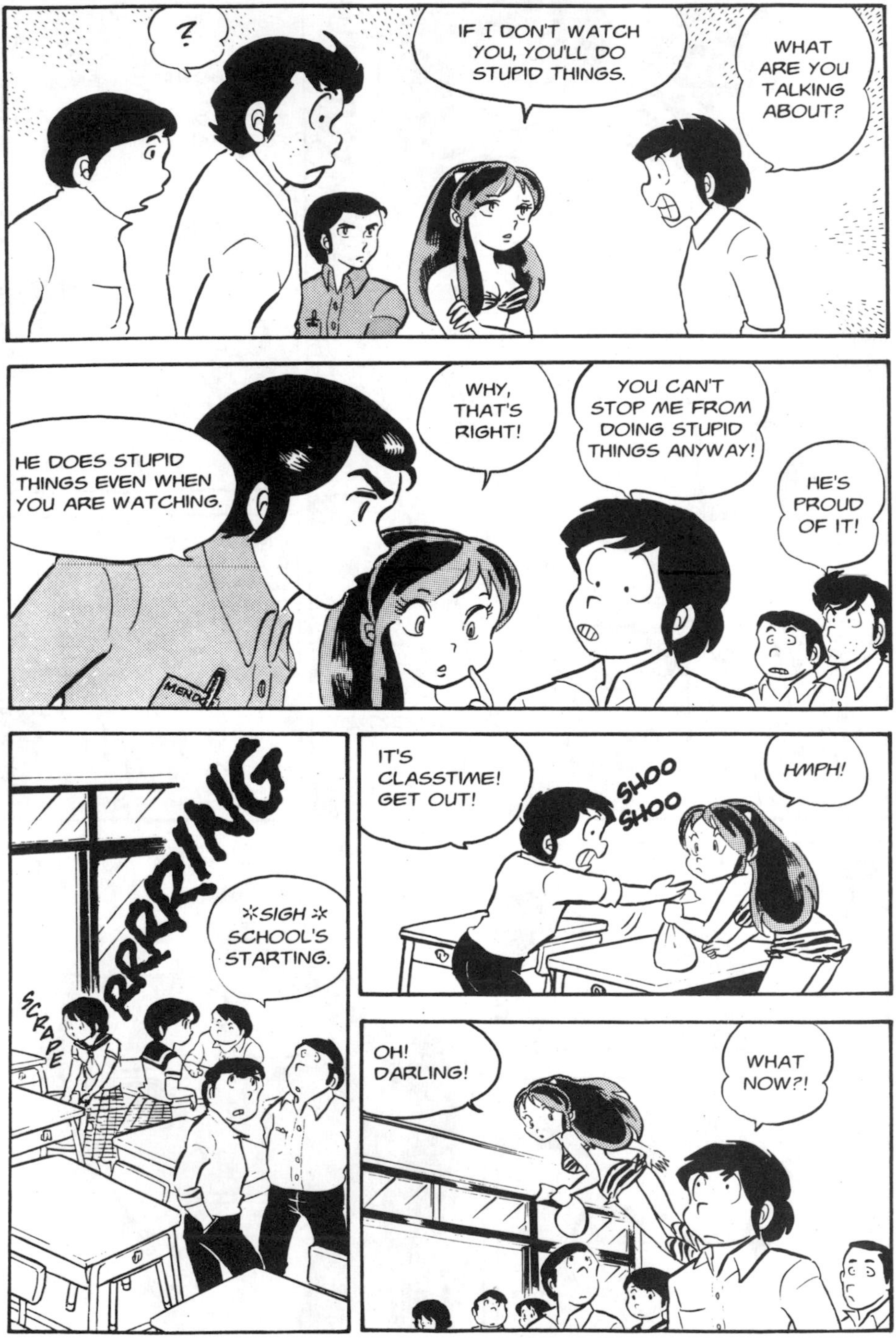
?
IF I DON'T WATCH YOU, YOU'LL DO STUPID THINGS.
WHAT ARE YOU TALKING ABOUT?
HE DOES STUPID THINGS EVEN WHEN YOU ARE WATCHING.
WHY, THAT'S RIGHT!
YOU CAN'T STOP ME FROM DOING STUPID THINGS ANYWAY!
HE'S PROUD OF IT!
MENDO
RRRING
SIGH SCHOOL'S STARTING.
SCRAPE
IT'S CLASSTIME! GET OUT!
SHOO SHOO
HMPH!
OH! DARLING!
WHAT NOW?!

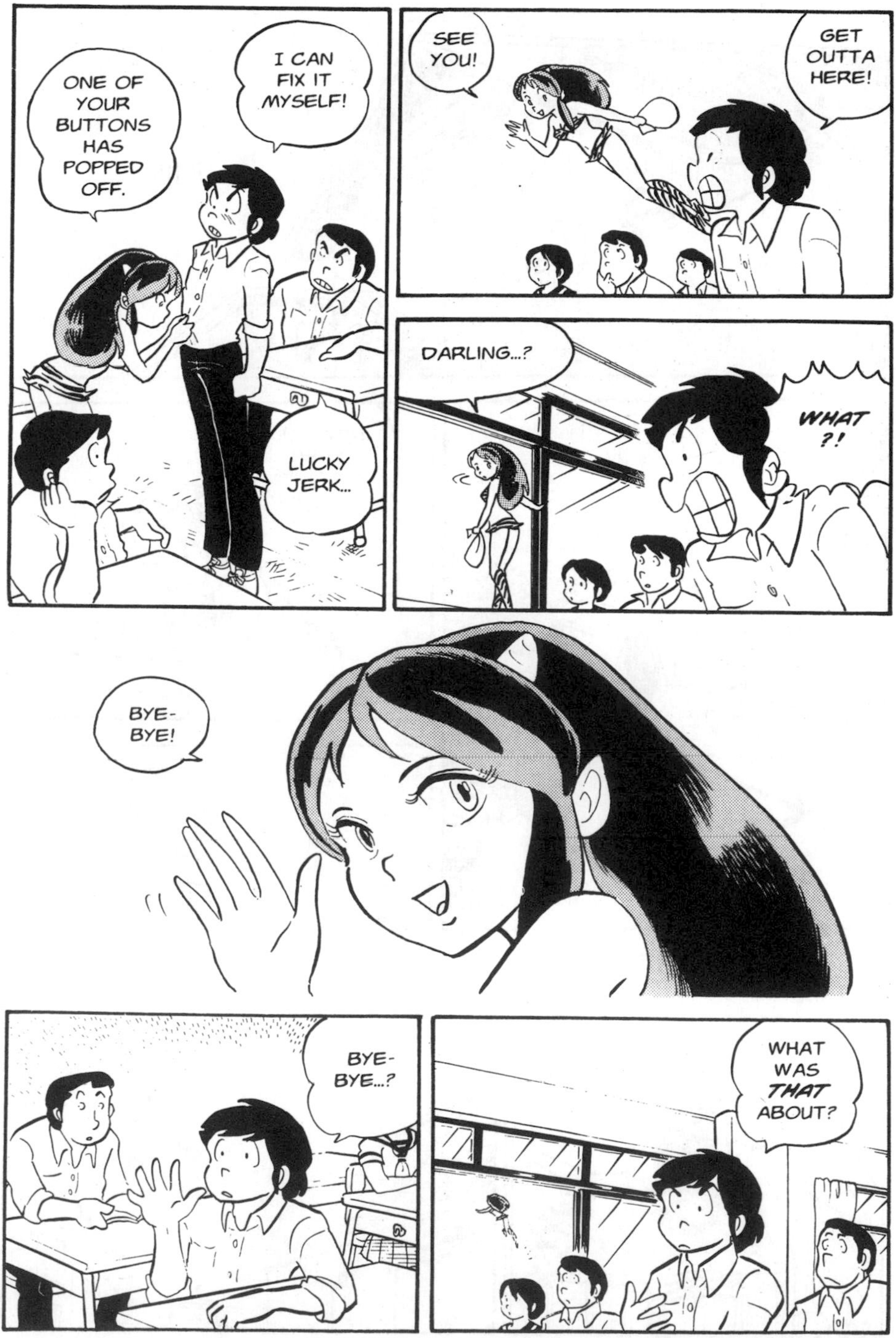
ONE OF YOUR BUTTONS HAS POPPED OFF.
I CAN FIX IT MYSELF!
LUCKY JERK...
SEE YOU!
GET OUTTA HERE!
DARLING...?
WHAT ?!
BYE-BYE!
BYE-BYE...?
WHAT WAS THAT ABOUT?

NOW YOU KEEP DARLING COMPANY IN MY PLACE!

WELL...

TIME FOR ME TO GO!

SHAA-AH

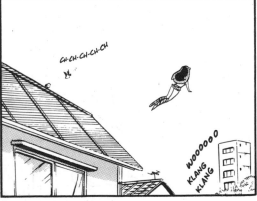
CH-CH-CH-CH-CH

WOOOOOO KLANG KLANG KLANG

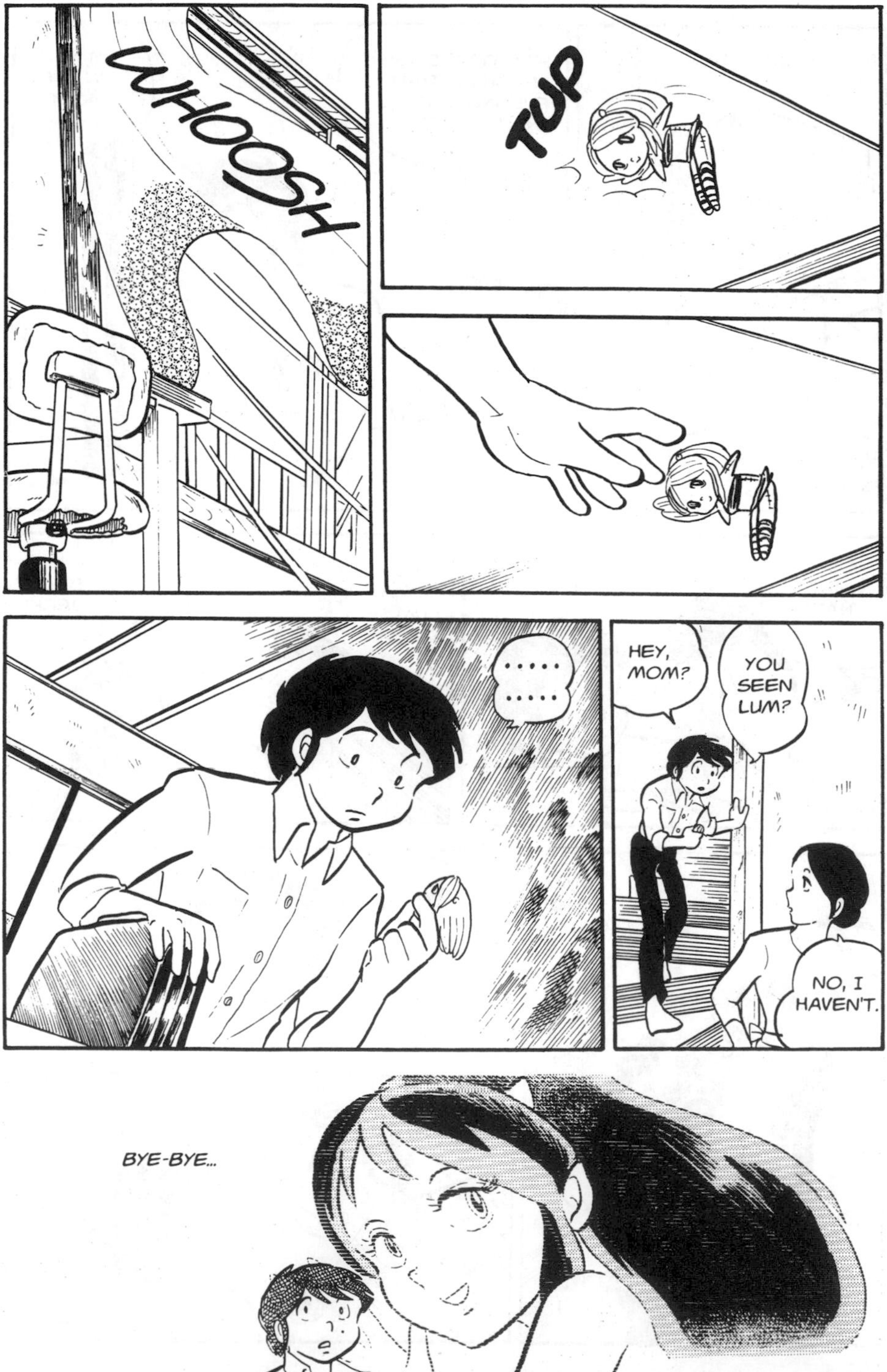
WHOOSH
TUP
......
......
HEY, MOM?
YOU SEEN LUM?
NO, I HAVEN'T.
BYE-BYE...

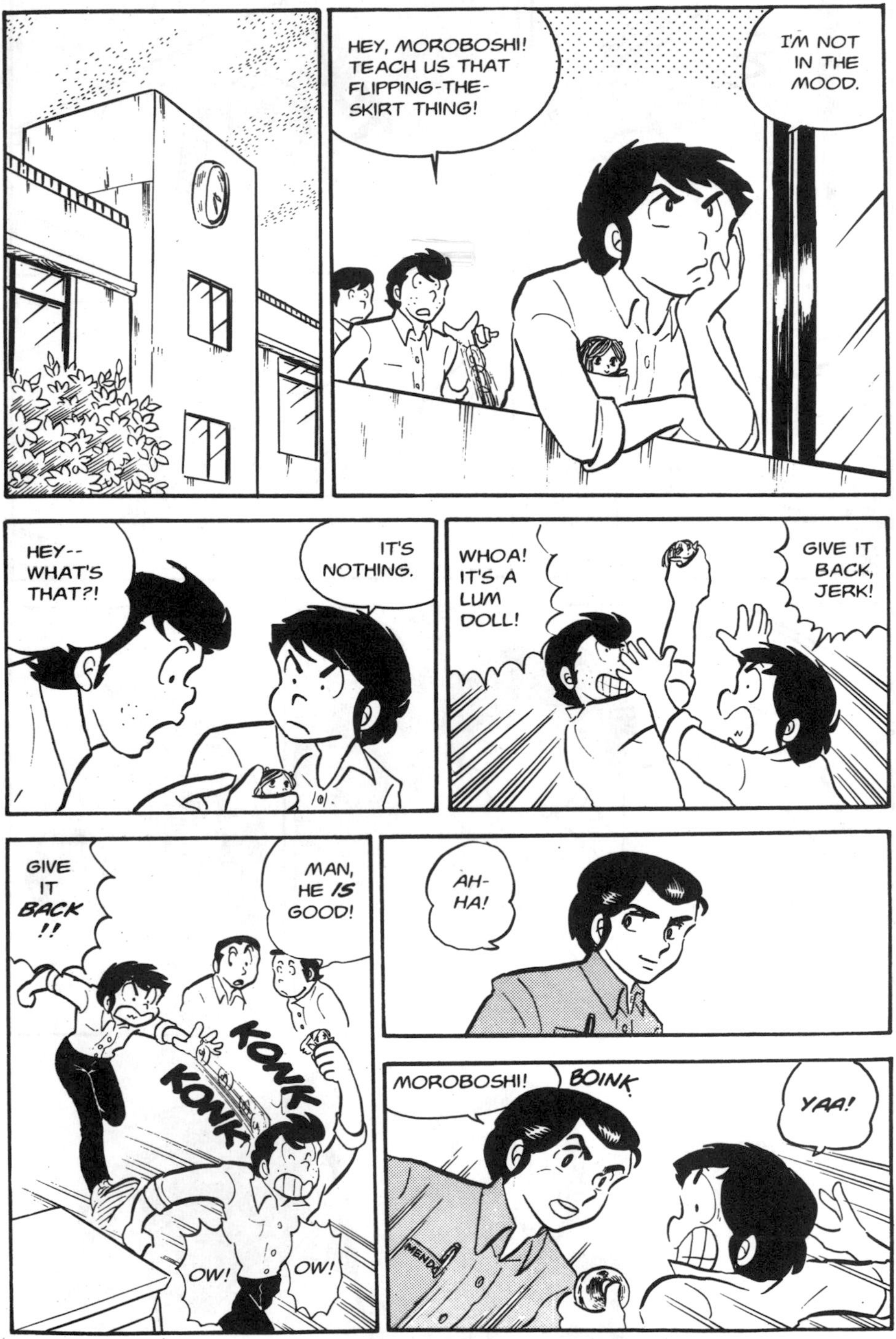
HEY, MOROBOSHI! TEACH US THAT FLIPPING-THE-SKIRT THING!
I'M NOT IN THE MOOD.
HEY--WHAT'S THAT?!
IT'S NOTHING.
WHOA! IT'S A LUM DOLL!
GIVE IT BACK, JERK!
GIVE IT BACK!!
MAN, HE IS GOOD!
KONK
KONK
OW!
OW!
AH-HA!
MOROBOSHI!
BOINK
YAA!
MENDO

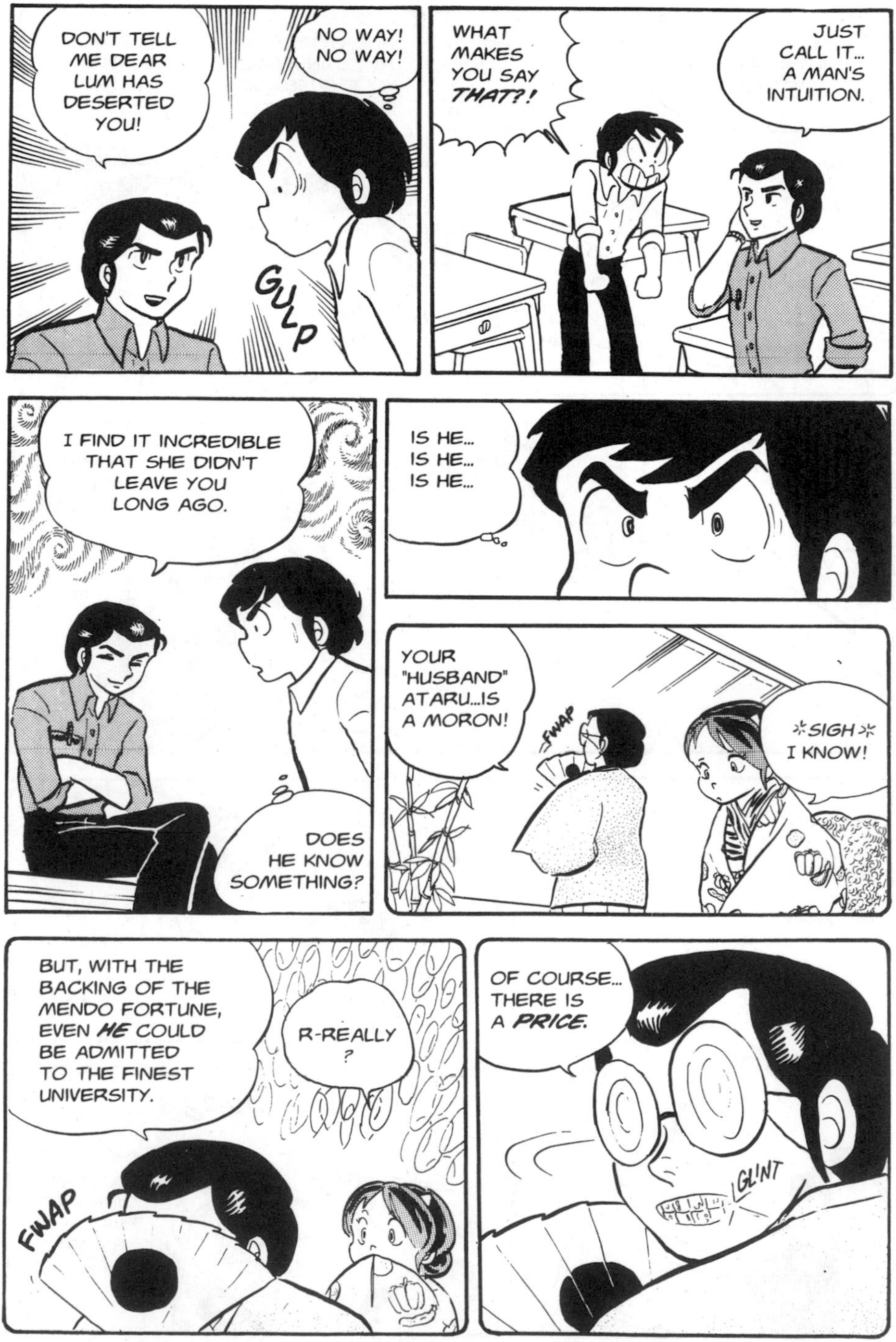
DON'T TELL ME DEAR LUM HAS DESERTED YOU!
NO WAY! NO WAY!
GULP
WHAT MAKES YOU SAY *THAT?!*
JUST CALL IT... A MAN'S INTUITION.
I FIND IT INCREDIBLE THAT SHE DIDN'T LEAVE YOU LONG AGO.
DOES HE KNOW SOMETHING?
IS HE... IS HE... IS HE...
YOUR "HUSBAND" ATARU...IS A MORON!
FWAP
SIGH I KNOW!
BUT, WITH THE BACKING OF THE MENDO FORTUNE, EVEN *HE* COULD BE ADMITTED TO THE FINEST UNIVERSITY.
R-REALLY ?
FWAP
OF COURSE... THERE IS A *PRICE*.
GLINT

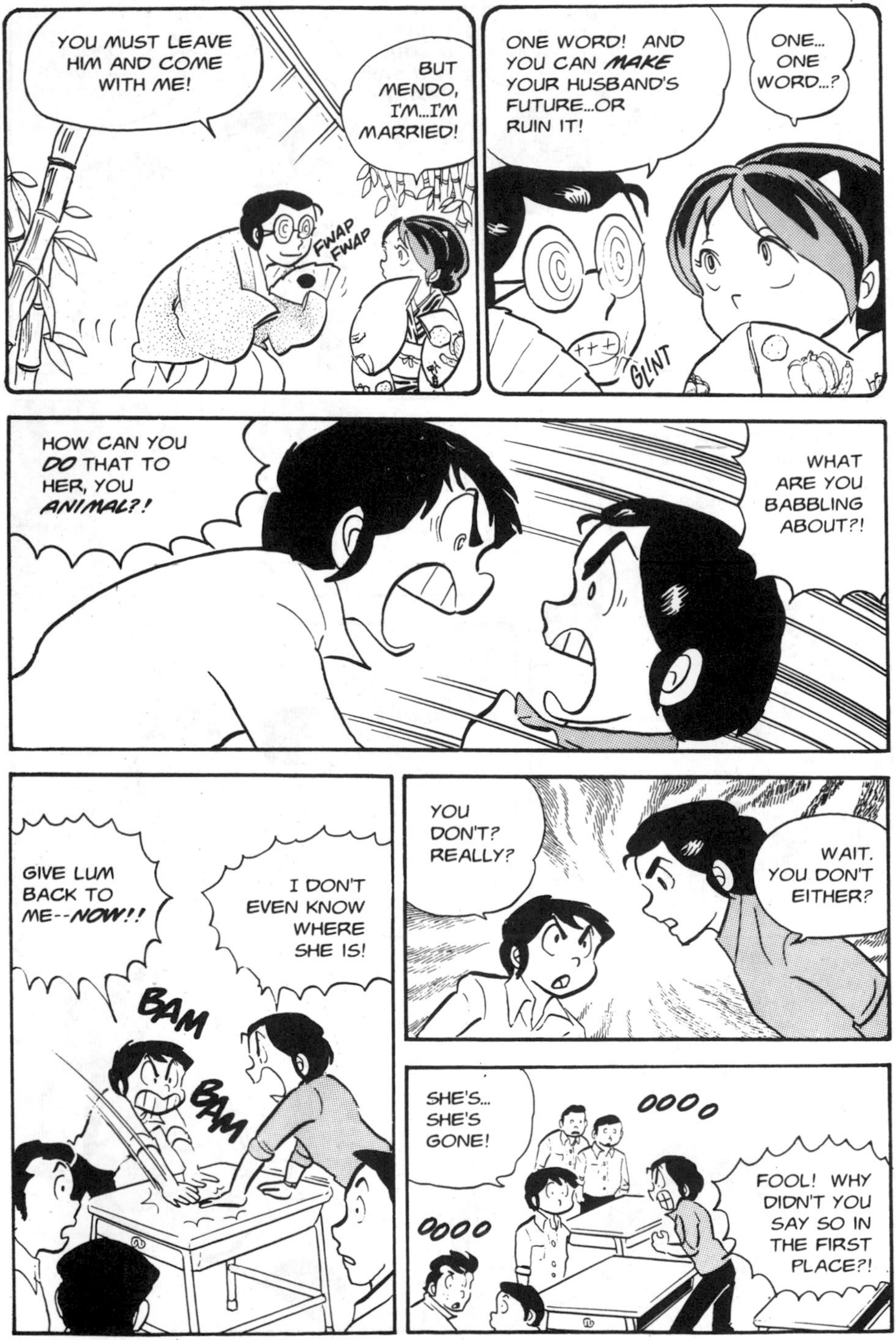

YOU MUST LEAVE HIM AND COME WITH ME!
BUT MENDO, I'M...I'M MARRIED!
FWAP FWAP
ONE WORD! AND YOU CAN MAKE YOUR HUSBAND'S FUTURE...OR RUIN IT!
ONE... ONE WORD...?
GLINT
HOW CAN YOU DO THAT TO HER, YOU ANIMAL?!
WHAT ARE YOU BABBLING ABOUT?!
GIVE LUM BACK TO ME--NOW!!
I DON'T EVEN KNOW WHERE SHE IS!
BAM
BAM
YOU DON'T? REALLY?
WAIT. YOU DON'T EITHER?
SHE'S... SHE'S GONE!
OOOO
OOOO
FOOL! WHY DIDN'T YOU SAY SO IN THE FIRST PLACE?!

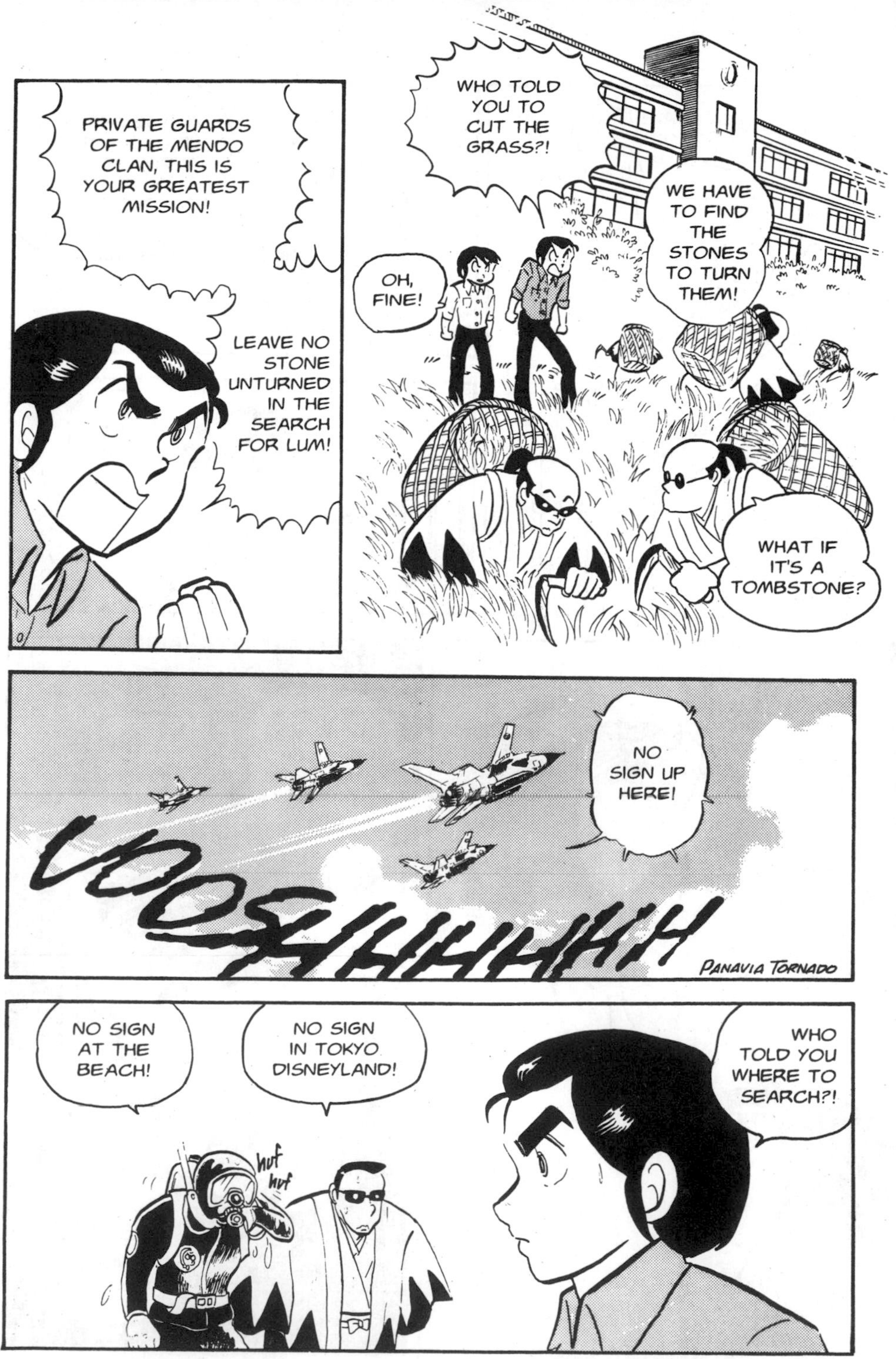
PRIVATE GUARDS OF THE MENDO CLAN, THIS IS YOUR GREATEST MISSION!
LEAVE NO STONE UNTURNED IN THE SEARCH FOR LUM!
WHO TOLD YOU TO CUT THE GRASS?!
OH, FINE!
WE HAVE TO FIND THE STONES TO TURN THEM!
WHAT IF IT'S A TOMBSTONE?
NO SIGN UP HERE!
VOOSHHHHHH
PANAVIA TORNADO
NO SIGN AT THE BEACH!
NO SIGN IN TOKYO DISNEYLAND!
WHO TOLD YOU WHERE TO SEARCH?!
huf huf

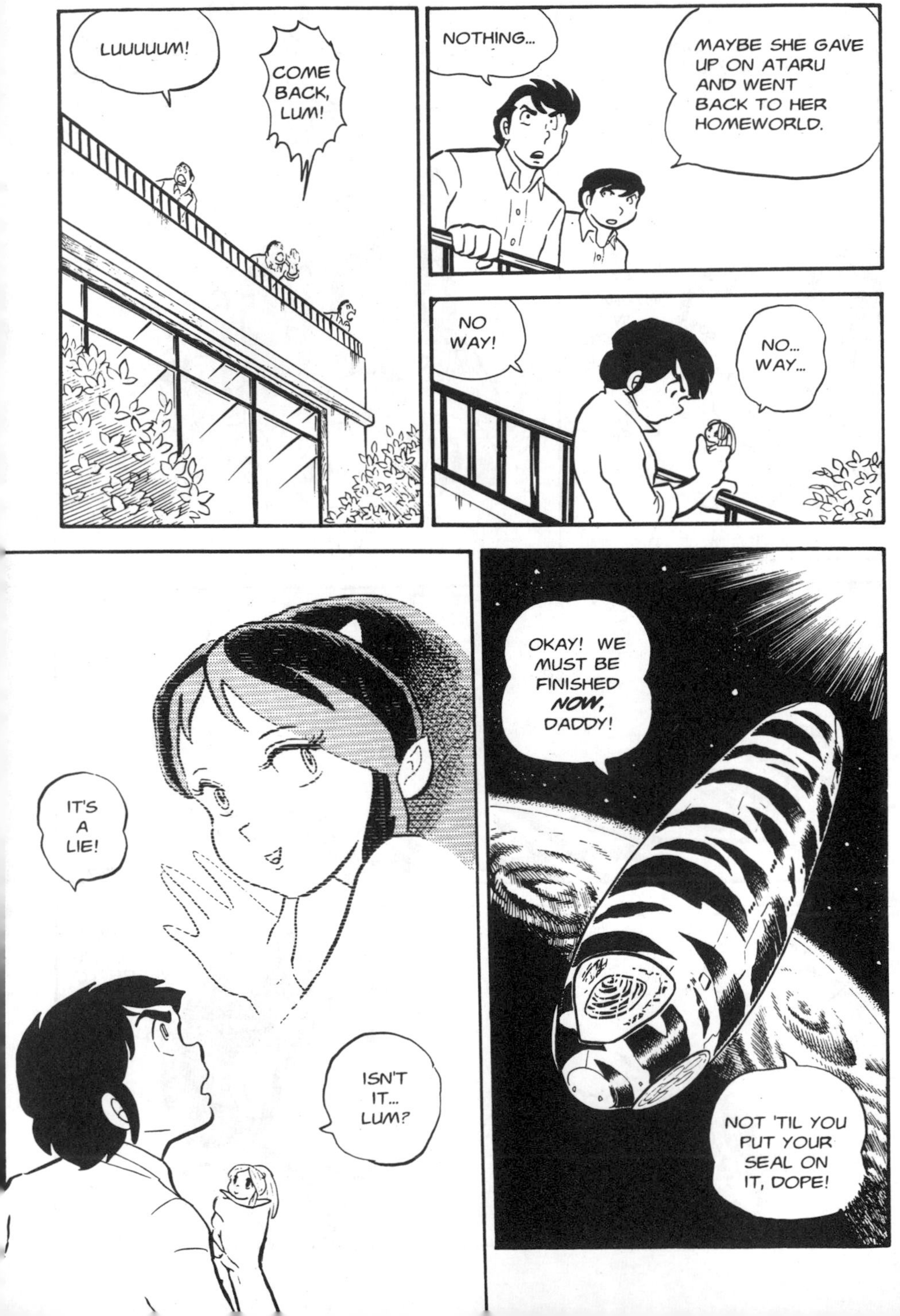
LUUUUUM!
COME BACK, LUM!
NOTHING...
MAYBE SHE GAVE UP ON ATARU AND WENT BACK TO HER HOMEWORLD.
NO WAY!
NO... WAY...
IT'S A LIE!
ISN'T IT... LUM?
OKAY! WE MUST BE FINISHED ***NOW,*** DADDY!
NOT 'TIL YOU PUT YOUR SEAL ON IT, DOPE!

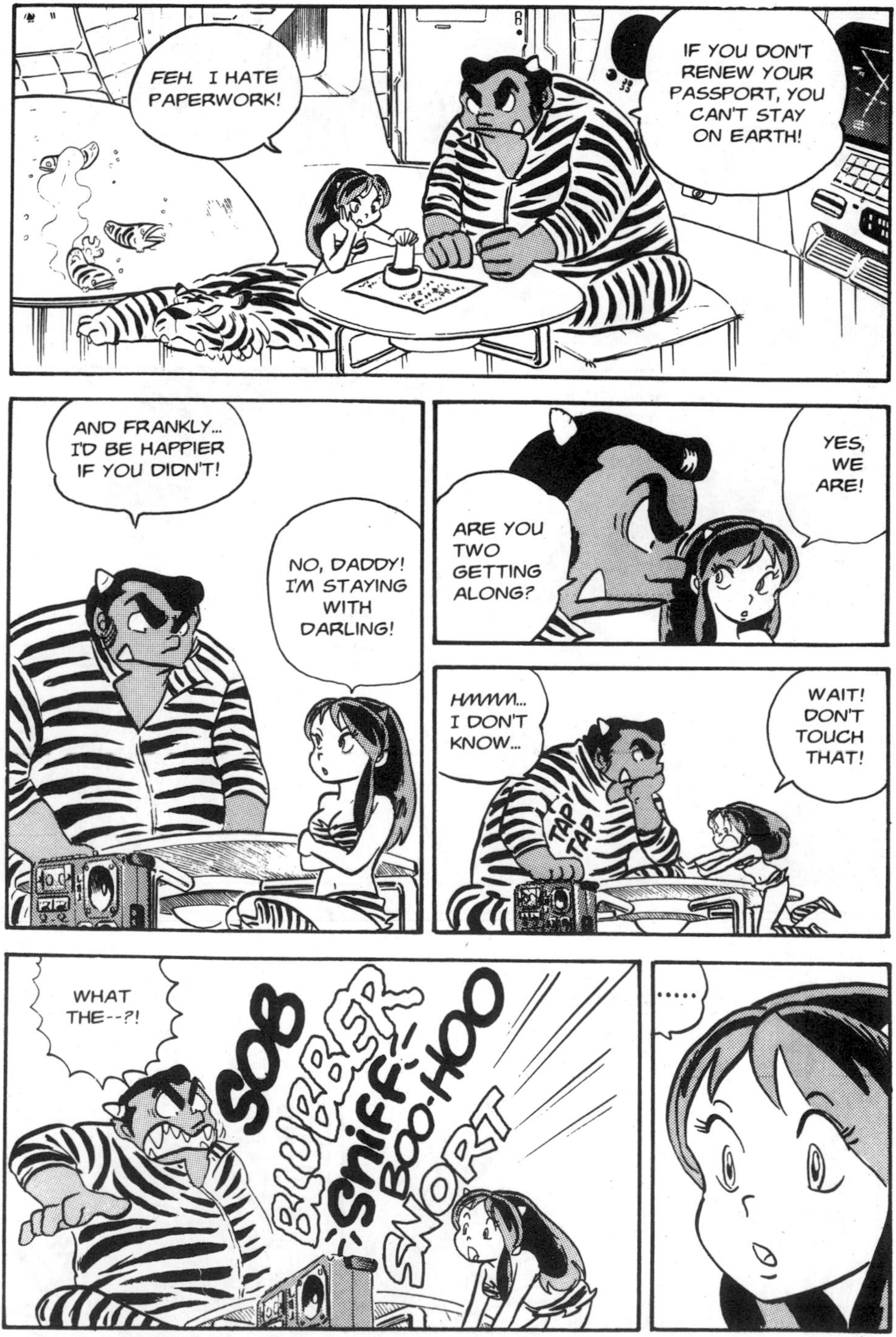
FEH. I HATE PAPERWORK!
IF YOU DON'T RENEW YOUR PASSPORT, YOU CAN'T STAY ON EARTH!
AND FRANKLY... I'D BE HAPPIER IF YOU DIDN'T!
NO, DADDY! I'M STAYING WITH DARLING!
ARE YOU TWO GETTING ALONG?
YES, WE ARE!
HMMM... I DON'T KNOW...
TAP TAP
WAIT! DON'T TOUCH THAT!
WHAT THE--?!
SOB
BLUBBER
SNIFF
BOO-HOO
SNORT
......

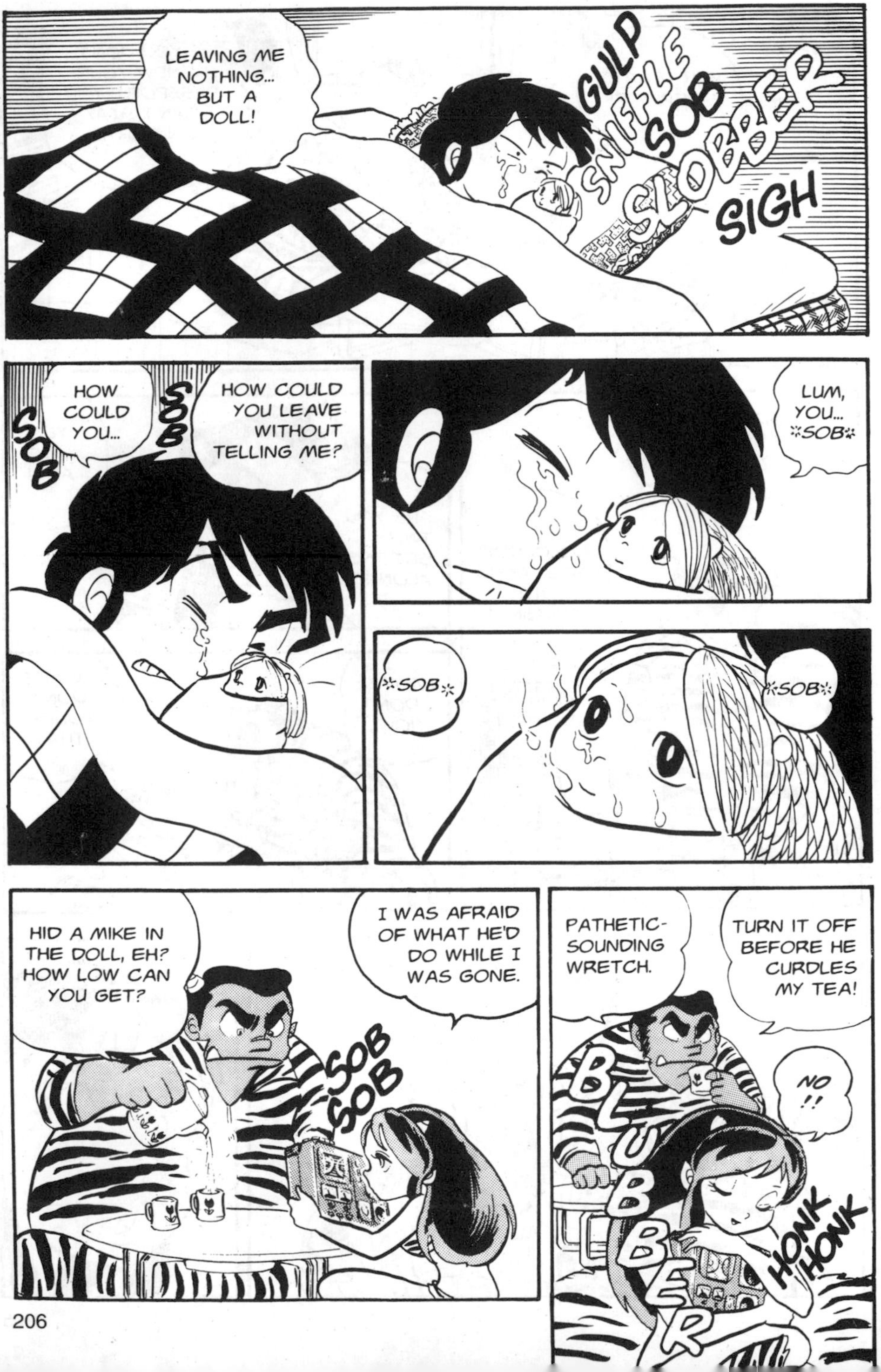
LEAVING ME NOTHING... BUT A DOLL!
GULP
SNIFFLE
SOB
SLOBBER
SIGH
HOW COULD YOU...
SOB
SOB
HOW COULD YOU LEAVE WITHOUT TELLING ME?
LUM, YOU... *SOB*
SOB
SOB
HID A MIKE IN THE DOLL, EH? HOW LOW CAN YOU GET?
I WAS AFRAID OF WHAT HE'D DO WHILE I WAS GONE.
SOB SOB
PATHETIC-SOUNDING WRETCH.
TURN IT OFF BEFORE HE CURDLES MY TEA!
BLUBBER
NO !!
HONK HONK

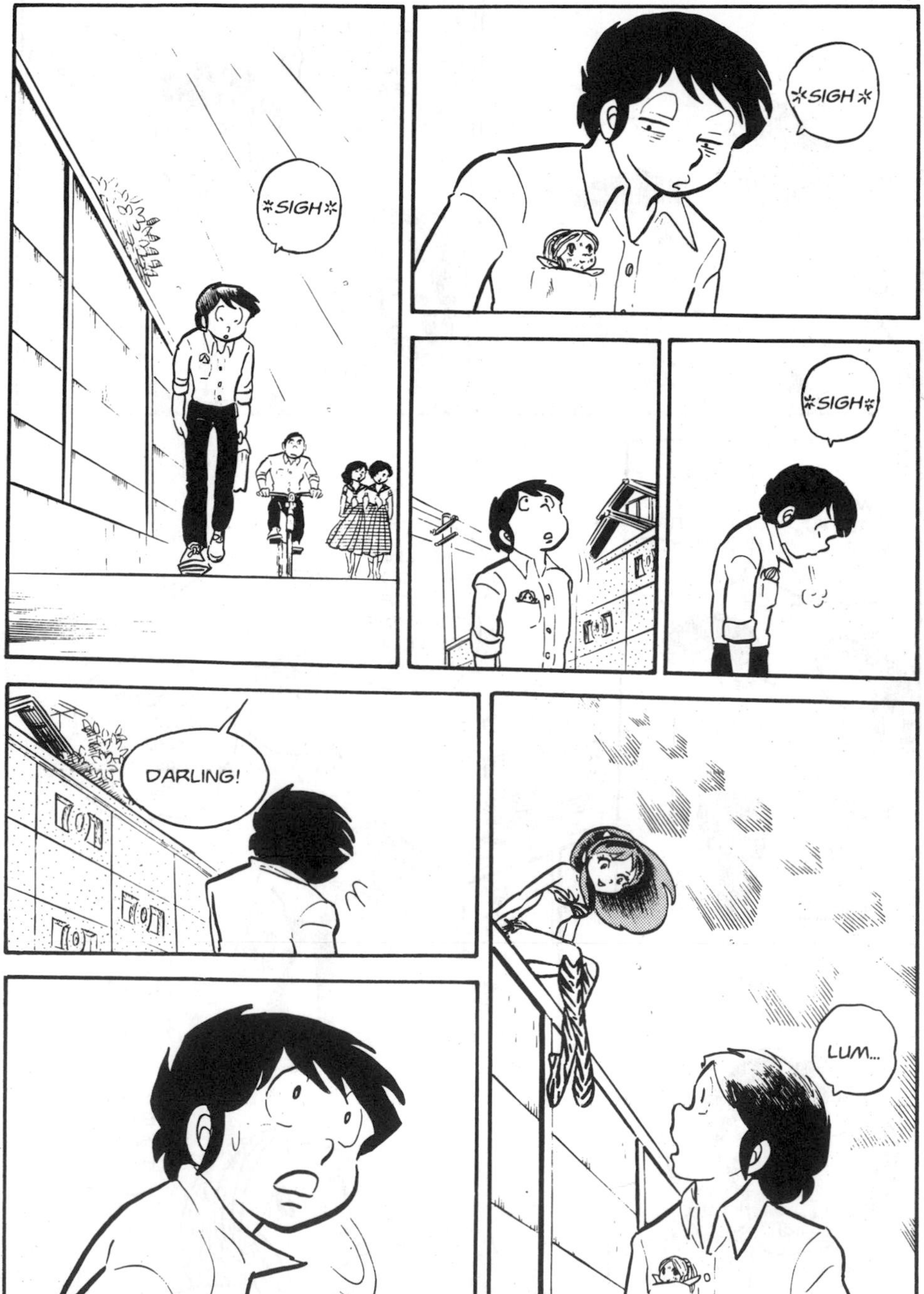
SIGH
SIGH
SIGH
DARLING!
LUM...

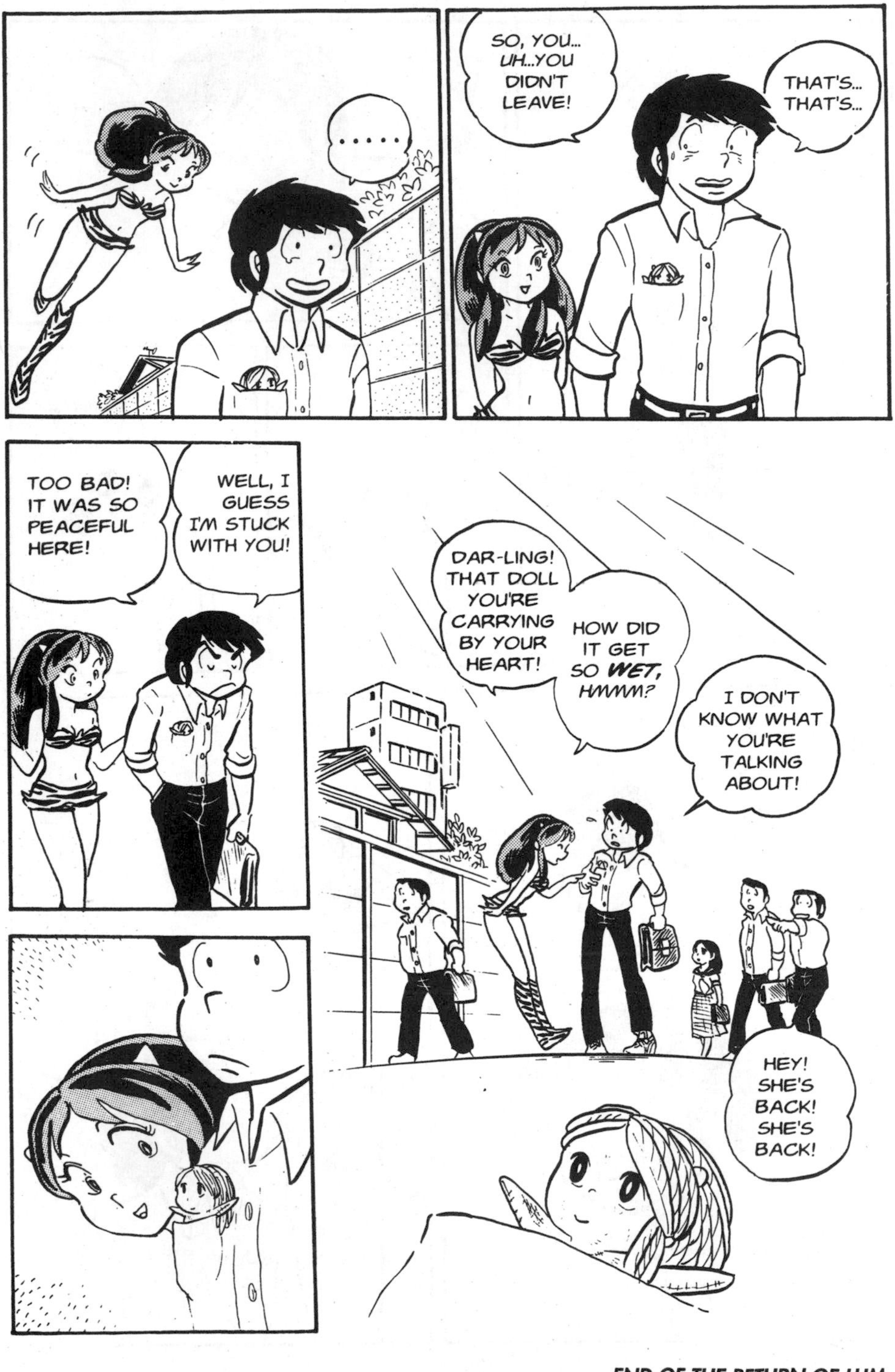
......
SO, YOU... UH...YOU DIDN'T LEAVE!
THAT'S... THAT'S...
TOO BAD! IT WAS SO PEACEFUL HERE!
WELL, I GUESS I'M STUCK WITH YOU!
DAR-LING! THAT DOLL YOU'RE CARRYING BY YOUR HEART!
HOW DID IT GET SO *WET*, HMMM?
I DON'T KNOW WHAT YOU'RE TALKING ABOUT!
HEY! SHE'S BACK! SHE'S BACK!

END OF THE RETURN OF LUM